Solutions to Violence

Edited By: Colman McCarthy

Center For Teaching Peace
Washington, D.C.

*Blessed are the
Peacemakers.
Blessed, too, are those
who wake up and
study them.*

Introduction

Studying nonviolence is not for the faint or weak of heart, nor conformists, quick-fixers, tremblers or the close-minded. So who does that leave? Not many, for sure. If you are among the few who are still hanging on, hanging in, hanging out and not yet hanging it up, welcome to some bracing peacemakers and peacebuilders. They are believers in the philosophy of pacifism, that little-heeded but ever-powerful creed that stands as the only effective alternative to violence.

Every problem we have, every conflict, fight or war, whether among those we know or don't know, whether among friends or perceived enemies, or internationally among governments, will be addressed through either violent force or nonviolent force. No third option exists. It's either fists, guns, armies, bombs or nukes—which is the conventional way, the violent way, the failed or flawed way—or the force of nonviolence: the force of justice, the force of organized resistance against corrupt power, the force of ideas and the force of love.

To read the essays in this anthology, and to absorb them intellectually and then act on them, is to understand that nonviolence is as much about getting the bombs out of our hearts as it is about getting them out of the global arsenal. The effort to develop a philosophy of nonviolent force demands strength from the intellect, patience from the heart and faith from the soul.

The journey will be eased—brightened even—by the intellectual companionship of such committed peacemakers as Gandhi, Tolstoy, Dorothy Day, Joan Baez, Carol Ascher, Sargent Shriver, Grace Yoder, Gene Sharp, Mary Roodkowsky, Martin Luther King, Jr., and others in this book. The literature of peace is vast. Gandhi's writings alone are collected in 95 books. Yet only a few of the nation's 78,000 elementary schools, 28,000 high schools and 3,000 colleges and universities offer courses in peace studies or put nonviolent conflict resolution classes in the curriculum.

The result of this academic neglect? Peace illiteracy and a culture awash in violence. Military violence that sees as many as 35,000 to 40,000 people killed monthly in the world's 35 current wars or conflicts—the poor killing the poor. Handgun violence. School massacre violence. Social violence that sees a crime committed every 17 seconds nationally. High rates of spousal violence, mostly men against women. Violence to animals: about 10 million a day killed for food, plus the toll taken by gunners, trappers, circuses, lab experimenters. Media violence: 95 percent of children's TV cartoons have violent themes. Environmental violence, from habitat destruction to corporations deliberately polluting our land, air and water.

We end up either as problem-describers or solution-finders. If you are in the second-group or want to be, read on. The authors are offering solutions to violence. Accept the ideas or reject them, but at least consider them. And at most, you will take them to heart and lead a life of moral purpose.

TABLE OF CONTENTS

To find the way to make peace with ourselves and to offer it to others, both spiritually and politically, is the most important kind of learning. To accept our abilities and limitations, and the differences in others; this is the contentment that gives life its highest value. It frees us to grow without restraint and to settle without pressure.

Wendy Schwartz

The first things to be disrupted by our commitment to nonviolence will be not the system but our own lives.

Jim Douglass

If We Listen Well

by Edward Guinan

For too long we have considered peace as the absence of conflict. We have approached the issue with this limited perspective and have directed our attention to the prevailing conflict of the moment, attempting to discover ways of reducing the destructiveness of the event. This approach is both necessary and desirable, but insufficient as we continue to approach the problem in a fragmented and isolated way. We continue to deal in symptomatic terms as if war and destruction and violence are the extensions and natural outgrowths of malignant attitudes, values, relationships, and beliefs that we continue to embrace.

Peace

Conflict will always be an integral part of human life but our methods of dealing with it need to change. We must be willing to develop an ongoing critical view of our values, operating premises and relationships, and a sensitivity to those about us.

Peace demands that one anticipate the effects of his views and actions on others and the unifying or destructive effects they may have. Most importantly one comes to realize that the "end" does not justify the "means": we get what we do, not what we hope for or intend. You cannot improve a man through punishment, nor can you bring peace through war or brotherhood through brutalization.

Finally one comes to appreciate the reality that there can be no "we's" and "they's" in our lives, but only brothers and sisters—all children of God—all sacred and dignified. Destruction of any one of these God-gifts means a certain destruction of oneself, and a mystery that is gone forever from this small, fragile world.

Violence

Violence can be seen as destructive communication. Any adequate definition must include physical, verbal, symbolic, psychological, and spiritual displays of hostility and hatred. The definition must include both our acts and our inactions and that which is done directly to people or indirectly to them through what they esteem. Many forms will take on a combination of these characteristics.

Violence should then include physical acts against another (i.e., the range of acts from personal attack to war which violate human autonomy and integrity); verbal attacks that demean and humiliate; symbolic acts that evoke fear and hostility; psychological attitudes that deny one's humanity and equality (legal, institutional, and moral); spiritual postures that communicate racism, inferiority, and worthlessness (i.e., beliefs and values that demean or categorize). Violence then becomes a dynamic rather than merely an act.

Hunger, poverty, squalor, privilege, powerlessness, riches, despair, and vicarious living are forms of violence—forms that a society approves and perpetuates. We have been too willing to discuss violence in terms of ghetto uprisings, student unrest, street thievery, and trashing, and have been unwilling to direct our attention to the more pathological types of violence that are acceptable—the types that daily crush the humanity and life from untold millions of brothers and sisters.

In the sixties we spoke with alarm of the "increase of violence" in our society, which may have been a half-truth: violence became more democratic in the decade of the sixties. Instead of resting exclusively with those who construct and maintain ghettos, keep food from the mouths of children, and coerce the young through educational programming and into war, violence became the tool of a widely divergent group seeking equality, power, and redress.

Under the umbrella of violence there reside two distinctively different phenomena. First, there is the violence of men and women who act out of frustration, hopelessness, and anger in an attempted grasp at life—the act of the slave braking the chains, which is understandable and inevitable as long as some humans are in bondage. The other type of violence is the violence of the respectable, the violence of the powerful that seeks personal gain and privilege by maintaining inhuman conditions. It is the violence of the board rooms, legislators, and jurists—the white-collar violence that pours surplus milk down sewers, robs workers of their wages, maintains prisons of infamy, lies to children, discards the weak and old, and insists that some should half-live while others rape and ravage the earth. This latter type of violence is what we must become aware of and actively dismantle if the future is to hold any possibilities for peace and a world where   all men and

1

women have a right to live and develop and participate by reason of their humanity, not by reason of their class, productive ability, or shrewdness.

Nonviolence

Nonviolence cannot then be understood as passivity or indifference to the dynamic of life (i.e., communication between men). It is not the posture of removing oneself from conflict that marks the truely nonviolent man, but, quite on the contrary, it is placing oneself at the heart of that dynamic. Nonviolence means taking the responsibility for aiding the direction of human communication and brotherhood. Nonviolence means an active opposition to those acts and attitudes that demean and brutalize another and it means an active support of those values and expressions that foster human solidarity. Nonviolence, in essence, means taking a stand in favor of life and refusing to delegate individual moral responsibility to another person or group; it means taking control on one's life and aiding others in doing likewise. Nonviolence is an attempt to find truth and love even in the midst of hatred, destruction, and pride.

As the means cannot be separated from the desired ends, nonviolence cannot be separated from peace, for it is the value system and dynamic that makes peace possible.

The Times

The past has not been given to us; it is not ours to breathe or exhale. We live within the smallest perimeter, which we call today, and into this brief moment, into this small space we beckon and command the future.

These are not good times, but good times do not mold great people. The sins of our excesses and arrogance can destroy us, or these failings can humble us to sainthood. Such are the times.

If the great virtues and teachings of the martyrs, resisters, and saints are relegated to a utopian or future-oriented condition, then indeed, they have little value for us at all. But the great heritage that this "community of liberation" has left us is not some unreal, impossible dream. It is this: Love can, and must, be lived today, despite the pain and difficulty of such life. Tomorrow will carry the tenderness and peace which we live now. Do not compromise today. It is all, dear brothers and sisters, that we have. This assembled community of peacemakers have paid dearly for their belief in such words and their lives form a chronicle of inspiration. They have been demeaned and laughed at; they have been dragged through jails and courtrooms and prisons; a few have paid the price of peace with their lives.

The Themes and People

The first signs of a violent society appear in its basic inability to communicate. Words lose their meaning and become hollow. They are twisted and deformed as tools of manipulation and servitude. Noble words such as truth, goodness, and love may come to mean despotism, obedience, and death. Peace becomes another name for multiheaded war missiles, and nonviolence is wrenched to mean silence, or lack or opposition, to thievery, privilege, and the status quo.

The Spiritual

A line from a contemporary song pleads: "Help me make it through the night." We find our existence framed in terms of aloneness rather than solidarity, struggles rather than consummations, departures rather than arrivals, questions rather than answers, and most importantly, night rather than daylight.

We cry out for fear the night will absorb us, yet we are unsure of any presence; we sing so as not to be crushed, yet the tones reflect the endless chant of the nightingales; we dance so as not to fall prey to these awesome interludes of emptiness; and most of all we pray so as not to lie. And these are the words we might use: "Help us make it through the night." Yet in the aloneness and struggle, in the departures and questions, in the cries and songs, in the dances and prayers there are imprints of heroic men and women, there are weavings of beauty, there are caresses of God. Traced through the faces of the old are messages of dignity and tenderness. The wail of the newborn is proof of silent breaths conspiring together. Each "forgive me" and "I love you" is prefaced by the warm tides of grace. Saints are born in Harlem in precise rhythm. Young people hurdle concrete mazes to touch and remember. Children weep for lost birds. Monks and mystics pray the sun up in the morning and call the evening dew. There are still wonderment, wishes, and dreams.

You must never forget that you are the brother or the sister of a carpenter and the child of a king. You must remember that all life is unfulfilled without you. You may learn that life is mysterious and sacred and that you must never, never destroy it. And if you listen well you will hear the chanting of others, and they are singing to you: "Help us make it through the night."

A Force More Powerful

By Peter Ackerman and Peter York

In mid-September, 2000, PBS ran a two-part, three hour television documentary on the definitive history of nonviolent conflict resolution in the 20th century. "A Force More Powerful" was edited by Peter Ackerman and filmed by Steve York. In the following interview they reflect on the philosophy of nonviolence and their work on the film.

Q: How did "A Force More Powerful" get started?

Ackerman: As a graduate student at the Fletcher School of Law and Diplomacy in the late 60s and early 70s, I was interested in 'asymmetric' conflicts,' where one side had the preponderance of military power but still lost. New factors were in play that were more psychological and political than material. Guerilla warriors like Ho Chi Minh and Che Guevara were, for many in liberation movements, the heroes then. At that time, I began to wonder about conflicts in which the asymmetry was total—that is to say, when one side fighting for their lives, freedom, or rights had no viable military option whatsoever. What did they do? In many places, they used nonviolent strategies, including strikes, noncooperation, and an infinite variety of protests and even nonviolent sabotage. In the 1980s, these nonviolent techniques came increasingly into play as country after country was transformed into a working democracy, culminating with the fall of the Berlin Wall and the victory over apartheid in South Africa. To my way of thinking there was not enough acknowledgment by foreign policy elites that these were not isolated events. These were successful 'wars,' but the brilliant part was that the winning sides weren't fighting with guns and bombs but with innovative nonviolent methods. Sure there was violence happening all over the world in the 20th century, but nonviolent power was prevailing too.

Q: How did you put all that scholarship and strategy on screen—and do people want to see that?

York: What you put on screen are stories and people. You show ideas personified. The drama is in the history. When I was in India, I walked along the dusty road leading to the beach where Gandhi broke the salt law. It looks about the same as it did in 1930 and it's nothing special, but what Gandhi did there is remarkable, and it gives the place a quiet sense of power. I'm not talking about the kind of power we associate with presidents or prime ministers; I mean the power of moral courage and personal action.

I'm still amazed at what James Lawson, at the age of 30 was able to accomplish in Nashville in 1960, and what Mkhuseli Jack accomplished in South Africa in the early 1980s at the age of 27. They're not considered 'powerful' people, even today, but they understood the power of ideas. Being in the presence of people like that is an incredible reminder that ideas matter, and that human intelligence and ingenuity can prevail.

Q: Why does nonviolent conflict resolution work?

Ackerman: Part of the underlying force of nonviolent resistance is that people who undertake it believe wholeheartedly in what they're doing, because they deeply feel the justice of their cause. In contrast, conventional warfare is often waged for greedy, aggressive purposes and fought by persons who have been conscripted into the fight by their government. Nonviolent action always has the potential to prevail against ruthless opponents because it can be conducted on a huge scale and involves every citizen who wants to play a part. Its techniques flow from the disruption of the everyday normalities that the tyrant counts on to maintain power. You see it time and again, in India, in Poland, in Chile, in South Africa—millions of people became part of these movements as much as by what they refused to do as by what they did.

That's not to say that nonviolent conflict is easy to wage. It involves willingness to suffer and to be hurt but not to retaliate and cause others to hurt. Gandhi often said there were many things he was willing to die for, but nothing he was willing to kill for. In nonviolent conflict, people are willing to be beaten, or jailed, or even killed, and they will only defend themselves with their convictions, their willingness to persevere and the force of their strategy. The result of this discipline, over time, is to make the aggressor see that what he wins militarily or through terror he cannot keep for every long without massively increasing the resources required to suppress all aspects of civil society.

York: Nonviolent movements often form in response to out-and-out tyranny, but rather than subduing people, repression often energizes them. It rouses public sentiment from the center, the core, that moderate middle that won't act until the extremes are cast into dramatic relief. The tide turned in Nashville, for example, when the home of a prominent black lawyer was bombed. Such acts of violence fueled the nonviolent ranks of the civil rights movements, rallied the African-American community, engaged the white community, and caught the attention of media and government, because the contrast was devastating.

Q: So why, as you claim, is nonviolent action so misunderstood and under appreciated?

Ackerman: Several reasons, but I think the main one is that government wages war, or some organized authority uses violence, whereas nonviolent action is a diffused people's action, and so it's not easily seen and followed. And because, in small groups, people can be brought out to protest almost anything, there's a 'fringe element' that taints some of these ideas. For example, I heard recently that certain animal rights activists protested an episode of the 'Survivor' television show because someone on the program roasted a rat for dinner, and these protestors were defending the rights of rats. Now the animal rights people have actually waged a very successful campaign over the past 20 years to get people to stop wearing fur, to lessen cruelty to animals in mean and gratuitous ways, to make people more sensitive to the feelings and lives of other creatures besides humans, and that's a good thing. But then you get a group of people marching in front of CBS screaming "Save the Rats,' the media jump on it and people think: 'Aha! Crazy activists.' So there's this impression that the only bona fide power struggles are those that are fought militarily and that nonviolent strategy can only be used by powerless fringe groups, which are barely tolerated in benign societies.

Another important aspect of why nonviolent conflict is misunderstood and under-appreciated is because it's so diverse in its practice and methods and participants. The media, much less historians, don't know how to recognize where it is operating. If country A sends troops into country B, the sides are clearly defined and, literally, the battle lines are drawn. If you're not dealing with international conflict between huge armies, but rather with efforts to undermine the entrenched power of the autocrat or invader, and you combine that with cumulative action by many people on many fronts—a boycott here, a demonstration there, a petition, a work slowdown—the location is no longer clear. Where do the media send cameras, or how does a historian frame a simple narrative?

Q: The media often focus on leaders. Is that a good way to delve into nonviolent movements?

Ackerman: There are two important things about leadership in these conflicts. One is that the leaders themselves are often reluctant leaders and even more reluctant heroes. They're not power mad, they're not looking for glory—some of them don't especially want to be leaders. They just want to stop the tyranny or the inequity, whatever. Which brings us to the second point, which is that when there is no clear leadership, movements lose their focus and momentum.

York: The American civil rights movement has become identified with Martin Luther King Jr., who was a phenomenal leaders. But he wasn't alone. In Nashville, Jim Lawson and Bernard Lafayette were central the Nashville protests. Lawson was, in fact, one of the architects of the civil rights movement, because he trained students and other demonstrators in nonviolent tactics that he himself learned from Gandhi's people in India. But in many nonviolent conflicts, a paramount leader may not be necessary, because ordinary people on their own initiative can take nonviolent action.

Q: Both of you speak exclusively of nonviolent conflict, nonviolent action, but you never use the terms 'nonviolence' or 'passive resistance.' Why?

Ackerman: This is something I feel strongly about. It's not a semantic distinction; it's the critical difference between action and inaction. What Gandhi did and what the people in Chile did and what Lech Walesa did was anything but passive. They didn't just sit there. They went out and did productive things. They held strikes and they organized boycotts and they put themselves in harm's way precisely because their actions punished their military oppressors. You can attach the word 'nonviolent' to all kinds of initiatives, including unorthodox techniques of seeking influence in a parliamentary setting. But the term, '*nonviolent conflict*' makes it clear that you're talking about non-violent *weapons*, nonviolent activism, in the most serious battles for fundamental human rights. Confusion can sometimes be created with the term *nonviolence*. For example, UNESCO has designated this as the Decade of Peace and Nonviolence, which is about people being good to each other, changing personal behavior to reflect lifestyle choices that acknowledge the common good defining one's own ethical positions. Now that's fine, good work. But we're talking about strategic

nonviolent conflict, the use of nonviolent strategies, whether people have access to violent weapons or not. There have been many cases of people who have chosen nonviolent approaches even when they had military options, and this is very important to understand. People in nonviolent struggles
are not unarmed—they are simply not armed with *violent* weapons, but make no mistake, they have formidable resources that flow from the fabric of their society. They are not necessarily principled advocates of nonviolence or other forms of peacemaking. Nonviolence seeks to make the conflict go away by virtuous behavior, while nonviolent strategists seek to win by aggressive engagement with an opponent.

York: Absolutely. Most people think of Gandhi as a saint. Perhaps he was, but that was only one facet of the man. He was much more. Our film shows that he was a brilliant political strategist. He understood power, the source of power and how to exercise power.

Q: *What about Tiananmen Square in China? Street protests in America? Can these be considered examples of strategic nonviolent conflict?*

Ackerman: Not really. First, successful nonviolent resistance reflects strategy, which implies a cumulative series of nonviolent actions or tactics intended to effect change. One kind of sanction, such as the demonstrations in Beijing, no matter how forceful or dramatic, cannot produce permanent change. But a strategic, well-managed campaign of nonviolent events can. Nonviolent strategy may include protests, but it will also include boycotts, strikes, noncooperation, and other tactics knitted together over time. Secondly when we talk about strategic nonviolent conflict, we're using the same context as we are when we talk about strategic violent conflict—that is, action directed against oppressors or invaders. So far the latest street demonstrations in America, such as in Seattle, haven't shown that a real movement with a real strategy has formed.

Q: What do you want viewers to take away from watching your film?

York: A sense of hope and a sense of appreciation for what's been accomplished, and what they themselves can do. We know from activists around the world, whom we've spoken to in the course of making our film, that many leaders, many participants, saw Attenborough's film about Gandhi and it inspired them to embark on nonviolent campaigns of their own.

I hope that people will see that not every leader has to be a Gandhi or a King, but that they can help effect change on a small or local scale and succeed. One of the other things said is that what we do at a particular time may seem insignificant, but eventually it can have an effect, and so it's very important to do it

There's a feeling, in this country and elsewhere, that problems are so great and the powers to mighty, that nothing that one person, or even a group of people, can do will change things. 'A Force More Powerful' is a reminder that violence is the weapon of the frightened, the unimaginative, the self-serving; while nonviolent weapons represent human power in its mightiest and most noble form.

Nonviolent Response to Assault

by Gerard A. Vanderhaar

I've never been mugged–at least not yet. I have often thought, though, about what I would do if someone jumped out of the shadows with a knife and demanded my wallet. Or if that pair of teenagers on the isolated New York subway platform swaggered over and asked for twenty dollars. Or if when I was stalled on an empty freeway a car suddenly pulled in front of me and the driver stepped out pointing a gun.

I don't know what I *would* do, and I'll never know until something like that happens. But right now, when I can think about it coherently, I know what I would *like* to do: remain calm. I would like to save my life, of course, and avoid whatever would trigger violence in my assailants. I would want to do whatever would defuse the confrontation and turn it around.

Like automobile accidents, fires, tornadoes, and earthquakes, the possibility of personal assault is a fact of life today. We are all potential victims of a sudden attack on our persons, our possessions, our life. Everyone should be prepared to face it.

Conventional wisdom says that if we can't get away, we should either submit or fight back strongly. "Save your skin." Self-preservation is nature's first law, we're told. Get by with the least damage to ourselves. An empty wallet is better than a slit throat. Losing one's virtue is better than losing one's life.

Or we are advised to use force if possible. A Memphis police lieutenant who runs clinics on how to cope with rape gives his advice: "First, try to escape or scare away the assailant by wrenching free or yelling. If the criminal doesn't let go, then you have to either give in, or hurt him in the most effective and efficient manner possible." This means gouge out an eye. Kick hard at the groin. Shoot, if you have a gun, and shoot to kill. His advice has a point for people not sensitive to nonviolence or not practiced in its ways. Essentially he offers the two traditional modes of survival in time of danger: flight or fight.

If we really believe, however, that active nonviolence is an effective alternative to flight or fight in other areas of life, we need to explore how we can respond nonviolently in this most critical of all personal dangers, when an assault occurs. Here are some true stories about people who were not experienced in nonvio-lence, not committed to ahimsa, but who did just the right nonviolent thing at the right time.

Three Events

A woman with two children in a disabled car late one night on the New Jersey turnpike looked up to see a man pointing a gun through her window. He ordered her to let him in the car. Instead of panicking, she looked him in the eye and, like an angry mother, commanded, "You put that gun away and get in your car and push me to the service area. *And I mean right now!*" He looked startled, put the gun away, went back to his car, and did as she ordered: pushed her car to the service area.

A colleague of mine walking late one winter afternoon was jumped by two young men hiding in the bushes under a viaduct. They demanded money. He said he didn't have any. They began punching him, repeating their demand for money. He felt helpless and didn't know what to do. Then it flashed into his mind to call for the only assistance he could think of. He rolled his eyes and started shouting, "Jesus, help me. Jesus, help me!" They stopped hitting him and looked at him as if he were crazy. Then they ran away.

A lady drove into the parking garage of Memphis' largest hospital one afternoon to visit a friend. As she eased her car into a space she noticed a strange-looking man lurking nearby. No one else was in sight. She usually kept a gun in her glove compartment, she said later, but that day she had left home without it. She had to think fast. She got out of the car, and as the man came over, she looked squarely at him and said in as firm a voice as she could muster, "I'm so glad there's a man around. Could you walk me to the elevator?" He replied meekly, "Yes, ma'am." She thanked him, got on the elevator alone–and practically collapsed out of fear and relief.

Although none of the three people were committed to nonviolence, they had improvised what we recognize as a truly nonviolent response. They did not act like victims. They engaged the potential assailants as human beings, and in two of the incidents managed to evoke a sense of decency that resulted in their being helped rather than hurt.

Since we are faced with the possibility of being subject to assault–I prefer to say "subject to" assault rather than "victim of"–there is much we can do nonviolently to keep ourselves from becoming victims.

Prevention

It is very nonviolent, not to mention practical, to do everything we reasonably can to avoid being attacked in the first place. That includes locking doors, walking with others rather than alone, avoiding high risk areas, and being alert to potential danger wherever we are.

For a person tuned into nonviolence, prevention is not being cowardly, but realistic. We are not helping ourselves or any potential assailants in the vicinity by naively thinking that everything will be all right all the time. Out of *ahimsa*, the desire for non-harm, we need to avoid making ourselves easy objects for attack. We should not tempt others to attack us.

If we see an attack coming, we should avoid it or seek cover. A woman in Hungerford, England, who was at the scene when a gunman began firing his rifle at marketplace strollers, killing sixteen people said she survived because she "dove for cover."

Our safety precautions send a strong signal to anyone who would do us harm. It is not that we are scared, but that we are alert and prepared to take care of ourselves. Two strange men entered an aerobics class in which my wife was participating and began talking loudly, distracting the exercisers. No one knew what they wanted, but they seemed capable of creating mischief. One of the exercisers went over to speak to them. He told them quietly how serious the class was, and that anyone who wanted to take part had to sign a waiver form and pay a fee. They were welcome to join if they wanted. He didn't accuse or threaten; he just spoke straightforwardly, matter-of-factly. They listened, saw his seriousness, then turned away and left the room. No trouble. It was an exercise in prevention.

Restraint

If we are up against an attacker who is crazed by drug or drink, or who is schizophrenic, or temporarily insane, nonviolent human interaction is nearly impossible. If we have the opportunity, restraint may be our only recourse.

One man told me about his wife who had been mentally ill. She would fly into rages. "I looked into her eyes, and it seemed like she wasn't there," he said. She would scream and curse and throw things and was incapable of listening to anyone. She refused to see a doctor or do anything to help herself. Then one night,

in one of her fits, she took a knife from the kitchen and started toward their child's bedroom. "That was the end of the line," he said. "I had to stop her." He bounded across the room and, as gently as possible but as firmly as necessary, he wrapped one arm around her from behind, grabbed the wrist of the hand that held the knife and squeezed until she dropped it. Then, still holding her, he dialed the emergency telephone number and waited for the ambulance to take her to the hospital. He said it was the hardest thing he ever had to do in his life.

When I think of restraining somebody nonviolently, I would like to do it as strongly and effectively–and as lovingly–as that man did his wife.

Self-Possession

As a remote preparation long before any attack occurs, we can sharpen our ability for an effective nonviolent response by increasing the power of our personhood. We believe that we are important, we are valuable and we want others to believe it about themselves. We are not victims; we are not cowering and cringing before life's challenges, fearfully looking over our shoulder to see what might be pursuing us. We stand straight, eyes calm, alert, moving ahead. We walk confidently, not with cockiness, which is a way of compensating for insecurity, but in a straightforward and open manner. We are not rash or brash; we don't take unnecessary risks, blind to danger. We are who we are, and we present ourselves to the world that way.

The caricature of the swaggering sheriff with a pistol strapped on one side, a heavy flashlight on the other, a billy club dangling from his belt, so loaded down that he walks with his elbows pointed outward, is the image of a fearful man, so lacking in self-confidence that he needs all this hardware to protect himself.

If we are so dominated by fear that we arm ourselves to hurt those who would attack us, we have sunk to the level of the assaulter. We have become like the enemy in our desperation to overcome the enemy.

In principle, people committed to nonviolence don't carry weapons. It is because we believe in *ahimsa*, but it is also because we believe that in a crisis our personal ability is more effective than a gun. Truth, righteousness, and readiness are powerful nonviolent weapons. Armed with these, our personal power increases.

These weapons, more than guns and knives, have a deterrent effect on a would-be attacker. Think of a robber lurking in a doorway late at night watching

8

potential marks approaching down the street. The robber will want to pick out those who look like easy victims: timid, uncertain, fearful, unprotected. Someone who appears in command, confident, will not be as appealing a target. If I am this person, I'm likely to be passed over in favor of an easier target (and I'll probably never know how close I came to being attacked).

A large-statured friend of mine, a long-time peace activist, wasn't passed over once. In a small town in South Dakota, on a sidewalk in full daylight he was suddenly faced with a much smaller man flashing a knife and demanding money. My friend, who had very little money anyway, said that the first thing he thought of was the incongruity of their sizes. "All I could do was laugh," he said. He didn't feel any fear, although later he said he was surprised he hadn't. His self-confidence was deep. The assailant glanced up at him, looked puzzled, then turned and ran away.

If an attack does occur, this kind of self-possession, this awareness of our personal power, this confidence in our nonviolent armor is the foundation of defense. But it's only the foundation. An understanding of what is likely to happen and some practice in nonviolent techniques can give us a truly effective defense against personal assault.

Human Nature Isn't Inherently Violent

by Alfie Kohn

Peace activists can tell when it is coming: Tipped off by a helpless shrug or a patronizing smile, they brace themselves to hear the phrase yet again. "Sure, I'm in favor of stopping the arms race. But aren't you being idealistic? After all, aggression is just"—here it comes—"part of human nature."

Like the animals—"red in tooth and claw," as Tennyson put it—human beings are thought to be unavoidably violent creatures. Surveys of adults, undergraduates, and high school students have found that about 60 percent agree with the statement, "Human nature being what it is, there will always be war."

It may be part of our society's folk wisdom, but it sets most of the experts' heads to shaking. Take the belief, popularized by Sigmund Freud and animal researcher Konrad Lorenz, that we have within us, naturally and spontaneously, a reservoir of aggressive energy. This force, which builds by itself, must be periodically drained off—by participating in competitive sports, for instance—lest we explode into violence.

It is an appealing model because it is easy to visualize. It is also false. As the respected animal behaviorist John Paul Scott, professor emeritus at Bowling Green State University in Bowling Green, Ohio, has written: "All of our present data indicate that fighting behavior among higher mammals, including man, originates in external stimulation and that there is no evidence of spontaneous internal stimulation."

Clearly, many individuals—and whole cultures—manage quite well without behaving aggressively, and there is no evidence of the inexorable buildup of pressure this "hydraulic" model would predict.

The theory also predicts that venting aggressive energy should make us less aggressive—an effect known as "catharsis," which follows Aristotle's idea that we can be purged of unpleasant emotions by watching tragic dramas. But one study after another has shown that we are likely to become more violent after watching or participating in such pastimes.

Although the hydraulic model has been discredited, the more general belief in an innate human propensity for violence has not been so easily shaken. Among the arguments one hears are these: Animals are aggressive and we cannot escape the legacy of our evolutionary ancestors; human history is dominated by tales of war and cruelty, and certain areas of the brain and particular hormones are linked to aggression, proving a biological basis for such behavior.

First, we should be cautious in drawing lessons from other species to explain our own behavior, given the mediating force of culture and our capacity for reflection.

But even animals are not as aggressive as some people think—unless the term "aggression" includes killing to eat. Organized group aggression is rare in other species, and the aggression that does exist is typically a function of the environment in which animals find themselves.

Scientists have discovered that altering animals' environment, or the way they are reared, can have a profound impact on the level of aggression found in virtually all species. Furthermore, animals cooperate both within and among species far more than many of us may assume on the basis of watching nature documentaries.

When we turn to human history, we find an alarming number of aggressive behaviors, but we do not find reason to believe the problem is innate. Here are some of the points made by critics of biological determinism:

• Even if a given behavior is universal, we cannot automatically conclude it is part of our biological nature. All known cultures may produce pottery, but that does not mean there is a gene for pottery-making.

• Aggression is nowhere near universal. Many hunter-gatherer societies in particular are entirely peaceful. And the cultures that are "closer to nature" would be expected to be the most warlike if the proclivity for war were really part of that nature. Just the reverse seems to be true.

• While it is indisputable that wars have been fought, the fact that they seem to dominate our history may say more about how history is presented than about what actually happened.

• Many people have claimed that human nature is

aggressive after having lumped together a wide range of emotions and behavior under the label of aggression. While cannibalism, for example, is sometimes perceived as aggression, it might represent a religious ritual rather than an expression of hostility.

It is true that the presence of some hormones or the stimulation of certain sections of the brain has been experimentally linked with aggression. But after describing these mechanisms in some detail, K.E. Moyer, a physiologist at Carnegie-Mellon University in Pittsburgh, emphasizes that "aggressive behavior is stimulus-bound. That is, even though the neural system specific to a particular kind of aggression is well activated, the behavior does not occur unless an appropriate target is available (and even then) it can be inhibited."

Regardless of the evolutionary or neurological factors said to underlie aggression, "biological" simply does not mean "unavoidable." The fact that people voluntarily fast or remain celibate shows that even hunger and sex drives can be overridden.

All this concerns the matter of aggressiveness in general. The idea that war in particular is biologically determined is even more far-fetched.

But if humans have the potential to be peaceful, why is the belief in a violent human nature so widespread?

To begin with, we tend to make generalizations about the whole species on the basis of our own experience. "People in a highly warlike society are likely to overestimate the propensity toward war in human nature," says Donald Granberg, a sociologist at the University of Missouri.

The historical record, according to the Congressional Research Service, shows the United States is one of the most warlike societies on the planet, having intervened militarily around the world more than 150 times since 1850. Within such a society, not surprisingly, the intellectual traditions supporting the view that aggression is more a function of nature than nurture have found a ready audience.

The mass media also play a significant role in perpetuating outdated views on violence, according to Jeffrey Goldstein, a psychologist at Temple University in Philadelphia. Because it is relatively easy to describe and makes for a snappier news story, reporters seem to prefer explanations of aggression that invoke biological necessity, he says. An international conference of experts concluded in 1986 that war is not an inevitable part of human nature. When one member tried to convince reporters that this finding was newsworthy, few news organizations in the United States were interested. One reporter told him, "Call us back when you find a gene for war."

Leonard Eron, a psychologist at the University of Illinois in Chicago, observes, "TV teaches people that aggressive behavior is normative, that the world around you is a jungle when it is actually not so." In fact, research at the University of Pennsylvania's Annenberg School of Communications has shown that the more television an individual watches, the more likely he or she is to believe that "most people would take advantage of you if they got a chance."

The belief that violence is unavoidable, while disturbing at first glance, actually holds a curious attraction for many people. It also allows individuals to excuse their own acts of aggression by suggesting that they have little choice.

"In order to justify, accept, and live with war, we have created a psychology that makes it inevitable," says Dr. Bernard Lown, co-chairman of International Physicians for the Prevention of Nuclear War, which received the Nobel Peace Prize in 1985. "It is a rationalization for accepting war as a system of resolving human conflict."

To understand these explanations for the war-is-inevitable belief is to realize its consequences. Treating any behavior as inevitable sets up a self-fulfilling prophecy: By assuming we are bound to be aggressive, we are more likely to act that way and provide evidence for the assumption. People who believe that humans are naturally aggressive may also be unlikely to oppose particular wars.

The evidence suggests, then, that humans do have a choice with respect to aggression and war. To an extent, such destructiveness is due to the mistaken assumption that we are helpless to control an essentially violent nature.

"We live in a time," says Lown, "when accepting this as inevitable is no longer possible without courting extinction."

from Detroit Free Press, *August 21, 1988*

Axioms of Nonviolence

by Lanzo del Vasto

"Peace" is a strong word. It has the same root as "pact" and presupposes agreement confirmed by sworn faith and the law. It has the same root as "pay" (*pacare* means "to appease") and so implies measured compensation. It is an act, an act that costs an effort. It belongs to the same family as "compact" and implies solidity and coherence.

This simple consideration of the meaning of words reveals the oneness of peace with justice which is stability, balance, and law.

Everyone knows that injustice makes peace impossible, for injustice is a state of violence and disorder which cannot and must not be maintained. It asserts itself through violence, holds sway through violence, and leads to the violence of revolt, which shows that if justice is the reason for peace, it is at the same time the cause of revolution and war, acts that always draw their justification from the defense or conquest of rights and the abolition of injustice.

But we started off from justice the foundation of peace, and here we come to justice the cause of all conflict. Are there two justices then?

Yes, the true and the false.

The true, which is one as truth is one. True justice is at one with truth. It is above everything, in everything, inscribed in the order of things, exists by itself and is God.

False justice is double and contradictory and, like mental aberration, engenders illusion and idols. But men cling to these phantoms more tenaciously than to reality, and so are tormented and torn asunder and hurled against each other in the perpetual war named history.

Let no one say of justice what is commonly said of truth: that it is inaccessible. Say rather that it is inevitable, obvious as light to the eye, and all error claims its support.

How does true justice lapse into false?
By means of these three arguments:

1. That we have the right to render evil for evil and to call the evil rendered good and just.

2. That the end justifies the means and good ends justify bad means.

3. That reason, agreement, and consent do not suffice to maintain justice and that it is just to have recourse to fear, compulsion, and force, not only in exceptional cases, but by means of permanent institutions.

These three arguments are tenets of faith for the common man, for the good as for the wicked. They are never called into doubt, never discussed, and on them people base their civil law and rules of behavior.

It has seldom been noticed that they are self-contradictory and can only lead to endless conflict.

Therefore justice and truth require us to disentangle ourselves from these arguments and their consequences. We must free ourselves from them under penalty of death. For the fact is that if today we cannot find other means of solving human conflict, we are all condemned to die.

The good news that must be announced in our time is that these means have been found. They are the arms of justice, or active revolutionary nonviolence.

The nonviolent can be distinguished by their refusal of the three arguments everyone repeats in order to justify violence. Nonviolence says:

1. No, evil is not corrected or arrested by an equal evil, but doubled, and to have recourse to it is to become a link in the chain of evil.

2. No, the end does not justify the means. Evil means spoil the best causes. If the end is just, the means must be so too.

3. No, fear, compulsion, and force can never establish justice, any more than they can teach us truth. They can only twist conscience. Now, the righting of conscience is what is called justice.

The nonviolent directly adhere to and act from the justice that is one, universal, and as simple as two-and-two-make-four. Hunger and thirst for justice are what make them act. They are servants of justice and do not make justice their servant so as to justify acts dictated by the motives mentioned earlier or reactions dictated by the adversary's attitude.

That is why Gandhi names direct nonviolent action "satyagraha," that is to say, an act of fidelity to truth. The victory the nonviolent seek is to convince the enemy and bring about a change of heart, to convert him by fighting him and, in the end, to make a friend of him.

Is the thing possible? How can it be done? Who has ever done it? In what circumstances, and with what results? I shall not answer here. Whole books have been written on the subject.

The first thing is to learn and understand what it is; the second, to try it out for oneself. But it cannot be learned like arithmetic or grammar. Learning and understanding nonviolence are done from within. So the first steps are self-recollection, reflection on the principles, and conversion, that is to say, turning back against the common current.

For if the purpose of your action is to make the adversary change his mind without forcing him to, how can you do so unless you yourself are converted? If the purpose is to wrest the enemy from his hatred and his evil by touching his conscience, how can you do so if you have not freed yourself from hatred, evil, and lack of conscience? You want to bring peace into the world, which is very generous of you; peace to the uttermost ends of the earth, for you are great-hearted, but do you know how to bring peace into your own house? Is there peace in your heart? Can one give what one does not possess?

As for justice, can you establish it between yourself and others, even those who are strangers and hostile to you, if you cannot succeed with your nearest and dearest? And what is more, if you cannot establish it between you and yourself?

But do not jump to the discouraging conclusion that in order to enter nonviolent combat one must be a saint or a wise man, or perfect. This form of combat is for one and all, and we can enter it as we are, with our indignities (and even all the better as we are fully conscious of them). But we should know that in principle, if not in fact, we must prepare ourselves as for all struggle. Here, however, preparation must be inward.

On the other hand, the struggle itself and the tribulations it involves are exercises that will help our transformation, and self-mastery is a pledge of victory over evil.

Peace and justice are a harmonious adjustment which does not come about by itself but is the fruit of effort and work upon oneself, before and during confrontation. That is why Vinoba says, "The training ground for nonviolence is man's heart."

But drill is not enough, nor courage, nor reason. There must also be music and a sense of harmony.

Let us proceed to the other tenets of every man's faith:

4. All violence, including murder, becomes lawful in the case of self-defense. Another argument that no one calls in doubt. Do you? Yes. Because self-defense is legitimate, a right and a duty, but murder, which is offense, not defense, is not.

Therefore one should not speak of legitimate defense, but of justified offense, which is self-contradictory.

I have no more right to take someone's life in order to defend mine than I have to take his wife in order to ensure my own happiness.

Let it rather be called "natural" or "animal" defense. It is of capital importance not to drag the law into this matter.

For if we consider legitimate the exceptional case where one can see no other means of staving off aggression than killing, we shall build upon it a whole system of legislation and institutions whose sole office will be to prepare and perpetuate murder.

And that is what we have done. The army, the police, and criminal law are that and nothing else.

Defense will no longer be natural and for that reason excusable; it will be premeditated and systematic crime, and there will no longer be any moral restraint or limit to killing and cruelty.

5. Murder is not only permissible, but a duty when common welfare requires it. Now the "common welfare" in question is not the welfare of all. It is the welfare of a limited group, even if it includes millions of people (the number involved makes no difference). Common welfare cannot be achieved at anyone's expense. Common welfare is justice and charity toward every human being.

14

6. Technology, economy, and politics are morally neutral. They obey their own natural laws. Here is how men build the gigantic machinery in which they are caught and crushed. That efficiency is good and always necessary for doing something goes without saying, but it is senseless to attribute value to it in itself. If efficiency lies in doing evil, then the better it is, the worse it is.

7. Justice is established order. This seventh argument, unlike those that have gone before, is not accepted by everyone. There is no regime which does not have its rebels. But the conviction of the greater number is such that the ordinary citizen is ready to kill and die through obedience to law and power.

Now the law fixes morals. Morals are the effect of a certain balance of force between tribes and classes, hard-won pacts which make possible civil life and work in common.

By the standards of absolute justice, the law always has lamentable shortcomings, in addition to which holders of power commit errors and abuses, all of which is coated over by habit and ignorance. But should the balance or power shift, consciences awake, and there ensues revolt which results in the creation of other states of injustice.

There must therefore always be a law to correct the law, and the law is constantly having to be amended and adjusted, as in liberal regimes.

But liberal regimes are unstable and continually shaken by rivalry, so that governments have more to do to stay in power than to govern. Nevertheless, they still have enough strength to abuse their power, and the people, enough passion and blindness to abuse their right of opposition. The liberal regime is no doubt more humane than others, but criticism by the opposition is less pure because it requires less courage. Legal and licit means exist of denouncing injustice in the press and raising questions in parliament, but the rich, the powerful, and the intriguers remain masters of the game.

That is why one must have no fear of resorting to direct nonviolent action and, if necessary, of breaking the law openly, seeking legal punishment and undertaking fasts and other sacrifices, so that the justice which is above all law may dawn in men's consciences.

This does not mean that direct nonviolent action is impossible in nonliberal regimes. To be sure, it is more difficult, and victory less certain.

But whoever does not attempt it at a relatively easy stage deserves to fall into bondage and undergo dictatorship.

Murderous rebellion, disorder, and cowardly acquiescence alike foster tyrannical regimes.

The fact is that in order to do, one must first be, and that has been our endeavor. We do not regard spiritual preparation as a means, but as something intrinsically more important than any outer demonstration or victory. Bringing man face to face with God and face to face with himself is what matters and is desirable for its own sake. When the Tree of Life has been found again, our acts will fall from it like ripe fruit full of savor.

Much more than going into the street, distributing tracts, speaking to crowds, knocking on doors, leading walks and campaigns, invading bomb factories, undertaking public fasts, braving the police, being beaten and jailed (all of which is good on occasion and which we gladly do), the most efficient action and the most significant testimony in favor of nonviolence and truth is living: living a life that is one, where everything goes in the same sense, from prayer and meditation to laboring for our daily bread, from the teaching of the doctrine to the making of manure, from cooking to singing and dancing around the fire; living a life in which there is no violence or unfairness, neither hidden violence nor brutal violence, neither legal and permitted unfairness, nor illegal unfairness. What matters is to show that such a life is possible and even not more difficult than a life of gain, nor more unpleasant than a life of pleasure, nor less natural than an "ordinary" life. What matters is to find the nonviolent answer to all the questions man is faced with today, as at all epochs, to formulate the answer clearly and do our utmost to carry it into effect. What matters is to discover whether there is such a thing as a nonviolent economy, free of all forms of pressure and closed to all forms of unfairness; whether there is such a thing as nonviolent authority, independent of force and carrying no privileges; whether there is such a thing as nonviolent justice, justice without punishment, and punishment without violence; such things as nonviolent farming, nonviolent medicine, nonviolent psychiatry, nonviolent diet.

And to begin with, what matters is to make sure that all violence, even of speech, even of thought, even hidden and disguised, has been weeded out of our religious life.

from Warriors of Peace: Writings on the Techniques of Nonviolence, *Knopf, New York, 1974*

Students Astutely Aware

by Colman McCarthy

Teaching has its heartfelt and resounding moments, and for me one of them came on the morning of January 17 when I was leaving Bethesda-Chevy Chase High School. Some students from my daily 7:40-8:30 a.m. class were taking control of their lives. Independent control.

I had just finished meeting with my class, 40 juniors and seniors in a course called "Alternatives to Violence." On the eastern edge of the school's front lawn about 150 students had gathered around the wide stump of an oak tree. Atop it was a young woman giving a speech. When I moved closer, I recognized her as a student from my class. She was speaking to a rapt audience about the war in the Gulf and the need to give nonviolent sanctions a chance.

The evening before, as U.S. bomber pilots began attacking Iraq, George Bush had announced that the world could "wait no longer." He was wrong. This part of the world could wait, as small and peripheral as it seemed on the lawn fronting the school. All semester, while reading and discussing essays on pacifism by Gandhi, Martin Luther King, Jr., Dorothy Day, Tolstoy, and a long list of other practitioners of nonviolence, the Pentagon's preparation for war hovered over the collective consciousness of the class.

Now that the bombing and killing had begun, as more than three-fourths of the class had predicted it would by a show of hands one moning in October, the time had come for action. I looked among the students at the rally. I knew about 20. Some I would have figured to be there, because I had listened to their anti-war views throughout the semester. Others suprised me - reserved ones who had not said much in class one way or the other about the Gulf.

The senior girl who had been speaking when I came over was in that group. I listened in amazement. Where did all that passion come from? And what inner fires had been burning in the next speaker, a senior boy who spoke knowledgeably about draft resistance. Be aware of your rights, he said, and went on to tell about the national groups that provide counseling on conscientious objection.

When the rally dispersed, four students took a large sign – "Honk for Peace" – and stood behind it on the highway in front of the school. A clamor of honks began. The group, joined by others, decided to cut classes and go be educated in democracy by visiting the anti-war protest in front of the White House.

They learned there that they were not alone, that resistance to the Gulf war was spreading daily in their country and in Europe. Mr. Bush has vowed that "this will not be another Vietnam." Wrong again. It took less than a week for America's streets, from San Diego to Boston, to be filled with citizens expressing their opposition and contempt for the same kind of war ethic that dragged the United States into Vietnam.

It is common of late for Vietnam veterans to return to Southeast Asia, in exercises of catharsis and reconciliation, and in many cases to ask forgiveness of the villagers who were bombed and sprayed by American soldiers. In 20 years, it could happen that today's U.S. bomber pilots will be returning to Iraq seeking reconciliation and peace. The anti-war demonstrators are saying rightly: Let's seek it now.

Up against the might of a war-approving Congress and the domination of the media by the Pentagon's version of events, plus television's one-sided reliance on ex-generals turned "military analysts" (why no peace analysts on these programs?), a few high school kids making speeches on a stump and holding peace signs is indeed small. Gandhi, as usual, had a thought: "Nonviolence is the finest quality of the soul, but it is developed by practice. Almost anything you do will seem insignificant but it is important that you do it."

Three days after war began in the Gulf, the semester was over and class ended. We tell our children not to fight in the schoolyard, not to hit brothers, sisters, or playmates, and to use reason and dialogue to settle conflicts. Seek alternatives to violence. It's a sound message, except that all this school year much of America's adults supported politicians and warriors who pushed the opposite ethic in the Middle East.

Three of my students, articulate and spunky even at 7:40 a.m., were consistently skeptical about nonviolence, but they were willing to push themselves and the rest of us to think freshly about old problems. Moving beyond patented or conventional boundaries, and see-

17

ing life differently and acting in the riskiness of that
new vision, is a breakthrough to be celebrated, not
minimized. Wherever the newness leads, the students
will go into adulthood as discoverers, not imitators and
least of all followers.

from Washington Post, *January 24,1991*

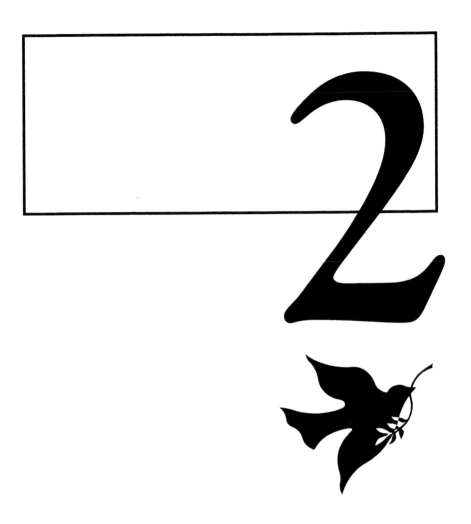

No one has a right to sit down and feel hopeless. There's too much work to do.

Dorothy Day

Love Is the Measure

by Dorothy Day

We confess to being fools and wish that we were more so. In the face of the approaching atom bomb test (and discussion of widespread radioactivity is giving people more and more of an excuse to get away from the philosophy of personalism and the doctrine of free will); in the face of an approaching maritime strike; in the face of bread shortages and housing shortages; in the face of the passing of the draft extension, teenagers included, we face the situation that there is nothing we can do for people except to love them. If the maritime strike goes on there will be no shipping of food or medicine or clothes to Europe or the Far East, so there is nothing to do again but to love. We continue in our 14th year of feeding our brothers and sisters, clothing them and sheltering them, and the more we do it, the more we realize that the most important thing is to love. There are several families with us, destitute families, destitute to an unbelievable extent, and there, too, is nothing to do but to love. What I mean is that there is no chance of rehabilitation, no chance, so far as we see, of changing them; certainly no chance of adjusting them to this abominable world about them—and who wants them adjusted, anyway?

What we would like to do is change the world— make it a little simpler for people to feed, clothe, and shelter themselves as God intended them to do. And to a certain extent, by fighting for better conditions, by crying out unceasingly for the rights of the workers, of the poor, of the destitute—the rights of the worthy and the unworthy poor, in other words—we can to a certain extent change the world; we can work for the oasis, the little cell of joy and peace in a harried world. We can throw our pebble in the pond and be confident that its ever-widening circle will reach around the world.

We repeat, there is nothing that we can do but love, and dear God—please enlarge our hearts to love each other, to love our neighbor, to love our enemy as well as our friend.

Whenever I groan within myself and think how hard it is to keep writing about love in these times of tension and strife which may, at any moment, become for us all a time of terror, I think to myself: What else is the world interested in? What else do we all want, each one of us, except to love and be loved, in our families, in our work, in all our relationships? God is Love. Love casts our fear. Even the most ardent revolutionist, seeking to change the world, to overturn the tables of the money changers, is trying to make a world where it is easier for people to love, to stand in that relationship to each other. We want with all our hearts to love, to be loved. And not just in the family, but to look upon all as our mothers, sisters, brothers, children. It is when we love the most intensely and most humanly that we can recognize how tepid is our love for others. The keenness and intensity of love brings with it suffering, of course, but joy too because it is a foretaste of heaven.

When you love people, you see all the good in them. There can never be enough thinking about it. St. John of the Cross said that where there was no love, put love and you would draw love out. The principle certainly works. I've seen my friend Sister Peter Claver with that warm friendliness of hers which is partly natural, but is intensified and made enduring by grace, come into a place which is cold with tension and conflict, and warm the house with her love.

And this is not easy. Everyone will try to kill that love in you, even your nearest and dearest; at least, they will try to prune it. "Don't you know this, that, and the other thing about this person? He or she did this. If you don't want to hear it, you must hear. It is for your good to hear it. It is my duty to tell you, and it is your duty to take recognition of it. You must stop loving, modify your loving, show your disapproval. You cannot possibly love—if you pretend you do, you are a hypocrite and the truth is not in you. You are contributing to the delinquency of that person by your sentimental blindness. It is such people as you who add to the sum total of confusion and wickedness and soft appeasement and compromise and the policy of expediency in this world. You are to blame for Communism, for industrial capitalism, and finally for hell on earth!"

To see only the good, the Christ, in others! Perhaps if we thought of how Karl Marx was called "Papa Marx" by all the children on the street, if we knew and remembered how he told fairy stories to his children, how he suffered hunger and poverty and pain, how he sat by the body of his dead child and had no money for coffin or funeral, perhaps such thoughts as these would make us love him and his followers. Dear God, for the memory of that dead child, or that faithful wife, grant his stormy spirit "a place of refreshment, light, and peace."

And then there was Lenin. He hungered and thirsted and at times he had no fixed abode. Mme. Krupskaya, his widow, said that he loved to go into the peace of the pine woods and hunt mushrooms. He lived one time in the slums of Paris and ate horsemeat. He started schools for the poor and workers. "He went about doing good." Is this blasphemy? How many people are dying and going to God their Father and saying sadly, "We have not so much as heard that there is a Holy Spirit." And how will they hear if none preaches to them? And what kind of shepherds have many of them had? Ezekiel said in his day, "Woe to the shepherds that feed themselves and not their sheep!"

from By Little and By Little, the Selected Writings of Dorothy Day
Knopf, New York

Poverty and Precarity

by Dorothy Day

It is hard to write about poverty.

We live in a slum neighborhood. It is becoming ever more crowded with Puerto Ricans, those who have the lowest wages in the city, who do the hardest work, who are small and undernourished from generations of privation and exploitation.

It is hard to write about poverty when the backyard at Chrystie Street still has the furniture piled to one side that was put out on the street in an eviction in a next-door tenement.

How can we say to these people, "Rejoice and be exceedingly glad, for great is your reward in heaven," when we are living comfortable in a warm house, sitting down to a good table, decently clothed? Maybe not so decently. I had occasion to visit the city shelter last month where homeless families are cared for. I sat there for a couple of hours, contemplating poverty and destitution - a family with two of the children asleep in the parents' arms and four others sprawled against them; another young couple, the mother pregnant. I made myself known to a young man in charge. (I did not want to appear to be spying on them when all I wanted to know was the latest on the apartment situation for homeless families.) He apologized for making me wait, explaining that he had thought I was one of the clients.

We need always to be thinking and writing about poverty, for if we are not among its victims its reality fades from us. We must talk about poverty, because people insulated by their own comfort lose sight of it. So many decent people come in to visit and tell us how their families were brought up in poverty, and how, through hard work and cooperation, they managed to educate all the children—even raise up priests and nuns to the Church. They contend that healthful habits and a stable family situation enable people to escape from the poverty class, no matter how mean the slum they may once have been forced to live in. So why can't everybody do it? No, these people don't know about the poor. Their conception of poverty is of something as neat and well ordered as a nun's cell.

No one working with the *Catholic Worker* gets a salary, so our readers feel called upon to give and help us keep the work going. And then we experience a poverty of another kind, a poverty of reputation. It is said often and with some scorn, "Why don't they get jobs and help the poor that way? Why are they living off others, begging?"

I can only explain to such critics that it would complicate things to give a salary to Roger for his work of 14 hours a day in the kitchen, clothes room, and office; to pay Jane a salary for running the women's house and Beth and Annabelle for giving out clothes, for making stencils all day and helping with the sick and the poor, and then have them all turn the money right back in to support the work. Or to make it more complicated, they might all go out and get jobs, and bring the money home to pay their board and room and the salaries of others to run the house. It is simpler just to be poor. It is simpler to beg. The main thing is not to hold on to anything.

But the tragedy is that we do, we all do hold on—to our books, our tools, such as typewriters, our clothes; and instead of rejoicing when they are taken from us we lament. We protest when people take our time or privacy. We are holding on to these "goods" too.

Occasionally, as we start thinking of poverty—often after reading the life of such a saint as Benedict Joseph Labre—we dream of going out on our own, living with the destitute, sleeping on park benches or in the city shelter, living in churches, sitting before the Blessed Sacrament as we see so many doing from the Municipal Lodging House around the corner. And when such thoughts come on warm spring days when the children are playing in the park, and it is good to be out on the city streets, we know that we are only deceiving ourselves, for we are only dreaming of a form of luxury. What we want is the warm sun, and rest, and time to think and read, and freedom from the people who press in on us from early morning until late at night. No, it is not simple, this business of poverty.

"Precarity," or precariousness, is an essential element in true voluntary poverty, a saintly priest from Martinique has written us. "True poverty is rare," he writes. "Nowadays religious communities are good, I am sure, but they are mistaken about poverty. They accept, admit poverty on principle, but everything must be good and strong, buildings must be fireproof. Precarity is everywhere rejected, and precarity is an essential element of poverty. This has been forgotten.

Here in our monastery we want precarity in everything except the church. These last days our refectory was near collapsing. We have put several supplementary beams in place and thus it will last maybe two or three years more. Someday it will fall on our heads and that will be funny. Precarity enables us better to help the poor. When a community is always building, enlarging, and embellishing, there is nothing left over for the poor. We have no right to do so as long as there are slums and breadlines somewhere."

from By Little and By Little, the Selected Writings of Dorothy Day
Knopf, New York

This Money Is Not Ours

by Dorothy Day

Editor's note:

A principle, Dorothy Day believed, remains abstract until it costs us something. In 1961, she welcomed the opportunity to test the value of one of her convictions in a gesture of disarming originality. The cost was $3,579.39.

For years the *Catholic Worker* had repeated Peter Maurin's defense of the medieval ban on usury. The acceptance of the belief that value resides in currency rather than labor, he believed, was a turning point in the transition from a functional to an acquisitive society. The *Catholic Worker* could not single-handedly reverse this process, but it could at least issue a solitary protest, and make what Peter would call a "point."

The Catholic Worker
39 Spring Street
New York 12, N.Y.

Treasurer   July 1960
City of New York

Dear Sir:

We are returning to you a check for $3,579.39 which represents interest on the $68,700 which we were awarded by the city as payment for the property at 223 Chrystie Street which we owned and lived in for almost 10 years, and used as a community for the poor. We did not voluntarily give up the property—it was taken from us by right of eminent domain for the extension of the subway which the city deemed necessary. We had to wait almost a year and a half for the money owed us, although the city permitted us to receive two-thirds of the assessed valuation of the property in advance so that we could relocate. Property owning having been made impossible for us by city regulations, we are now renting and continuing our work.

We are returning the interest on the money we have recently received because we do not believe in "money lending" at interest. As Catholics we are acquainted with the early teaching of the Church. All the early councils forbade it, declaring it reprehensible to make money by lending it out at interest. Canon law of the Middle Ages forbade it and in various decrees ordered that profit so obtained was to be restored. In the Christian emphasis on the duty of charity, we are commanded to lend gratuitously, to give freely, even in the case of confiscation, as in our own case—not to resist but to accept cheerfully.

We do not believe in the profit system, and so we cannot take profit or interest on our money. People who take a materialistic view of human service wish to make a profit but we are trying to do our duty by our service without wages to our brothers as Jesus commanded in the Gospel (Matthew 25). Loaning money at interest is deemed by one Franciscan as the principal scourge of civilization. Eric Gill, the English artist and writer, calls usury and war the two great problems of our time.

Since we have dealt with these problems in every issue of the Catholic Worker *since 1933—man's freedom, war and peace, man and the state, man and his work—and since Scripture says that the love of money is the root of all evil, we are taking this opportunity to live in practice of this belief, and make a gesture of overcoming that love of money by returning to you the interest.*

Insofa as our money paid for services for the common good, and aid to the poor, we should be very happy to allow you to use not only our money without interest, but also our work, the Works of Mercy which we all perform here at the headquarters of the Catholic Worker without other salary or recompense than our daily food and lodging, clothes, and incidental expenses.

Insofar as the use of our money paid for the time being for salaries for judges who have condemned us and others to jail, and for the politicians who appointed them, and for prisons, and the execution chamber at Sing Sing, and for the executioner's salary, we can only protest the use of our money and turn with utter horror from taking interest on it.

Please also be assured that we are not judging individuals, but are trying to make a judgement on the system under which we live and with which we admit that we ourselves compromise daily in many small ways, but which we try and wish to withdraw from as much as possible.

Sincerely yours,
Dorothy Day, Editor

It is not easy, having acted upon principle, to explain it in ways acceptable and understood by others. An instance is our recent sending back of the interest on the money given us for St. Joseph's House on Chrystie Street.

During the course of the month we have received a few letters, not very many, of criticism of our act. One letter, from a generous benefactor who had given us a large sum when her father died, pointed out that if her parent had not invested his money wisely she and her mother would not have had anything left to live on; also that we probably received many donations which came from dividends, interest, etc.

I only try to answer as best I can. But sometimes one confuses others the more by trying to answer objections. When we wrote our letter to the city, and published it in the paper, we also printed some excerpts from the teaching of St. Thomas Aquinas on interest and money-lending. We used some of Peter Maurin's easy essays on the subject, and an article by Arthur Sheehan on credit unions, which, however, ask for a small interest on their loans. How can this be reconciled with the "gesture" we made of returning to the city the large check which represented the interest for a year and a half on the money paid us for our property on Chrystie Street? First of all, we asked with Chesterton: Whose money is this interest which the city was paying us? Where did it come from? Money does not breed money; it is sterile.

To answer our correspondent: Of course we are involved, the same as everyone else, in living off interest. We are all caught up in this same money economy. Just as "God writes straight with crooked lines," so we too waver, struggle on our devious path—always aiming at God, even though we are conditioned by habits and ancestry, etc. We have free will, which is our greatest gift. We are free to choose, and as we see more clearly, our choice is more direct and easier to make. But we all see through a glass darkly. It would be heaven to see Truth face to face.

We are publishing a paper in which ideas are discussed and clarified, and illustrated by act. So we are not just a newspaper. We are a revolution, a movement, as Peter Maurin used to say. We are propagandists of the faith. We are the Church. We are members of the Mystical Body. We all must try to function healthily. We do not all have the same function, but we all have a vocation, a calling. Ours is a "prophetic" one, as many priests have said to us. Pope John recently cited the courage of John the Baptist as an example for today. Prophets made great gestures, did things to call attention to what they were talking about. That was what we did; we made a gesture, when we returned the money to the city. It was calling attention to a great unsolved problem in which we are all involved, Church, State, corporation, institution, individual.

There is no simple solution. Let the priests and the economists get to work on it. It is a moral and an ethical problem. We can work on the lowest level, the credit union in the parish, for instance. Through the credit union families have been taught to resist the skillful seductions of the advertising men and by doing without many things, to attain to ownership, homes, workshops, tools, small factories, and so on. These things have happened in Nova Scotia, in missions throughout the world, and this is one way to combat what the bishops call the all-encroaching State. It is the beginning of the decentralist society.

So primarily, our sending back the money was a gesture. It was the first time we had to do so with so large a sum of money. We were being reimbursed by the city—and generously, as far as money went—for the house and our improvements on it. (They had taken over the property by the right of eminent domain because a subway extension was going through.) One can argue that the value of the property went up, that the city had the 18 months' use of our money, that money purchases less now, and so on. The fact remains that the city was doing what it could to pay off each and every tenant in the two tenement houses from which they were being evicted, giving bonuses, trying to find other lodgings, though these were usually unacceptable, being in other neighborhoods or boroughs.

We agree that slums need to be eliminated, but that an entire neighborhood, which is like a village made up of many nationalities, should be scattered, displaced—this is wanton cruelty, and one of the causes of the juvenile delinquency of our cities. Also, it is terribly bad and ruthless management on the part of the city fathers.

Is Robert Moses responsible? He is the planner. But he deals recklessly with inanimate brick and cement at the expense of flesh and blood. He is walking ruthlessly over brokenhearted families to make a great outward show of a destroyed and rebuilt city. He has been doing what blockbusters and obliteration bombing did in European and British cities. Right now an entire neighborhood just south of Tompkins Square where some of our poor friends live is being demolished and the widows and fatherless are crying to heaven. The city fathers try to recompense them, try to give them bonuses to get out quickly. But what good does the money do them when there is no place to go? They do not want to go to another neighborhood or even to another block. Actually, as piled-up furniture on the streets testifies, many cling to their poor homes until the last moment, and probably forfeit the 200 or 300 dollars they are offered, rather than be exiled. That money means as much to them as the 2,000 or 3,000 thousand did to us.

There is talk about doing things economically, yet money is poured out like water in all directions and scandals are always being unearthed of cheating and graft in high places. This extends down to the smallest citizen, too, trying to get in on the big deal and get his— from the building inspector who expects to be tipped, to the little veteran around the corner who is speculating in the real estate by buying and improving and renting and then selling back his property to the city at exorbitant prices. "It doesn't matter if it is going to be torn down in a year or so," he assured us. "Rent out all the apartments and stores and then you can ask more from the city." Big deal! Everyone is trying to get in on the Moses big deal.

So to put it on the natural but often most emotional plane of simple patriotism, love of country or city, this feeling, too, prompted us to send back the interest. We do not want to participate in this big deal. "Why are there wars and contentions among you? Because each one seeketh his own."

We considered this a gesture, too, toward peace, a spiritual weapon which is translated into action. We cannot talk about these ideas without trying to put them into practice, though we do it clumsily and are often misunderstood.

We are not trying to be superior, holier than thou. Of course we are involved in paying taxes, in living on money which comes from our industrial capitalist way of life. But we can try, by voluntary poverty and labor, to earn our living, and not to be any more involved than we can help. We, all of us, partake in a way in the sin of Sapphira and Ananias, by holding back our time, our love, our material resources even, after making great protestations of "absolutism." May God and you, our readers, forgive us. We are, in spite of all we try to do, unprofitable servants.

from By Little and By Little, the Selected Writings of Dorothy Day
Knopf, New York

Undeclared War to Declared War

by Dorothy Day, 1942

Dear Fellow Workers in Christ:

Lord God, merciful God, our Father, shall we keep silent, or shall we speak? And if we speak, what shall we say?

I am sitting here in the church on Mott Street writing this in your presence. Out on the streets it is quiet, but you are there too, in the Chinese, in the Italians, these neighbors we love. We love them because they are our brothers, as Christ is our Brother and God our Father.

But we have forgotten so much. We have all forgotten. And how can we know unless you tell us. "For whoever calls upon the name of the Lord shall be saved." How then are they to call upon Him in whom they have not believed? But how are they to believe Him whom they have not heard? And how are they to hear, if no one preaches? And how are men to preach unless they be sent? As it is written, "How beautiful are the feet of those who preach the gospel of peace." (Romans X)

Seventy-five thousand *Catholic Workers* go out every month. What shall we print? We can print still what the Holy Father is saying, when he speaks of total war, of mitigating the horrors of war, when he speaks of cities of refuge, of feeding Europe …

We will print the words of Christ who is with us always, even to the end of the world. "Love your enemies, do good to those who hate you, and pray for those who persecute and calumniate you, so that you may be children of your Father in heaven, who makes His sun to rise on the good and the evil, and sends rain on the just and unjust."

We are at war, a declared war, with Japan, Germany, and Italy. But still we can repeat Christ's word, each day, holding them close in our hearts, each month printing them in the paper. In times past, Europe has been a battlefield. But let us remember St. Francis, who spoke of peace and we will remind our readers of him, too, so they will not forget.

In the *Catholic Worker* we will quote our Pope, our saints, our priests. We will go on printing the articles which remind us today that we are all "called to be saints," that we are other Christs, reminding us of the priesthood of the laity.

We are still pacifists. Our manifesto is the Sermon on the Mount, which means that we will try to be peacemakers. Speaking for many of our conscientious objectors, we will not participate in armed warfare or in making munitions, or by buying government bonds to prosecute the war, or in urging others to these efforts.

But neither will we be carping in our criticism. We love our country and we love our President. We have been the only country in the world where men of all nations have taken refuge from oppression. We recognize that while in the order of intention we have tried to stand for peace, for love of our brother, in the order of execution we have failed as Americans in living up to our principles.

We will try daily, hourly, to pray for an end to the war, such an end, to quote Father Orchard, "as would manifest to all the world, that it was brought about by divine action, rather than by military might or diplomatic negotiation, which men and nations would then only attribute to their power or sagacity."

"Despite all calls to prayer," Father Orchard concludes, "there is at present all too little indication anywhere that the tragedy of humanity and the desperate need of the world have moved the faithful, still less stirred the thoughtless masses, to turn to prayer as the only hope for mankind this dreadful hour.

"We shall never pray until we feel more deeply, and we shall never feel deeply enough until we envisage what is actually happening in the world, and understand what is possible in the will of God; and that means until sufficient numbers realize that we have brought things to a pass which is beyond human power to help or save.

"Those who do feel and see, however inadequately, should not hesitate to begin to pray, or fail to persevere, however dark the prospects remain.

"Let them urge others to do likewise; and then, first small groups, and then the Church as a whole and at last the world, may turn and cry for forgiveness, mercy, and deliverance for all.

"Then we may be sure God will answer, and effectually; for the Lord's hand is not shortened that it cannot save, nor His ear heavy that it cannot hear."

Let us add, that unless we combine this prayer with almsgiving, in giving to the least of God's children, and fasting in order that we may help feed the hungry, and penance in recognition of our share in the guilt, our prayer may become empty words.

Our works of mercy may take us into the midst of war. As editor of the *Catholic Worker*, I would urge our friends and associates to care for the sick and the wounded, to the growing of food for the hungry, to the continuance of all our works of mercy in our houses and on our farms. We understand, of course, that there is and that there will be great differences of opinion even among our own groups as to how much collaboration we can have with the government in times like these. There are differences more profound and there will be many continuing to work with us from necessity, or from choice, who do not agree with us as to our position on war, conscientious objection, etc. But we beg that there will be mutual charity and forbearance among us all.

This letter, sent to all our Houses of Hospitality and to all our farms, and being printed in the January issue of the paper, is to state our position in this most difficult time.

Because of our refusal to assist in the prosecution of war and our insistence that our collaboration be one for peace, we may find ourselves in difficulties. But we trust in the generosity and understanding of our government and our friends, to permit us to continue, to use our paper to "preach Christ crucified."

May the Blessed Mary, Mother of love, of faith, of knowledge and of hope, pray for us.

from By Little and By Little, the Selected Writings of Dorothy Day
Knopf, New York

Reflections in Jail

by Dorothy Day

One of the peculiar enjoyments I got out of jail was in being on the other side for a change. I was the one working in a laundry, ironing uniforms of jailers. I was the one sitting in the sewing room turning the collar and mending the uniform of an officer. It gave me a chance to tell the other prisoners about Tolstoy, and how he said the first move toward reform was to do one's own work. Everyone regarded the officers as members of the parasite class, though they would not use that word. How much more respect they would have had for the officers, and for the work they themselves had to do, if they had seen the officers sitting mending their own clothes. If they had seen them working to help their fellows. Perhaps it would have meant a beginning of the philosophy of work which Peter Maurin used to say was so sadly lacking today. If prisoners and officers had worked together to make the prison a happier place, what a change there might have been in the hearts of those confined.

The officers sat all day at their desks, watching, directing, always expecting the worst, always looking for some small infraction, always seeing the women as criminals. They did not see that which is of God in every person, as the Friends put it. St. John of the Cross said, "Where there is no love, put love, and you will find love." The officers looked for the criminal and found the criminal.

The women got away with what they could. They fought, they lied, they stole when they could. While working in the laundry, I saw a girl put a folded dress, which she wanted for herself, up between her legs, under her skirt. When she spoke of it afterward to some of the other prisoners on our corridor, they jeered. "That's nothing," one said, "I've seen girls who worked in the kitchen get away with a turkey or a ham." Judith made us all hilarious by immediately getting up and trying to impersonate a girl walking out of the kitchen with a turkey or ham held thus.

Looking back on these last paragraphs, I see that I have gone from the sublime to the ridiculous, even to the vulgar and, for some, the revolting. But beauty and joy often spring from the dung heap.

I have said that I enjoyed being on the other side for a time. People come into the Catholic Worker in such numbers: 800 a day for food; hundreds of men, women and children coming in for clothes. When all the beds in the house are full, we often give out "flop" money–the fifty cents a night it costs to sleep on the Bowery. All that we give is given to us to give. Nothing is ours. All we have to give is our time and our patience, our love. In the movie, *Monsieur Vincent*, the saint tells a young nun that she has to love the poor very much for them to forgive her the bread she gives them. How often we have failed in love, how often we have been brusque, cold and indifferent. "Roger takes care of the clothes; you'll have to come back at ten o'clock." Or "Just sit in the library and wait." "Wait your turn, I'm busy." So it often goes. And now I was getting pushed here and there, told what I could do or could not do, hemmed in by rules and regulations and red tape and bureaucracy. It made me see my faults but it also made me see how much more we accomplish at the Catholic Worker in our own direct way, by not asking questions or doing any investigating, but by cultivating a spirit of trust. The whole experience of jail was good for my soul. I realized again how much ordinary kindness can do. Graciousness is an old-fashioned word but it has a beautiful religious tradition. "Grace is participation in the divine life," according to St. Peter.

Most of the time we were treated like dumb beasts–worse, because it was with indifference and contempt. "You'll be back" was the common farewell to the prisoner. It was, in effect, wishing her not to fare well. There was no goodbye, "*God be with you,*" because there was not enough faith or hope or charity to conceive of a forgiving and loving God being with anyone so lost in vice and crime as prostitutes, drug addicts and other criminals are supposed to be.

One great indignity is the examination given all women for drugs. There is certainly no recognition of the fact of political imprisonment. All of us were stripped and searched in the crudest way– even to the tearing of tissues so that bleeding resulted. Then there is the matter of clothing–the scanty garments, the crude wrappers which scarcely wrap around one, the floppy cloth slippers which are impossible to keep on! In Russia, in Germany, and even in our own country, to strip the prisoner, to humiliate him, is a definite part and purpose of a jail experience. Even in the Army, making a man stand naked before his examiners is to treat him like a dumb beast or a slave.

A great courtesy accorded us was a visit from the warden himself. Never had anything like that happened before, one of the girls assured us. He wanted to know about our demonstration, why we had done it. He was a Hungarian Catholic so perhaps it was easy to understand his confusion about our pacifism. What man does not wish to resist a foreign aggressor, to defend his home and family? But the problem of the means to an end had never occurred to him. Nowadays, it is pretty generally accepted that the end justifies the means. To his mind, one just could not be a pacifist today. It was an "impossible" position.

As to our attitude toward the prison and the prisoners, he could not understand our love for them, our not judging them. The idea of hating the sin and loving the sinner seemed foreign to him. Of course, he did not hate the sinner but he had to look upon them as evil; otherwise his job would be meaningless. When we talked of the good we found there, in spite of perversion, prostitution, and drugs, he looked at us strangely and wanted to know if we were Christian Scientists. At least he did not call us communists. He was too intelligent for that. But we seemed to him to be denying the reality of evil, because we were upholding the prisoner. The evil was there, all right, frank and unabashed. It was inside and also outside the jail.

One of the greatest evils of the day is the sense of futility. Young people say, "What can one person do? What is the sense of our small effort?" They cannot see that we can only lay one brick at a time, take one step at a time; we can be responsible only for the one action of the present moment. But we can beg for an increase of love in our hearts that will vitalize and transform these actions, and know that God will take them and multiply them, as Jesus multiplied the loaves and fishes.

Next year, perhaps, God willing, we will again go to jail and, perhaps, conditions will be the same. To be charitable we can only say that the prison officials do the best they can, according to their understanding. In a public institution, they are not paid to love the inmates, they are paid to guard them. They admit that the quarters are totally inadequate, that what was built for a House of Detention for women awaiting trial is now being used for a workhouse and penitentiary.

Dorothy Day (1890-1980)

by Colman McCarthy

NEW YORK — The funeral procession of Dorothy Day, her body in a pinewood coffin, moved out of Maryhouse on Third Street on the way to a requiem mass at Nativity Catholic Church, a half-block away. Someone wondered aloud why more of the poor were not present. The street, as mean as any in this cloister of harshness on the edge of the Bowery, was certainly not overflowing with homeless souls come to mourn the woman who had served them in a personal ministry for half a century. A few men and even fewer women—blank-eyed, dressed in tatters—stood in clusters, while others wandered down the street from the city shelter for derelicts, one of Manhattan's unseen hellholes. But that was all. Most of the 800 people following the coffin were either old friends of Miss Day who live outside the neighborhood or members of the Catholic Worker community who run St. Joseph's and Maryhouse, the two local shelters for the homeless.

Large numbers of the poor did not come, for a reason as obvious as the open sores on the face of a wino opposite Maryhouse: they are too busy trying to fight death themselves. To mark the passing of someone who loved them—accepted them totally by living here, raising money for them through her newspaper, the *Catholic Worker*—would, of course, make sense in the rational world of the comfortable, where public tribute to the deceased great and the seemingly great is the proper way of dealing with grief. But here on this street that is full of the homeless and jobless, death was not needed for grief. Hope gets buried every day.

If the turnout of the poor was not strong, there was also an almost total absence of Catholic officialdom. This was the genuine affront. Few of the faithful in this century were more committed than Dorothy Day to the church's teachings, both in its social encyclicals—on the distribution of wealth, the evils of the arms race—and its calls to private spirituality. She was a daily communicant at mass, rising early to read the Bible and pray the rosary.

Dorothy Day used her faith as a buffer against burnout and despair. Fittingly, it will have to be taken on faith that her life of service made a difference. She issued no progress reports on neighborhood improvement, summoned no task forces on how to achieve greater efficiency on the daily soup line.

Nor did she ever run "follow-up studies" on whether the derelicts of the Bowery renounced their drunken and quarrelsome ways. As her favorite saint, Theresa of Lisieux, taught, results don't matter to the prayerful.

On the subject of results, Dorothy Day had a philosophy of divine patience: "We continue feeding our neighbors and clothing and sheltering them, and the more we do it the more we realize that the most important thing is to love. There are several families with us, destitute to an unbelievable extent, and there, too, is nothing to do but love. What I mean is that there is no chance of rehabilitation—no chance, so far as we see, of changing them, certainly no chance of adjusting them to this abominable world about them, and who wants them adjusted, anyway?"

That was from the June, 1946, issue of the *Catholic Worker* newspaper, a monthly that has been a voice of pacifism and justice since 1933. The jobless and homeless are so thick in the streets that "Holy Mother City," as Miss Day called it, makes no pretense of even counting them.

It may be just as well. Counters get in the way when there is soup to be made. Even worse, getting too close to the government means a trade-off that Miss Day resisted in words and action. "The state believes in war," she said, "and, as pacifists and philosophical anarchists, we don't."

Because she served the poor for so long and with such tireless intensity, Dorothy Day had a national constituency of remarkable breadth. She was more than merely the conscience of the Left. Whether it was a young millionaire named John F. Kennedy who came to see her (in 1943) or one of the starving, she exuded authenticity.

It was so well-known that she lived among the poor—shared their table, stood in their lines, endured the daily insecurity—that the Catholic Worker became known as the one charity in which contributions truly did reach the poor. It is at St. Joseph's House, 36 E. 1st, New York 10003.

"It is a strange vocation to love the destitute and dissolute," Miss Day wrote a few years ago. But it is one that keeps attracting the young who come to the

Catholic Worker as a place to brew the soup and clean the toilets, which is also the work of peacemakers. They are against military wars for sure, but their pacifism resists the violence of the economic wars. "We refuse to fight for a materialistic system that cripples so many of its citizens," the Catholic Worker has been saying for half a century.

The only Catholic bishop of the church on hand was Terence Cardinal Cooke of New York. As the procession rounded the corner from Maryhouse and went on to the sidewalk leading to the church, the scarlet vestments of the cardinal came into view. The contrast was powerful. In a neighborhood of drab colors, where even the faces of the poor seem to be grayed with depression, the scarlet robes of the cardinal, his scarlet skullcap, had a touch of mock comedy to them; the vestments seemed almost the costume of a clown—a clown who was lost in the saddest of landscapes.

A Catholic Worker priest, a young Dominican who works at Maryhouse and was to celebrate the mass, made the best of the situation. At the head of the procession, he shook hands with Cardinal Cooke. The cardinal took over and prayed aloud, commending the soul of "dear Dorothy" to the mercy of the Lord. While cameramen from the *Associated Press*, the *Daily News*, and the *Religious News Service* clicked away—getting the coffin in the foreground—the cardinal finished praying in two minutes.

It was just enough time for many in the processing to think beyond the cardinal's brilliantly hued presence at the church door. Some recalled the pacifists from the Catholic Worker who have been standing for the past few months outside Cardinal Cooke's offices uptown and in front of the splendid St. Patrick's Cathedral. They have been leafleting the churchgoers on the immorality of the arms race and pleading with the unseen cardinal to issue a statement in favor of nuclear disarmament. In the most recent issue of the *Catholic Worker*, one of Dorothy Day's writers said sharply about the vigil at St. Patrick's last August: "We want to remember the victims of the [Hiroshima and Nagasaki] bombings, and to mourn the fact that the hierarchy of our archdiocese is so silent about nuclear disarmament, when statements from the Vatican Council, recent popes, and the U.S. Catholic Bishops Conference have been so clear in their condemnation of the arms race."

Six grandchildren of Miss Day, carrying her coffin, nodded their thanks to the cardinal and proceeded into the church. A moment later, John Shiel went up to Cardinal Cooke. Shiel, a short, half-toothless man who has been repeatedly jailed in peace protests, is something of a lay theologian who can quote every pope back to Boniface I on the subject of war and peace. A friend of Miss Day, he left Washington at 4 a.m. to be here for the mass.

"Hello, John," said His Eminence, who knew Shiel from his persistent lobbying for peace at the annual meetings of the hierarchy.

"Hello there, Cardinal," said Shiel. "When are you going to come out against nuclear weapons?"

His Eminence gave no answer, and shortly he was driven off in his limousine to "a previous commitment." The day before, according to a Catholic Worker staff member, Cardinal Cooke's secretary had phoned to request that the mass be held at 10 a.m., because it would then fit into the cardinal's schedule and he could preside. But Miss Day's daughter had already decided on 11 a.m. because that was when the soup kitchen was closed for the morning break between cleaning up after breakfast and getting ready for lunch. The cardinal's presence would be missed, the secretary was told, but with all due respect, feeding the poor came first.

Inside the church, with its unpainted cement-block walls and water-marked ceiling, the breadth of Dorothy Day's friendships was on view. In the pews were Cesar Chavez, Frank Sheed, Michael Harrington, Ed and Kathleen Guinan, Paul Moore, and Father Horace McKenna, the Jesuit who for decades has been serving the poor at his own soup kitchen in Washington.

In the back of the church, after the sermon, the undertaker, a friendly man, tall and properly somber-looking, was asked about the arrangements. "She was a lovely lady," he said. "We're doing this way below cost. The Worker gives us a lot of business, and besides, Miss Day is part of the community."

The undertaker said that the archdiocese was picking up the tab of $380 for opening the grave at the cemetery. If the patron saint of irony were listening in, he or she would call out to the heavenly choir: "Stop the music." During the archdiocese cemetery workers' strike in the mid-1950s, Dorothy Day was personally denounced by Cardinal Spellman for siding with the underpaid gravediggers.

After mass, a young Catholic Worker staff member, who was the candle-bearer at the head of the funeral procession, told the story of the candle—a thick white one, almost three feet tall. "We went around to neighborhood churches. We asked the sacristans for their old candle stubs that would be thrown out anyway. Then we melted them into this one large candle." Another form of brightness was present—a thought from one of Dorothy Day's books, printed on the bottom of the mass card: "We have all known the long loneliness and we have learned that the only solution is love and that love comes with community."

At about 12:30, some of the crowd drifted back to Maryhouse where lunch was being served. Pea soup was ladled from a 10-gallon kettle. Brown bread was on the table with milk, tea, and oranges: enough food for all.

from Washington Post, *December 2, 1980*

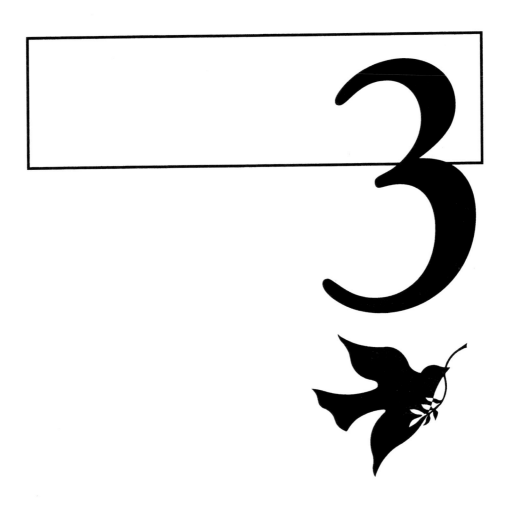

If we are to reach real pace in the world, we shall have to begin with children. And if they will grow up in their natural innocence, we won't have to struggle, we won't have to pass fruitless resolutions, but we shall go from love to love and peace to peace.

Gandhi

The Doctrine of the Sword

by Mohandas Gandhi

In this age of the rule of brute force, it is almost impossible for any one to believe that any one else could possibly reject the awe of the final supremacy of brute force. And so I receive anonymous letters advising me that I must not interfere with the progress of noncooperation, even though popular violence may break out. Others come to me and, assuming that secretly I must be plotting violence, inquire when the happy moment for declaring open violence is to arrive. They assure me that the English will never yield to anything but violence, secret or open. Yet others, I am informed, believe that I am the most rascally person living in India, because I never give out my real intention and that they have not a shadow of a doubt that I believe in violence just as much as most people do.

Such being the hold that the doctrine of the sword has on the majority of mankind, and as a success of noncooperation depends principally on absence of violence during its pendency and as my views in this matter affect the conduct of a large number of people, I am anxious to state them as clearly as possible.

I do believe that, where there is only a choice between cowardice and violence, I would advise violence. Thus when my eldest son asked me what he should have done, had he been present when I was almost fatally assaulted in 1908, whether he should have run away and seen me killed or whether he should have used his physical force, which he could and wanted to use, and defended me, I told him that it was his duty to defend me even by using violence. Hence it was that I took part in the Boer War, the so-called Zulu rebellion, and the late War. Hence also do I advocate training in arms for those who believe in the method of violence. I would rather have India resort to arms in order to defend her honor than that she should in a cowardly manner become or remain a helpless witness to her own dishonor.

But I believe that nonviolence is infinitely superior to violence, forgiveness is more manly than punishment. Forgiveness adorns a soldier. But abstinence is forgiveness only when there is the power to punish: it is meaningless when it pretends to proceed from a helpless creature. A mouse hardly forgives a cat when it allows itself to be torn to pieces by her. I therefore appreciate the sentiment of those who cry out for the condign punishment of General Dyer and his ilk. They would tear him to pieces if they could. But I do not believe India to be helpless. I do not believe myself to be a helpless creature. Only I want to use India's and my strength for a better purpose.

Let me not be misunderstood. Strength does not come from physical capacity. It comes from an indomitable will. An average Zulu is any way more than a match for an average Englishman in bodily capacity. But he flees from an English boy, because he fears the boy's revolver or those who will use it for him. He fears death and is nerveless in spite of his burly figure. We in India may in a moment realize that 100,000 Englishmen need not frighten 300 million human beings. A definite forgiveness would therefore mean a definite recognition of our strength. With enlightened forgiveness must come a mighty wave of strength in us, which would make it impossible for a Dyer and a Frank Johnson to heap affront upon India's devoted head. It matters little to me that for the moment I do not drive my point home. We feel too downtrodden not to be angry and revengeful. But I must not refrain from saying that India can gain more by waiving the right of punishment. We have better work to do, a better mission to deliver to the world.

I am not a visionary. I claim to be a practical idealist. The religion of nonviolence is not meant merely for the Rishis and saints. It is meant for the common people as well. Nonviolence is the law of our species as violence is the law of the brute. The spirit lies dormant in the brute and he knows no law but that of physical might. The dignity of man requires obedience to a higher law—to the strength of the spirit.

I have therefore ventured to place before India the ancient law of self-sacrifice. For satyagraha and its offshoots, noncooperation and civil resistance, are nothing but new names for the law of suffering. The Rishis, who discovered the law of nonviolence in the midst of violence, were greater geniuses than Newton. They were themselves greater warriors than Wellington. Having themselves known the use of arms, they realized their uselessness and taught a weary world that its salvation lay not through violence but through nonviolence.

Nonviolence in its dynamic condition means conscious suffering. It does not mean meek submission to the will of the evildoer, but it means the putting of one's whole soul against the will of the tyrant. Working under this law of our being, it is possible for a single individual to defy the whole might of an unjust empire to save his honor, his religion, his soul and lay the foundation for that empire's fall or its regeneration.

And so I am not pleading for India to practice nonviolence, because she is weak. I want her to practice nonviolence being conscious of her strength and power. No training in arms is required for realization of her strength. We seem to need it, because we seem to think that we are but a lump of flesh. I want India to recognize that she has a soul that cannot perish and that can rise triumphant above every physical weakness and defy the physical combination of a whole world. What is the meaning of Rama, a mere human being, with his host of monkeys, pitting himself against the insolent strength of 10-headed Ravan surrounded in supposed safety by the raging waters on all sides of Lanka? Does it not mean the conquest of physical might by spiritual strength? However, being a practical man, I do not wait till India recognizes the practicability of the spiritual life in the political world. India considers herself to be powerless and paralyzed before the machine guns, the tanks, and the aeroplanes of the English. And she takes up noncooperation out of her weakness. It must still serve the same purpose, namely, bring her delivery from the crushing weight of British injustice, if a sufficient number of people practice it.

I isolate this noncooperation from Sinn Feinism, for, it is so conceived as to be incapable of being offered side by side with violence. But I invite even the school of violence to give this peaceful noncooperation a trial. It will not fail through its inherent weakness. It may fail because of poverty of response. Then will be the time for real danger. The high-souled men, who are unable to suffer national humiliation any longer, will want to vent their wrath. They will take to violence. So far as I know, they must perish without delivering themselves or their country from the wrong. If India takes up the doctrine of the sword, she may gain momentary victory. Then India will cease to be the pride of my heart. I am wedded to India, because I owe my all to her. I believe absolutely that she has a mission for the world. She is not to copy Europe blindly. India's acceptance of the doctrine of the sword will be the hour of my trial. I hope I shall not be found wanting. My religion has no geographical limits. If I have a living faith in it, it will transcend my love for India herself. My life is dedicated to service of India through the religion of nonviolence which I believe to be the root of Hinduism.

Meanwhile, I urge those who distrust me not to disturb the even working of the struggle that has just commenced by inciting to violence in the belief that I want violence. I detest secrecy as a sin. Let them give nonviolent noncooperation a trial and they will find that I had no mental reservation whatsoever.

Gandhi in the Postmodern Age

by Sanford Krolick and Betty Cannon

The theory of nonviolence as an offspring of democracy is still in its infancy. Mohandas Gandhi, the master of this philosophy and its methods, was educated in Britain as a lawyer and learned well the principles of democracy. Throughout his years in South Africa and in the campaign for Indian independence, his efforts in dealing with conflict were consistent with the basic beliefs of democracy. While others fought revolutions promising that victory would bring democracy, Gandhi brought about revolutions using democratic principles and techniques; his victories were signified by the acceptance of democracy. Gandhi never tired of talking about the means and ends, claiming that the means used in settling the dispute between the Indian people and the British Government would determine the type of government India would evolve. He was fond of saying that if the right means are used, the ends will take care of themselves.

Gandhi called his philosophy satyagraha. In the United States it has been called nonviolence, direct action, and civil disobedience. These terms are inadequate because they only denote specific techniques Gandhi used. However, for the purposes of this discussion, we will use nonviolence to designate the philosophy and resisters to designate those who adopt this philosophy and carry out its methods.

The basic principle of nonviolence is to seek negotiations. The goal of a nonviolent movement is to establish an atmosphere that leads to a successfully negotiated agreement and thereby establishes the basis for compromise in the settlement of future conflicts.

The first step in a nonviolent campaign is for the resisters to define the minimum terms that they would accept in negotiations. Their minimum demands must be precisely that; every effort should be made to ensure that all resisters and opponents clearly understand this, because once at the negotiation table, these demands must not be conceded. They should reflect the fundamental principle involved. The price of bus fare was irrelevant to the freedom riders. The right of each individual to choose where he wished to sit was fundamental to the recognition of the principle of equal treatment regardless of race.

There are pragmatic as well as philosophical reasons for demanding the minimum terms. A statement of maximum demands can put the opponent on the defensive, and perhaps make him feel that the resisters have mapped out a master plan for the future that affords little latitude for expressing his ideas and needs. He would then believe that negotiations would result in his being forced to capitulate rather than in his gaining an honorable agreement.

Too many demands may be confusing. Dissatisfaction and disunity can result if serious negotiations reveal that the leaders and participants have different priorities. Furthermore, the opponent might seek a solution to what he believes is the main point but which is only of marginal importance to the resisters, and thus end up disgusted when his efforts do not yield settlement. More important, the opponent must clearly understand that the resisters cannot be "bought off" by minor or irrelevant concessions that do not recognize the fundamental principles involved. Thus the minimum demands must be stated at the beginning, repeated continuously, and upheld throughout the negotiations. The resisters must not accept any settlement that fails to recognize these demands unless they become convinced their position is incorrect. If the resisters are purists, as Gandhi was, they will also refuse to abide by an agreement to which the opponent concedes (possibly out of frustration) if he is not convinced of the validity of the resisters' position.

Publicity about the movement and its objectives is essential for educating the opponent, the participants, and the public. Resisters should pursue publicity with unrelenting enthusiasm, either on their own using a duplicating or copying machine or through newspapers and national television. They must publish the objectives, the strategy, and the tactics of the campaign. Secrecy has no place in a nonviolent campaign; it serves only to destroy communications with the participants and invite suspicion from the public and the opponent.

In a nonviolent campaign the opponent must always be informed ahead of time of the precise course of any action that is planned—for example, the exact route a demonstration intends to follow. This is particularly important if confrontation is likely since it reduces the possibility of violence through panic on either side. Of course, the authorities can thwart action by arresting resisters ahead of time, but plans that have been well publicized can arouse sympathy and attract support.

Publicity should also be understood as a form of communication that lays the groundwork for agreement. Until the opponent agrees to formal negotiations, publicity should be treated as a substitute. Honesty and accuracy are critical, as is the avoidance of any derogatory or slanderous statements. Insults from the opponent are best ignored. The movement will be judged by the honesty and fairness with which its case is presented.

The resisters' communications should indicate that they are listening as well as talking and are willing to admit a mistake or miscalculation. These steps must be continued throughout the movement until final agreement is reached. They are the basic tools for airing differences and settling disputes within a democratic framework.

Such activities may evoke a violent response from authorities who hope to quell the movement quickly. They might also bring a sympathetic offer to negotiate. However, it is most likely they will bring no response at all. Most nonviolent groups are destroyed by neglect, not by action. Finding their proposals are ignored, not even dignified by a response or reaction, resisters become stifled and the movement dissolves. Perhaps this is why pacifism has been considered weak and ineffective in America. It is all too easy for frustration to lead to violence. When this happens, the resisters have lost the initiative.

Keeping the Initiative

Gandhi's most important contribution to the theory of nonviolence was his insistence that the resisters must keep the initiative at all times. While the opponent must be given ample opportunity to consider the proposals, he must not be allowed to ignore them. Gandhi fully understood that half the battle, indeed often the most difficult part of the battle, is to convince the opponent that he must deal with resisters. Even in using force the opponent becomes involved in a relationship with the movement and makes a commitment to resolving the issue.

If the minimum demands of the resisters have been clearly formulated and extensively publicized, and if every avenue to the establishment of negotiations has been tried but the opponent has either refused to negotiate or will not deal with the minimum demands, then nonviolent direct action is necessary if the resisters are to keep the initiative. Direct action should be pursued only when all other alternatives, with the

exception of violence, have been tried. The focus of the action must be carefully chosen, for it must both demonstrate the problem and elicit a response from the opponent. The action must leave the opponent latitude for response; above all, it must allow for face-saving. While action should be dramatic, it should not be presented in a way that calls for surrender or capitulation of the opponent. A creatively negotiated settlement between equals remains the objective.

No matter what the response of the opponent may be, he must always be treated with the respect and dignity that the resisters are seeking for themselves. In actual practice, there are only a few times during a nonviolent campaign when direct action is truly necessary. During 25 years of almost continuous nonviolent activities, Gandhi used organized direct action fewer than 10 times.

The major techniques of direct action fall under two headings: noncooperation and civil disobedience. The techniques of noncooperation include mass rallies, strikes, picketing, and boycotts. The grape workers' campaign led by Cesar Chavez illustrates these techniques. The aim of the grape workers was honorable negotiations. They wanted to be recognized as a union with the right to bargain collectively with growers for wages, hours, and benefits. The workers established a union hall and held mass meetings throughout the campaign. When the growers were not willing to negotiate, the workers voted to go on strike, refusing to cooperate in harvesting the crop. The growers responded by hiring other migrants and some seasonal workers from Mexico.

The resisters then established picket lines near the farms in hope of gaining the cooperation of the strike breakers. Although this tactic continued daily for many months, it was not successful in preventing the harvest or in gaining negotiations with the growers. Chavez then decided to initiate a nationwide boycott of grapes. He sent the young people who had come to California to offer their support to the movement back to the cities to organize the boycott. This move widened the issue by creating interest and involvement across the nation. The individual shopper's decision about purchasing grapes was less crucial than the involvement of established union members who refused to cross picket lines to ship and handle grapes. In September 1966 the grape workers voted for the union with which the growers agreed to bargain.

The second method of direct action, more suitable to situations that do not involve economic relationships, is civil disobedience. This involves noncooperation with respect to a specific law or set of laws. In using this technique it is essential that all participants disobey only the law or laws specified, while obeying all others. The point is not to bring the opponent to his knees but to the negotiating table. Great care must be taken in selecting the law to be contravened. It can be central to the grievance or symbolic of it. The more important determinant is the involvement of the participants. From the resister's viewpoint, it should be a law that has regularly affected large groups. The number of people affected by the injustice is more important than the injustice done. This was understood by Martin Luther King, Jr., in singling out public lunch counters that refused service to black customers as the issue of the Birmingham, Alabama civil disobedience demonstration. Such humiliation had been experienced by many blacks. The issue emphasized the demand for equal treatment, and the action pointed to the local laws that violated the rights of black citizens.

Civil disobedience is serious business. The deliberate violation of a law is virtually guaranteed to evoke response from governmental authorities. The strength, determination, and cohesiveness of the resisters will be tested. Typically, arrests will be made. The ability of the movement to continue with disciplined resisters once the leaders are arrested is crucial. The aim is "to fill the jails," thus jamming the courts while retaining public interest and sympathy.

In Birmingham, King initiated the movement with only 20 resisters. Through nightly mass meetings, volunteers came forth in increasing numbers to fill the places of the men who were jailed. King testified that the turning point came when he called upon high school students to join the march to city hall, challenging the police barricades and courting arrest. The news service coverage of the march included a picture of a six-year-old being arrested. On May 7, 1963, the Senior Citizens Committee of 125 business leaders of Birmingham met with King. As they walked out on the street for lunch,

"...there were square blocks of Negroes, a veritable sea of black faces. They were committing no violence. They were just present and singing. Downtown Birmingham echoed to the strains of the freedom songs."

King states that when the meeting reconvened, "One of the men who had been in the most determined opposition cleared his throat and said: 'You know, I've been thinking this thing through. We ought to be able to work something out.'"

In their civil disobedience campaigns, both Gandhi and King focused on the ambiguity between the officially stated democratic principles and the clear violation of these principles in practice. These campaigns compelled the government authorities to choose between ideals and actions. Either they had to renounce their democratic ideals and suppress the resisters by force in order to maintain their dominance, or they had to affirm their ideals, honestly negotiate, and replace dominance with compromise. As the choice became increasingly clear, the response of the authorities to the resisters depended in part on the reaction of the majority of citizens. In this, nonviolence paid tremendous dividends. By 1947 the majority of British citizens were unwilling to support massive repression of India. In 1960 many in the South and North were unwilling to support massive repression of civil rights marchers.

In a direct action campaign it is essential that the resisters avoid using violence in any form. This is not an end in itself; it is a means of breaking the cycle of fear and repression in order to establish a basis for trust and democratic negotiation. An action cannot be characterized as nonviolent if it is performed out of fear, for that may lead to submission. As Gandhi was fond of saying, the mouse does not exercise nonviolence in allowing the pussycat to eat him. Gandhi also insisted that when one saw no choices except to respond with violence or to submit, violence was the better choice because it afforded more self-respect than did cowardly submission. He emphasized the third alternative, nonviolent resistance, as a conscious choice.

Nonviolence is sterile unless it is coupled with a program to bring about change. A firm commitment to refuse to respond with violence or to submit to fear comes from strength, courage, and self-discipline. Nonviolence is truly the conquest of violence.

Actors and Roles in Nonviolent Confrontation

Perhaps a clearer understanding of nonviolence can be gained if the conflict is viewed in terms of individuals. The average individual approaches a new relationship with mixed feelings. He hopes to gain understanding, respect, and appreciation; he fears that he may suffer rejection, disgrace, or humiliation. Most relationships contain a mixture of these feelings and reactions. The direction in which a relationship develops depends in large part on how conflicts that arise are resolved. If resolution based on understanding, mutual respect, and honesty is found, then a basis of trust is initiated. Each conflict that is resolved by these methods increases the trust and reinforces feelings of respect and understanding.

In contrast, if a conflict is not settled or is settled in a manner that leads one or both parties to believe that his basic rights and self-respect have been damaged, then feelings of misunderstanding and anger jeopardize the basis of trust. If this pattern is repeated in future conflicts, these feelings are reinforced. The ineffective means of resolving one conflict lays the foundation for dealing with the next, and this has a spiraling effect. Distrust, apprehension, and fear that stem from a lack of trust can come to govern the course of the relationship. As tension mounts each person becomes increasingly suspicious of the other's motives. Each then becomes afraid to yield his power and position because he imagines that his opponent will take advantage of him. Each clings to what he has, refusing to make concessions. Each believes any gain by the other is his loss. Each side thus becomes locked into a position, unable to move for fear of giving the advantage to the other.

Yet the strange part of such a relationship is that each becomes increasingly dependent upon the other. The negative feelings of distrust, anger, and fear tie them together like an invisible bond. Each perceives that he could or would change if he could trust the other, each looks to the other to make the first move for compromise, and each sees the possibility of resolving the situation as depending upon the other. The result is that both are deadlocked in a relationship that they find uncomfortable and threatening, yet one in which each has surrendered his own ability to solve the problem by assigning the other the responsibility for making the first move to end the deadlock. Each blames the other for the situation, which is only another way of assigning the opponent the power and responsibility for resolving the dispute. If the opponent has the power to create the problem, then he should have the power to resolve it. The ability to exercise creativity, individuality, and initiative is gone.

If the situation escalates, anger and fear build. Each party in the dispute begins to think of the other in dehumanizing ways. Each begins to imagine that the other is evil, and think and talk of him as sinister, scheming, devoid of human sympathy and honor. These thoughts can give rise to self-fulfilling actions; as each opponent spends considerable time scheming, entertaining uncharitable thoughts, and plotting revenge, he does become sinister and increasingly devoid of charity. Total victory—the ability to force the opponent into complete submission—is seen as the only way out of the situation. The appalling fact is that violence can so dehumanize people that they are willing to sacrifice their own lives in order to destroy an opponent.

Nonviolence is a program for breaking the cycle of fear while, at the same time, achieving the desired social or political ends. But it is not without its own risks. Personal injury, legal sanctions, and social criticism are always possibilities. Resisters have to weigh these costs when deciding whether their protest is worth it. Charles Evers, civil rights leader from Mississippi, weighed his participation this way:

"My life would be safe if I shuffled and tommed and said, 'Yassuh, Mr. Charlie, we niggers is real happy.' But then I'd be dead already. I'd rather die on my feet than live on my knees."

In summary, we have presented the basic tenets of nonviolence. Our object has been to describe those tactics that resisters need to follow if they are to engage in nonviolent protest. These include seeking negotiations (where minimum terms have been defined and the objectives of the protest made clear) and keeping the initiative both at the negotiating table and, if necessary, in the streets. Direct action such as noncooperation or civil resistance should be used only if the paths to negotiation are blocked.

These tactics are bound to create tensions in a democratic society. Obviously, if many actions were protested, the society would be in turmoil and the government would probably resort to more and more force to maintain order. Democracy might soon be ended under the guise of protecting it. On the other hand, if governmental decisions and social mores could not be protested, then the system could hardly be called democratic. While majority rule is a fundamental principle, so is the right of a minority to defend itself, its rights, and its interests. Jefferson proclaimed this in 1776. But unlike the tactics that he and his fellow colonists used, the nonviolent resisters of this century have protested within the structure and, for the most part, the rules of the system. For the sake of democracy, it is well that they have done so. Violence threatens the character of the system; nonviolence is a democratic means of conflict resolution.

Family Satyagraha

by Eknath Easwaren

Personal relationships offer fertile ground to learn and use satyagraha. Gandhi called this "domestic satyagraha." We get a clear idea of what he meant when we look at his early life in South Africa—not, interestingly enough, at satyagraha as he was to develop it later, but as it was used against him. Gandhi was a domineering, sometimes petulant husband during those years in Johannesburg, because he believed, as he recounts, that it was his right to impose his will upon his wife. When Kasturbai objected to his unilateral approach, Gandhi only became more adamant. But Kasturbai had an intuitive grasp of the properties of nonviolent love, and during those tumultuous years of domestic strife, she proved to be Gandhi's equal. Her attitude transformed his relationship with her and in the process revealed to him the beauty and the power of nonviolent resistance.

"I learnt the lesson of nonviolence from my wife, when I tried to bend her to my will. Her determined resistance to my will, on the one hand, and her quiet submission to the suffering my stupidity involved, on the other, ultimately made me ashamed of myself and cured me of my stupidity...in the end, she became my teacher in nonviolence."

Without knowing it, Kasturbai had used satyagraha's foremost weapons to win over her husband: a readiness to suffer rather than retaliate, and an implacable will.

Family satyagraha is founded, like all satyagraha, on this delicate balance of patience and determination, which, when rightly practiced, can become a cornerstone for deep personal relations between men and women. The discovery Gandhi made in his own household at the turn of the century in Johannesburg is of critical importance today, when these relationships have become fraught with competition and tension. Few homes today seem able to withstand even the predictable tensions of married life, so that estrangement and alienation have become common ingredients in the modern household. At this low ebb in family living, Gandhi's way rings especially true: forgive, forbear, support the other person always, and when it becomes necessary to resist, do so lovingly and without rancor. The apex of this ideal is reached when the wife's welfare becomes more important to the husband than his own happiness, and the husband's welfare takes on a similar importance to the wife. This kind of relationship marks one of the highest achievements of true ahimsa.

Between parents and children, satyagraha has a natural place. Here again, patience mingled with firmness frames the approach. The "irreducible minimum" in family satyagraha is that the welfare of the children comes first; their growth and development take precedence over everything else. It means making minor sacrifices of small pleasures at times or saying no, gently but firmly, more often than one wants to. Most important, in Gandhi's thinking, is that the example set by the parents be true to their ideals. When Gandhi moved to Tolstoy Farm in 1909, it was with a motley group of children whom he immediately took under his fatherly wing. They were an "ill-assorted" lot, but in Gandhi's eyes, he and they were "all one family." "I saw," he writes, "that I must be good and live straight, if only for their sakes." The seeds of family satyagraha were sown by Gandhi in the rich soil of Tolstoy Farm, and years of careful husbandry brought them into full bloom; in time, this demanding relationship with children became a natural, almost effortless attitude for him.

During the thirties a woman came to Sevagram asking Gandhi to get her little boy to stop eating sugar; it was doing him harm. Gandhi gave a cryptic reply: "Please come back next week."

The woman left puzzled but returned a week later, dutifully following the Mahatma's instructions. "Please don't eat sugar," Gandhi told the young fellow when he saw him. "It is not good for you." Then he joked with the boy for a while, gave him a hug, and sent him on his way. But the mother, unable to contain her curiosity, lingered behind to ask, "Bapu, why didn't you say this last week when we came? Why did you make us come back again?"

Gandhi smiled. "Last week," he said to her, "I too was eating sugar."

Gandhi was personal in all his relations. Even at the height of the freedom movement in India, he would not allow his campaigns to drift into non-personal postures. Regardless of how institutional his opponents might appear behind their marbled corridors and initialed titles, Gandhi's adversaries were always people first, "tarred with the same brush" and akin to him in their common humanity. Personal relationships were neither a luxury nor an imposition to Gandhi, but rather natural and vital expression of ahimsa; at each level of human interaction they build the forum in which satyagraha operates. It is interesting to watch Gandhi's circle of friendships gradually evolve from his immediate family in Porbandar and Johannesburg to his many followers living in his ashrams, until finally it included all India and much of the world.

One of the main features of satyagraha, as we have seen, is its "open-endedness," its capacity to adapt creatively to new contexts while adhering to its irreducible principles of truth and nonviolence. This flexibility has never been more important than today, when the challenges we face are so different from those Gandhi confronted. Merely to imitate the forms of Gandhi's political campaigns, such as strikes and demonstrations, would tragically limit satyagraha to the narrow context of political reform. The crises that threaten our lives today are not so much political as spiritual: personal and social matters of alienation, isolation, and increasing polarization between men and women, old and young. Consequently, our times require a determined movement towards nonviolence and unity in our families and communities.

from Gandhi the Man

Ahimsa

by Eknath Easwaran

Ahimsa, nonviolence, was the noblest expression of Truth for Gandhi—or, properly speaking, the way to Truth.

"Ahimsa and Truth are so intertwined that it is practically impossible to disentangle and separate them. They are like the two sides of a coin, or rather a smooth unstamped metallic disc. Who can say which is the obverse and which the reverse? Nevertheless ahimsa is the means; Truth is the end."

Ahimsa is the bedrock of satyagraha, the "irreducible minimum" to which satyagraha adheres and the final measure of its value.

In the traditional lore of India there is a story about an old sannyasi, a Hindu monk, who was sitting on the bank of a river silently repeating his mantram. Nearby a scorpion fell from a tree into the river, and the sannyasi, seeing it struggling in the water, bent over and pulled it out. He placed the scorpion back in the tree, but as he did so, the creature bit him on the hand. He paid no heed to the bite, but went on repeating his mantram. A little while later, the scorpion again fell into the water. As before, the monk pulled him out and set him back in the tree and again was bitten. This little drama was repeated several times, and each time the sannyasi rescued the scorpion, he received a bite.

It happened that a villager, ignorant of the ways of holy men, had come to the river for water and had seen the whole affair. Unable to contain himself any longer, the villager told the sannyasi with some vexation:

"Swamiji, I have seen you save that foolish scorpion several times now and each time he has bitten you. Why not let the rascal go?"

"Brother," replied the sannyasi, "the fellow cannot help himself. It is his nature to bite."

"Agreed," answered the villager. "But knowing this, why don't you avoid him?"

"Ah, brother," replied the monk, "you see, I cannot help myself either. I am a human being; it is my nature to save."

Ahimsa is usually translated as "nonviolence," but as we have seen, its meaning goes much beyond that. Ahimsa is derived from the Sanskrit verb root san, which means to kill. The form hims means "desirous to kill"; the prefix a- is a negation. So a-himsa means literally "lacking any desire to kill," which is perhaps the central theme upon which Hindu, Jain, and Buddhist morality is built. In the Manu Smriti, the great lawbook of Hinduism, it is written, *Ahimsa paramo dharma*: "ahimsa is the highest law". It is, as Gandhi puts it, the very essence of human nature.

"Nonviolence is the law of our species as violence is the law of the brute. The spirit lies dormant in the brute and he knows no law but that of physical might. The dignity of man requires obedience to a higher law—to the strength of the spirit."

The word nonviolence connotes a negative, almost passive condition, whereas the Sanskrit term ahimsa suggests a dynamic state of mind in which power is released. "Strength," Gandhi said, "does not come from physical capacity. It comes from an indomitable will." Therein he found his own strength, and there he exhorted others to look for theirs. Latent in the depths of human consciousness, this inner strength can be cultivated by the observance of complete ahimsa. Whereas violence checks this energy within, and is ultimately disruptive in its consequences, ahimsa, properly understood, is invincible. "With satya combined with ahimsa," Gandhi writes, "you can bring the world to your feet."

When Gandhi speaks of ahimsa as a law, we should take him at his word. Indeed, it was a law for him like gravity, and could be demonstrated in the midst of human affairs. Gandhi even characterized his practice of ahimsa as a science, and said once, "I have been practicing with scientific precision nonviolence and its possibilities for an unbroken period of over 50 years." He was a precise man, meticulous and exacting, fond of quoting a Marathi hymn that goes, "Give me love, give me peace, O Lord, but don't deny me common sense." He valued experience as the test of truth, and the nonviolence he pursued and called "true nonviolence" had to conform to experience in all levels of human affairs. "I have applied it," he declares, "in every walk of life: domestic, institutional, economic, political. And I know of no single case in which it has failed." Anything short of this total application did not interest

Gandhi, because ahimsa sprang from and worked in the same continuum as his religion, politics, and personal life. Only practice could determine its value, "when it acts in the midst of and in spite of opposition," and he advised critics to observe the results of his experiments rather than dissect his theories.

"...nonviolence is not a cloistered virtue to be practiced by the individual for his peace and final salvation, but it is a rule of conduct for society. To practice nonviolence in mundane matters is to know its true value. It is to bring heaven upon earth. I hold it therefore to be wrong to limit the use of nonviolence to cave dwellers [hermits] and for acquiring merit for a favored position in the other world. All virtue ceases to have use if it serves no purpose in every walk of life."

Gandhi's adherence to nonviolence grew from his experience that it was the only way to resolve the problem of conflict permanently. Violence, he felt, only made the pretense of a solution, and sowed seeds of bitterness and enmity that would ultimately disrupt the situation.

One needs to practice ahimsa to understand it. To profess nonviolence with sincerity or even to write a book about it was, for Gandhi, not adequate. "If one does not practice nonviolence in one's personal relationships with others, one is vastly mistaken. Nonviolence, like charity, must begin at home." The practice of nonviolence is by no means a simple matter, and Gandhi never intimated that it was. As a discipline, a "code of conduct," true nonviolence demands endless vigilance over one's entire way of life, because it includes words and thought as well as actions.

"Ahimsa is not the crude thing it has been made to appear. Not to hurt any living thing is no doubt a part of ahimsa. But it is its least expression. The principle of ahimsa is hurt by every evil thought, by undue haste, by lying, by hatred, by wishing ill to anybody. It is also violated by our holding on to what the world needs."

My Faith in Nonviolence

by Mohandas Gandhi

I have found that life persists in the midst of destruction and, therefore, there must be a higher law than that of destruction. Only under that law would a well-ordered society be intelligible and life worth living. And if that is the law of life, we have to work it out in daily life. Wherever there are jars, wherever you are confronted with an opponent, conquer him with love. In a crude manner I have worked it out in my life. That does not mean that all my difficulties are solved. I have found, however, that this law of love has answered as the law of destruction has never done. In India we have had an ocular demonstration of the operation of this law on the widest scale possible. I do not claim therefore that nonviolence has necessarily penetrated the 300 million, but I do claim that it has penetrated deeper than any other message, and in an incredibly short time. We have not been all uniformly nonviolent; and with the vast majority, nonviolence has been a matter of policy. Even so, I want you to find out if the country has not made phenomenal progress under the protecting power of nonviolence.

It takes a fairly strenuous course of training to attain to a mental state of nonviolence. In daily life it has to be a course of discipline though one may not like it, like, for instance, the life of a soldier. But I agree that, unless there is a hearty cooperation of the mind, the mere outward observance will be simply a mask, harmful both to the man himself and to others. The perfect state is reached only when mind and body and speech are in proper coordination. But it is always a case of intense mental struggle. It is not that I am incapable of anger, for instance, but I succeed on almost all occasions to keep my feelings under control. Whatever may be the result, there is always in me a conscious struggle for following the law of nonviolence deliberately and ceaselessly. Such a struggle leaves one stronger for it. Nonviolence is a weapon of the strong. With the weak it might easily be hypocrisy. Fear and love are contradictory terms. Love is reckless in giving away, oblivious as to what it gets in return. Love wrestles with the world as with the self and ultimately gains mastery over all other feelings. My daily experience, as of those who are working with me, is that every problem lends itself to solution if we are determined to make the law of truth and non-violence the law of life. For truth and nonviolence are, to me, faces of the same coin.

The law of love will work, just as the law of gravitation will work, whether we accept it or not. Just as a scientist will work wonders out of various applications of the law of nature, even so a man who applies the law of love with scientific precision can work greater wonders. For the force of nonviolence is infinitely more wonderful and subtle than the material forces of nature, like, for instance, electricity. The men who discovered for us the law of love were greater scientists than any of our modern scientists. Only our explorations have not gone far enough and so it is not possible for everyone to see all its workings. Such, at any rate, is the hallucination, if it is one, under which I am laboring. The more I work at this law the more I feel the delight in life, the delight in the scheme of this universe. It gives me a peace and a meaning of the mysteries of nature that I have no power to describe.

Practically speaking there will be probably no greater loss in men than if forcible resistance was offered; there will be no expenditure in armaments and fortifications. The nonviolent training received by the people will add inconceivably to their moral height. Such men and women will have shown personal bravery of a type far superior to that shown in armed warfare. In each case the bravery consists in dying, not in killing. Lastly, there is no such thing as defeat in nonviolent resistance. That such a thing has not happened before is no answer to my speculation. I have drawn no impossible picture. History is replete with instances of individual nonviolence of the type I have mentioned. There is no warrant for saying or thinking that a group of men and women cannot by sufficient training act nonviolently as a group or nation. Indeed the sum total of the experience of mankind is that men somehow or other live on. From which fact I infer that it is the law of love that rules mankind. Had violence, i.e., hate, ruled us, we should have become extinct long ago. And yet the tragedy of it is that the so-called civilized men and nations conduct themselves as if the basis of society was violence. It gives me ineffable joy to make experiments proving that love is the supreme and only law of life. Much evidence to the contrary cannot shake my faith. Even the mixed nonviolence of India has supported it. But if it is not enough to convince an unbeliever, it is enough to incline a friendly critic to view it with favor.

A Pause from Violence

by Colman McCarthy

In a memorable, joyous ceremony last week at Crosslands, Pennsylvania, the government of India bestowed its highest civilian honor on Horace Alexander, a 95-yearold British philosopher and peacemaker who was a friend, student, and biographer of Gandhi. Alexander, a Quaker and a conscientious objector in World War I, first involved himself in Indian affairs in 1926, when he spent a week with Gandhi at the Mahatma's ashram in Sabarmati.

His most recent involvement was a 1983 preface to the second edition of *Gandhi Through Western Eyes*, Alexander's 1969 classic book in which the Gandhian way—the nonviolent, courageous way—is explained as the world's only rational option for peace.

The Indian government's honoring of Alexander— he received the Decorated Lotus Award—comes late in this lovely man's long and inspiring life. But the honor breaks into the news when a pause from violence is desperately needed.

India itself in past weeks has seen a bloody revival of Sikh-Hindu hatred in the Punjab. In the United States, the Reagan administration has sent 400 Stinger antiaircraft missiles to Saudi Arabia. This latest arms shipment ensures that America's role as the world's leading weapons dealer will continue. In 1983, according to the Congressional Research Service, our share of the global arms market rose from 32 percent to 39 percent. The Soviet Union's declined from 26 percent to 16 percent.

Crosslands, Pennsylvania, 30 miles west of Philadelphia, is a Quaker retirement community. Horace Alexander has lived there for the past six years with his American wife. Except for a slight hearing problem, his health is fine and his wit is sharp. Over the phone the other afternoon, he said, "I never expected to live to this age—it's ridiculous!" On such current events as the shipment of missiles to Saudi Arabia, he sighed: "I think we're very good at wasting our money. We must change our whole attitude."

Alexander's memories of Gandhi are sharp. The two men were faithful letter-writers to each other. Their correspondence supplemented Alexander's regular visits to Gandhi from the 1920s to the 1940s. A photograph of the two peacemakers shows them crossing a field together near Gandhi's ashram. Alexander, tall and angular, is wearing a suit and tie and holds with his left hand a pair of bird-watching binoculars looped over his neck. Gandhi, barefoot and dressed in a white loincloth, carries a walking stick.

The two appear to be locked in conversation. It is easy to imagine them doing what only true friends can do for each other: disagreeing with gentleness. Alexander wrote of Gandhi that "to gain his respect, it was essential that you should show yourself to be at some point sharply critical of him."

During World War II, Alexander travelled to India as a staff member of the Friends (Quaker) Ambulance Unit. In 1943, he visited Gandhi during one of Ganfhi's prison fasts. The two shared a high moment in Calcutta on Independence Day in 1947. "I remained in India for some years after Gandhi's death," Alexander recalled, "and at one time considered making my home there. But I concluded that I really belonged in the West, and that my job in old age must be to help in interpreting India, or at least Gandhi's India, to Western people."

Few callings could be higher. Or more difficult. Schools in India offer no systematic teaching of Gandhi's philosophy of nonviolence and organized resistance. Honored, yes; studied, no. It is the same in the United States with Martin Luther King, Jr., whose life was turned around by the reading of Gandhi.

In the epilogue to *Gandhi Through Western Eyes*, Alexander describes Gandhi as a varicolored thinker. He was a conservative whose beliefs were "held together by a tradition of family interdependence and of village self-government." He was a liberal who saw his adversaries not as enemies to be defeated but as possible friends to be persuaded: "I am a born cooperator," Gandhi said repeatedly. He was a radical: "Unless the world accepts nonviolence, it will spell certain suicide for mankind."

Horace Alexander is also a conservative-liberal-radical. At 95, and deservedly honored, he has seen and heard it all. Nothing, though, has come into his mind that has made as much sense as the teaching from his Quaker parents and Gandhi that the peaceable kingdom is eminently possible.

from Washington Post, June 9, 1984

World peace starts right here. I will not raise my child to kill your child.

Barbara Choo

Feminism, Peace, and Power

by Mary Roodkowsky

"Who then will do it? The men are all fighting, and some women, too."— Betty Williams, Nobel Peace laureate, when asked why women created the People's Peace Movement in Ireland.

Fighting, vanquishing, attacking, and counterattacking are so-called masculine skills shed of the metaphors of business, sports, and social competition which usually clothe them. War creates heroes, supermen, known by their performance: true men, on whose chests medals and stripes glitter and ribbons flap. Strong men, whose very survival proves brains and brawn. Men in charge of their own lives, and with the power and authority to direct and mold the loves of others.

Victory in war derives from comparative advantage—no stronger or wiser for the battle, perhaps poorer than before—the conqueror is defined by his superior position, his lower losses. The loot consists mainly of positional goods, those which can be held only at the expense of others. Use and control over the opponent's natural resources and social status—the ability to determine if and how others will share in those resources.

Because it seems that conflict's only rationale is acquisition of goods or power from another, only those who are enfranchised, or who might hope to be, need involve themselves. No wonder, then, that women neither profit from nor join in wars. The round tables where strategic decisions are made never include women—in fact, women rarely approach them save with memos or coffee for the real decision makers.

While men wage war, women keep house and also the economy. Their perpetual care of the hearth and of the children maintains a social structure and ensures a home where soldiers may return. Women labor in factories and offices, in seats left vacant by men called to the front.

Women also take on new burdens in wartime. They sacrifice butter to churn out guns in factories, they expand their roles as society's washers, nurses, and caretakers, to include the extra destruction created by war. Women make and roll bandages, and then use them to bind wounds they never inflicted. At the war's close they comfort combat—tattered psyches, of both sides. Their wartime jobs—and the newly acquired

earning power it brought—are preempted by those to whom they really belong, the boys back from the front.

Thus, wars that are fought for goods and position benefit women little. In fact, rather than acquiring goods or position in war, women often are the goods, the spoils, acquired by war. Rape has been standard operating procedure during armed conflict, from the Trojan War to the Viet Nam War. In her book *Against Our Will*, Susan Brownmiller suggests that soldiers' abuse of women ranks along with looting, burning, and bombing as a means of subduing the enemy. Later, the women become part of the victor's booty:

"The body of a raped woman becomes a ceremonial battlefield, a parade ground for the victor's trooping of the colors. The act that is played out upon her is a message passed between men—vivid proof of victory for one and loss and defeat for the other."

Some of glory's light does shine on women, but indirectly and through their relationships to men, as in so many other areas of life. Army nurses who have bravely cared for wounded men may receive medals, and exceptional female military personnel may also be rewarded for their contributions. But the "glory" comes mostly through their men—the fathers, husbands, sons—"given" to the effort. All women in wartime must sacrifice those men's presence, as well as their contributions to home and family. Later, the ultimate honor consists in welcoming back the womb's fruit like the Spartan woman who will only greet her son with his shield, victorious, or on it, dead. Today's reward consists of a body in a bag, and a yearly appearance in the Memorial Day parade. While triumphant men split the spoils and bask in power, women replace their life's love and the result of their caring work with a Gold Star banner fluttering in the wind. Only one-half of the men in a battle can win, one side must lose; however, no woman, on either side of the battle line, can ever claim victory or its prerogatives.

Women Propose Peace

Given their suffering—in themselves, in the destruction of what is most important to them, in the violation of their bodies—and given that women receive little compensation for what they give, it is not surprising that many peace movements and movements for nonviolent change throughout history have

49

been led by women. A history of such involvement might include the imagery of Euripides' Lysistrata, or the way the Pilate's unnamed wife tried to save Christ; it could also tell of Angelina Grimke's impassioned pleas that women work for an end to slavery, without bloodshed; it might discuss Mrs. Rosa Parks' refusal to move to the rear of a bus in Montgomery, Alabama, sparking the civil rights movement; it might document the women's strike for peace during the Viet Nam War years, and describe Betty Williams and Mairead Corrigan and the other women in the Irish People's Peace Movement. It might discuss how the woman's suffrage movement of the 19th and 20th centuries in America diligently overturned law and social order, without violence. Given the deep state of powerlessness of most women and the extra effort it takes for women to work in the organized realms of government, law, and broad scale organization, this record is even more remarkable.

Winning Over Others

Nonviolence not only opposes war; it also upholds a way of living where conflict creates rather than destroys. Feminism, too, goes beyond its rejection of arms and battle, to suggest and to practice nondestructive patterns of conflict resolution. It is perhaps rooted in women's socialization, or perhaps due to women's economic and political powerlessness, or perhaps because of the common female roles. But whatever its source, feminist understandings of conflict can help to clarify and expand nonviolent theory.

One major aspect of Gandhi's nonviolence embodied a stance of non-injury, or ahimsa, to the enemy. Destruction of the opponent merely perpetuates the injustice one tries to overcome. Instead, the goal is to win the opponent over to one's own side. Gandhi wrote:

"We must try patiently to convert our opponents. If we wish to evolve the spirit of democracy out of slavery, we must be scrupulously exact in our dealings with opponents. We must concede to our opponents the freedom we claim for ourselves and for which we are fighting."

Ahimsa has been very much a part of women's attitudes, even with respect to the most emotional, basic issues of feminism. For instance, at the national convention sponsored by the State Department, the most volatile issues included abortion rights, the Equal Rights Amendment, and freedom for sexual preference (lesbian rights). All three passed, but not without debate, debate which adhered in various ways to nonviolent principles of respect for the opponent, and of wining over those with whom one disagrees.

Because of socialization from girlhood on, reinforced by the expectations of womanhood, a woman perceives her fate as intimately tied to that of others in a variety of ways—her choices are not always hers alone. A woman has far less decision-making power in the social structures that govern her, whether she lives in the United States, Ireland, Egypt, or India. Likewise, on an individual level, her husband, children, and other family steer her life's course. What happens to these people and to the dominant social structures affect her with a more conclusive impact than they do a man with more autonomy. Economically, for example, when a woman depends on a man for her sustenance, the political or social factors which increase or decrease his status will likely do the same for her—either directly, when he gets a raise, or indirectly, when a slow economy pushes the "least important" elements out of the work force, as after a war or when labor is costly. He may have alternative choices in his job, and hers depend upon his. Women's relationship to men, for better and usually for worse, is a derivative one. For women as a group this has led to a greater cognizance of the interrelatedness of all humans, with each other and with the earth. Women's relationships to other women likewise recognize such interrelatedness, but on a far more egalitarian basis. Contrary to stereotypes of calculating, competitive women, documentation of women in developing nations and histories of women in Western civilization demonstrate norms of cooperation, caring, and nurture among women.

For example, female midwives through the Middle Ages often expertly delivered children at minimal cost. When two male doctors introduced the forceps, many midwives scorned them—for their expense, and for the fact that they foresaw an era when less compassionate, more technological childbirth would become the norm. Women in many developing nations sustain informal exchanges of goods and services among themselves, swapping household foods and childcare on a cooperative, nonprofit basis. In contemporary society, wherever neighborhoods still exist and women's communities live despite pressures of urbanization, such bartering still occurs, despite the counterpressures of consumerism.

An adherent of nonviolence cannot injure another, because their fates intertwine. How, then, can women make a policy of winning their need and more by destroying or subjugating the adversary, when so much of their own well-being so clearly depends on the welfare of the adversary?

Not only are women's fates combined with those of

their community, but women's roles in society are constructed with a notion of responsibility to others and to the physical world—such accountability intrinsically leads to nonviolence.

Women bear the brunt of their own actions more directly than do men. Men's work is supported by others—by those lower on the social ladder, by secretaries and subordinates in the workplace, by women at home. A woman's work, however, receives no such subsidy. She takes final responsibility for the children's and the men's lifestyles and daily physical and material needs, as well as for her own, since there is no one further down the ladder to whom she can shunt the blame or the chores. Cooking dinner, washing laundry, feeding the baby, are all tasks created by the needs of many but only met by the work of one woman. Such "women's work" is not the whole of the females' responsibilities. The world over, women perform not only such womanly chores, but other "male" work as well. In Africa, 80 percent of the farmers are women; in the United States, 48 percent of women work or need work outside the home. Dual workloads complicate women's accountability and burden. A woman doctor in a remote Himalayan mountain area comments that women in her district "work three times as hard as men," for they must do all the things men do, and then care for the family.

Without someone down the line to blame, the unpleasant, ugly fallout of violent action might deter more women from participating in it. The desecration of the earth in strip-mining, for example, is encouraged and financed not by those displaced by or living near the site, but by corporations in cities. Nuclear power irresponsibly manufactures energy, allowing others—future generations—to grapple with the radioactive waste it creates. No one thoroughly socialized in female responsibilities could ever dream such a system.

Nonviolent action asserts the value and necessity of acting in support of the truth (the Satyagraha of Gandhi), that doing for self means also doing for others. The U.S. peace group, Mobilization for Survival, made four demands in 1977, the first three were all injunctions against violence: zero nuclear weapons, ban nuclear power, and stop the arms race; the fourth demand was the advocacy for the justice central to nonviolent action: fund human needs.

The psychology of women supports this policy of non-injury. A woman judges her own worth, and others judge her, in terms of how well she serves others. Rather than basing her worth on the domination of others or on comparative strength, the normative criteria have been sacrifice and service.

Such advocacy is in many ways the raison d'etre of the traditional female role. Psychoanalyst Jean Baker Miller states:

"In our culture serving others is for losers, it is low-level stuff. Yet serving others is a basic principle around which women's lives are organized; it is far from such for men. In fact, there are psychoanalytic data to suggest that men's lives are psychologically organized against such a principle, that there is a potent dynamic at work forcing men away from such a goal."

When conflict produces an either/or, have/have-not situation, a woman is apt to opt for the subordinate role. The ideal of service is so firmly implanted in the consciousness, in letting the other win—tennis, an argument, or a job—that not to do so is unfeminine, and therefore attacks the core of the woman's worth. Women's spirituality is beautifully described by the French mystic, Simone Wiel, who states that love is merely attention to the other's needs.

However, in doing such service, we can make another kind of connection between feminism on the one hand, and nonviolence on the other. This ideal of living-for-others not only has avoided overt violence aimed at others by women, its reverse side is the exploitation of that service by men, to hurt women, and women's extreme internalization of that ideal and the negation of their own needs.

Because nonviolence promotes action for justice, nothing can be less passive than its "truth-force." For their own sake women need to emphasize this active side far more than the avoidance of violence to others. Many ethics, nonviolent codes included, speak largely to the male psyche, to its aggressive, competitive, against-others nature. Applying ethical principles of self-denial and service to the already self-sacrificing woman can sometimes overwhelm her into increased living-for-others to the point where any living-for-self seems invalid. Jean Baker Miller writes that the unilateral assignation of women to a service role is the source of overwhelming problems for men and women alike, denying to the former (men), their justly due community responsibility, to the latter (women), a necessary and realistic understanding of self-worth.

Gandhi sometimes glorified suffering for the cause of truth. But he, and other nonviolent activists, also stressed the need for noncooperation with the forces of evil. Angelina Grimke urged her Christian sisters to throw away their submissive behavior in order to work to end slavery. Peace activist Dorothy Day illegally asserted herself against nuclear armaments and for the United Farm Workers' union struggle. Women can apply this principle of noncooperation to their oppression, and to those who hurt them. Nonviolence never assents to the demands of the oppressors, even though it may cause anger or resentment. It strips the oppressors of authority to which they are not entitled, at the same time ascertaining that all enjoy what they rightfully own.

Feminist and nonviolent activist Barbara Deming connects feminism with nonviolent cooperation in application of ahimsa to both the other and the self:

"We act out respect for ourselves by refusing to cooperate with those who oppress or exploit us. And as their power never resides in their single selves, always depends upon the cooperation of others—by refusing that cooperation…refusing our labor, our wits, our money, our blood upon their battlefields, our deference, we take their power away from them."

Our actions bear upon ourselves as well as on others. Injuring others means injuring ourselves—our capacity to love, to care, to create, and to learn. And this dynamic works in reverse: to respect ourselves will mean to respect others, to expect them to respect, learn, and create in return. Feminism has set in motion a process by which women—in caring, nonviolent ways—are learning to respect themselves, value their own work, and to evoke, expect, and demand that respect from others. In this way, another dichotomy— that between oppressor and oppressed, powerful and powerless—dissolves.

For women, such noncooperation with the degradation of sexism and the self-hatred it brings is nonviolent to others and to self. Doubtless, non-cooperation with sexist structures—refusal to make coffee, criticism of policies made by men with high-ego involvement in their work, insisting on equal wages; or going to school—will be threatening to men, who will then accuse women of being angry and even violent. Affirmative action in the U.S.A., for example, is really such noncooperation with the male WASP workworld. Yet, if women are not to continue to judge themselves with violence, noncooperation is essential.

Using Power Creatively

At their cores, both feminism and nonviolence perceive power differently from male-centered ideology and are alien to the reality principle that directs our world and which encourages violent struggles for position.

Power, as the dominant ideology understands it, cannot coexist with love or caring—it is an imposition over others, rather than a force to help us compose, or create, together.

Those who know that only one side can be victorious in war can well understand the corollary of this truism: that any concept of a loving or interdependent ethic must mean a relinquishing of social and positional goods and therefore, powerlessness. Power so conceptualized cannot be used for the general good of the society—only for the aggrandizement of an individual or state—hence, a state of war. Feminist philosopher Mary Daly suggests that this split degrades humanity: "Power split off from love makes an obscenity out of what we call love, forcing us unwillingly to destroy ourselves and each other."

Feminists and advocates of nonviolence live by the contrary force, the power of love, which compels us to ahimsa. Learning to use our human energies as a loving force is the process of empowerment—a process which enables us to act critically and creatively to end injustice, not accept it. Empowerment comes both from the community—in the consciousness-raising group or the affinity group—and from the individual's new reconceptualizing of his/her own loving capabilities.

For poet and feminist Adrienne Rich, motherhood dissolves many dichotomies between power and powerlessness. While a mother has ultimate power over, responsibility for, and control over her baby since the baby depends on the mother for all sustenance and warmth, the baby also controls the mother—her psyche and her body, as in the flow of milk from her breasts. Rich writes of the sense of confused power and powerlessness, of being taken over in the one hand and of touching new physical and psychic potentialities in the other, a heightened sensibility which can be exhilaration, bewildering, and exhausting. For Rich, motherhood dramatizes the interactions of "exclusive" opposites, impresses upon us, for example, that "love and anger can exist concurrently."

The women's health care movement generally, and feminist attitudes toward both specifically, understand the concurrence of power and powerlessness and use it as a principle in developing nonviolent attitudes toward the body. The women's health care movement seeks to change the physical alienation affecting women, replacing a variety of attitudes that deny the body's goodness and fear of its function. Rather than labelling menstruation "the curse," women are learning to accept and celebrate their cyclical rhythms. Instead of birth control pills which, although "sure," chemically dominate and sometimes injure the body, women are turning to methods that are perhaps more limited but far safer.

The movement toward home births and toward "childbirth without violence" integrates many principles of nonviolence in the relationships involved in childbirth. Modern technological obstetrics sterilizes, shaves, and generally obfuscates the nature of childbirth, dehumanizing the most profound of human experiences. Mothers become passive observers, while their bodies become objects. Babies likewise are objectified, not considered to be people affected by their environment. The goal of such obstetrics is, of course, total control through the domination of the doctor. The entire birth experience is subject to manipulation, not only its labor and its pain, but also its passion, creativity, and satisfaction. Home births have developed an alternative to this, where midwife, mother, child, father, and others all participate and cooperate with natural forces. The benefits of such non-injury to mother and child alike include physically healthy birth without drugs, less birth trauma for the baby, early development of emotional ties between mother, father, and baby. Beyond these, new attitudes toward birth signify the development of supportive and less destructive attitudes toward our bodies, and to the natural environment generally.

Feminism and Nonviolence as Creativity

New thinking by women shedding old oppressive roles, yet retaining the real joys of womanness, can become one of the most creative political forces society has ever known. Women, like all oppressed groups, have had to know well, and bargain with, the structures which hurt them. Feminism has helped to evoke new social understandings based on women's experience and sisterhood. Many of these are implicitly grounded in nonviolence. Sisterhood implies democracy, for the needs and points of view are all-important in community. Women's responsibility provides a rationale for self-reliance and an end to exploitation.

Perhaps, as men take on new roles which encourage human values, nonviolence will seem more realistic to them too. Those who care for children and who understand their value as derived from caring will be less willing to kill. Environmental accountability will be encouraged when men take more responsibility for their day-to-day actions, and deal more closely with the consequences. Competition may lose some of its importance to those with other priorities.

Life is not a zero-sum game, where some must win at the others' expense. Violence and sexism in their many forms destroy our bonds with each other and our standing on the earth. They are ideologies which deny the ways in which we need each other and our natural order, and attempt to do what cannot be done—discard human needs and emotions and the natural workings of the earth.

Rape Is All Too Thinkable for Quite the Normal Sort of Man

by Neal King and Martha McCaughey

Men have trouble discussing rape. Some men rape, say some men, imagining that members of a subspecies abuse women in this culture. But let's be honest and tell it like it is: Normal men rape.

We are not being metaphorical or loose with our terms; we mean this the way it sounds. The vast majority of men who rape are quite ordinary.

If this sounds absurd, let's review some facts.

Rape is the bodily penetration of an unconsenting person. Men need to be reminded what this means. It's not listening when your partner says "no"; it's getting your date drunk to get sex from her; it's taking advantage of an unconscious woman at a party; it's using your economic or political power to intimidate a coworker into sex. These forms of rape are far more common than the stereotypical scene of a stranger jumping out from the bushes and attacking a woman.

Nearly half of all American women have had at least one man try, successfully or not, to rape them. And many women have been attacked a number of times. The men who do this must be normal; there are not enough "abnormal" men in this society to accomplish abuse on that scale.

When a rape is grotesquely violent, or when it's perpetrated on the wife of another man or on a very young girl, many men get upset to the point of proclaiming their desire to kill the rapist. But people have grown so accustomed to the sexual coercion of women that most rapes go unnoticed, especially by the men who commit them.

Most rapists are not strangers or even strange; they are their victims' friends, acquaintances, co-workers, neighbors, dates, lovers, husbands, brothers, fathers. They are the everyday, run-of-the-mill normal men in the lives of normal women.

Male readers may be getting defensive at this point, thinking, "I'm not one of them!" And they may not be. But the fact is, most men do not know what rape is. To these men, forcing a woman who is not willing is part of the game, perfectly normal and, for many, especially satisfying. These men may acknowledge that using physical force is rape, but prevailing over a woman through trickery, blackmail, or other means is simply sex. This implies that men don't want to know—that rape may be a part of their normal sexual encounters. Normal men rape because they engage in normal sex—normal sex often being coercive and abusive to women.

Though these women feel injured and demeaned in such encounters, they are not supposed to feel that they have been raped. Men don't define the experience as rape, and men are oblivious to the pain they've inflicted. Many a man who forces his date to have sex will call her up the next day and ask her out again. Normal men can be that out of touch with women's feelings.

So often women hear men refer to rape as if it were some kind of compliment, "You're so attractive that I have to have you," or "She's too ugly to get raped," or, "You look so good, I can't control myself." The notion that rape can be normal is evident in the inevitable questions about what a woman was wearing at the time: "Dressed like that, what did she expect?"

If men respected women as peers, they would see the fixation on women's body parts as a fetish, the fascination with adolescent women as pedophilia, and the desire for female passivity as necrophilia. They would also see the sexual coercion of women for what it is—rape.

In this culture, sadly, a man can be normal in believing that sex is what women are for. But that is not what women are for.

If sex is not consensual, it is rape, and men must start learning the difference by looking at it from women's perspectives.

The man who can truthfully say that he has never forced or tricked a woman into sex may dismiss all of this—"It's not my concern." It is. All men must work to create a culture where sexual aggression is unthinkable for normal men. Men have to examine their own relationships with women and talk to other men about rape. The man who says that rape is a women's issue is part of the problem. The wall of silence that men have put up against this "normal" violence must come down. Normal men rape, and normal men, together, have the responsibility to stop it.

from Los Angeles Times, *August 13, 1989*

Narrowing the Battlefield

by Carol Ascher

The attitude of nonviolence stems from a reverence and respect for life. It is the Commandment, "Thou Shalt Not Kill," understood in its widest meaning: physical and psychic harm, short of death, are included on the assumption that in this bountiful world there can be sufficient space, time, and resources for each of us to get what we need without violently taking from others. There is an appealing optimism in this attitude, and I believe also truth. Its complications arise, of course, when there is or appears to be a scarcity, when there are vast differences in the power to procure or command resources, and when violence is proclaimed the order of the day. At times like this, when editorial writers congratulate their readers for getting over the "Vietnam Syndrome," as if a reluctance to kill people and destroy another country were a disease, nonviolence can seem like a sweet pipedream.

The irony of the nonviolent attitude, of course, is that it only has living meaning in exactly those moments when an individual or group has the power to kill or destroy, or when a person's or a group's safety is threatened.

When we talk about women and men in relation to nonviolence, I think we are talking about an urgent and ultimate good for both. But because of real differences in strength and power created by both nature and society, the nonviolent attitude has had a quite different meaning for women than for men. Most obviously, for men in our society, nonviolence means relinquishing physical and mechanical powers to which they usually have had easy access, and probably have even learned to believe they have a right: it means deciding not to go to war, to carry weapons, or to hit their wives. For women, on the other hand, a nonviolent world immediately conjures images of walking in safety and ease on the street, feeling unafraid to argue heatedly with a lover, not worrying about the loss of husbands or sons in war. If women must give up anything to accept a nonviolent world, it seems to me, it is their age-old standards for judging "manliness" in men. At the risk of bifurcating the world too sharply, I suspect that when you ask a man to picture a gun, he most often imagines himself holding it; while, to a woman, the gun in the picture is pointed at her or at someone she loves.

The problem for women who want to take a nonviolent stance in this still extremely violent world is, in fact, rather like the problem for men who decide to become pacifists while on the battlefield. They must invent tactics, strategies, and states of mind which take them out of real-world and internalized victimization. Insofar as it is possible to get off the battlefield, they must do so. But men can shoot their guns into the air, volunteer to drive an ambulance, or go AWOL. Women in their homes and in the cities of today have a more difficult time discovering the demarcations of the battlefield. What are the equivalents for women of shooting a gun into the air? I myself am not always sure.

It will come as a surprise that for thousands of years, without being pacifists, women have largely taken a defensive position towards violence. Whether they believed violence was right or wrong, they knew they could get killed; and having children under their wing, they stayed out of the line of fire. In primitive societies, women cultivate the soil while the men hunt or make war. There is no value system which judges the men's activities as pejorative; on the contrary, they are most often accorded a higher status exactly because of their closeness to death. It is the connection between men's higher status and their activities as hunters and warriors that made Simone de Beauvoir write in *The Second Sex* that, "If blood were but a nourishing fluid, it would be valued no higher than milk. For it is not in giving life but in risking life that man is raised above the animal; that is why superiority has been accorded in humanity not to the sex that brings forth but to that which kills." Although I think we are deeply embedded in nature exactly because of both our violence and the oppression of women which our consciousness could enable us to overcome, I believe that the two phenomena are linked.

In our urbanized industrial society, beyond the very real dangers which women rationally try to avoid, an elaborate culture has developed through which women indicate their inferiority to men at the same time as showing their "sensitivity" to violence. The hands over the eyes during the murder scene at the movies, squeamish shrieks in the face of bugs that must be removed or killed, an avoidance of certain kinds of articles on the front page of the newspaper or stories on the evening news—these are the images that rush to my mind. But again, these sensitivities do not reflect more than the dullest adherence to the Commandment against killing; and I doubt that the connection is more than rarely even made. Instead, all this acting out is largely ritualized drama, a kind of pageant play affirming men's important role as gun bearers, bug squashers, and decision-makers on those front-page issues of destruction and violence. The women will wash and clean up and bear whatever life and death bring them.

Of course, the men have their reciprocal role: they not only risk their lives to "defend" the homeland (experiencing "life" and friendship at its peak while out alone with their buddies), but with due chivalry they protect their women from knowing the grisly and glorious truths about the violent atrocities they may have committed away from home.

A wave of American feminism arose out of the ashes of the anti-draft and anti-war movement of the 1960s. Women, gaining political skills at the same time as a new understanding of their second place in the violent world of men, began to strike out on their own. During the 1970s, as a result of the women's movement, a change occurred in this country in women's relationship to violence. In large part, women lessened their fear of it, but they themselves at times also became more involved in it. Early on there was the anger that men had controlled the streets too long with their threats of mugging and rape, and the cry that women had to reclaim the right to walk about freely at night. I recall vigilante squads of women who, for a time, tried to ensure other women's safety in the dark hours. One friend of mine joined a women's group which organized regular rifle practice so that women could become at ease with the control side of a gun. I myself took karate lessons—a chance to learn the limits of my own physical power and to lose my feminine fear of violence, I thought—until after three months its militaristic elements repelled me too much to continue. For the first time, too, there were publicized cases of women who defended themselves against rape with guns and knives. Joanne Little became a legend when, herself already a prisoner, she killed a guard who had tried to rape her, using his own weapon. Women became sensitive to the cultural violence against them, and some began to picket in front of theaters which showed images of sexual violence against women. I attended uncomfortable meetings where women admitted to being battered wives and asked other women for help. And there was the drive by women to join the military, and the resulting machinations for and against the Equal Rights Amendment and the revival of the draft.

On the other side, although it sometimes seems less publicized, has been an active feminist-pacifist movement. Feminists with a nonviolent perspective have been at the core of anti-nuclear organizing, and their sensitivity to the preciousness of life has made them turn up at the forefront of a variety of ecological issues from Love Canal to uranium mining on Native American territories. The idea of nonviolence has been extended from the relationship between people to the ties between human beings and our delicate earth. A significant number of feminist-pacifists have also chosen to live in rural areas, in women's communities, without men. They have said, in effect: it is too hard to live one's private life ethically and comfortably on the battlefield.

Strangely, there is one area of battle and conflict that women carry with them even unto the furthest rural reaches. Within feminist-pacifist circles, the issue of abortion has been upsetting and unresolved. Most feminists without a nonviolence perspective, perhaps wisely, argue in public for women's right to control their own bodies, including their reproductive systems, and reserve their sadness and moral concern about the fate of a fetus for quiet discussions, behind closed doors. But feminist-pacifists have made a commitment to sanctify life, and so some feel they cannot so simply argue the expedience of first winning a right for women that they then may pronounce unethical to use. There have been angry and hurtful interchanges among these women, but more recently also open discussion, including an enormously interesting transcribed discussion among several feminist-pacifists in the August 1, 1980 issue of *WIN*, the War Resisters League magazine.

I believe a nonviolent approach to the universe is more urgent than ever before. But I also believe that both the "violent" as well as the nonviolent aspects of the women's movement over the past decade have been largely to the good. Both sides, each in its way, have worked to narrow the gap and so have an effect on the violent world of men. I suspect there are fewer women now than 10 years ago who worship men's capacity for violence from afar, while denigrating their own life-giving activities—however much noise Phyllis Schafly, Maribel Morgan, and the men who finance them may be making. Also, psychologically, many women may need to move from seeing themselves as passive victims of violence through a phase of anger and violence before they can become nonviolent activists. From this perspective, even women entering the military may have some good results. The problem is: do we have time, given our capacity for destruction, for women to get this experience, and can it be gotten without creating its own added waves of violence?

I said before that I hold to the connection between the sharp bifurcation of genders, with its concomitant oppression of women, and the violence and destruction we experience throughout the world. In her book *The Mermaid and the Minotaur*, one of the great theoretical contributions of this wave of the women's movement, Dorothy Dinnerstein has elaborately argued how female-dominated child-rearing guarantees "male insistence upon, and female compliance with, a double standard of sexual behavior," including male aggression and violence and "certain forms of antagonism—rampant in men, and largely shared by women as well—against women." Turning away from their mothers, who they must not be like, men also run from their own softness and nurturance, their "fleshy mortality," the memory of infancy when they experienced both boundlessness and helpless passion. With their infantile longings neither satisfied nor transcended, war and conquest are the "amoral greed of infancy" turned loose on the world; and the death and destruction which they create is the fear of both which they must deny in themselves. Arguing the urgency for men to share in child-rearing with women, Dinnerstein writes, "They cannot be our brothers until we stop being their mothers: until, that is, we stop carrying the main responsibility—and taking the main blame—for their early introduction to the human condition." Of course, as she adds, what also stops true solidarity among women is that women share men's anti-female feelings.

If Dinnerstein is right, as I believe she is, then a nonviolent world must be worked toward at home, in a differently structured family, as well as on the street and in the recruitment center. The battlefield that must be narrowed includes those widely differing roles deemed appropriate for men and women. This is an enormously difficult task: when one talks to people about murder, most will have to concede that it is wrong; but there are still many who see nothing amiss with one-half the world, women, taking full responsibility for bringing to adulthood each new generation of human beings. Yet the enormity of the task is matched by the risks on the other side, as men continue to develop technology that can not only wipe out an entire hemisphere of our planet but also make life impossible for countless future generations.

from "Confrontation," Winter 1991
Long Island University Literary Journal

Patriarchy: A State of War

by Barbara Hope

Why weren't we prepared for this – the imminence of nuclear holocaust. The final silencing of life. The brutal extinction of the planet. Surely there have been substantial clues throughout history. Male supremacy. Wars. Witch-burning. Male religious myths. Weapons of increased destructive capacity. Institutionalized greed. The enslavement of half the human race. Centuries of violence.

Why weren't we prepared for this? We have lived with violence for so long. We have lived under the rule of the fathers so long. Violence and patriarchy: mirror images. An ethic of destruction as normative. Diminished love for life, a numbing to real events as the final consequence. We were not even prepared.

Mary Daly, in *Gyn/Ecology: The Metaethics of Radical Feminism*, writes: "The rulers of the patriarchy–males with power–wage an unceasing war against life itself. Since female energy is essentially biophilic, the female spirit/body is the primary target in the perpetual war of aggression against life. Women must understand that the female self is the enemy under fire from the patriarchy." She further writes that "clearly the primary and essential object of aggression is not the opposing military force. The members of the opposing team play the same war games and share the same values. The secret bond that binds the warriors together is the violation of women, acted out physically and constantly replayed on the level of language and shared fantasies."

We needn't look far for evidence to support her theory. Recall the U.S. Army basic training jingle; "This is my rifle (slaps rifle). This is my gun (slaps crotch). One is for killing, the other for fun." The language of war is the language of genocide. Misogynist obscenities are used to train fighters and intensify feelings of violence. War provides men with a context to act out their hatred of women without the veneer of chivalry or civilization. War is rape.

In the male world of war, toughness is the most highly–prized virtue. Some even speak of the "hairy chest syndrome." The man who recommends violence does not endanger his reputation for wisdom, but a man who suggests negotiation becomes known as soft, as willing to settle for less. To be repelled by mass murder is to be irresponsible. It is to refuse the phallic celebration. It is to be feminine, to be a dove. It means walking out of the club of bureaucratic machismo. To be a specialist in the new violence is to be on the frontier. It is no accident that patriarchy related history as the history of war; that is precisely their history. In remembering their battles, the fathers recall the deep experience of their own violent proclivities and relive the ecstatic euphoria of those ultimate moments of male bonding.

The history of war speaks volumes about national will in a patriarchal culture. Wars are nothing short of organized killing presided over by men deemed the best. The fact is– they are. They have absorbed, in the most complete way, the violent character of their own ethos. These are the men who design missiles and technologies as extensions of themselves. These men are ready to annihilate whole societies. These are the men honored as heroes with steel minds, resolute wills, insatiable drives for excellence, capable of planning demonic acts in a detached non-emotional way. These are the dead men, the hollow men, capable of nothing but violence.

It is significant that, after the accident at Three Mile Island, women were more concerned about the danger than men; women felt that they were being lied to about the real-life effects of nuclear technology. Women were resistant to the repeated declarations of the male decision-makers that everything was under control, that there was nothing to be alarmed about, that nuclear engineers could solve any difficulties. Women felt the lies. Women know and feel the lies that maintain nuclear technology because we have been lied to. We are the victims of patriarchal lies. We know the deceit that grounds patriarchal colonization of women. We know, feel and intuit the deep truth that falsehoods, deceptions and lies form the very character of male rule. Women are the first victims of the patriarchal state of war.

Violence to our bodies: A woman is raped every three minutes. A woman is battered every eighteen seconds. Women are physically threatened by a frightening social climate structured in male might. Women are depicted in pornography as objects to be beaten, whipped, chained and conquered. The myth prevails that women like it.

Violence to our hearts: The positing of male comradeship as the model of human relationships. The systematic separation of women from one another. The degradation of women's culture. The erasure of women's history. The sanctifying of the heterosexual norm with its rigid understanding of the giving and receiving of affection.

Violence to our spirit: The dismemberment of the goddess and the enthronement of the male god. The ripping of women away from a life in tune with natural patterns of rhythm and flow in the universe. The ongoing patriarchal work of rendering women unconscious to ourselves.

Violence to our work: The exploitation and devaluation of women's labor. The relegation of women to supportive, maintenance roles. The deliberate structure of women's economic dependence. Violence to women. Under the patriarchy, women are the enemy. This is a war across time and space, the real history of the ages.

In this extreme situation, confronted by the patriarchy in its multiple institutional forms, what can women do? We can name the enemy: patriarchy. We can break from deadly possession by the fathers. We can move from docility, passivity and silence to liberation, courage and speech. We can name ourselves, cherish ourselves, courageously take up our lives. We can refuse to sell our bodies and we can refuse to sell our minds. We can claim freedom from false loyalties. We can band with other women and ignite the roaring fire of female friendship.

This much we have learned from our living: life begets life. Life for women, life for the earth, the very survival of the planet is found only outside the patriarchy. Beyond their sad and shallow definitions. Beyond their dead and static knowledge. Beyond their amnesia. Beyond their impotence. Beyond their wars. Wars which unmask the fear, insecurity and powerlessness that form the very base of patriarchal rule.

To end the state of war, to halt the momentum toward death, passion for life must flourish. Women are the bearers of life-loving energy. Ours is the task of deepening that passion for life and separating from all that threatens life, all that diminishes life. Becoming who we are as women. Telling/living the truth of our lives. Shifting the weight of the world.

Will such measures put an end to war? What we already know is that centuries of other means have failed. In the name of peace, war is raged, weapons developed, lives lost. Testimonies are announced. Treaties signed. Declarations stated. Pronouncements issued. And the battle still goes on. The patriarchy remains intact. Women are not free. Nothing changes. This time the revolution must go all the way. In the words of the poet:

> *This is what we are watching: watching the*
> *spider rebuild–patiently, they say,*
>
> *but we recognize in her*
> *impatience–our own–*
>
> *the passion to make and make again*
> *where such unmaking reigns*
>
> *The refusal to be a victim*
> *we have lived with violence so long*

> —Adrienne Rich, Natural Resources

from Peacework; Twenty Years of Nonviolent Social Change, *Edited by Pat Farren, American Friends Service Committee, 1991*

An American Shero of 1941

by Colman McCarthy

Washington — For those feeling glutted with Pearl Harbor tales and left cold by them — I'm freezing — the worthier anniversary is on Dec. 8. On that day in 1941, Rep. Jeannette Rankin, brave and defiantly sensible, stood alone in Congress to vote against America's entry into World War II.

The Montana Republican, 61 at the time and a lifelong pacifist, went to the House floor believing that "you can no more win a war than win an earthquake." The vote was 338-1.

Miss Rankin was hissed. Colleagues asked her to reconsider and make the vote unanimous. After declining, she left the House floor and avoided assault from power zealots by hiding in a phone booth.

Miss Rankin would later explain her vote: "There can be no compromise with war; it cannot be reformed or controlled; cannot be disciplined into decency or codified into common sense, for war is the slaughter of human beings, temporarily regarded as enemies, on as large a scale as possible."

Were Jeannette Rankin a member of Congress in modern times, she would have joined the minority who opposed American militarism in Grenada, Libya, Panama, and Iraq, as she did in 1969 when leading a peace march in Washington to protest the Vietnam War.

She would be vocal, too, about current preparations for America's next war against whoever dares cross it. Miss Rankin's stand in 1941 had the strength of consistency. On April 6, 1917, she had voted against U.S. involvement in World War I, saying, "We cannot settle disputes by eliminating human beings."

That was the first vote of the first woman in Congress. For defying the military ethic, a *New York Times* editorialist saw Miss Rankin as "almost final proof of feminine incapacity for straight reasoning."

A majority of Montanans apparently agreed. They gave her only one term in 1917 and only one after the 1941 vote. Both times, Miss Rankin found the rejections as bothersome as pebbles in her shoe. She marched ahead, combining her pacifism with the feminism she had championed in her first term when introducing suffrage legislation that would give federal voting rights to women in the 19th amendment.

Between the two wars, Miss Rankin fortified her ideals by a life of study and service. She moved to Georgia, living near Athens in Thoreau-like simplicity in a cabin with no phone, electricity, or running water but plenty of books.

She founded the Georgia Peace Society and taught "peace habits" to local children. For her toil, she received a high honor from the Atlanta post of the American Legion: The old boys called her a Communist.

Neither Jeannette Rankin nor her politics has wafted off into obscurity. On May 1, 1985, 500 Montanans, historians, politicians, and a few pacifists gathered in the rotunda of the Capitol for the unveiling of bronze likeness of Miss Rankin.

In a speech, Rep. Pat Williams, the Montana Democrat who represents the congresswoman's old district, offered a a memorable line: Miss Rankin "realized and brought us to understand the meaning of the power and influence of an individual in this democracy carrying out her conscience."

The following year, some Rankinites in Missoula, the congresswoman's hometown, organized to form the Jeannette Rankin Peace Resource Center. In five years, it has become nationally known for carrying on the kind of educational, social justice, and conflict resolution programs that Miss Rankin believed in. At a ceremony last April, the center reminded the citizens of Missoula County what it cost them to live in militaristic America: $344,284 a day — the Pentagon's share of the local federal tax haul.

The event prompted the chairman of the economics department at the University of Montana to state the most obvious political reality of our day: Military spending is the "crushing burden that has substantially decreased our ability to take care of our basic needs." Pure Rankin, pure truth.

Internationally, knowledge of this American hero grows. The Japanese have been reading the 1989 book *A Single Dissenting Voice: The Life of Jeannette Rankin.* Its author, Yunosuke Ohkura of the Tokyo Broadcasting Co., was in Washington in May 1973 and read the obituary of Miss Rankin, who died at 93. He was astonished to read of her stand in 1941.

"We are a nation of unity," Yunosuke Ohkura, now a professor at Tokyo University, told *Montanan* magazine last year. "I've never heard of a single dissenting vote in Japanese life. But in the United States, even after this powerful attack, there was a person against the war. I was amazed."

Professor Ohkura's book, soon to be translated into English, will join two other full biographies of Miss Rankin. More are needed — as are more of her kind in Congress when war hysteria next arises.

from Washington Post, *December 6, 1991*

But there are some things in our social system to which all of us ought to be maladjusted. I never intended to become adjusted to the madness of militarism and the self-defeating method of physical violence.

Martin Luther King, Jr.

Martin Luther King, Jr.

by Charles De Benedetti

Between 1955 and 1968, a black-led civil rights movement emerged across the United States, and especially in the American South, struggling to end racial segregation and to allow blacks fuller access to the largest promises of the national life. Joining millions of people from all races, creeds, and regions, this movement grew from several deep and tangled historical roots, including: the long black quest for freedom and equality; the egalitarian values inherent in the Declaration of Independence and other fundamental American documents; the strong emphases on social justice of many of America's religious faiths; and, most recently, the labor and liberal reform movements of the 1930s and 1940s. This movement found in Martin Luther King, Jr. a leader capable of transforming millions of inchoate aspirations into an engine of peaceful social change.

The movement's largely peaceful methods and positive results were not preordained. Almost certainly, in view of long-building black frustrations, there would have been a major civil rights movement in the 1950s and 1960s, with or without the Reverend King. Yet, without King's leadership and moral authority, this movement might well have taken a far different course, perhaps even toward a racial bloodbath and severe political repression. Instead, King stepped into history and aggressively deployed the power of Christian nonviolence to move the country away from racial injustice and toward reconciliation. As was noted in a eulogy at his funeral in April 1968, he appeared as "a peaceful warrior who built an army and a movement that is mighty without missiles, able without an atomic arsenal, ready without rockets, real without bullets; an army tutored in living and loving and not in killing." He was that rare phenomenon— "a leader who was willing to die, but not willing to kill." In the process of fighting for civil rights, he helped to shepherd his country through a time of trial and progress in race relations.

Fundamentally, King was an inclusive peacemaker. He sought not only to include as many supporters as possible within the civil rights movement, but also to bring about an eventual reconciliation with their opponents. He saw the circle of support for social justice, which he termed the "beloved community," expanding until it included virtually all Americans. Furthermore, King was an inclusive peacemaker in the sense that he strove to overcome his personal limitations for the sake of greater moral and political effectiveness.

The basic outline of King's life before the Montgomery Alabama bus boycott of 1955-56 can be summarized briefly. He was born in Atlanta on January 15, 1929. His parents were Alberta Williams King, the daughter of the pastor of the Ebenezer Baptist Church, and Martin Luther "Daddy" King, the assistant pastor who became pastor upon the death of his father-in-law in 1931. Ebenezer was a thriving church, and Martin grew up in a family with middle-class comforts. He attended church faithfully and sang hymns at church meetings at a young age. Growing up in Atlanta, he also experienced white racism firsthand.

A precocious youth, King skipped his senior year in high school and entered the predominantly black Morehouse College in Atlanta at age 15. After graduating from Morehouse with a degree in sociology in spring 1948, he entered the largely white Crozier Theological Seminary in suburban Philadelphia. Three years later, as valedictorian of his graduating class, he won a scholarship to attend the graduate school of his choice. That fall King entered Boston University's prestigious School of Theology, which awarded him the Ph.D. degree in 1955. In the meantime, he married Coretta Scott, a student at the Boston Conservatory, and accepted an appointment as minister of the Dexter Avenue Baptist Church in Montgomery, beginning in the summer of 1954.

As a youth, King's most difficult problem involved the choice of a vocation. He wanted to serve others and to make his mark in the world, but he was not sure how he should proceed. While attracted in some ways to the ministry, he did not like the pressure his father was putting on him to succeed him as pastor at Ebenezer, and he doubted the relevance of his church's fundamentalist religion in modern America. He toyed with the idea of becoming a doctor, and after a bad personal experience with discrimination on a train trip, he considered becoming a lawyer so that he could help in breaking down the legal barriers that trapped blacks in a segregated subcaste.

In sum, during his first 27 years King developed numerous qualities that proved invaluable to him as a peacemaker. He felt a deep concern for the plight of the black masses, especially in his native South. He sustained a strong religious faith combined with a quest for greater spiritual depth and understanding. He maintained a continuing interest in his own intellectual growth and in learning about ways to bring about peaceful social change. He had an ability to communicate with people of diverse racial and educational backgrounds. And, perhaps most significant, he developed a commitment, strengthened in a time of crisis, to continue to work for social justice even if it meant forfeiting his own life.

The decade beginning with the Montgomery bus boycott in fall 1955 and ending with the Voting Rights Act in summer 1965 marked the glory days for King—and for the civil rights movement as a whole. It was during these years that King, the inclusive peacemaker, was most effective. The story of the civil rights movement during these years has been told many times; here the focus is on some key reasons for King's effectiveness, followed by a closer look at the two great events in civil rights in 1963: the springtime Birmingham Alabama campaign and King's "I Have a Dream" speech in Washington, D.C. in August.

One reason for King's effectiveness during these years was his continuing personal and intellectual growth. He broadened himself by visiting West Africa in 1957 and India in 1959. The visit to the "land of my father's fathers" was memorable, and led to what King called a "nonviolent rebirth" and to a continuing interest in Africa's welfare. His trip to India deepened his commitment to Gandhian principles, including an effort upon his return to put less emphasis on material comforts in his own life. In the midst of a hectic schedule, King took time for writing and reflection. In addition to many articles, he published two books about the movement—*Stride Toward Freedom: The Montgomery Story* (1958) and *Why We Can't Wait* (1964)—and a deeply spiritual book of sermons, *Strength to Love* (1964). During these years King was especially interested in learning more about human behavior and the psychological underpinnings of racism and violence. The relatively brief periods of time that King set aside for travel and for personal renewal helped to keep his speeches and writings fresh and cogent, and helped him, at least until the mid-1960s, to avert a clear danger facing prominent peacemakers—exhaustion or burnout.

During 1966, King largely refrained from criticizing the Vietnam War. He was preoccupied with the Chicago campaign, and distracted by growing demands of young black militants for black power. He made some guardedly critical statements regarding U.S. war policy. But it was not until early 1967, after doing careful study of the history of the conflict, that he made the war the theme of several major addresses. In February, he told an audience in Los Angeles that "the bombs in Vietnam explode at home: they destroy the hopes and possibilities for a decent America." In a sermon at his church in Atlanta, he said that he could "study war no more," and urged blacks opposed to the war to "challenge our young men with the alternative of conscientious objection." "The world now demands a maturity of America that we may not by able to achieve," King continued. "The New Testament says, 'Repent.' It is time for America to repent now." Before a crowd of 3,000 in New York's Riverside Church on April 4, he portrayed the war as a moral tragedy perpetrated by "the greatest purveyor of violence in the world today—my own government." Americans had failed to recognize the Vietnamese opposition to the Vietnam war was still a minority view even among his liberal civil rights allies and supporters. Black leaders, including Roy Wilkins of the NAACP and Whitney Young of the National Urban League, attacked King's position, while normally sympathetic newspapers like the *New York Times* and the *Washington Post* blasted the Southern Christian Leadership Conference leader for commenting on matters they considered irrelevant to social justice issues. King, however, believed that his opposition to the war was consistent with his concern about the oppressed and his commitment to nonviolence. He thus decided to stand on principle against a war that was draining so much of the power and potential of black America.

Like Vietnam, the rise of black nationalism presented difficult dilemmas for King. He supported many of the ideals of Stokely Carmichael and other black nationalists: pride in black history, emphasis on unity and improvement of living conditions within the black community, and constructive use of black economic and political power. But he did not like the slogan "Black Power" that had corrupted the imagination of many young blacks after Carmichael first used it at a Mississippi rally in 1966. King believed that the slogan had too many negative connotations, and that it would feed the growing white backlash against civil rights. He also believed that it would be impossible for blacks to continue to improve their status in American society without white support. And, even if they could make it on their own, Black Power's emphasis on separatism and its implicit endorsement of violence went against King's commitment to an inclusive Christian community.

King responded in detail to Black Power ideas during winter 1967 in his last full-length book, *Where Do We Go From Here: Chaos or Community?* He was careful to acknowledge the Black Power arguments that whites had systematically oppressed blacks, and that blacks had made many gains through self-help and racial pride. But he strongly rejected black nationalism's basic premises:

"In the final analysis the weakness of Black Power is its failure to see that the black man needs the white man and the white man needs the black man. However much we may try to romanticize the slogan, there is no separate black path to power and fulfillment that dies not intersect white paths, and there is no separate white path to power and fulfillment, short of social disaster, that does not share that power with black aspirations for freedom and human dignity. We are bound together in a single garment of destiny. The language, the cultural patterns, the music, the material prosperity, and even the food of America are an amalgam of black and white."

King's book epitomized the changes in the black movement during the time since he had completed *Why We Can't Wait* three years earlier. In that book, King had written primarily about the black struggle for equal rights. Now he was writing much more about the systemic problem of economic inequality and the need for massive federal expenditures to "fight poverty, ignorance, and slums." Equally important, in *Why Can't We Wait*, King was speaking for white liberals and for the overwhelming majority of blacks, North and South, with only the relatively small Black Muslim movement in serious opposition. Now he clearly was writing to respond to the growing nationalist movement and to rally the supporters of his nonviolent, integrationist approach. King still possessed a respected voice, but increasingly it was one voice among many.

King's insistence in *Where Do We Go From Here* on large-scale federal programs to end poverty in America provided the focus for the last year of his life. Clearly his vision was now more radical, for he was advocating not only equal rights but also a coalition of the poor to demand economic justice. Earlier, as he was maintaining his coalition of blacks and white liberals (including wealthy white contributors), he had not talked about restructuring the economic system. Now he did so. As he told journalist David Halberstam in spring 1967, "I labored with the idea of reforming the existing institutions of the South, a little change here, a little change there. Now I feel quite differently. I think you've got to have a reconstruction of the entire society, a revolution of values."

This vision, which David Levering Lewis recently called "the promise of nonviolent populism," informed King's planning for the Poor People's Campaign in Washington in 1968. In order to force the government to face up to the continuing problem of poverty in America, King proposed to bring poor blacks, whites, Puerto Ricans, Indians, and Chicanos to the capital. Initially, plans called for people to come from various parts of the nation and demand the passage of SCLC's $12 billion "Economic Bill of Rights," which included such things as guaranteed jobs for the able-bodied, livable incomes for the legitimately unemployed, and a firm federal commitment to open housing and integrated education. If their efforts failed, thousands more would come and create "major massive dislocations" in the city.

King was unable to carry out what he had called his "last, greatest dream." He was shot down by a white racist assassin on April 4, 1968, in Memphis, Tennessee, where he had gone to lend support to the city's striking garbage workers. Yet, even if he had not been killed, the odds were against the success of the Poor People's Campaign. For one thing, the attitudes of most officials and northerners were extremely hostile. For another, it would have been very difficult to unite poor people of such diverse ethnic and regional backgrounds and to raise the funds required to sustain them in Washington until victory was achieved. But King had not gone with the odds in his other campaigns. Under incessant threat of death, he did not ever have good reason to believe that he would live through them. In faith, he had strived since 1955 to help to bring about the "beloved community." In faith, he would continue to do so until he was "free at last."

On Sunday, February 4, 1968, exactly two months before his death, King delivered a very personal message to the congregation at Ebenezer Baptist Church in Atlanta, where he and his father served as co-pastors. The topic was what he would want said at his own funeral, what he believed his life added up to. Because his words bear so directly on assessing King as peacemaker, they deserve quoting at some length:

"Tell them not to mention that I have a Nobel Peace Prize. That isn't important. Tell them not to mention that I have three or four hundred other awards. That's not important. Tell them not to mention where I went to school. I'd like somebody to mention that day that Martin Luther King, Jr. tried to give his life serving others. I'd like for somebody to mention that day that Martin Luther King, Jr. tried to love somebody. I want you to say the day that I tried to be right on the war question. I want you to be able to say that I did try to feed the hungry. I want you to be able to say that day that I did try in my life to clothe those who were naked. I want you to say that I tried to love and serve humanity. Yes, if you want to say that I was a drum major, say that I was a drum major for justice. Say that I was a drum major for peace. That I was a drum major for righteousness. And all of the other shallow things will not matter. I won't have any money to leave behind. I won't have the fine and luxurious things of life to leave behind. But I just want to leave a committed life behind. And that's all I want to say."

The clearest, most powerful theme in this message is King's desire to be remembered as a person who sought to live his Christian faith, to obey God's word as he understood it. Although he appears to have succeeded in this quest, King was far from perfect. He knew the ordinary pressures and temptations of life. He suffered a deep sense of guilt, and periodically knew the agony of depression. He lived through jailings, failures, hatred, and abuse, most of it delivered by his fellow Christians. Yet, as he affirmed in his sermon, he tried to remain faithful to his Christianity and to hope for fuller human community which he believed that it nurtured.

How effective was King as a peacemaker? He surely was correct in his contention that peace within societies is not merely the absence of overt violence (what he called "negative peace"); instead, peace must involve conscious efforts to build community and bring about greater social justice ("positive peace"). He also was correct to note that means and ends are interrelated, that only nonviolent methods are likely to lead to a more just and peaceful society. Like Gandhi, King's teachings and actions are likely to be studied and discussed as long as there are nonviolent movements for social change.

from Peace Heroes, *Indiana University Press, Bloomington, Indiana*

Declaration of Independence from the War in Vietnam

by Martin Luther King, Jr.

Over the past two years, as I have moved to break the betrayal of my own silences and to speak from the burnings of my own heart, as I have called for radical departures from the destruction of Vietnam, many persons have questioned me about the wisdom of my path. At the heart of their concerns this query has often loomed large and loud: Why are you joining the voices of dissent? Peace and civil rights don't mix they say. Aren't you hurting the cause of your people, they ask. And when I hear them, though I often understand the source of their concern, I am nevertheless greatly saddened, for such questions mean that the inquirers have not really known me, my commitment, or my calling. Indeed, their questions suggest that they do not know the world in which they live.

There is at the outset a very obvious and almost facile connection between the war in Vietnam and the struggle I, and others, have been waging in America. A few years ago there was a shining moment in that struggle. It seemed as if there was a real promise of hope for the poor—both black and white—through the Poverty Program. Then came the build-up in Vietnam, and I watched the program broken and eviscerated as if it were some idle political plaything of a society gone mad on war, and I knew that America would never invest the necessary funds or energies in rehabilitation of its poor so long as Vietnam continued to draw men and skills and money like some demonic, destructive suction tube. So I was increasingly compelled to see the war as an enemy of the poor and to attack it as such.

Perhaps the more tragic recognition of reality took place when it became clear to me that the war was doing far more than devastating the hopes of the poor at home. It was sending their sons and their brothers and their husbands to fight and to die in extraordinarily high proportions relative to the rest of the population. We were taking the young black men who had been crippled by our society and sending them 8,000 miles away to guarantee liberties in Southeast Asia which they had not found in Southwest Georgia and East Harlem. So we have been repeatedly faced with the cruel irony of watching Negro and white boys on TV screens as they kill and die together for a nation that has been unable to set them together in the same schools. So we watch them in brutal solidarity burning the huts of a poor village, but we realize that they would never live on the same block in Detroit. I could not be silent in the face of such cruel manipulation of the poor. I knew that I could never again raise my voice against the violence of the oppressed in the ghettos without having first spoken clearly to the greatest purveyor of violence in the world today—my own government.

Somehow this madness must cease. I speak as a child of God and brother to the suffering poor of Vietnam and the poor of America who are paying the double price of smashed hopes at home and death and corruption in Vietnam. I speak as a citizen of the world, for the world as it stands aghast at the path we have taken. I speak as an American to the leaders of my own nation. The great initiative in this war is ours. The initiative to stop must be ours.

This is the message of the great Buddhist leaders of Vietnam. Recently, one of them wrote these words: "Each day the war goes on, the hatred increases in the hearts of the Vietnamese and in the hearts of those of humanitarian instinct. The Americans are forcing even their friends into becoming their enemies. It is curious that the Americans, who calculate so carefully on the possibilities of military victory, do not realize that in the process they are incurring deep psychological and political defeat. The image of America will never again be the image of revolution, freedom, and democracy, but the image of violence and militarism."

In 1957 a sensitive American official overseas said that it seemed to him that our nation was on the wrong side of a world revolution. During the past 10 years we have seen emerge a pattern of suppression which now has justified the presence of U.S. military "advisors" in Venezuela. The need to maintain social stability for our investments accounts for the counterrevolutionary action of American forces in Guatemala. It tells why American helicopters are being used against guerrillas in Colombia and why American napalm and Green Beret forces have already been active against rebels in Peru. With such activity in mind, the words of John F. Kennedy come back to haunt us. Five years ago he said, "Those who make peaceful revolution impossible will make violent revolution inevitable.

"I am convinced that if we are to get on the right side of the world revolution, we as a nation must undergo a radical revolution of values. When machines and computers profit and property rights are considered more important than people, the giant triplets of racism, materialism, and militarism are incapable of being conque. The Western arrogance of feeling that it has everything to teach others and nothing to learn from them is not just. A true revolution of values will lay hands on the world order and say of war: "This way of settling differences is not just." This business of burning human beings with napalm, of filling our nation's homes with orphans and widows, of injecting poisonous drugs of hate into the veins of people normally humane, of sending men home from dark and bloody battlefields physically handicapped and psychologically deranged, cannot be reconciled with wisdom, justice, and love. A nation that continues year after year to spend more money on military defense than on programs of social uplift is approaching spiritual death.

There is nothing, except a tragic death wish, to prevent us from reordering our priorities, so that the pursuit of peace will take precedence over the pursuit of war. There is nothing to keep us from molding a recalcitrant status quo until we have fashioned it into a brotherhood.

This kind of positive revolution of values is our best defense against communism. War is not the answer. Communism will never be defeated by the use of atomic bombs or nuclear weapons.

We must not engage in a negative anti-communism, but rather in a positive thrust for democracy, realizing that our greatest defense against communism is to take offensive action in behalf of justice. We must with positive action seek to remove those conditions of poverty, insecurity, and injustice which are the fertile soil in which the seed of communism grows and develops.

These are revolutionary times. All over the globe men are revolting against old systems of exploitation and oppression, and out of the wombs of a frail world, new systems of justice and equality are being born. The shirtless and barefoot people of the land are rising up as never before. "The people who sat in darkness have seen a great light." We in the West must support these revolutions. It is a sad fact that, because of comfort, complacency, a morbid fear of communism, and our proneness to adjust to injustice, the Western nations that initiated so much of the revolutionary spirit of the modern world have now become the arch anti-revolutionaries. This has driven many to feel that only Marxism has the revolutionary spirit. Therefore, communism is a judgment against our failure to make democracy real and follow through on the revolutions

that we initiated. Our only hope today lies in our ability to recapture the revolutionary spirit and go out into a sometimes hostile world declaring eternal hostility to poverty, racism, and militarism.

Here is the true meaning and value of compassion and nonviolence—when it helps us to see the enemy's point of view, to hear his questions, to know his assessment of ourselves. For from his view we may indeed see the basic weaknesses of our own condition, and if we are mature, we may learn and grow and profit from the wisdom of the brothers who are called the opposition.

An address at Riverside Church,
New York City, Tuesday, April 4, 1967

Loving Your Enemies

by Martin Luther King, Jr.

The following sermon was delivered at the Dexter Avenue Baptist Church in Montgomery, Alabama, at Christmas, 1957. Martin Luther King wrote it while in jail for committing nonviolent civil disobedience during the Montgomery bus boycott.

Let us be practical and ask the question, How do we love our enemies?

First, we must develop and maintain the capacity to forgive. He who is devoid of the power to forgive is devoid of the power to love. It is impossible even to begin the act of loving one's enemies without the prior acceptance of the necessity, over and over again, of forgiving those who inflict evil and injury upon us. It is also necessary to realize that the forgiving act must always be initiated by the person who has been wronged, the victim of some great hurt, the recipient of some tortuous injustice, the absorber of some terrible act of oppression. The wrongdoer may request forgiveness. He may come to himself, and, like the prodigal son, move up some dusty road, his heart palpitating with the desire for forgiveness. But only the injured neighbor, the loving father back home, can really pour out the warm waters of forgiveness.

Forgiveness does not mean ignoring what has been done or putting a false label on an evil act. It means, rather, that the evil act no longer remains as a barrier to the relationship. Forgiveness is a catalyst creating the atmosphere necessary for a fresh start and a new beginning. It is the lifting of a burden or the canceling of a debt. The words "I will forgive you, but I'll never forget what you've done" never explain the real nature of forgiveness. Certainly one can never forget, if that means erasing it totally from his mind. But when we forgive, we forget in the sense that the evil deed is no longer a mental block impeding a new relationship. Likewise, we can never say, "I will forgive you, but I won't have anything further to do with you." Forgiveness means reconciliation, a coming together again. Without this, no man can love his enemies. The degree to which we are able to forgive determines the degree to which we are able to love our enemies.

Second, we must recognize that the evil deed of the enemy-neighbor, the thing that hurts, never quite expresses all that he is. An element of goodness may be found even in our worst enemy. Each of us has something of a schizophrenic personality, tragically divided against ourselves. A persistent civil war rages within all of our lives. Something within us causes us to lament with Ovid, the Latin poet, "I see and approve the better things, but follow worse," or to agree with Plato that human personality is like a charioteer having two headstrong horses, each wanting to go in a different direction, or to repeat with the Apostle Paul, "The good that I would I do not: but the evil which I would not, that I do."

This simply means that there is some good in the worst of us and some evil in the best of us. When we discover this, we are less prone to hate our enemies. When we look beneath the surface, beneath the impulsive evil deed, we see within our enemy-neighbor a measure of goodness and know that the viciousness and evilness of his acts are not quite representative of all that he is. We see him in a new light. We recognize that his hate grows out of fear, pride, ignorance, prejudice, and misunderstanding, but in spite of this, we know God's image is ineffably etched in his being. Then we love our enemies by realizing that they are not totally bad and that they are not beyond the reach of God's redemptive love.

Third, we must not seek to defeat or humiliate the enemy but to win his friendship and understanding. At times we are able to humiliate our worst enemy. Inevitably, his weak moments come and we are able to thrust in his side the spear of defeat. But this we must not do. Every word and deed must contribute to an understanding with the enemy and release those vast reservoirs of goodwill which have been blocked by impenetrable walls of hate.

Let us move now from the practical how to the theoretical why: Why should we love our enemies? The first reason is fairly obvious. Returning hate for hate multiplies hate, adding deeper darkness to a night already devoid of stars. Darkness cannot drive out darkness; only light can do that. Hate cannot drive out hate; only love can do that. Hate multiplies hate, violence multiplies violence, and toughness multiplies toughness in a descending spiral of destruction. So when Jesus says "Love your enemies," he is setting forth a profound and ultimately inescapable admonition. Have we not come to such an impasse in the modern world that we must love our enemies—or else? The chain reaction of evil—hate begetting hate, wars producing more wars—must be broken, or we shall be plunged into the dark abyss of annihilation.

Another reason why we must love our enemies is that hate scars the soul and distorts the personality. Mindful that hate is an evil and dangerous force, we too often think of what it does to the person hated. This is understandable, for hate brings irreparable damage to its victims. We have seen its ugly consequences in the ignominious deaths brought to six million Jews by a hate-obsessed madman named Hitler, in the unspeakable violence inflicted upon Negroes by bloodthirsty mobs, in the dark horrors of war, and in the terrible indignities and injustices perpetrated against millions of God's children by unconscionable oppressors.

But there is another side which we must never overlook. Hate is just as injurious to the person who hates. Like an unchecked cancer, hate corrodes the personality and eats away its vital unity. Hate destroys a man's sense of values and his objectivity. It causes him to describe the beautiful as ugly and the ugly as beautiful, and to confuse the true with the false and the false with the true.

A third reason why we should love our enemies is that love is the only force capable of transforming an enemy into a friend. We never get rid of an enemy by meeting hate with hate; we get rid of an enemy by getting rid of enmity. By its very nature, hate destroys and tears down; by its very nature, love creates and builds up. Love transforms with redemptive power.

The relevance of what I have said to the crisis in race relations should be readily apparent. There will be no permanent solution to the race problem until oppressed men develop the capacity to love their enemies. The darkness of racial injustice will be dispelled only by the light of forgiving love. For more than three centuries American Negroes have been battered by the iron rod of oppression, frustrated by day and bewildered by night by unbearable injustice, and burdened with the ugly weight of discrimination. Forced to live with these shameful conditions, we are tempted to become bitter and to retaliate with a corresponding hate. But if this happens, the new order we seek will be little more than a duplicate of the old order. We must in strength and humility meet hate with love.

My friends, we have followed the so-called practical way for too long a time now, and it has led inexorably to deeper confusion and chaos. Time is cluttered with the wreckage of communities which surrendered to hatred and violence. For the salvation of our nation and the salvation of mankind, we must follow another way.

While abhorring segregation, we shall love the segregationist. This is the only way to create the beloved community.

To our most bitter opponents we say: "We shall match your capacity to inflict suffering by our capacity to endure suffering. We shall meet your physical force with soul force. Do to us what you will, and we shall continue to love you. We cannot in all good conscience obey your unjust laws, because noncooperation with evil is as much a moral obligation as is cooperation with good. Throw us in jail, and we shall still love you. Bomb our homes and threaten our children, and we shall still love you. Send your hooded perpetrators of violence into our community at the midnight hour and beat us and leave us half dead, and we shall still love you. But be ye assured that we will wear you down by our capacity to suffer. One day we shall win freedom, but not only for ourselves. We shall so appeal to your heart and conscience that we shall win you in the process, and our victory will be a double victory."

Pilgrimage to Nonviolence

by Martin Luther King, Jr.

Often the question has arisen concerning my own intellectual pilgrimage to nonviolence. In order to get at this question it is necessary to go back to my early teens in Atlanta. I had grown up abhorring not only segregation but also the oppressive and barbarous acts that grew out of it. I had passed spots where Negroes had been savagely lynched, and had watched the Ku Klux Klan on its rides at night. I had seen police brutality with my own eyes, and watched Negroes receive the most tragic injustice in the courts. All of these things had done something to my growing personality. I had come perilously close to resenting all white people.

I had also learned that the inseparable twin of racial injustice was economic injustice. Although I came from a home of economic security and relative comfort, I could never get out of my mind the economic insecurity of many of my playmates and the tragic poverty of those living around me. During my late teens I worked two summers, against my father's wishes—he never wanted my brother and me to work around white people because of the oppressive conditions—in a plant that hired both Negroes and whites. Here I saw economic injustice firsthand, and realized that the poor white was exploited just as much as the Negro. Through these early experiences I grew up deeply conscious of the varieties of injustice in our society.

So when I went to Atlanta's Morehouse College as a freshman in 1944 my concern for racial and economic justice was already substantial. During my student days at Morehouse I read Thoreau's *Essay on Civil Disobedience* for the first time. Fascinated by the idea of refusing to cooperate with an evil system, I was so deeply moved that I reread the work several times. This was my first intellectual contact with the theory of nonviolent resistance.

Not until I entered Crozer Theological Seminary in 1948, however, did I begin a serious intellectual quest for a method to eliminate social evil. Although my major interest was in the fields of theology and philosophy, I spent a great deal of time reading the works of the great social philosophers. I came early to Walter Rauschenbusch's *Christianity and the Social Crisis*, which left an indelible imprint on my thinking by giving me a theological basis for the social concern which had already grown up in me as a result of my early experi-ence. Of course there were points at which I differed with Rauschenbusch. I felt that he had fallen victim to the 19th-century "cult of inevitable progress" which led him to a superficial optimism concerning man's nature. Moreover, he came perilously close to identi-fying the Kingdom of God with a particular social and economic system—a tendency which should never befall the Church. But in spite of these shortcomings Rauschenbusch had done a great service for the Chris-tian Church by indicating that the gospel deals with the whole man, not only his soul but his body, not only his spiritual well-being but his material well-being. It has been my conviction ever since reading Rauschenbusch that any religion which professes to be concerned about the souls of men and is not concerned about the social and economic conditions that scar the soul is a spiritu-ally moribund religion only waiting for the day to be buried. It well has been said: "A religion that ends with the individual, ends."

After reading Rauschenbusch, I turned to a serious study of the social and ethical theories of the great philosophers, from Plato and Aristotle down to Rousseau, Hobbes, Bentham, Mill, and Locke. All of these masters stimulated my thinking—such as it was—and, while finding things to question in each of them, I nevertheless learned a great deal from their study.

During the Christmas holidays of 1949 I decided to spend my spare time reading Karl Marx to try to understand the appeal of communism for many people. For the first time I carefully scrutinized *Das Kapital* and *The Communist Manifesto*. I also read some interpretive works on the thinking of Marx and Lenin. In reading such Communist writings I drew certain conclusions that have remained with me as convictions to this day. First I rejected their materialistic interpretation of history. Communism, avowedly secularistic and mate-rialistic, has no place for God. This I could never accept, for as a Christian I believe that there is a creative personal power in this universe who is the ground and essence of all reality—a power that cannot be explained in materialistic terms. History is ulti-mately guided by spirit, not matter. Second, I strongly disagreed with communism's ethical relativism. Since for the Communist there is no divine government, no absolute moral order, there are no fixed, immutable principles; consequently almost anything—force, vio-lence, murder, lying—is a justifiable means to the "millennial" end. This type of relativism was abhorrent to me. Constructive ends can never give absolute moral justification to destructive means, because in the final analysis the end is pre-existent in the mean. Third, I opposed communism's political totalitarianism. In communism the individual ends up in subjection to the state. True, the Marxist would argue that the state is an "interim" reality which is to be eliminated when the classless society emerges; but the state is the end while it lasts, and man only a means to that end. And if any man's so-called rights or liberties stand in the way of that end, they are simply swept aside. His liberties of expression, his freedom to vote, his freedom to listen to what news he likes or to choose his books are all restricted. Man becomes hardly more, in communism, than a depersonalized cog in the turning wheel of the state.

This deprecation of individual freedom was objectionable to me. I am convinced now, as I was then, that man is an end because he is a child of God. Man is not made for the state; the state is made for man. To deprive man of freedom is to relegate him to the status of a thing, rather than elevate him to the status of a person. Man must never be treated as a means to the end of the state, but always as an end within himself.

Yet, in spite of the fact that my response to communism was and is negative, and I considered it basically evil, there were points at which I found it challenging. The late Archbishop of Canterbury, William Temple, referred to communism as a Christian heresy. By this he meant that communism had laid hold of certain truths which are essential parts of the Christian view of things, but that it had bound up with them concepts and practices which no Christian could ever accept or profess. Communism challenged the late Archbishop and it should challenge every Christian—as it challenged me—to a growing concern about social justice. With all of its false assumptions and evil methods, communism grew as a protest against the hardships of the underprivileged. Communism in theory emphasized a classless society, and a concern for social justice, though the world knows from sad experience that in practice it created new classes and a new lexicon of injustice. The Christian ought always to be challenged by any protest against unfair treatment of the poor, for Christianity is itself such a protest, nowhere expressed more eloquently than in Jesus' words: "The Spirit of the Lord is upon me, because he hath anointed me to preach the gospel to the poor, he hath sent me to heal the brokenhearted, to preach deliverance to the captives and recovering of sight to the blind, to set at liberty them that are bruised, to preach the acceptable year of the Lord."

I also sought systematic answers to Marx's critique of modern bourgeois culture. He presented capitalism as essentially a struggle between the owners of the productive resources and the workers, whom Marx regarded as the real producers. Marx interpreted economic forces as the dialectical process by which society moved from feudalism through capitalism to socialism, with the primary mechanism of this historical movement being the struggle between economic classes whose interests were irreconcilable. Obviously this theory left out of account the numerous and significant complexities—political, economic, moral, religious, and psychological—which played a vital role in shaping the constellation of institutions and ideas known today as Western civilization. Moreover, it was dated in the sense that the capitalism Marx wrote about bore only a partial resemblance to the capitalism we know in this country today.

But in spite of the shortcomings of his analysis, Marx had raised some basic questions. I was deeply concerned from ny early teen days about the gulf between superfluous wealth and abject poverty, and my reading of Marx made me ever more conscious of this gulf. Although modern American capitalism had greatly reduced the gap through social reforms, there was still need for a better distribution of wealth. Moreover, Marx had revealed the danger of the profit motive as the sole basis of an economic system: capitalism is always in danger of inspiring men to be more concerned about making a living than making a life. We are prone to judge success by the index of our salaries or the size of our automobiles, rather than by the quality of our service and relationship to humanity—thus capitalism can lead to a practical materialism that is as pernicious as the materialism taught by communism.

In short, I read Marx as I read all of the influential historical thinkers—from a dialectical point of view, combing a partial yes and a partial no. In so far as Marx posited a metaphysical materialism, an ethical relativism, and a strangulating totalitarianism, I responded with an unambiguous "no" but in so far as he pointed to weaknesses of traditional capitalism, contributed to the growth of a definite self-consciousness in the masses, and challenged the social conscience of the Christian churches, I responded with a definite "yes."

My reading of Marx also convinced me that truth is found neither in Marxism nor in traditional capitalism. Each represents a partial truth. Historically capitalism failed to see the truth in collective enterprise and Marxism failed to see the truth in individual enterprise. Nineteenth-century capitalism failed to see that life is social and Marxism failed and still fails to see that life is individual and personal. The Kingdom of God is neither the thesis of individual enterprise nor the antithesis of collective enterprise, but a synthesis which reconciles the truths of both.

During my stay at Crozer, I was also exposed for the first time to the pacifist position in a lecture by Dr. A. J. Muste. I was deeply moved by Dr. Muste's talk, but far from convinced of the practicability of his position. Like most of the students of Crozer, I felt that while war could never be a positive or absolute good, it could serve as a negative good in the sense of preventing the spread and growth of an evil force. War, horrible as it is, might be preferable to surrender to a totalitarian system—Nazi, Fascist, or Communist.

During this period I had about despaired of the power of love in solving social problems. Perhaps my faith in love was temporarily shaken by the philosophy of Nietzsche. I had been reading parts of *The Genealogy of Morals* and the whole of *The Will to Power*. Nietzsche's glorification of power-in his theory—all life expressed the will to power—was an outgrowth of his contempt for ordinary morals. He attacked the whole of the Hebraic-Christian morality—with its virtues of piety and humility, its otherworldliness, and its attitude toward suffering—as the glorification of weakness, as making virtues out of necessity and impotence. He looked to the development of a superman who would surpass man as man surpassed the ape.

Then one Sunday afternoon I traveled to Philadelphia to hear a sermon by Dr. Mordecai Johnson, president of Howard University. He was there to preach for the Fellowship House of Philadelphia. Dr. Johnson had just returned from a trip to India, and, to my great interest, he spoke of the life and teachings of Mahatma Gandhi. His message was so profound and electrifying that I left the meeting and bought a half-dozen books on Gandhi's life and works.

Like most people, I had heard of Gandhi, but I had never studied him seriously. As I read I became deeply fascinated by his campaigns of nonviolent resistance. I was particularly moved by the Salt March to the Sea and his numerous fasts. The whole concept of "Satyagraha" (Satya is truth which equals love, and agraha is force; "Satyagraha," therefore, means truth-force or love-force) was profoundly significant to me. As I delved deeper into the philosophy of Gandhi my skepticism concerning the power of love gradually diminished, and I came to see for the first time its potency in the area of social reform. Prior to reading Gandhi, I had about concluded that the ethics of Jesus were only effective in individual relationship. The "turn the other cheek" philosophy and the "love your enemies" philosophy were only valid, I felt, when individuals were in conflict with other individuals; when racial groups and nations were in conflict a more realistic approach seemed necessary. But after reading Gandhi, I saw how utterly mistaken I was.

Gandhi was probably the first person in history to lift the love ethic of Jesus above mere interaction between individuals to a powerful and effective social force on a large scale. Love for Gandhi was a potent instrument for social and collective transformation. It was in this Gandhian emphasis on love and nonviolence that I discovered the method for social reform that I had been seeking for so many months. The intellectual and moral satisfaction that I failed to gain from the utilitarianism of Bentham and Mill, the revolutionary methods of Marx and Lenin, the social-contracts theory of Hobbes, the "back to nature" optimism of Rousseau, and the superman philosophy of Nietzsche, I found in the nonviolent resistance philosophy of Gandhi. I came to feel that this was the only morally and practically sound method open to oppressed people in their struggle for freedom.

But my intellectual odyssey to nonviolence did not end here. During my last year in theological school, I began to read the works of Reinhold Niebuhr. The prophetic and realistic elements on Niebuhr's passionate style and profound thought were appealing to me, and I became so enamored of his social ethics that I almost fell into the trap of accepting uncritically everything he wrote.

About this time I read Niebuhr's critique of the pacifist position. Niebuhr had himself once been a member of the pacifist ranks. For several years, he had been national chairman of the Fellowship of Reconciliation. His break with pacifism came in the early thirties, and the first full statement of his criticism of pacifism was in *Moral Men* and *Immoral Society*. Here he argued that there was no intrinsic moral difference between violent and nonviolent resistance. The social consequences of the two methods were different, he contended, but the differences were in degree rather than kind. Later Niebuhr began emphasizing the irresponsibility of relying on nonviolent resistance when there was no ground for believing that it would be successful in preventing the spread of totalitarian tyranny. It could only be successful, he argued, if the groups against whom the resistance was taking place had some degree of moral conscience, as was the case in Gandhi's struggle against the British. Niebuhr's ultimate rejection of pacifism failed to do justice to the reformation doctrine of justification by faith, substituting for it a sectarian perfectionism which believes "that divine grace actually lifts men out of the sinful contradictions of history and establishes him above the sins of the world."

At first, Niebuhr's critique of pacifism left me in a state of confusion. As I continued to read, however, I cane to see more and more the shortcomings of his position. For instance, many of his statements revealed that he interpreted pacifism as a sort of passive nonresistance to evil expressing naive trust in the power of love. But this was a serious distortion. My study of Gandhi convinced me that true pacifism is not nonresistance to evil, but nonviolent resistance to evil. Between the two positions, there is a world of difference. Gandhi resisted evil with as much vigor and power as the violent resister, but he resisted with love instead of hate. True pacifism is not unrealistic submission to evil power, as Niebuhr contends. It is rather a courageous confrontation of evil by the power of love, in the faith that it is better to be the recipient of violence than the inflicter of it, since the latter only multiplies the existence of violence and bitterness in the universe.

The next stage of my intellectual pilgrimage to nonviolence came during my doctoral studies at Boston University. Here I had the opportunity to talk to many exponents of nonviolence, both students and visitors to the campus. Boston University School of Theology, under the influence of Dean Walter Muelder and Professor Allen Knight Chalmers, had a deep sympathy for pacifism. Both Dean Muelder and Dr. Chalmers had a passion for social justice that stemmed, not from a superficial optimism, but from a deep faith in the possibilities of human beings when they allowed themselves to become coworkers with God. It was at Boston University that I came to see that Niebuhr had overemphasized the corruption of human nature. His pessimism concerning human nature was not balanced by an optimism concerning divine nature. He was so involved in diagnosing man's sickness of sin that he overlooked the cure of grace.

I studied philosophy and theology at Boston University under Edgar S. Brightman and L. Harold DeWolf. Both men greatly stimulated my thinking. It was mainly under these teachers that I studied personalistic philosophy—the theory that the clue to the meaning of ultimate reality is found in personality. This personal idealism remains today my basic philosophical position. Personalism's insistence that only personality—finite and infinite—is ultimately real strengthened me in two convictions: it gave me metaphysical and philosophical grounding for the idea of a personal God, and it gave me a metaphysical basis for the dignity and worth of all human personality.

Just before Dr. Brightman's death, I began studying the philosophy of Hegel with him. Although the course was mainly a study of Hegel's monumental work, *Phenomenology of Mind*, I spent my spare time reading his *Philosophy of History* and *Philosophy of Right*. There were points in Hegel's philosophy that I strongly disagreed with. For instance, his absolute idealism was rationally unsound to me because it tended to swallow up the many in the one. But there were other aspects of his thinking that I found stimulating. His contention that "truth is the whole" led me to a philosophical method of rational coherence. His analysis of the dialectical process, in spite of its shortcomings, helped me to see that growth comes through struggle.

In 1954 I ended my formal training with all of these relatively divergent intellectual forces converging into a positive social philosophy. One of the main tenets of this philosophy was the conviction that nonviolent resistance was one of the most potent weapons available to oppressed people in their quest for social justice. At this time, however, I had merely an intellectual understanding and appreciation of the position, with no form determination to organize it in a socially effective situation.

When I went to Montgomery as a pastor, I had not the slightest idea that I would later become involved in a crisis in which nonviolent resistance would be applicable. I neither started the protest nor suggested it. I simply responded to the call of the people for a spokesman. When the protest began, my mind, consciously or unconsciously, was driven back to the Sermon on the Mount, with its sublime teachings on love, and the Gandhian method of nonviolent resistance. As the days unfolded, I came to see the power of nonviolence more and more. Living through the actual experience of the protest, nonviolence became more than a method to which I gave intellectual assent; it became a commitment to a way of life. Many of the things that I had not cleared up intellectually concerning nonviolence were now solved in the sphere of practical action.

Since the philosophy of nonviolence played such a positive role in the Montgomery movement, it may be wise to turn to a brief discussion of some basic aspects of this philosophy.

First, it must be emphasized that nonviolent resistance is not a method for cowards; it does resist. If one used this method because he is afraid of merely because he lacks the instruments of nonviolence, he is not truly nonviolent. This is why Gandhi often said the if cowardice is the only alternative to violence, it is better to fight. He made this statement conscious of the fact that there is always another alternative: no individual or group need submit to any wrong, nor need they use violence to right the wrong; there is the way of nonviolence resistance. This is ultimately the way of the strong man. It is not a method of stagnant passivity. The phrase "passive resistance" often gives the false impression that this is a sort of "do-nothing method" in which the resister quietly and passively accepts evil. But nothing is further from the truth. For while the nonviolent resister is passive in the sense that he is not physically aggressive toward his opponent, his mind and emotions are always active, constantly seeking to persuade his opponent that he is wrong. The method is passive physically, but strongly active spiritually. It is not passive nonresistance to evil, it is active nonviolent resistance to evil.

A second basic fact that characterizes nonviolence is that it does not seek to defeat or humiliate the opponent, but to win his friendship and understanding. The nonviolent resister must often express his protest through noncooperation or boycotts, but he realizes that these are not ends themselves; they are merely means to awaken a sense of moral shame in the opponent. The end is redemption and reconciliation. The aftermath of nonviolence is the creation of the beloved community, while the aftermath of violence is tragic bitterness.

A third characteristic of this method is that the attack is directed against forces of evil rather than against persons who happen to be doing the evil. It is evil that the nonviolent resister seeks to defeat, not the persons victimized by evil. If he is opposing racial injustice, the nonviolent resister has the vision to see that the basic tension is not between races. As I like to say to the people in Montgomery: "The tension in this city is not between white people and Negro people. The tension is, at bottom, between justice and injustice, between the forces of light and the forces of darkness. And if there is a victory, it will be a victory not merely for 50,000 Negroes, but a victory for justice and the forces of light. We are out to defeat injustice and not white persons who may be unjust."

A fourth point that characterizes nonviolent resistance is a willingness to accept suffering without retaliation, to accept blows from the opponent without striking back. "Rivers of blood may have to flow before we gain our freedom, but it must be our blood," Gandhi said to his countrymen. The nonviolent resister is willing to accept violence if necessary, but never to inflict it. He does not seek to dodge jail. If going to jail is necessary, he enters it "as a bridegroom enters the bride's chamber."

One may well ask: "What is the nonviolent resister's justification for this ordeal to which he invites men, for this mass political application of the ancient doctrine of turning the other cheek?" The answer is found in the realization that unearned suffering is redemptive. Suffering, the nonviolent resister realizes, has tremendous educational and transforming possibilities. "Things of fundamental importance to people are not secured by reason alone, but have to be purchased with their suffering," said Gandhi. He continued: "Suffering is infinitely more powerful than the law of the jungle for converting the opponent and opening his ears which are otherwise shut to the voice of reason."

A fifth point concerning nonviolent resistance is that it avoids not only external physical violence but also internal violence of spirit. The nonviolent resister not only refuses to shoot his opponent but he also refuses to hate him. At the center of nonviolence stands the principle of love. The nonviolent resister would contend that in the struggle for human dignity, the oppressed people of the world must not succumb to the temptation of becoming better or indulging in hate campaigns. To retaliate in kind would do nothing but intensify the existence of hate in the universe. Along the way of life, someone must have sense enough and morality enough to cut off the chain of hate. This can only be done by projecting the ethic of love to the center of our lives.

In speaking of love at this point, we are not referring to some sentimental or affectionate emotion. It would be nonsense to urge men to love their oppressors in an affectionate sense. Love in this connection means understanding, redemptive good will. Here the Greek language comes to our aid. There are three words for love in the Greek New Testament. First, there is *eros*. In Platonic philosophy *eros* meant the yearning of the soul for the realm of the divine. It has come now to mean a sort of aesthetic or romantic love. Second, there is *philia* which means intimate affection between personal friends. *Philia* denotes a sort of reciprocal love; the person loves because he is loved. When we speak of loving those who oppose us, we refer to neither *eros* nor *philia*; we speak of a love which is expressed in the Greek word *agape*. *Agape* means understanding, redeeming good will for all men. It is an overflowing love which is purely spontaneous, unmotivated, groundless, and creative. It is not set in motion by any quality or function of its object. It is the love of God operating in the human heart.

Agape is disinterested love. It is a love in which the individual seeks not his own good, but the good of his neighbor (I Cor. 10:24). Agape does not begin by discriminating between worthy and unworthy people, or any qualities people possess. It begins by loving others for their sakes. It is an entirely "neighbor-regarding concern for others," which discovers the neighbor in every man it meets. Therefore, agape makes no distinction between friend and enemy; it is directed toward both. If one loves an individual merely on account of his friendliness, he loves him for the sake of the benefits to be gained from the friendship, rather than for the friend's own sake. Consequently, the best way to assure oneself that love is disinterested is to have love for the enemy-neighbor from whom you can expect no good in return, but only hostility and persecution.

Another basic point about agape is that it springs from the need of the other person—his need for belonging to the best in the human family. The Samaritan who helped the Jew in the Jericho Road was "good" because he responded to the human need that he was presented with. God's love is eternal and fails not because man needs his love. St. Paul assures us that the loving act of redemption was done "while we were yet sinners"—that is, at the point of our greatest need for love. Since the white man's personality is greatly distorted by segregation, and his soul is greatly scarred, he needs the love of the Negro. The Negro must love the white man, because the white man needs his love to remove his tensions, insecurities, and fears. Agape is not a weak, passive love. It is love in action. Agape is love seeking to preserve and create community. It is insistence on community even when one seeks to break it. Agape is a willingness to sacrifice in the interest of mutuality. Agape is a willingness to go to any length to restore com-munity. It doesn't stop at the first mile, but it goes the second mile to restore community. It is a willingness to forgive, not seven times, but seventy times seven to restore community. The cross is the eternal expression of the length to which God will go in order to restore broken community. The resurrection is a symbol of God's triumph over all the forces that seed to block community. The Holy Spirit is the continuing community creating reality that moves through history. He who works against community is working against the whole of creation. Therefore, if I respond to hate with a reciprocal hate I do nothing but intensify the cleavage in broken community. I can only close the gap in broken community by meeting hate with love. If I meet hate with hate, I become depersonalized, because creation is so designed that my personality can only be fulfilled in the context of community. Booker T. Washington was right: "Let no man pull you so low as to make you hate him." When he pulls you that low he brings you to the point of working against community; he drags you to the point of defying creation, and thereby becoming depersonalized.

In the final analysis, agape means a recognition of the fact that all life is interrelated. All humanity is involved in a single process, and all men are brothers. To the degree that I harm my brother, no matter what he is doing to me, to that extent I am harming myself. For example, white men often refuse federal aid to education in order to avoid giving the Negro his rights; but because all men are brothers they cannot deny Negro children without harming their own. They end, all efforts to the contrary, by hurting themselves. Why is this? Because men are brothers. If you harm me, you harm yourself.

Love, agape, is the only cement that can hold this broken community together. When I am commanded to love, I am commanded to restore community, to resist injustice, and to meet the needs of my brothers.

A sixth basic fact about nonviolent resistance is that it is based on the conviction that the universe is on the side of justice. Consequently, the believer in nonviolence had deep faith in the future. This faith is another reason why the nonviolent resister can accept suffering without retaliation. For he knows that in his struggle for justice he has cosmic companionship. It is true that there are devout believers in nonviolence who find it difficult to believe in a personal God. But even these persons believe in the existence of some creative force that works for universal wholeness. Whether we call it an unconscious process, an impersonal Brahman, or a Personal Being of matchless power and infinite love, there is a creative force in this universe that works to bring the disconnected aspects of reality into a harmonious whole.

King and Pacifism: The Other Dimension

by Colman McCarthy

Why the uproar over the remarks of Jesse Helms on Martin Luther King, Jr.? The North Carolina senator, in raising questions about King's character and his links with Communists, was temperate compared with what we have heard before. J. Edgar Hoover said that King was "the most notorious liar in the country." In 1965, Sheriff Jim Clark, the keeper at the time of Alabama's attack dogs and water hoses, said that "an agitator" like King "is the lowest form of humanity."

During the Senate debate on whether to honor King with a national holiday, Helms, in his twisted way, actually helped the cause. His speeches assured publicity. Without the oversized mouth of Helms, the issue might have passed unnoticed.

King's reputation was damaged more by the supporters of the holiday legislation than by its opponents. He was praised as only a civil rights leader. Sen. Edward Kennedy said that "King worked tirelessly to remove the stain of discrimination from our nation."

King was much, much more than that. At the core of both his thinking and of his commitment as a Christian clergyman was pacifism, as practiced through the techniques of organized nonviolent confrontation. His constituency was not limited to blacks. Liberals like Kennedy do a disservice to King. In limiting their praise of him to civil rights they sanitize the record.

It was King the pacifist who said in April 1967 that "the greatest purveyor of violence in the world today [is] my own government." That statement was not quoted on the Senate floor. Nor was his statement that we are "a society gone mad with war.... If Americas's soul becomes totally poisoned, part of the autopsy must read 'Vietnam.' It can never be saved so long as it destroys the deepest hopes of men the world over."

At some moment, the city of Washington will need a statue of King to go along with his national holiday. Several of King's thoughts are suitable to be chiseled into stone, with a number of sites around town being appropriate for the statue.

In front of the Pentagon, why not a bronzed King saluting the flag with these words underneath: "War is not the answer. Communism will never be defeated by the use of atomic bombs or nuclear weapons."

Or perhaps the King statue should be placed between the Treasury and the Department of Commerce, with this thought: "Capitalism may lead to a practical materialism that is as pernicious as the theoretical materialism taught by communism."

Maybe Congress will want the King presence on the lawn before the Capitol. If so, King's quote— uttered in early 1968 when the House and Senate were cutting social programs and increasing military spending—is fit: "The Congress is sick."

For a fourth possible site, there is the new memorial for the 59,000 Americans who died in Vietnam. Put in stone King's memorable words about the troops being sent to Southeast Asia: "Before long they must know that their government has sent them into a struggle among Vietnamese, and the more sophisticated surely realize that we are on the side of the wealthy and the secure while we create a hell for the poor.

"These aren't the soothing nosegays found in quotation books under "Patriotism" where the comments of George Washington, our only other leader to be honored with a national holiday, can be found be schoolchildren. By categorizing King as only a civil rights leader, the Senate of 1983 has pulled off what King himself would not allow his detractors to get away with in the 1960s. After his tactics of nonviolence led to the passage of the 1961 civil rights law, voices of respectability told King to stick to race and leave antiwar dissent to others.

It was the new way of telling blacks to stay in their place. King replied that racism and militarism are diseases spread by the same germ: the contempt of the powerful for the weak. With the world armed with nukes, he said, "It will be worthless to talk about integration if there is no world to integrate."

If the Senate liberals avoided the real King, Ronald Reagan will certainly do so when he signs the bill for the holiday. That leaves it up to the followers of King. To accept him as anything less than a revolutionary pacifist will mean that we are getting just another irrelevant plastic hem.

from Washington Post, October 30, 1983

Far more violence to human beings in history has been done in obeying the law than in breaking the law.

Howard Zinn

On the Duty of Civil Disobedience

by Henry David Thoreau

I heartily accept the motto— "That government is best which governs least"; and I should like to see it acted up to more rapidly and systematically. Carried out, it finally amounts to this, which also I believe— "That government is best which governs not at all"; and when men are prepared for it, that will be the kind of government which they will have. Government is at best but an expedient; but most governments are usually, and all governments are sometimes, inexpedient. The objections which have been brought against a standing army, and they are many and weighty, and deserve to prevail, may also at last be brought against a standing government. The standing army is only an arm of the standing government. The government itself, which is only the mode which the people have chosen to execute their will, is equally liable to be abused and perverted before the people can act through it. Witness the present Mexican war, the work of comparatively a few individuals using the standing government as their tool; for, in the outset, the people would not have consented to this measure.

Unjust laws exist; shall we be content to obey them or shall we endeavor to amend them, and obey them until we have succeeded, or shall we transgress them at once? Men generally, under such a government as this, think that they ought to wait until they have persuaded the majority to alter them. They think that, if they should resist, the remedy would be worse than the evil. But it is the fault of the government itself that the remedy is worse than the evil. It makes it worse. Why is it not more apt to anticipate and provide for reform? Why does it not cherish its wise minority? Why does it cry and resist before it is hurt? Why does it not encourage its citizens to be on the alert to point out its faults, and do better than it would have them? Why does it always crucify Christ, and excommunicate Copernicus and Luther, and pronounce Washington and Franklin rebels?

If the injustice is part of the necessary friction of the machine of government, let it go, let it go: perchance it will wear smooth—certainly the machine will wear out. If the injustice has a spring, or a pulley, or a rope, or a crank, exclusively for itself, then perhaps you may consider whether the remedy will not be worse than the evil, but if it is of such a nature that it requires you to be the agent of injustice to another, then, I say, break the law. Let your life be a counter-friction to stop the machine. What I have to do is to see, at any rate, that I do not lend myself to the wrong which I condemn.

As for adopting the ways which the State has provided for remedying the evil, I know not of such ways. They take too much time, and a man's life will be gone. I have other affairs to attend to. I came into this world, not chiefly to make this a good place to live in, but to live in it, be it good or bad. A man has not everything to do, but something; and because he cannot do everything, it is not necessary that he should do something wrong. It is not my business to be petitioning the Governor or the Legislature any more than it is theirs to petition me; and, if they should not hear my petition, what should I do then? But in this case the State has provided no way: its very Constitution is the evil. This may seem to be harsh and stubborn and unconciliatory; but it is to treat with the utmost kindness and consideration the only spirit that can appreciate or deserves it. So is all change for the better, like birth and death, which convulses the body.

I do not hesitate to say that those who call themselves Abolitionists should at once effectually withdraw their support, both in person and property, from the government of Massachusetts, and not wait till they constitute a majority of one, before they suffer the right to prevail through them. I think that it is enough if they have God on their side, without waiting for that other one. Moreover, any man more right than his neighbors constitutes a majority of one already.

I meet this American government, or its representative, the State government, directly, and face to face, once a year—no more—in the person of its tax-gatherer; this is the only mode in which a man situated as I am necessarily meets it; and it then says distinctly, Recognize me; and the simplest, the most effectual, and, in the present posture of affaire, the indispensablest mode of treating with it on this head, of expressing your little satisfaction with and love for it, is to deny it then. My civil neighbor, the tax-gatherer, is the very man I have to deal with—for it is, after all, with men and not with parchment that I quarrel—and he has voluntarily chosen to be an agent of the government. How shall he ever know well what he is and does as an officer of the government, or as a man, until he is obliged to consider whether he shall treat me, his neighbor, for whom he has respect, as a neighbor and well-disposed man, or as a maniac and disturber of the peace, and see if he can get over this obstruction to his neighborliness without a ruder and more impetuous thought or speech corresponding with his action. I know this well, that if 1,000, if 100, if 10 men whom I could name—if 10 honest men only—aye, if one honest man, in this State of Massachusetts, ceasing to hold slaves, were actually to withdraw from this copartnership, and be locked up in the county jail therefor, it would be the abolition of slavery in America. For it matters not how small the beginning may seem to be: what is once well done is done forever. But we love better to talk about it: that we say is our mission. Reform keeps many scores of newspapers in its service, but not one man. If my esteemed neighbor, the State's ambassador, who will devote his days to the settlement of the question of human rights in the Council Chamber, instead of being threatened with the prisons of Carolina, were to sit down the prisoner of Massachusetts, that State which is so anxious to foist the sin of slavery upon her sister—though at present she can discover only an act of inhospitality to be the ground of a quarrel with her—the Legislature would not wholly waive the subject the following winter.

Under a government which imprisons any unjustly, the true place for a just man is also a prison. The proper place today, the only place which Massachusetts has provided for her freer and less desponding spirits, is in her prisons, to be put out and locked out of the State by her own act, as they have already put themselves out by their principles. It is there that the fugitive slave, and the Mexican prisoner on parole, and the Indian come to plead the wrongs of his race, should find them; on that separate, but more free and honorable ground, where the State places those who are not with her, but against her—the only house in a slave State in which a free man can abide with honor. If any think that their influence would be lost there and their voices no longer afflict the ear of the State, that they would not be as an enemy within its walls, they do not know by how much truth is stronger than error, nor how much more eloquently and effectively he can combat injustice who has experienced a little in his own person. Cast your whole vote, not a strip of paper merely, but your whole influence. A minority is powerless while it conforms to the majority; it is not even a minority then; but it is irresistible when it clogs by its whole weight. If the alternative is to keep all just men in prison, or give up war and slavery, the State will not hesitate which to choose. If a thousand men were not to pay their tax bills this year, that would not be a violent and bloody measure, as it would be to pay them and enable the State to commit violence and shed innocent blood. This is, in fact, the definition of a peaceable revolution, if any such is possible. If the tax-gatherer, or any other public officer, asks me, as one has done, "But what shall I do?" my answer is, "If you really wish to do anything, resign your office." When the subject has refused allegiance, and the officer has resigned his office, then the revolution is accomplished. But even suppose blood should flow. Is there not a sort of blood shed when the conscience is wounded? Through this wound a man's real manhood and immortality flow out, and he bleeds to an everlasting death. I see this blood flowing now.

The only obligation which I have a right to assume, is to do at any time what I think right. It is truly enough said, that a corporation has no conscience; but a corporation of conscientious men is a corporation with a conscience. Law never made men a whit more just; and, by means of their respect for it, even the well-disposed are daily made the agents of injustice. A common and natural result of an undue respect for law is that you may see a file of soldiers, colonel, captain, corporal, privates, power-monkeys, and all, marching in admirable order over hill and dale to the wars, against their wills, aye, against their common sense and consciences, which makes it very steep marching indeed, and produces a palpitation of the heart. They have no doubt that it is a damnable business in which they are concerned; they are all peaceably inclined. Now, what are they? Men at all? of small movable forts and magazines, at the service of some unscrupulous man in power? Visit the Navy Yard, and behold a marine, such a man as an American government can make, or such as it can make a man with its black arts—a mere shadow and reminiscence of humanity, a man laid out alive and standing, and already, as one may say buried under arms with funeral accompaniments, though it may be—

"Not a drum was heard, not a funeral note,
    As his corse to the rampart we hurried;
Not a soldier discharged his farewell shot
    O'er the grave where our hero we buried."

The mass of men serve the state thus, not as men mainly, but as machines, with their bodies. They are the standing army, and the militia, jailers, constables, posse comitatus, etc. In most cases there is no free exercise whatever of the judgment or of the moral sense; but they put themselves on a level with wood and earth and stones; and wooden men can perhaps be manufactured that will serve the purpose as well. Such command no more respect than men of straw or a lump of dirt. They have the same sort of worth only as horses and dogs. Yet such as these even are commonly esteemed good citizens. Others—as most legislators, politicians, lawyers, ministers, and officeholders—serve the state chiefly with their heads; and, as they rarely make any moral distinctions, they are as likely to serve the Devil.

War Tax Resistance: One Story

by Andrea Ayvazian

The single most significant statement I have heard about war tax resistance was made confidently and in simplicity by Alan Eccleston at a 1981 workshop: "When you are ready to engage in war tax resistance you *know* it." I was slightly skeptical at the time because someone had given me the same advice about marriage and it had not proven correct.

But now, five years into the process of war tax resistance, I believe Alan was absolutely right. When you are ready to become a war tax resister, you know it deep inside with little doubt or fear. I knew it–almost suddenly–on a visceral level in 1982 and, since that time, nothing that has unfolded due to my resistance has been too great a burden to carry; nothing has been too frightening or overwhelming. Once I was ready, I was ready–and I have welcomed all of it.

War tax resistance for me has involved always owing the government money in April–several hundreds of dollars in fact. As April 15th draws close, I meticulously complete my 1040 form, calculate exactly what I owe and mail my form in on time with a detailed letter explaining why my 1040 does not have an accompanying check. Everyone who is engaged in any aspect of tax resistance does it in her or his own way–there is no one way, and certainly no correct or incorrect way. Withholding money every April has worked for me, and my story has its difficult, funny and touching moments, as any tax resister can confirm.

The first year I engaged in war tax resistance, I happened to owe almost $1,000. I withheld the entire amount, sent it to an escrow fund, wrote an impassioned letter about war, peace, social injustice, Quakerism, feminism, nonviolence, and everything else I could fit on two typed pages, and settled back to see what would unfold.

Alan had told me that it could take the IRS two weeks to catch up with me, or two years, or nothing might ever happen. I returned from work one day in May to find a discreet little card stuck in my apartment door, saying that an IRS agent had been to visit and he would be back. Actually, I was delighted. I thought: "Why wait for him to return and find me gone again? I'll just call him on the phone and find out what's cooking." So I did, and that began what has been a long, tumultuous, fairly intense relationship with Bob, "my" IRS agent.

Bob came to my apartment the next week and I explained with great emotion why I could not pay for the weapons of war, how I dreamed of and worked for a world of peace and equity. I carried on at great length, with Bob nodding and actually looking sympathetic. At the end of my monologue he asked if I was interested in hearing about their easy payment plan.

Bob and I do not see eye-to-eye. After several threatening letters, another visit, and an audit in Springfield, Bob visited my bank and withdrew the $1,000 I had withheld, plus, 5% penalty and 15% interest (this is now reduced to 9%). The bank wrote me a cursory note informing me that my account was reduced by almost $1,500.

The years since 1982 have been full of tax resistance adventures, and I have had the opportunity to see a good deal of Bob. The pattern each year has been generally the same. After I write my letter explaining why I am withholding part of my federal income tax, I receive a series of computer letters. The first is fairly benign–informing me that I owe the IRS some money (as if my withholding were simply an oversight on my part). The letters escalate with increasingly threatening language until the "ten-day notice" arrives saying that decisive action is about to be taken. About six weeks after that letter arrives, they actually do something. Every year Bob has called, and, most years, he has visited. He has tried to talk me into simply paying the IRS what he says I owe so that he can "close my file." Every year, money has been taken from my bank account–the amount withheld, plus interest and penalty.

In 1984, when Bob went to my account, I did not have enough money there to cover what he said I owed. He emptied and closed my account and called me to review my next options. We actually decided to meet over breakfast (he paid the bill) and, told me directly, the next step was to put a lien on my paychecks so that the IRS would begin receiving a large portion of each check until my "debt" to them was covered. This made me feel very insecure–I live paycheck to paycheck–so I asked him instead to take my car.

Following that meeting, I called for a Clearness Committee with some Friends from Mt. Toby Meeting. With their help, I decided to sell my car immediately to a friend who needed a reliable vehicle, give her a good bargain, put the money in the bank and let Bob take it. He called wondering what happened to my car. I told him I had sold it, so he went directly to the bank for the money.

Probably the most touching moment came in 1985 after my account had been ravished or closed so many times that I finally went to see the president of my bank. At eight o'clock one morning, the president met me at a side door and led me through the dark, deserted bank to his office. I sat across from him and told him why I was a war tax resister. I told him I was not there to convince him of anything, to defend myself or to make a case; I simply had a story that I found I needed to tell him. During the 45 minutes that we spent together, his whole body language changed. His posture eased, his voice softened, he leaned forward and asked me probing questions–and he let me tell my whole story.

Before leaving, I said: "I want to ask your forgiveness for being compelled to engage in a protest that is a nuisance for you and your staff." He stood up, shook my hand and said: "And I want to ask your forgiveness for my being compelled to comply."

People have asked me why I let the IRS seize money from my account. In my mind, I am never willingly paying the military portion of my federal income tax due in April–the IRS must come find me and take the money from me. I have chosen to live my life as I wish, with *them* responding and reacting to *my* behavior, not the other way around. I do not move my money around or close my account when I know they are coming because I do not wish to be further consumed by this process. Also, I know that, if they do not find the money in the bank, they will come after my paycheck or what little property I own, and I have always found those options more frightening. I believe that the IRS spends all the money it gains from the interest and penalties simply to track down and seize assets from resisters like me. The benefit to them is negligible.

Every war tax resister has her or his tales to tell; mine is not unusual or heroic. Like others, I keep on with this noncooperation because I believe it is a powerful teaching tool, because I think it makes my other work for peace and justice more credible, because it gives me a forum to talk to bank presidents and IRS auditors, because it helps make congruent my beliefs and actions, and mainly because I could no longer force myself to write that check in April believing it would buy bullets, tanks and nuclear warheads.

I believe that by each of us taking the small steps that we individually can, we will quietly, but most effectively, transform the world.

The Judge & the Bomb

by Judge Miles Lord

The following is a statement by U.S. District Judge Miles Lord at his sentencing of two persons convicted of destroying war-related computer equipment at a Sperry plant in Minnesota.

It is the allegation of these young people that they committed the acts here complained of as a desperate plea to the American people and its government to stop the military madness which they sincerely believe will destroy us all, friend and enemy alike.

As I ponder over the punishment to be meted out to these two people who were attempting to unbuild weapons of mass destruction, we must ask ourselves: Can it be that those of us who build weapons to kill are engaged in a more sanctified endeavor than to see who would by their acts attempt to counsel moderation and mediation as an alternative method of settling international disputes? Why are we so fascinated by a power so great that we cannot comprehend its magnitude? What is so sacred about a bomb, so romantic about a missile? Why do we condemn and hang individual killers while extolling the virtues of warmongers? What is that fatal fascination which attracts us to the thought of mass destruction of our brethren in another country? How can we even entertain the thought that all people on one side of an imaginary line must die and, if we be so ungodly cynical as to countenance that thought, have we given thought to the fact that in executing that decree we will also die? Who draws these lines and who has so decreed?

How many people in this democracy have seriously contemplated the futility of committing national suicide in order to punish our adversaries? Have we so little faith in our system of free enterprise, our capitalism, and the fundamental concepts that are taught us in our constitutions and in our several bibles that we must, in order to protect ourselves from the spread of foreign ideologies, be prepared to die at our own hands? Such thinking indicates a great deal of lack of faith in our democracy, our body politic, our people, and our institutions.

There are those in high places that believe Armageddon is soon to be upon us, that Christ will soon come to earth and take us all back with him to heaven. It would appear that much of our national effort is being is devoted to helping with the process. It may even be a celebration of sorts. When the bombs go off, Christ won't have to come to earth—we will all, believers and nonbelievers alike, meet him halfway.

The anomaly of this situation is that I am here called upon to punish two individuals who were charged with having caused damage to the property of a corporation in the amount of $33,000. It is this self-same corporation which only a few months ago was before me accused of having wrongfully embezzled from the U.S. government the sum of $3.6 million. The employees of this company succeeded in boosting the corporate profits by wrongfully and feloniously juggling the books. Since these individuals were all employees of the corporation, it appears that it did not occur to anyone in the office of the Attorney General of the United States that the actions of these men constituted a criminal conspiracy for which they might be punished. The government demanded only that Sperry pay back a mere 10 percent of the amount by which the corporation had been unlawfully enriched. Could it be that these corporate men who were working to build weapons of mass destruction received special treatment because of the nature of their work?

I am now called upon to determine the amount of restitution that is to be required of the two individuals who have done damage to the property of Sperry. The financial information obtained by the probation officers indicates that neither of the defendants owes any money to anyone. While Ms. Katt has no assets, Mr. LaForge is comparatively well endowed. He owns a 1968 Volkswagen, a guitar, a sleeping bag, and $200 in cash.

The inexorable pressure which generates from those who are engaged in making a living and a profit from building military equipment and the pork barreling that goes on in the halls of Congress to obtain more such contracts for the individual state will in the ultimate consume itself in an atomic holocaust. These same factors exert a powerful pressure upon a judge in my position to go along with the theory that there is something sacred about a bomb and that those who raise their voices or their hands against it should be struck down as enemies of the people, no matter that in their hearts they feel and know that they are friends of the people.

Now conduct of this sort cannot be condoned under the guise of free speech. Neither should it be totally condemned as being subversive, traitorous, or treasonous in the category of espionage or some other bad things. I would here in this instance take the sting out of the bomb, attempt in some way to force the government to remove the halo with which it seems to embrace any device which can kill, and to place instead thereon a shroud, the shroud of death, destruction, mutilation, disease, and debilitation.

If there is an adverse reaction to this sentence, I will anxiously await the protestations of those who complain of my attempts to correct the imbalance that now exists in a system that operates in such a manner as to provide one type of justice for the rich and a lesser type for the poor. One standard for the mighty and another for the weak. And a system which finds its humanness and objectivity is sublimated to military madness and the worship of the bomb.

A judge sitting here as I do is not called upon to do that which is politically expedient or popular but is called upon to exercise his calm and deliberate judgment in a manner best suited to accomplish and accommodate and vindicate the rights of the people acting through its government and the rights of those people who are the subject matter of such actions. The most popular thing to do at this particular time would be to sentence them to a 10 year period of imprisonment, and some judges might be disposed to do just that. [Thereupon, sentence was imposed: Six months in prison, was suspended, six months on probation.]

I am also aware of the thrust of the argument which would say this would encourage others to do likewise.

If others do likewise, they must be dealt with at that time.

I am also impressed with the argument that this might in some way constitute a disparity of sentence, that you individuals have not been properly punished for your offense because some others might not be deterred from doing that.

I really wonder about the constitutionality of sentencing one person for a crime that may be committed by another person at another time and place.

It is also difficult for me to equate the sentence I here give you—for destroying $36,000 worth of property, because you have been charged — with those who stole $3,600,000 worth of property and were not charged, demoted, or in any way punished.

My conscience is clear.

We will adjourn the Court.

from Northern Sun News

Planning for Economic Conversion

by Seymour Melman and Lloyd J. Dumas

It's time to start planning the conversion of America's defense economy to civilian work. By conversion we mean political, economic and technical measures for ensuring the orderly transformation of labor, machinery and other economic resources now being used for military purposes to alternative civilian uses. The political impetus for conversion is gaining momentum as a result of the relaxation of cold war tensions. Another stimulus to action is America's deteriorating competitive position in the world economy.

A major factor in America's decline to the status of a second-class industrial power has been the voracious appetite of the military-industrial complex, which employs 6.5 million civilian and military personnel in more than 135,000 factories, laboratories and bases. From 1947 to 1989 this country diverted to military purposes resources whose value exceeded the fixed reproducible, tangible wealth of the entire civilian economy. Tens of thousands of factories became virtual wards of the Pentagon; sheltered from the discipline of the marketplace, they adopted inefficient and costly methods. An indirect consequence of the larger share of tax dollars funneled into the military establishment was a diminution of public investment in the infrastructure and its resulting decay. The debilitating effect of all those developments on American industrial strength is readily apparent.

Labor productivity, a key indicator of long-term efficiency, has significantly declined. Between 1968 and 1988 labor productivity (measured by the dollar value of output per hour of workers in the nonagricultural business sector) rose by 24 percent, approximately one-third of the gain between 1948 and 1968.

In every year between 1894 and 1970 the United States ran a trade surplus—exporting more goods than it imported. In 1971 these surpluses turned into deficits. By 1987 the foreign trade deficit had hit a peak of $170 billion, more than 160 percent above the record level set only four years earlier. "Made in the U.S.A." once meant well-made, high-quality, reasonably priced goods produced by industrial workers earning the highest wages in the world. Now U.S. trade deficits reflect in part a decline in quality and productive efficiency.

In 1982 the American economy plunged into its worst economic downturn since the Great Depression.

By the end of the 1980s, however, the unemployment rates fell to a more tolerable levels. Inflation remained well below the double-digit rates of the late 1970s. And the real gross national product grew more than 25 percent between 1982 and the third quarter of 1988, when it passed the $4 trillion mark. Supposedly, the country is in the midst of the strongest economic recovery since World War II.

But that is an illusion. We have merely pumped up the economy with a huge infusion of public and private debt. This facade of prosperity is not based on the efficient production that drove the economy's remarkable growth throughout much of America's industrial history–an expansion whose benefits were spread among the population rather than going to one small segment of it at the expense of all the rest.

Between fiscal 1980 and fiscal 1989 the national debt more than tripled, from $914 billion to $2.8 trillion. In less than three years after 1985, the federal government added nearly $780 billion in debt, an amount equal to more than 85 percent of the *total* national debt as of 1980. State and local government debt, and the private debt of households and nonfinancial institutions, soared from nearly $3 trillion in 1980 to more than $6 trillion by September 1988. Between 1980 and 1987 the United States went from being the world's largest creditor nation, to whom $106 billion was owed, to being the world's largest debtor nation, with a net international debt approaching $400 billion.

All that borrowing served temporarily to paper over deep-seated economic problems, giving us a fleeting reprieve. But it has also created a "bubble of debt" on top of a steadily eroding economic base, adding the possibility of a sudden collapse to the continuing long-term deterioration in American economic performance.

Conversion to What?

What could the 6.5 million employees of the military-serving institutions do for a living beyond their work for the Pentagon? There are three major areas of work that could be done by these people. The first is repairing the American infrastructure. This includes building and repairing roads, railroads and bridges; constructing waste disposal plants; cleaning up toxic and nuclear wastes; erecting new housing to make up for the enormous shortfall in construction and repair during the past decades; refurbishing libraries, public school buildings, university facilities and so on. In New York City alone, there are 1,000 public school buildings, of which 83 percent require major repairs. Bridges and highways have been crumbling for want of proper maintenance, and the country's railroads are more like the Tonerville Trolley of cartoon fame than modern high-speed facilities. The cost of repairing the infrastructure could amount to more than $5 trillion. The work to be done would surely extend over several decades.

House Resolution 101 includes a provision for a Cabinet-level council that would be charged with encouraging state, city and county governments to prepare capital budgets for renovating the public works and services under their jurisdiction. If carried out, this would set in motion a thoroughly decentralized set of nationwide planning operations for projects that would have employment needs beyond the size and capabilities of the existing work force.

The second area of new work for the converted military labor force would involve producing in the United States many of the products that are now imported. There is no law of nature or economics that prevents factories in the United States from once again becoming competent producers of shoes, for example; we now import 80 percent of our supply. An infusion of fresh investment and talent into the machine-tool industry could restore our former ability to produce high-quality machinery. The United States now buys 50 percent of its new machine tools from Japan, Germany and South Korea.

The third area is new ideas, a sphere in which American engineers and technicians once excelled.

A uniquely large proportion of engineers and administrators are employed in the military-serving industries. For those occupations some special conversion prospects will surely be in order. Teachers of mathematics and the sciences are in notoriously short supply in American high schools and junior colleges. The major teachers colleges could design appropriate programs for training some of these men and women to teach the young, an activity that would have long-range benefits for society. Many engineers could be retrained as civil engineers to work in American communities. The addition of an engineer to a city's or a town's staff would mean a substantial improvement in the ability of local governments to cope with the array of public works that are their responsibility.

The Process of Economic Conversion

The ideology of the free-market economy argues that the labor and facilities no longer needed in the military-serving sector will flow smoothly and efficiently toward an expanding civilian sector once military spending is cut. The market will take care of the transition. There is no need for special attention and certainly no need for advance preparation.

But this isn't true. The world of military industry is very different from the world of commercial industry. For one thing, military-serving firms do not operate in anything like a free-market environment. In the military production system, the nature, quantity and price of output are not determined by impersonal market forces. The are set by the interaction of the Pentagon's central planners and the managers of the military-industrial firms. Military industry, unlike any civilian industry, has only one customer—the Defense Department. Even when military firms sell to other nations, they typically sell products initially designed and produced to satisfy the needs of the Defense Department and can sell abroad only with its permission. Furthermore, the vast majority of defense contracts are negotiated rather than awarded through true price-competitive bidding.

More important, competition in the civilian commercial marketplace provides a crucial element of cost discipline that is largely absent in military industry. In practice, most major military contractors operate on a cost-plus basis, being reimbursed for whatever they have spent plus a guaranteed profit. In such an environment, there are no real penalties for inefficient production. In fact, company revenues can be increased by jacking up costs. Such cost escalation would spell bankruptcy for firms operating in a free market.

The sales function of a typical civilian company involves dealing with large numbers of potential customers, ranging from perhaps a few dozen for firms purveying industrial products to millions for consumer goods producers. For military firms the sales function means knowing the Armed Services Procurement Regulations, developing contacts within the Defense Department and being adept at lobbying. The most crucial job of managers in civilian industries is keeping costs down while producing good quality products. Managers in defense firms need pay relatively little attention to cost, but they must try to manufacture products capable of operating under extreme conditions while delivering every possible increment of performance.

It is not a question of one kind of management

being easier or harder than the other. The point is that they are very different. It is simply not reasonable to expect a manager used to operating in one of these worlds to perform efficiently in the other without undergoing substantial retraining and reorientation. This takes time and will not happen automatically. Civilian firms may well prefer to hire inexperienced civilian managers instead of facing the costs involved in retraining an experienced military manager for civilian work. The same consideration holds for engineers and scientists—the other main component of the military-serving labor force—who would require substantial retraining and reorientation.

The products of military industry are notorious for their poor reliability, despite requirements that only components meeting stringent military specifications be used. These components are not only remarkably costly but also certified to withstand extraordinary extremes of shock, temperature and so on. Poor reliability is an unavoidable consequence of the increasing complexity of military weaponry. Thus sophisticated military aircraft have been in repair a third or more of the time. That's bearable when the cost of maintenance is not a limiting factor. But city transportation systems cannot accept vehicles that are "not mission capable" a third of the time. Hence the retraining of military-experienced engineers and managers is an essential aspect of economic conversion. Of course, the physical facilities and equipment of military industry will require modification as well.

Planning for Conversion

Advanced contingency plans for moving into alternative civilian-oriented activity could help carry the nation smoothly through the transition to a demilitarized economy and protect militarily-dependent communities against the considerable economic disruption they will otherwise experience. The transformation of a facility and its work force to civilian production must be planned locally, by those who know them best—not by distant "experts." Even at its best such a planning process will be lengthy. A great many details must be worked through to ensure that the transition is smooth and that the resulting facility and work force are properly restructured to be an efficient civilian producer, able to operate profitably without continuing subsidies. It is long past time to get this process underway.

A bill now before Congress, House Resolution 101, would institutionalize a nationwide system of highly decentralized contingency planning for economic conversion at every military facility in the United States. The resolution, called the Defense Economic Adjustment Act, sponsored by Representative Ted Weiss, would require the establishment of labor-management

Alternative Use Committees at every military facility with 100 or more people. These local committees would be empowered to draw up detailed technical and economic plans for shifting to viable alternative civilian activity. Funds would be provided for services such as income support, continued health insurance and pension benefits during any actual transition resulting from military cutbacks.

There are two reasons why military-industry workers should be especially protected, even though workers in other industries are not. First, such protection is vital to breaking the hold of the politically powerful "jobs" argument, which raises the specter of lost jobs to the constituents and thus damage to the political careers of representatives who vote against any military programs. The second is that the special obstacles to conversion of military industry must be overcome to allow the infusion of resources into civilian activity that will ultimately revitalize the whole of U.S. industry, and not just the prospects of converted defense workers and firms.

By moving military-sector resources into profitable civilian activity through a carefully planned process of economic conversion, the nation can break its decades-long addiction to military spending and build a stronger and more secure economic base. Without such a revitalization of civilian production, it is difficult to see how America can climb out of the deep hole of production incompetence, deficit and debt it dug for itself in the 1980s and reverse the deterioration of its economic performance and competitive position in the global marketplace.

Perestroika and Glasnost

The remarkable changes in the Soviet Union and Eastern Europe offer great promise of substantial arms reduction. We have seen only a beginning, but it is a hopeful one. The prospect of a 50 percent reduction in strategic nuclear arsenals—even talk of the total elimination of nuclear weapons within a decade or two—has moved from the realm of an impossible dream to the real world of negotiations. Progress toward reduction of conventional forces has begun.

Each of the three forces we have been discussing has its counterpart in the Soviet Union, which has finally admitted that it too is plagued by out-of-control budget deficits. The military's diversion of critical resources from the country's civilian industrial base has played no small part in rendering those industries hopelessly inefficient. At the same time, the attention of the nations of Western Europe has turned increasingly to economic integration rather than military adventurism. As far as the Soviet Union is concerned, this surely diminishes the threat to their security.

Obstacles to Conversion

Nevertheless, there are strong institutional and ideological barriers to implementation of economic conversion. The most prominent of these are the managements in central government offices and the private firms that are dependent on the military economy. Government departments are ordinarily viewed as "bureaucracies"; however, the central management in the Defense Department that controls the operations of 35,000 prime contracting establishments is, functionally, a central administrative office. This central administrative office is probably the largest such entity in the world and performs the same functions as similar offices in large corporations.

Furthermore, the management of the Pentagon's central office controls the largest block of finance capital in the hands of any single American management. Every year since 1951 the new capital made available to the Defense Department has exceeded the combined net profits of all U.S. corporations. The top managers in the Pentagon and their subordinates are endowed with the usual managerial imperative to maintain and enlarge their decision-making power. Accordingly, they have consistently opposed all proposals for economic conversion planning in the United States.

This managerial opposition to conversion planning is not specific to any particular social structure, political ideology or management technique. Thus the managers of the U.S. military economy perform their command function via allocation of money resources, while those of the Soviet Union perform the command function by direct physical resource pre-emption and allocation. The results in each case are similar: preemption of major resources from civilian production and powerful pressures for operating in an unproductive, cost-maximizing way.

The workforce and surrounding communities of factories, bases and laboratories that serve the military are another institutional barrier to economic conversion. In the United States 3.5 million men and women work in the military industry. An additional 1 million are employees of the Pentagon, including civilian workers on bases, and there are 2 million in the armed forces. For these 6.5 million people and their families and surrounding communities, the military-serving facilities have been the principal sources of jobs for most of their lives. The skills they have developed and the relationships with which they are familiar are powerful incentives to continue working for the military. The

people in such enterprises know that even the appearance of an interest in the idea of economic conversion would bring the disfavor of the Pentagon's top managers.

The nation's organized engineering societies include large numbers of engineers beholden to the military economy. This has a significant effect on the contents of society meetings, the subject matter of journals and learned papers, and the network of contacts available for employment opportunity. At this writing no single engineering society has ventured to propose contingent conversion planning for its members as a way of coping with the possible reversal of military budget growth. In its November 1989 issue, *Spectrum*, a journal of the Institute of Electrical and Electronics Engineers, published a special report titled "Preparing for Peace," a serious, courageous attempt to survey the military engineers' prospects during a subsiding cold war.

Finally, there are the universities, particularly the larger ones, which have grown accustomed to receiving major R&D grants from the Defense Department and to administering major research institutions, like the Lawrence Livermore and Los Alamos nuclear weapons laboratories, for the Pentagon. At the same time the departments of universities that might be expected to have some connection with civilian production, the engineering and business schools, have become less production-oriented during the long cold war period. Some schools are beginning to make an effort to reestablish the importance of civilian production in their curriculums, but the emphasis is small compared with the military-oriented research activities. The universities also contain large departments and schools—such as political science and international relations—whose faculties and curriculums have focused on training cold war technicians, researchers and administrators.

Alongside these direct economic ties to the military at the universities there are a number of ideological commitments that play an important part in sustaining support for military institutions. Among economists, for example, it is generally accepted that money equals wealth, that the proper measure of economic product is in money terms, that the money value of an economic activity denotes its value independent of the usefulness of the product. Military goods and services are thus counted as additions to real wealth despite the fact that they do not contribute to the central purpose of the economy—to provide the material standard of living. They add neither to the present standard of living (as do ordinary consumer goods) nor to the future standard of living by increasing the economy's capacity to produce (as do industrial machinery, equipment and the like).

Since the Great Depression, economists, and indeed the larger society, have defined the central problem of the U.S. economy as the maintenance of proper levels of market demand, and thereby of income and employment. From this perspective, expenditures that generate market demand are critical, regardless of the nature of the product. A consensus formed that military spending is the best way to accomplish this effect. Thus, most economics textbooks do not differentiate between firms producing military goods and civilian enterprises.

Collecting the Peace Dividend

Apart from the planning of economic conversion, its actual execution will be heavily dependent on the timing and the size of the peace dividend that would result from the reduction of military budgets. Savings can be expected from two sources: first, and early on, reduction of certain military activities (such as base closings and elimination of marginal weapons programs) at the initiative of the federal government; second, de-escalation of military spending and the size of the military-serving institutions as a result of international agreements setting in motion a programmed reduction of the arms race. The first of these approaches could yield possible savings of several billion dollars annually. The New York Times editorialized on March 8 in favor of weapons and force cuts starting with $20 billion per year and reaching $150 billion annually after ten years. That would bring down annual military spending to a level comparable to that in President Carter's budgets. But a thoroughgoing military de-escalation would require international disarmament agreements.

A program for reversing the arms race was laid out by President Kennedy in April 1962 in a document called "Outline of Basic Provisions of a Treaty on General and Complete Disarmament in a Peaceful World." This plan called for a ten-year period to accomplish a significant reversal of the arms race among nations and the parallel establishment of international institutions for inspecting the disarmament process, for coping with international conflict by nonmilitary means and for developing an international peacekeeping force. If this blueprint is implemented, a ten-year cumulative peace dividend of $1.5 trillion is within reach. That is the magnitude of resources needed to start serious economic conversion and to rebuild the infrastructure and industry of the country.

Up Against the Arms Merchants

by Colman McCarthy

One of the Sperry Corporation's efforts to be both a good servant of the Pentagon and of its shareholders is the production of computer equipment for nuclear weapons.

Sperry, a major military contractor that recently pleaded guilty to three counts of fraudulently overcharging the government, currently gets $1.3 billion from the Pentagon to develop, among other things, computer components for the Trident II missile. This is a multi-kiloton weapon able to explode a holocaust many times more violent than the bombs dropped by America on Japan in 1945. In its current annual report, Sperry boasts of being "well established in the electronic-warfare business."

In August, John LaForge, 28, and Barb Katt, 26, entered a Sperry plant in Eagan, Minn., and began hammering at the computers. LaForge is a former Eagle Scout and a graduate of Bimidji State University who served 18 months as a VISTA volunteer. Katt, who graduated from Bimidji State with a degree in Philosophy, has worked with mentally-impaired adults. Both have made deep commitments to peace, whether in the form of comforting a poor person or of trying to stop the military's idolatrous faith in the bomb.

LaForge and Katt have been involved in civil disobedience for four years. They are also students of the history of arms escalation.

The disarmament conference convened by the pair in the Sperry weapons plant went at first unnoticed by the employees. LaForge and Katt had entered the place peacefully, were unarmed and wore the clothes of corporate respectability: blue suits and shined shoes.

During the disabling of the computer, workers were at first confused. Finally, LaForge recalled, "Someone said, 'Shouldn't someone call security?' They thought we were employees gone bonkers."

Security was called. LaForge and Katt were arrested. Two months later, in mid-October, both were found guilty by a jury of a felony. Two days ago, Judge Miles Lord, sympathetic to the defendants, gave them six months suspended sentences.

The case of the Sperry Software Pair, as it is called, deserves attention. A number of facts converge to make it larger than only a Minneapolis case, and a number of ideas were presented by LaForge and Katt that make them more than two well-meaning rebels.

The destruction of a weapons system at Sperry – causing about $35,000 damage – is one of at least a dozen recent actions against the government's war preparations. In Syracuse, seven members of the Griffiss Plowshares, who had damaged a B52 fitted with cruise missiles, were hit with two- and three-year prison terms. In Orlando, eight peace activists were each sentenced to three years for damaging a missile launcher at the Martin-Marietta plant. Jail terms were given to four members of Friends for a Nonviolent World for trespassing at an Air Force base in Grand Forks, N.D. In Bangor, Wash., three citizens are serving 90-day sentences for blocking a train carrying nuclear missiles to a military base.

In all, more than 30 peace activists are in prison or jail for civil disobedience against the arms race.

In cities such as Minneapolis and Orlando, the trials of these cases receive media attention. But nationally, there is little. Trees in the forest are falling as never before, but because the media choose to put their ears elsewhere, the noise never happened. Americans are told more about the protests occurring in places like England, where the women of Greenham Common are saying "no" to nuclear weapons. Petra Kelley of West Germany is better known to Americans than Elizabeth McAlister, now locked away for three years in the Federal Women's Prison in Alderson, W. Va.

McAlister and the others in jail, as well as John LaForge and Barb Katt, are not off-the-wall crazies. All of the them are well-educated, mature, prayerful, and caring citizens who came to civil disobedience in the same spirit that Gandhi, King, and Thoreau defied the might of the state. Many are parents, some are teachers, a few are priests or nuns. Todd Kaplan, 26, in a Florida prison, describes himself as "a faithful Jew struggling to follow God's call to bring *shalom* (peace) and *tzedekah* (justice) to this world."

By delivering stiff sentences to resisters like Kaplan,

the courts give credibility to the Pentagon's argument that the Bomb is sacred. Destroying the property of death that could destroy the ultimate property—the world—is somehow, twistedly, seen as criminal.

from Washington Post

War, Property & Peace

by Colman McCarthy

When John LaForge spoke to the jury in a Federal District Court about why he and a companion did $35,000 damage to a nuclear-weapons system in a Sperry warfare plant, he discussed choices. "We are not romantic idealists, naive of the real cat-eat-bird world," he said. "In this world, Sperry prototypes are built to operate in a harsh radiation environment. The living beings of this world cannot. So we have spoken as loudly as possible, without harming anyone, to this dark time of planned human extinction. . . in which billions of dollars are spent to make nuclear war happen, and practically nothing is spent to keep it from happening."

The jury rejected the argument. It found LaForge and his friend guilty of the destruction of federal property.

Convictions are common these days for the artisans of anti-war civil disobedience. Out of a dozen recent trials, more than 30 peace activists are now in prison or jail because they have entered weapons plants and disabled one bomb part or another. With clumsy determination, most judges, viewing the defendants as publicity seekers or outright loonies, hurry them through the courts and into jail as though national security is being undermined every minute they walk free.

This case in Minneapolis is different. Judge Miles Lord, aware that the militarism needs to be put away and not the citizens of cast-iron conscience who oppose it, gave the two defendants six-month suspended sentences. For once, a courtroom is presided over by a jurist who respects both the tradition of civil disobedience and the arguments made for it by peacemakers who have been damaging the weapons. Lord, best known for his judicial firmness against corporate criminals, gave LaForge a full forum for his views. Lord said, "I was very impressed with the plausibility of the argument of the defendants when they said that international law made it illegal to manufacture these atomic weapons that indiscriminately kill and wipe out whole civilian populations."

Lord is not a romantic idealist either. He was not surprised by the jury's verdict of guilty: "A good motive doesn't count. The jury is required to follow the law." However, in court last Thursday, Lord said, when setting the pair free, that he wanted "to take the sting out of the bomb and remove the halo over any device that can kill." What most juries, as well as most people, find troublesome about the actions of war resisters in weapons plant is their destructiveness. How can they call themselves nonviolent peacemakers, it is asked, when they are unpeacefully doing violence to someone's property?

A fair question, except how can anti-property property be respected? Nuclear weapons, stacked like firewood and ready to burn the final conflagration, are pieces of property that threaten the world, the common property of everyone. The war resisters who have smashed everything from warhead nose cones to Trident II missile tubes believe they are acting against anti-life property. They ask that if a gun is held to your head or the head of someone you love, don't you have the right – or obligation – to dismantle, destroy, or get rid of the gun.

In the Sperry trial, it was reported that Judge Lord told the prosecutors to stop their repetitious talk of violent acts against Sperry. Stressing that this wasn't an assault case, Lord was quoted in a Minnesota newspaper as saying that the acts were like a person "going into a National Forest and cutting down an expensive tree that didn't fall on anyone." La Forge spoke up (in another court he would likely have been silenced) to extend the analogy: The felled tree was diseased and threatened to destroy all the forests of the Earth.

Weapons that kill indiscriminately have been outlawed by such international agreements as the 1977 Geneva Protocol. The Nuremberg Principles talk of "crimes against peace," namely, "planning, preparation, initiation, or waging of a war of aggression." Nuremberg does not absolve a citizen from responsibility to stop such crimes, "provided a moral choice was in fact possible for him."

Martin Luther King, Jr., when asked whether his civil disobedience was efficient or politically shrewd, answered that efficiency or shrewdness wasn't the point. The issue is: Is it right or wrong?

If King is unpersuasive, there is the Buddist tale of the spiritual master who went to the town square every day to cry out against war and injustice. Disciples, seeing that he was having no effect, said, "No one is listening, everyone's insane. It's time to stop." "No," said the master, "I will keep crying out so I won't go insane."

from Washington Post

I was 8 years old when my father was murdered. It is almost impossible to describe the pain of losing a parent to a senseless murder. And in the aftermath, it is similarly impossible to quiet the confusion: "Why him? Why this? Why me?" But even as a child one thing was clear to me: I didn't want the killer, in turn, to be killed. I remember lying in bed and praying, "Please, God. Please don't take his life, too." I saw nothing that could be accomplished in the loss of one life being answered with the loss of another. And I knew, far too vividly, the anguish that would spread through another family—another set of parents, children, brothers and sisters thrown into grief.

M. Kerry Kennedy

Ministering to the Condemned

by Joseph B. Ingle

I am firmly convinced that if the citizens of the United States fully understood the nature and effects of the death penalty, we would no longer allow the punishment to be imposed. Unfortunately, however, many people have been misinformed or have closed their minds about this issue, and the media coverage of executions, if present at all, is steadily shrinking. Furthermore, the media that still provide coverage have continually failed to describe what the inmate is actually like and what he and his family experience during his final hours. We learn about the final meal, the last statement, and the body's reaction when it is electrocuted, but not about the actual ways in which people experience their own or their loved one's planned death.

For the last 13 years, I have traveled throughout the South ministering to inmates condemned to death. This work led to the establishment of a prison reform organization called the Southern Coalition on Jails and Prisons, with affiliate offices now located in eight states. In the course of this work, I have formed several close relationships with condemned inmates and their families.

In this essay, I would like to describe David Washington, a man I came to love and respect, and the events surrounding his execution in Florida in July 1984 (Magee, 1980:149-161). David's crimes were horrible, and I am no less appalled by them than are the strongest death penalty advocates. I do not believe, however, that the Christian command to forgive is a conditional directive; nor does the commandment "thou shalt not kill" add "except in retribution." David Washington would be happy to know that others, with varying stands on the question of capital punishment, might learn more about death (and life) by hearing a little bit about his final days.

The Person

We called him Pee Wee. It was a nickname coined on the streets of Miami, and one that David Washington brought with him to Florida State Prison's death row. It was an odd nickname, as he was not a small man – he stood six feet tall and was acknowledged to be one of the best basketball players on death row. His smooth, caramel skin and dark eyes were regularly accompanied by a warm smile. As his many friendships in Miami confirmed, Pee Wee radiated a genuine charm.

The events that sent David to the electric chair involved the deaths of three victims. A product of Liberty City, the black ghetto in Miami, David was a street-wise youth, but he never used his social background as an excuse for his crimes. Rather, he readily admitted his full responsibility to the police and to the courts. He turned himself in to the police, fully cooperated with their investigations, and pleaded guilty. Pee Wee threw himself on the mercy of the court, waiving his right to a jury trail. But the court had no mercy and, in 1976, David was sentenced to three consecutive death sentences.

In my visits with David over the years, I found a deeply troubled soul. He was so distressed over his crimes that occasionally he would sit in his cell in a nearly catatonic state, refusing any outside contacts. If my visit coincided with one of these retreats, he would refuse to come out to see me, and would instead remain in the solace of his cell, reflecting over his crimes and the lives of the people he had murdered, seeking an understanding and forgiveness that could only come from within. In a real sense, David carried these victims with him until the hour of his death. They were his burden to bear, and like most other death-row prisoners I have known, David felt remorse and pain in living with the responsibility for his crime.

When Pee Wee was sociable, his kindness and concern were second to no one else's in the prison. In a very meaningful sense, he was not the same person who committed those horrible crimes on the streets, indeed, though many will choose not to believe this. I found that David resonated a sweetness of character and true humility. David was not some rabid dog; like the rest of us, he was a unique individual who had both good and bad parts.

David, unlike many people on death row, rarely discussed his legal proceedings with me. He had accepted his guilt on a personal level, and whatever the courts did could not affect those feelings. The guilt and responsibility he experienced were real no matter what any court did to him. Thus, almost all our visits were personal and spiritual in nature. We came to care a great deal for one another, to hate the sin but love the sinner.

In the course of one visit, Pee Wee struggled to

explain why he had not come out for my last visit: "Joe, I want you to know that it has nothing to do with you. Sometimes I just get back there thinking about those people I killed, and I don't say nothing to nobody. I just sit there for days, waiting for it all to go through me so I can feel right again."

In a sense, it was as if all three victims were alive and inhabiting David's soul. Talking with Pee Wee was often like talking with someone who had lost a family member to murder. David never forgot his victims; his struggle was to accept himself and to learn forgiveness for what he had done, and to try to repay a debt he knew he never could. It was a difficult pilgrimage that Pee Wee had undertaken.

It is often stated that when the lives of the saints are examined, their souls become windowpanes through which we can see God. Saints are able to become transparent so that others can experience or see God through their lives. While David was no saint, his suffering served as a reminder to others on death row, and those of us on the outside who came to know him, of the presence of his victims in our lives. He was a living reminder of the value of life. David became a windowpane through which we could see God acting in the world, working for reconciliation, forgiveness, and the preservation of life. Through him, I reinforced my view that destruction of life, whether in a random street killing or in the electric chair, must be stopped. Responsibility for these needless deaths must be borne by those involved in them; it is only when we come to see our complicity in murder and our responsibility for it that we can move onto the level of a forgiveness and a reconciliation that transcend the wrongful deed. David taught others this painful and difficult lesson by his example as he lived out his days in his 50-square-foot death-row cell.

Pee Wee arrived on death row in November, 1976. The first person he befriended upon his arrival, the person who took him under a protective wing, was John Spenkelink, who was executed less than three years later. In Pee Wee's words: "I was ignorant when I came to death row. I didn't know nothing about it. John Spenkelink spent time with me. He explained the way things worked, introduced me to the guys, eased my way. He was a real friend to me and a lot of the guys. He was quiet, calm – a real leader. If we wanted changes made, we came to John. He made sure things were right."

I will leave it to other contributors to this volume to explain the struggles faced by men on death row when their close friends are taken to the electric chair.

In this case, with the help of John Spenkelink, David became familiar with the routine of death row: the countless hours locked in a cell, with televisions and radios blaring, the loud conversations, the Florida heat, and, worst of all, the waiting and the uncertainty of dealing with impending death and the pain of watching his family trying to cope. Simply sitting there alone, David was unable to explain to himself or to his God why he had murdered. Sometimes he would cry. Weeping for what he had done, he quietly worked his way through his guilt. As the years passed, the suffering he endured was impossible to escape. He did make his peace with God; he had sought forgiveness and knew that although his community could not grant it, his God could. But he could never forget what he had done, so the suffering remained with him. How can any of us live our own lives, or face our death, when there is no way to rectify the errors we have made, and there is no societal support for the forgiveness we ask? Capital punishment dooms all of its victims to death with important unfinished business remaining. It is a lonely death.

Meanwhile, David's legal situation steadily deteriorated. His case was chosen by the Supreme Court to determine standards for effective assistance of counsel in death penalty cases and, in 1984, the court ruled unfavorably (Strickland v. Washington, 466 U.S. 668 [1984]). At that time, we were quite sure that David had only a few months to live, and the roller coaster of preparation for death started to accelerate. In mid-June, Governor Bob Graham signed David's death warrant, setting the execution date for 12 July. It was David's third death warrant, and thus the third time his possessions were packed and he was moved to a holding cell, under 24-hour personal guard, next to the death chamber.

Life Under a Death Warrant

While there is always uncertainty for those on death row (Radelet et al., 1983), the uncertainty reaches its apex after a death warrant has been issued (roughly a month before the scheduled execution). Condemned inmates on "death watch," as it is called in Florida, are fortunate because opponents of the death penalty have taken great pains to ensure that the death will not be faced alone. Thus, when I arrived in Florida State Prison on 9 July, three days before the scheduled execution, David was not alone. A paralegal, Margaret, and an attorney who has taken hospice training, Susan, had seen him frequently in the preceding weeks.

The legal prognosis was poor, but still somewhat unpredictable. Although we knew that David would probably be put to death, the arbitrariness that characterizes the imposition of the death penalty in

Florida (Bowers and Pierce, 1980; Gross and Mauro, 1984; Radelet, 1981; Radelet and Mello, 1986; Radelet and Pierce, 1985) also seems to characterize the odds of winning an appeal (Radelet and Vandiver, 1983) and of getting a stay of execution once a warrant is signed. If his legal papers were seen by the right judge on the right day, a stay might be granted. Thus, there was reason to hope, but we had to guard against the risk that this hope might cloud David's ability to deal with the reality of his impending death.

In this case, the unexpected indeed happened. David obtained a stay of execution from the Trial Court on 6 July. However, the state immediately appealed this action to the Florida Supreme Court. This court, in turn, using imperative judicial language, urged the Trial Court to lift its stay. By remanding the case to the Trial Court, the Supreme Court's message was clear: it's time to execute David Washington, and let's get on with it. When I left for the prison on the night of 9 July, we were awaiting a response from the Trial Court judge to this demand.

Before I entered the prison, the Trial Court had acted – and acted in a way that rebuffed the State Supreme Court and underscored the mockery of the ping-pong game the Appellate Courts play with human life. Rather than lift the stay, the trial judge vacated all three death sentences. Thus, as I entered the prison, I found a jovial atmosphere.

During the death watch, at a time when the inmate needs so clearly to be near those who love him (and vice versa), the inmate is separated from his family and friends by a glass barrier (cynics might argue that this barrier creates the impression that his loved ones, rather than the state, are the ones trying to put him to death). Pee Wee and I thus greeted each other by placing our palms on opposite sides of the glass window. He was smiling as I asked him to repeat what his lawyer had just told him on the phone. He relayed the conversation, and I leaned back in my chair and expressed, in relief, disbelief that it had really happened.

As the evening progressed, the effects of being free from the sentence of death for the first time in eight years revealed themselves in Pee Wee. He was light-hearted, joyous, laughing, and teasing. The joy and happiness we experienced had rarely been felt in the bowels of the prison. We did not talk seriously about our fear (indeed, our confidence) that the state would appeal this last ruling to the Florida Supreme Court, but David had a very realistic appraisal of the slim odds he would have if such an appeal was launched. He

expected the state to prevail upon appeal, but decided to worry about that prospect when and if it developed. This night, for the first time since we had met, David was unburdened by a death sentence. Along with the volunteer lawyer and paralegal who had come to visit, we celebrated the persistent efforts of his attorneys and David's freedom from death. As the volunteers and I left the prison two hours later, we radiated David's joy; seldom have I exited a prison so hopeful and joyous. If only for a few hours, we relished David's freedom from the manacles of death.

During the 40-mile drive back to Gainesville, we speculated on prospective events in the courts. We all agreed that despite the outstanding work of David's lawyer, the State Supreme Court would in all likelihood reinstate the death sentences. But it was as if David's dwelling wholly in the present had communicated itself to us. We would let tomorrow take care of itself; this night was for celebration.

The volunteer paralegal put it best as she described David's attitude toward adverse legal rulings in his case: "David received news about the legal proceedings very gracefully. He was glad there were people who cared about him and who were making the effort for him, but he had no attachment to the results of what happened in court. He had a tremendous serenity, a kind of holy indifference, as to the outcome of any of the legal proceedings. It was not the most important thing going on with him. He never manifested more than a polite indifference about the legal issues. At the same time, he received news of the legal efforts gratefully but in no way could anything that happened in the court disturb what was happening in him."

The next evening provided a delightful interlude, as I visited friends who had nothing to do with the death penalty. Regrettably, however, the telephone interrupted our conversation. David's death sentences had been reinstated by the State Supreme Court. Although expected, the news that I knew would lead to the taking of my friend's life was piercingly painful.

The Last Visits

The next day, a Federal District Court judge granted David a 24-hour stay of execution; the execution was rescheduled for 7:00 a.m., 13 July. I sought to maintain a facade of indifference to these complicated legal proceedings, as did David, as I ministered to him and his family. We still had hope, but tried to keep that hope from dominating our time together.

On the evening of 11 July, the volunteer attorney,

the paralegal, and I joined 11 members of David's family for a visit with him. There were 36 more hours to live. For three hours, we crowded into the non-contact visiting area and talked with him through the glass barrier. Three small children, aged three through five, enlivened the occasion by talking with their uncle through the glass. David teased them, put happy smiles on their faces, and sought to uplift all of our spirits. His stepfather, a quiet and large man, radiated strength for all of us. David's mother relived some of the memories she shared with her son. David spoke intently to his younger brother, who was clearly having an especially difficult time. At one point, David asked me to take special care in helping his brother make it through the ordeal. Although all the family members suffered, the pain of David's 12-year-old daughter was perhaps the most visible. She had not seen her dad in years, and she had difficulty expressing her love amid the horror of this occasion. She broke down in tears several times, and it was only David's constant support and encouragement that kept her intact.

At one point during the visit, I joined David's brother at a window overlooking the prison parking lot. He was standing, silently crying, while gazing toward the wing that housed the electric chair. As we stood there passively staring, I spoke quietly with him. After several minutes, he stopped crying long enough to tell me that he simply could not take it. I assured him that there was no reason he should; it was an insane situation, and the important thing was to remember David's request that he not do anything stupid or rash. He nodded and again we stood in silence. He did not return to the prison the following night.

We bade David adieu when our visiting time was expended. We knew that there was to be another day for us and for David. We went over the final visiting plans for the next day, David's last full day on earth, and parted for the night.

The next evening all of David's family returned, with the exception of his brother. In contrast to the previous night, when we knew there would be another day, the finality of this night enveloped us all. The three children cried throughout most of the visit, not fully understanding why they and all the adults in the room were so sad. David summoned each of us to the glass to talk privately. In seeking to comfort his loved ones, he poured himself out to each. At one point, he asked Margaret, Susan, and me to come to the glass. As Margaret later recalled: "David said that apart from his family, we had shown him more love than anyone else. He tried to express his gratitude and told us also of his concern for us. He was worried because we were being

hit so hard by every execution and personally involved with each one. We immediately let David know how very much he and the other men had given us and that we were doing what we were doing because we wanted to do it. He had given us more than we could ever return to him, and more than the state could ever take away by executing him."

During the course of the conversation, David mentioned how much this assurance meant to him. I echoed the sentiments, and we talked about love being the uniting reality through life and earth. It was clear that David was comfortable and spiritually at ease.

At midnight, David's mother and daughter, along with Susan and me, were permitted to have a one-hour contact visit with him. The remainder of the family and Margaret remained on the other side of the glass partition. After each of us hugged him, we sat in chairs around him. As he had done throughout the death warrant, he proceeded to minister to us. He began with his mother: "I ain't believing this! I ain't believin' you're crying! You've always been the strong one – I never expected this. Now come on, we can't have this. You dry those tears and sit up straight."

His mother, forcing a smile through her sobs, looked at David and said, "But you're my baby." David, his voice catching, almost overcome with tears himself, embraced her despite the handcuffs. There were no words to be said as mother and son hugged each other a final time.

David's primary concern was for his daughter. He agonized over her having to endure the horror of his execution. He sat her on his lap, her lanky body draping his. She was crying openly, the tears streaming down her face, and David spoke to her: "I want you to make me proud. I don't want you messin' up like I did. You listen to your grandmother and do what she tells you. I want you to do better than I did. I didn't listen, and you see what happened to me. Now I want you to get your books – to study. School is important and I want you to do well. Don't you be makin' the mistakes I did, thinkin' school wasn't important."

As Pee Wee spoke softly to his daughter, he wiped her tears away. I sat in my chair, stricken by the pathos of the moment. Father was saying goodbye to daughter, imparting advice to help her survive in this world after his death. He was trying to leave a legacy to stand with her through the years. As I looked at his daughter's stricken face, gazed at his mother with her handkerchief crumpled to hide her tears, I heard a soft sobbing, I looked to the window and there, peering through the glass, was the three-year-old niece. Her face was pressed against the glass, a river of tears flowing down her cheeks. As I saw her and felt her tears, I realized that she and I were equally unable to fathom the events at hand. Neither of us, though bearing witness to the final parting, was able to understand it. Why was Pee Wee going to his death? Why was this unnecessary pain deemed necessary by our fellow citizens? The dispenser of so much love and grace, the sufferer of such grief, was going to be taken from those who loved him. Was the only thing our society could do for the families of homicide victims to double the number of innocent families who experience the tragic loss of a loved one?

Soon it was almost one o'clock, and we were saying our final goodbyes. We knew that David would be put to death in six hours. David once again thanked us for our friendship. As we filed out the door, each of us hugged him one last time. The guards handcuffed David's hands behind his back and led him down the hallway. As David was led away, I gazed about me. His daughter was sobbing in Susan's firm embrace, watching her father leave for the last time, shouting, "Please don't kill my daddy." The small children were near hysterics, his mother's shoulders were heaving with sorrow, and his stepfather tried to comfort us all. As David neared the door that would take him from us, I called down the prison corridor, "We love you," and several others echoed these words. David looked back over his shoulder, looking at this family for the last time. His expression was tender and sorrowful. His gaze rendered us speechless, and a gentle smile creased his smooth face. Then he was gone.

We remained transfixed. None of us moved. It was as if by holding the moment, by not moving, we could retain David with us. We stood planted in the middle of the prison corridor like fixtures. Then a prison colonel, the head of the execution team, entered the hall and walked through our midst. The spell was broken, and we stumbled to the parking lot, wailing, grief-stricken, and inconsolable. Society's retribution had produced a family bereaved, a wounded child, and another mourning mother.

The only conclusion I can offer from the above case, and from the many others like it that remain untold, is that capital punishment takes the lives of people who can be quite remarkable despite their appalling crimes, and that its pains touch many more people than the individual inmate himself. It is a punishment done in all our names, and although crimes of the prisoner have caused immense suffering to the innocent, I fail to see how that suffering is alleviated by creating a whole new family of innocent people who mourn the loss of a loved one.

The Pains of Life

Joseph M. Giarratano

Seven years ago, I began the process of awaiting my man-made appointment with death. Since being condemned to death, my days have been spent dealing with the guilt of having been convicted of taking the lives of two human beings, confronting the very real possibility of my own violent death, and coping with the anger, resentment, frustration, helplessness, and grief of having five friends taken from my side to be ritualistically exterminated. These have been nine long years of fighting to maintain my sanity, of growing, and of holding onto a sense of humanity in an environment maintained specifically for the purpose of bombarding the senses with hopelessness.

It is almost impossible to maintain a sense of humanity in a system that ignores the fact that you are a living, breathing human being – a system where you are recognized only as a number, a compilation of legal issues open for debate, a 20-to-50-page legal brief before tribunals that will determine your fate without ever knowing you, as something nonhuman – a piece of tainted meat to be disposed of.

These nine years, I've lived on death row, a unit isolated not only from the outside world, but also from the rest of the prison population. Contact with others not "like" me is very limited: visits with friends or family that take place in an isolated cubical the size of a telephone booth, with thick security glass separating me from those who still recognize my humanness. There are also contact visits with those who work to save my life through the legal channels. These are individuals who continue to acknowledge my humanity and whom I've come to love as family. When I am permitted to visit these friends, I leave my "home" escorted by an elite group of guards; the black uniforms and combat boots distinguish them from the ordinary correctional officers (whose uniform is light blue). But the true essence of life and death is in the unit where my days are spent. Here, 24 hours a day, is where I experience and interact with the basic emotions of life, and face the reality of death.

On the night of 31 July 1986, four guards came to my unit, with handcuffs and waist-chain, to escort me to the telephone. It was a call that I had been dreading, because I would be saying my final goodbye to another friend. Within three hours after that call, Mike Smith, a man whom I shared a life bond with for seven years,

would be coldly strapped into an electric killing machine. Then, 2,700 volts of raw current would fry the life out of his body.

Even now, I feel the anger I felt at his death, and the pain of having a friend coldly taken from me to be ritualistically put to death. As I walked down the hallway, several guards commented on the wrongness of killing my friend, and stated that Mike was a good man. Fighting back the tears was hard because of the helplessness I experienced at not being able to save him. Memories of the times Mike and I had spent together flooded through me. I wanted to understand why Mike was being taken from me, but it was impossible. Each day I have to interact with the same guards who came to the unit and took him from me. These guards were the same guards who were telling me, "Joe, Mike is a good man. They shouldn't kill him." Each time I heard a guard say that, I could feel the anger churning within me. What they were saying made no sense to me. I wanted to scream, "NO!" I wanted to tear down the prison walls and make them stop. I hated them.

As I lifted the phone to my ear and heard my friend's voice, I didn't know what to say. Other than quick hellos, our conversation consisted of a few scattered questions tied together with long silences. I could feel the tears leaking from my eyes as the hopelessness overwhelmed me. I wanted to tell Mike to fight the guards until the last second – to take some of them down with him – but all I could say was, "I love you, my friend. I'm sorry I can't stop this." Mike's reply still rings in my ear: "I'll be fine, Joe. You know that I'm going home. Please don't do anything that you might regret later. You have to forgive them."

Walking back to my cell, I could barely move - it felt as if every muscle in my body were cramped. I could hear the guards asking me questions, but I knew that if I responded, my hatred would spew out at them. I felt the helplessness and hopelessness in the pit of my stomach - I wanted to pull my friend back. It wasn't until later that I noticed the blood on my wrists where the cuffs bit into my flesh. I tried to pull Mike back, and I couldn't.

Before that day, four other friends had been executed; men whom I ate with, talked with, played with, argued with – men whom I came to know as friends and shared a life bond with. Men whom no matter what their crimes, I could not see as anything but human beings – whom I could not see as animals or pieces of meat. James and Linwood Briley, Morris Mason, and Frank Coppola are the men whose tears I saw, whose flesh I touched, whose pain I still feel. I still know the hopelessness, I am still with the guards who took them away to be executed, and I am still trying to understand.

I know the pain that I brought to my victim's family. I know their loss, their anger, their frustration, hatred, and despair. I know their feelings of helplessness and hopelessness. I know these emotions as they, the families of my friends who have been executed, and my family and friends do – a twisted cycle of continuing violence, loss, pain, grief and helplessness. Unlike those whom we invest with authority, I have learned that killing people is wrong.

Hope is such a frail thing when hopelessness constantly bombards the senses. You can hear its empty sound in the clanging of the steel doors, in the rattle of chains, in the body searches, in the lack of privacy, in the night sounds of death row, and you can see it in the eyes of the guards who never really look at you, but are always watching to see that you do not commit suicide. You can feel the hopelessness each time you are asked to state your number, when you are holding the hand of a friend in chains who is being pulled away from you, never to be seen again. You can hear it in the echo of a system where humanity is constantly denied. Eventually I, like all human beings, will die. But for now I am very much alive and, until death touches me, I will feel the pain, anger, frustration, despair and grief at the loss of those close to me. I will feel the fear of my own predetermined death. For Mike's family, life must go on, as is true for all who have lost loved ones. The focus shifts back to life, and the death grows more remote as time passes. But here on the row, where life goes on, death is never distant. Here life and death are one. Both are ever-present; while there are times when death seems distant, it is only an illusion; at any time an announcer on television or radio may tell you that your death or the death of a friend is one step closer. You may read about your death in the daily newspaper, or a letter from a court clerk, or hear about it when the guards announce "Let's go, _____." Here one can never forget about death for long – on the row where hope and hopelessness coexist daily.

All of these emotions are very real to me, and I can see them in the eyes of the human beings around me, condemned and executioner alike. Anyone who stays on a death row, comes to know someone on the row; anyone who visits regularly can feel the passion of these emotions pulsating in the air. One can hear the sound of guards and prisoners laughing together, talking, sharing meals. There are the ministers who come to visit through the bars – some trying to save our souls, all praying and telling us not to give up hope, but none telling us how this can be done. Many share in our helplessness for a time, but they also have their lives to contend with. The condemned and executions live together is a strange paradox.

I have spoken with many of the guards, most of whom avoid the subject of my death, the possible deaths of the men around me, and their own role in this death ritual. There are a few who will avoid my eyes and say: "Joe, it's not my doing. I don't want to see you die. There are others who deserve it more than you." Many find it easy to avoid the subject, since they will not be the ones who actually pull the switch – they will only escort me to the death house and let their coworkers take over. But their eyes tell all that needs to be said. They have very human eyes, just like the other human beings around me and just like those of my dead friends. Yet, they will do their jobs. Standing in this house of death among all these human beings – some who come to visit, some who come to stay, and some never to be seen again – life is not cogent.

Each day, I yearn to touch, hold, and be with my loved ones, just as they want me with them. The closeness of death makes me more aware of my human feelings, and constantly adds fuel to a passion for life. It makes me more aware of how much time I have wasted in life, how very responsible we all must be, and how precious each day of living must be. Each day, I hear Mike Smith's words to me: "You must forgive them. I love you, too." Hearing these words does not allow me to ignore the humanity around me, not that of the condemned or the executioner(s). On 31 July 1986, I hated them. Each day here as been an experience in life. Although death will eventually come, it has not overtaken me yet and, until it does, I live. Where there is life, there is hope, as both thrive through the recognition of humanity – both yours and mine. Each day I spend here is an experience in Life, as well as Death.

Joseph M. Giarratano is currently under sentence of death in Virginia. During his ten years on death row, he has been active in death penalty litigation/abolition. He is currently client advisor to the Virginia Coalition on Jails and Prisons.

Another Attorney for Life

by Michael Mello

As the number of condemned prisoners in the United States grows, so does the problem of finding competent attorneys to handle death penalty cases when the execution date draws near (Mello, 1988). In this essay, I would like to reflect on the motivations, rewards, and frustrations connected with this type of work, based on my five years of defending those who live under a sentence of death in Florida.

"Why do you represent people who are sentenced to death? Isn't it depressing?" I have been asked such questions so often, by so many different people with different degrees of seriousness, that I have tried to find some pat answers, or at least one pat answer suitable for wineglass repartee. My attempts have been unsuccessful. This is not because I am ashamed of what I do or because I am unwilling to debate the merits of the death penalty. It is because I have been unable to find a way to express succinctly the intensity, the emotional highs and lows, of working for people who are litigating for their lives. I lack the words to describe how rewarding, as well as how frightening and stressful, this work can be.

This essay presents the same problem. I spend most of my working days (and a few nights) writing legal briefs, petitions, and memoranda in capital cases. Yet this reflective essay is the most difficult death penalty writing assignment I have ever undertaken. I wonder if questions of motives would be so difficult were I a construction worker, a secretary, or a nuclear physicist. Jobs can have several different rewards, including money, prestige, education, and variety. Such reasons have only limited relevance in explaining why attorneys would ever want to handle death penalty cases.

Yet there are few other paying jobs that would permit me to spend all of my working time and energy fighting the system of government-sponsored homicide. I believe this system is an unambiguous disgrace to civilized humanity. My cases involve not so much debates about the wisdom of the death penalty in theory—its abstract morality or immorality—but rather case-by-case technical attacks upon a legal system that selects which citizens have lost their entitlement to live. As Charles Black demonstrated more than a decade ago in *Capital Punishment: The Inevitability of Caprice and Mistake* (2nd ed., 1981), the probability of mistake and the omnipresence of arbitrariness in the imposition of the death penalty pervade this system. My experience supports Black's thesis that the death penalty can never be administered in a fair and even-handed way. A clear sense of the system's basic unfairness is an important motivating factor for my work.

A second motivation is the belief that effective advocacy can reveal latent injustices and therefore force the system to work as it should, even in the most apparently hopeless and seemingly clear-cut cases. For example, Theodore Bundy, infamous as Tallahassee's Chi Omega killer, has been consistently portrayed by the national media as the essence of evil itself. Death penalty supporters cite Bundy as the ultimate justification for the death penalty. I have heard some people who generally oppose capital punishment say that they would make an exception for Theodore Bundy. Such death penalty opponents take care to distance themselves from Bundy's case, carefully pointing out that most capital cases are not nearly so heinous.

Yet Bundy's present attorneys, who are representing him without fee, have pieced together a picture of the case quite different from the media's portrayal of the former law student turned mass murderer. Bundy has never been charged with, much less convicted of, most of the crimes attributed to him. He has been convicted of, and sentenced to death for, two crimes. He might well be innocent of at least one; the prosecution's case at trial depended on hypnotically-created and unreliable testimony. Concerning the other crime, the sentencing jury (culled of all death penalty opponents and drawn from a community that had been saturated for months with prejudicial pretrial publicity) initially split six to six on whether Bundy should receive the death penalty. The jury had never been told that a tie vote on penalty was permissible (and would be treated as a recommendation of life imprisonment), so they continued to deliberate. One juror finally switched sides, making the vote seven to five for death. In both cases, the state had been willing to accept pleas of guilty in exchange for sentences of life imprisonment, but Bundy refused to plea-bargain. There is a good argument that his decision was itself the product of mental illness and incapacity.

Post-trial investigation almost always discloses

important factual information not discovered by trial attorneys, who often work with extremely limited resources (Goodpaster, 1983). Sometimes new evidence of innocence is found (Bedau and Radelet, 1987). Sometimes the crime may be explained, at least in part, by factors beyond the inmate's control, such as mental illness or a childhood of extreme abuse or neglect. Sometimes evidence of a defendant's positive qualities is found, making it less simple to reduce him or her to a subhuman object who has no right to live.

A major problem I regularly encounter is that the courts may be unwilling to revisit the case in light of such newly discovered evidence. However discouraging it may be when courts reject such legal claims, the litigation is still making a record for the future. Taken as a whole, these cases form a historical record of whom the state is killing and under what circumstances. The cases document that the "modern" death penalty is just as unfair as ever, that the new procedures are merely cosmetic, and that fundamental flaws in the system still exist (Amnesty International, 1987). I sometimes take the view that I am litigating for the historians, the sociologists, and the anthropologists, in addition to litigating for the courts.

Questions about my motives are most difficult to answer when they come from someone I represent. Our relationship will be greatly influenced by how far along in the legal process the inmate's case is when we first meet. All have already been sentenced to death. At the early stages, when we can expect that the execution will not happen for several years-if it happens at all-our relationship evolves at its own speed. It is, of course, impossible to generalize, as every case is unique. Sometimes we become close; in other cases we do not. Some inmates are intensely interested in every legal development; others want to know, but they want the attorney to bring the subject up and pursue it; still others want to talk only about their families, their lives on death row, or the state of the world in general. Many inmates are mentally ill in one form or another, ranging from gentle neurosis to flamboyant psychoses, severe retardation, and neurological impairment (Lewis et al., 1986). Early in the legal process, the death penalty does not eclipse all else, although it provides the subtext for much of our conversation. We can be expansive and talk about a wide range of subjects, including my reasons for being there.

In most cases, however, the client and I have not had the luxury of getting to know each other through a slowly developing relationship. The scarcity of death row attorneys in Florida and the frequency with which execution dates have been scheduled by its governors

have meant that I often meet the inmate for the first time when the execution date has been set for the forthcoming month. I must get to know the inmate fast and gain his trust so that he will rely on my judgment and, more importantly, share information with my colleagues and me. The first step in most postconviction efforts is to compile a complete life history of the inmate. Often the information needed is of the most intimate sort and may require the inmate to confront and share painful feelings and long-buried memories. The urgency of an impending execution date means that the legal team must develop, and sometimes force, trust and closeness at an accelerated pace.

The cases that are most difficult are those in which the inmate is running out of legal possibilities for relief. Such cases have been through the entire legal process in both state and federal courts at least once, and are therefore called "successors." When an execution date is set in a case requiring successive litigation, both the inmate and the lawyer know that the chances of obtaining a stay of the execution are slim. We must strike a balance between ephemeral hope and hard reality.

The improbability of securing a stay of execution, which is linked to the increasing hostility of the courts to successors, presents lawyers with intractable dilemmas. Should scarce legal resources be expended on cases in which we will probably not succeed in preventing the execution? The effort requires an enormous investment of time, work, and emotional energy. For me, one important component of this decision is the impact on the inmate of a last-ditch effort: does the litigation effort which inevitably raises the inmate's hopes that he will escape his imminent execution date, impede his ability to work through the (uncertain) fact of impending death? Does such litigation-such literally last-minute litigation-foster denial of the reality of the possibility of death?

Perhaps the most chilling questions involve what a lawyer should do if the inmate decides not to pursue further attempts to ward off the executioner. I can appreciate that a person could conclude that death is preferable to the uncertainty of death row and even to life imprisonment in a maximum-security prison (Bluestone and McGahee, 1962; Gallemore and Panton, 1972; R. Johnson, 1981; Radelet et al., 1983). Assuming that the inmate is mentally competent and that the decision is an informed one, should the attorney give effect to his client's wishes? If so, then is the lawyer respecting the inmate's human dignity and his right to make the most personal and intimate life choice, one of the few such choices permitted to death row inmates (K. Johnson, 1981)? Or is the lawyer simply acquiescing in the inmate's suicide and, thus, making it easier for the state to execute others who do not want to die (Strafer, 1983; White, 1987)? How does one balance the choices and desires of one's client with the interests of other death row inmates in resisting executions?

I am thankful that I have not yet encountered a client who did not want to fight in the courts until the end, since Florida inmates have thus far refused to be volunteers for execution. From my perspective, legal resources must be spent in all cases, even in those where there is small likelihood of even temporary success. This is so because the legal system that decides who lives and who dies operates in no small measure on the basis of chance, luck, and arbitrariness. From time to time, albeit rarely, courts do grant stays in successors. The stakes, not the odds, are what is important. Even when the stays are temporary and even when they do not result in eventual victory–a life sentence or a new trial–this sort of litigation can buy the inmate time, sometimes as little as five hours and sometimes as much as years. This may not be what lawyers usually mean when they talk of "winning." But redefinition of the notion of winning is an important way of coping with a system that is often indifferent and increasingly hostile. To win time is to win. During that time, new evidence beneficial to the condemned person's case may come to light. Also during that time, the condemned, like the rest of us, feel joy and sorrow, have hopes and dreams, grow and change. In short, they live their lives.

Living one's life, even in the close confines of death row, is always much more than a legal matter. This is particularly so in the weeks and months prior to a scheduled execution date. It is essential that the human, extralegal needs of the inmates are recognized and, where necessary, advocated; often the attorneys challenging the inmate's underlying conviction and sentence are not the best ones to fulfill this role. In Florida, death row inmates are fortunate to have a few people who assist them and their families in coping with the psychological and spiritual process of preparing for possible death. This nonlegal counseling and support help turn death from an abstract principle to concrete reality, and also help the inmate take care of the unfinished business of this lifetime. This places the legal struggle in perspective. We fight not only death, but also despair. My goals are to ensure that the inmate knows that all hope is not lost–that the battle continues and that he will not be abandoned–but also that the outlook is grim and that he should be preparing himself to die.

Nevertheless, because of the nature of crisis advocacy, this perspective has only limited utility to me as a lawyer. To be a forceful advocate, one can never view the impending execution as inevitable. While a realistic appraisal of the legal situation is essential to effective lawyering, the zealous presentation of the case before the courts requires a belief in victory. The litigation at this stage is uniquely rough and tumble, with many of the trappings of judicial decorum suspended. Often, virtually all of the other actors in the system, from prosecutors to judges to courtroom personnel to prison officials, expect the execution to go forward and resent the interference by the inmate and his lawyer. Stopping that momentum requires a belief that the scheduled execution will not occur.

This belief has retarded my own process of dealing with the death of my clients. This was brought home to me forcefully in the case of Ronald Straight, who was executed in May 1986 following a round of successive litigation. I had become especially close to Mr. Straight and his mother in the last month of his life, and I strongly believed that his execution would offend the constitutional rights that protect us all. The Supreme Court ultimately denied a stay of execution (by a vote of five to four) less than five minutes before the scheduled time of execution. There was no time to assimilate the reality (of losing by only one vote) and the finality (of there being nothing left that lawyers could do to switch the one vote needed to save Ronnie Straight's life). Straight was being strapped into the electric chair. I will never forget the waves of helpless rage that washed over me as the clerk of the Supreme Court read me the orders denying the stay. It would have been easy-too easy-to blame the Court as an institution, the five Justices who voted to deny the stay, or the one Justice who could have changed his or her mind. Instead, I found that the real target of my rage was myself: a participant in the system of legal homicide. I am a participant who advocates for the condemned, but a participant nonetheless. Was I serving to legitimize the system by helping to provide sanitized executions, executions with the aura of legalism and therefore the appearance of fairness?

As a lawyer, I am constrained by the rules of the game I have chosen to play. Although a skilled manipulator of these rules can meet with success, to be "effective," a lawyer must understand and accept, at least tacitly, the system and its principles. On a personal level, the most frustrating principle to accept is one of the most fundamental: *stare decisis*, the doctrine of precedents. In the minds of a majority of the Justices on the Supreme Court, the constitutionality of the death penalty itself is no longer a serious question. The system of capital punishment still requires fine tuning, but the fundamental issues have been resolved by the Court in favor of the constitutionality of the death penalty. The cases upholding it have been affirmed repeatedly over the past decade, indicating that capital punishment is here to stay, at least for the foreseeable future. While it is certainly untrue to say that precedents are eternal, given the present political climate and the current personnel on the Supreme Court, there is little likelihood of the Court's redefining the death penalty as unconstitutional.

To be sure, important legal issues remain to be resolved in individual cases. Such issues, however, are different from the basic, systemic issues that once typified death penalty litigation. Prior issues revolved around such questions as whether retribution is a legitimate goal of the penal system, whether the death penalty is arbitrary, whether the imposition of capital punishment is racist, and whether capital punishment deters crime more effectively than lengthy imprisonment. This narrowing of issues from the systemic to the individual is exemplified by the present state of litigation surrounding deterrence. It is no longer viable to litigate that the evolving social scientific evidence demonstrates that the death penalty does not deter. Instead, advocacy concerns the right of an individual defendant to present social scientific evidence at his or her own trial. The goal is to save the individual defendant rather than to attack the core assumptions or constitutionality of the death penalty itself. In fact, to the extent that specific cases present issues of broader application, I often try to de-emphasize the larger questions. The question I most often dread at oral argument is, "Counsel, if we rule your way, won't we also have to grant relief in a lot of other cases that present the same claim?"

I do not mean to suggest that there is a clear line between "systemic" defects in capital punishment and "individual" defects in specific cases. The unfairness of a particular death penalty sentence is often symptomatic of more general flaws in the death penalty system itself. There has, however, been a shift in the ways that courts and litigants understand and confront these problems. The courts are no longer interested in broad-based attacks on the death penalty. Thus, the fight is for one life at a time. The irony is the need to convince the courts that granting relief in a particular case will not "open the floodgates" to granting relief in many other cases.

The precedents that define the landscape of present litigation on the death penalty form the world within which the zealous advocate must operate. It is a world within which killing is accepted as legally permissible. Resistance to executions therefore becomes paradoxical. The system is attacked, but this attack becomes institutionalized and thus, to some extent, domesticated.

Yet the ironies inherent in the system of capital punishment are not confined to death row inmates and their advocates. For example, in 1985 the Florida legislature created and funded the Office of the Capital Collateral Representative (CCR) to represent those Florida death row inmates who did not otherwise have lawyers. The legislature did so at the behest of State Attorney General Jim Smith, who argued forcefully that giving inmates lawyers would make the system work more smoothly and would speed up executions. The legislative debates on CCR are extraordinary, as the following exchange illustrates:

Attorney General Smith: . . . [The federal courts have] made it clear they are going to exhaustively review every death case and if the people of Florida want to continue to have capital punishment, and I think they do, this is something we're going to have to do.

Senator Crawford: . . . What you're saying basically is if you support the death penalty [and if you think the] State has a right to utilize that in a timely manner, that we should support this legislation?

Attorney General Smith: Yes, sir. (Elvin, 1986; Florida Senate, 1985)

However, once CCR became operational and succeeded in preventing a string of executions, some legislators grumbled that the office had violated the legislative intent behind its creation. It was apparently not foreseen that the attorneys and other personnel employed by CCR would be effective advocates who could win stays of execution for their clients.

The shifting of the battleground from the broad issue to the individual case, and the increasing impatience with capital cases generally, must be understood in terms of a burgeoning death row. There are presently over two thousand men and women under sentence of death in the United States, spread over 34 states. There are nearly three hundred in Florida alone. State and federal courts in the southeastern United States, where the concentration of condemned inmates is the greatest, have in the past decade been swamped by the sheer number and complexity of the appeals and collateral proceedings that reach them. Judges, being human, may begin to tire of these cases. It is easy to become numbed by the volume. I fear that our society's desire to make executions easier has made us forget that we are dealing with people's lives. The taking of life becomes routine.

Given the number and the emotional power of these cases, death row attorneys have been attacked as unethical and unprofessional by opposing attorneys representing the state. What is more disturbing is that some of this almost prosecutorial rhetoric is finding its way into the utterances of judicial officers. The most common charges include the intentional thwarting of justice by raising frivolous claims and the use of all available procedures to obtain a stay. In particular, it is becoming common to hear accusations that legal papers are intentionally filed so close to the scheduled execution date that courts must grant stays simply to consider the claims raised–which usually turn out to lack merit anyway.

The American adversarial system of justice is based on the notion that lawyers on each side will use every legitimate means to win on behalf of their clients. In the words of the Code of Professional Responsibility, an attorney should represent a client zealously within the bounds of the law. More fundamentally, I do not see how an attorney could do otherwise, especially when a client's very life is at stake. Certainly a commercial or corporate litigator trying to prevent one company from acquiring another company would be expected-and indeed professionally required-to employ all available legal procedures for the client's benefit. Timing of actions, much criticized in death penalty defense work, is equally important in the realm of corporate acquisition practice, where the "life or death" of a company is often at stake. It seems to me that human life can be considered no less valuable. Those who criticize death penalty lawyers for using what they label "dilatory tactics" would see the issue quite differently if the case involved their client or their loved one.

Human life cannot be assigned a value, because it can never be replaced. I believe that the criminal justice system decides life and death on the basis of chance, racism, and financial resources and therefore has no business deciding who lives and who dies. I believe that the death penalty is an anathema to civilization. I believe that basic morality negates any justification of homicide, whether institutionalized or not. And if I cannot and do not say these things in casual conversation, it is because they are not casual.

Michael Mello is an assistant professor at Vermont Law School. His research interests focus on capital punish-

ment. At the time he drafted his contribution to this collection, Mr. Mello was an attorney with the Office of the Capital Collateral Representative in Tallahassee, Florida, where his legal practice consisted solely of representing condemned inmates on Florida's death row.

An Inhumane Way of Death

by Willie Jasper Darden, Jr.

Ironically, there is probably more hope on death row than would be found in most other places. Each of us has been convicted of murder. Some are guilty and a few are innocent. But the one thing we all have in common is that we await our demise side by side-the innocent and the guilty alike. We hope because it would be so easy for our fate to be changed. Hope is one thing we have in common with those stricken with a terminal illness.

Every person in our society is capable of murder. Who among us can say that they have never been so angry that they did foolish things, or that they have not wished for the death of one who destroyed their happiness? Isn't it true that those who advocate the use of capital punishment are just as guilty of homicide as the person executed? Isn't it dangerous for society to preach a message that some of its citizens deserve to die? Like those stricken with a terminal illness, I want to understand.

Before the Colosseum "games" of ancient Rome, the condemned gladiators stood before the royal podium and said, "We who are about to die salute you, Caesar." Humans on death row do not have that immediacy of struggle or that intimacy with their impersonal foe on the field of battle. We are humans who face death because of the faulty wording of a legal appeal or the capriciously bad stomach of a judge or juror. If we executed all murderers, we would execute twenty thousand per year; we face execution because we are the scapegoats. Like those stricken with a terminal illness, I feel I was chosen at random. And, while morally it is no worse to execute the innocent than to execute the guilty, I will proclaim until the electric chair's current silences me that I am innocent of the charge that sent me here.

Our society executes as much "for the person" as "for the crime." We execute for heresy–for being different, or for being at the wrong place at the wrong time. We execute for the traits of the person found guilty. If the person is black, uneducated, poor, outspoken, slightly retarded, eccentric, or odd, he stands a much higher chance of being executed than do those convicted of even worse crimes than he. Juries find it hard to convict one of their own, so middle-class whites are rarely in our ranks. Like those stricken with a terminal illness, I feel a tremendous sense of injustice.

Unlike others preparing to die, empirical studies have been conducted by the best minds in America to show that I am right.

I have been on death row for 14 years and can honestly say that the only description of this place is hell. We send people to prisons to suffer, and prisons have been highly successful in achieving this goal. We live in a society that fosters the belief that inhumanity, revenge, and retribution are legitimate goals of the state. Like those stricken with a terminal illness, I fight my own anger.

Most, if not all, of the humans on death row have souls that can be made clean through love, compassion, and spirituality. However, to acknowledge this threatens our ability to execute, as we must dehumanize before we can kill in such a predetermined fashion. It takes concern and understanding to identify with one of God's own. Didn't Jesus glorify the shepherd who left his whole flock just to rescue one lamb? I believe it is the duty and obligation of all of God's children to save, heal, and repair the spirit, soul, mind, and body of others. When Jesus said, "Love your neighbor," I don't think he was talking about those whom it is easy to love. Like others preparing for death, I need community.

The one thing all humans want and need is to love and be loved. I often sit and just watch the men here. I watch them change. I watch, and I feel great pity for them. I feel shame, too. Shame because many of my Christian brothers and sisters in society allow this to continue in their names.

One of the most profound teachings of Jesus is, "Judge not that ye be not judged." I think that before we can hold up the lamp of understanding to others, we must hold it up to ourselves. That, I believe, is what death is all about.

Willie Jasper Darden, Jr., was sentenced to death in 1974. On March 15, 1982, despite worldwide protest, widespread belief in his innocence, and allegations of prosecutorial racism (including features on ABC's "20/20" and CBS's "West 57th Street"), Mr. Darden was executed.

More Than a Reasonable Doubt

by Colman McCarthy

Amenities in the Virginia State Prison include a cooling room. On the basement level, it is a few yards from the death chamber that holds Virginia's best-functioning piece of judicial furniture, its electric chair. After people are killed–247 since 1908–their bodies are scorchingly hot from taking 2,500 volts of electricity in as many surges as needed. In the cooling room, corpses have their temperatures lowered for handling and shipping.

Into this scene of modern barbarity, a shackled and cuffed Joseph Giarratano was led the other morning for an interview. It was a makeshift arrangement. The prison, a hellhole built before the Civil War and recently closed except for the death chamber, no longer has a functioning visitors' room. The cooling room is all.

Giarratano is the 34-year-old former drug addict scheduled to be electrocuted February 22 for the 1979 apartment-house knifing of Toni Kline of Norfolk, Virginia, and the rape and strangling of her 15-year-old daughter, Michelle.

Few modern death-penalty cases have received as much national and international attention. Coverage has ranged from page one stories in major U.S. dailies to in-depth segments on network television. Giarratano, who came into death row as a semiliterate suicidal loner and loser, has transformed himself into a constitutional scholar who has written successful briefs on behalf of fellow prisoners. His articles have run in disparate forums, from the *Los Angeles Times* op-ed page to the current *Yale Law Review*.

This was my fourth visit with Giarratano in the past 22 months. I'm one of a large and growing number of people who have scrutinized the record of this case–pre- and post-conviction procedures, transcripts, appeals–and concluded that Giarratano is either innocent or deserves a new trial.

Evidence obtained in the past three years that raises doubts, according to Giarratano's lawyer, includes the following: Bloody shoe prints found in the apartment did not match Giarratano's boots, which had no blood on the soles; the stabbing and strangling were done by a right-handed person, while Giarratano is left-handed; hair found on the rape victim did not match Giarratano's; the autopsy report was changed after Giarratano's confession to corroborate the confession. Attempts to introduce this evidence in appeal have been rejected by state and federal courts due to procedural rules.

Giarratano's conviction, after a three-hour trial in which he was represented by an inexperienced court-appointed lawyer, turned on his confessions. Five were given– each inconsistent with the others and each made while in a delusional state. A state psychiatrist has testified that the confessions were made up– "confabulated" –as the result of Giarratano's psychotic mental state.

What's known about the crime is that on February 4, 1979, Giarratano, blacked out from alcohol and drugs, awoke from a living-room sofa to find the two bodies, one bloodied from a slit throat, the other strangled. Assuming that he must have killed the two, Giarratano fled by bus to Florida. There, overcome with guilt and remorse, he turned himself in.

In the cooling room of the state prison, I asked Giarratano the question that most perplexes people who have yet to take sides on the case: If it's so certain that you're innocent or deserving of a new trial, why haven't the courts, after 10 years of considering your well-crafted appeals, said so? He answered: "It isn't that the courts weren't convinced one way or the other, but they're bound by the procedural rules they created. It's a court rule that if the defense attorney didn't make proper objections during the trial, then the error cannot be raised on appeal. The second procedural rule states that any new evidence must be raised within 21 days of the trial's conclusion, otherwise the review is forever barred. Federal courts must defer to state procedural rules. Because of all this, no court has ever ruled on the merits of my case."

Gerald Zerkin, Giarratano's Richmond attorney, says that Virginia has the nation's narrowest and most unresponsive appeal system: "In recent years, our state courts have reviewed about 50 cases in post-conviction appeals and have not overturned one death sentence. Nationally, the overturn rate is more than 40 percent. Instead of its being seen as someone's life is at stake and therefore we need more due process, in Virginia it's the opposite: because we need to kill them, we should give them less due process."

Several thousand letters have come into the office of Virginia Governor L. Douglas Wilder, including two from me and with no courtesy of a reply for either. Wilder, once an opponent of capital punishment but now an advocate, has authority to grant a conditional pardon that would permit a new trial based on new evidence and doubts about Giarratano's guilt. Nationally, 23 innocent people have been executed between 1900 and 1985.

At interview's end, Giarratano said he was hopeful of winning his freedom. Why?, I asked. He told me of meeting Douglas Wilder a few years ago, when the then state senator, outspoken in his opposition to executions, toured death row to publicize his views. "Conditions at the prison were pretty bad," Giarratano recalled, "and Wilder came to the row to see for himself. When he left, he turned to us and said, 'Don't give up hope.'"

Giarratano hasn't. Much of the world now looks on to see if Wilder is concerned with procedures or justice.

from Washington Post, *February 16, 1991*

The animals of the world exist for their own reasons. They were not made for humans any more than black people were made for whites, or women created for men.

Alice Walker

The Ethics of Nonviolent Eating

by Helen Nearing

I wonder of what sort of feeling, mind, or reason, that man was possessed who was first to pollute his mouth with gore, and to allow his lips to touch the flesh of a murdered being; who spread his table with the mangled forms of dead bodies, and claimed as daily food and dainty dishes what but now were beings endowed with movement, with perception, and with voice?

Plutarch, **On the Eating of Flesh**, *70 A.D.*

This book on simple food is vegetarian, of course. It is the simplest, cleanest, easiest way to eat. I take it for granted that to live on plants and fruits, seeds and nuts is the way for rational, kindly and perceptive people to live. By the time mankind has fully advanced from complex back to simple living, flesh will have been dropped from the diet and that cruel costly fare will be left to the carnivores. The readers of this book may be beyond that repulsive custom, but for those who are not, I set down what I consider legitimate arguments for a vegetable diet. However, I realize in advance I shall make little dent upon the general public, long-time confirmed in its savage custom.

The sight of slabs of flesh should horrify and disgust any sensitive person if they exercised their inborn compassion. Habit has dimmed their native kindliness. Their palates have become abnormally corrupted and conditioned by a taste for dead food, its flavoring and odors. People who eat slaughtered creatures every day find it hard to imagine what to substitute for meat, not realizing that meat is the substitute for vegetables.

Nature has provided man with an abundance of food for full nourishment instead of putrefying corpses, which repugnant diet decent folk would abhor if generation upon generation had not, through use and custom, habituated themselves to the ghoulish practice of making their stomachs the burial ground for dead bodies.

The word "vegetarian" derives from the Latin *vegetus*–whole, sound, fresh, lively. The meat humans eat is neither whole, sound, fresh, or lively. It is dis-limbed, tainted, decaying, stale and dead. A diet consisting of green leafy vegetables, root crops, grains, berries, nuts and fruits supplies all the body needs for strength and well-being. It is healthful food, aesthetic, economical, harmless to our brother animals, easy to grow, to prepare and to digest.

Flesh-eating by humans is unnecessary, irrational, anatomically unsound, unhealthy, unhygienic, uneconomic, unaesthetic, unkind and unethical. May I elaborate?

Unnecessary: Meat is not a necessity, but a cultivated want. We need not butcher our fellow creatures for food. Millions of people throughout the world and through the ages have lived their whole lives on plant food and been none the worse; in fact, they have probably been in better health because of their abstemious diet. I had the good sense to be born in a vegetarian family and have lived into my seventies in good health and strength, without meat. Scott became a vegetarian in his mid-thirties and has lived into his nineties, hale and hearty, with plenty of brain and brawn, and without meat. It is obviously not necessary to eat cooked flesh.

A vegetarian friend, Henry Bailey Stevens, wrote some *Rhymes for Meat-Eaters*, from one of which I quote:

*With lentils, tomatoes and rice, olives
and nuts, and bread,
Why does a man care to gnaw a slice of
something bleeding and dead?*

Irrational: The argument is frequently made that if we did not kill and eat animals, the creatures would take over and cover the earth. This is not necessarily so. The process of natural selection would intervene as it does with wild animals. If we stopped breeding and cozening domestic animals, the rate of their population growth would immediately and drastically diminish.

Animals need not be bred; they need not be killed; they need not be eaten. "But it is natural for us to eat animals" is the usual remark—"Animals were made for us." That is hardly logical. Animals were on earth aeons before man. They waited long before their devourers arrived.

I have no doubt that it is a part of the destiny of the human race, in its gradual improvement, to leave off eating animals, as surely as the savage tribes have left off eating each other.He will be regarded as a benefactor of his race who shall teach man to confine himself to a more innocent and wholesome diet.

Henry David Thoreau, **Walden**, 1854

If it were so natural, why not catch and kill your own animal, cut a slice from the carcass or tear a leg off the living beast and eat it "naturally," fresh and whole? You could do that with a fruit or vegetable, but not with your pet cat or dog's quivering flesh. Many who claim to love animals and have them for pets would never kill and eat their own Bunny Boy. But others' pets, other animals' offspring and parents that have been murdered by others, can be put into the stew pot and callously consumed.

Most meat-eaters have a squeamish limit beyond which even they will not go. They will not eat worms, slugs, garden snails (though they are said to be an excellent source of protein), or insects, mice, rats, cats or dogs, horses, or human beings. "The Samoans, who eat dogs, despise eggs and chickens. Similarly, the Qitoto of Brazil, who eat rats, frogs, lizards, snakes and turtles, eat the eggs of reptiles but despise those of birds." Bernard Shaw spoke of meat-eating as "cannibalism with its heroic dish omitted."

And Bronson Alcott remarked to Emerson who was dilating upon the horrors of cannibalism while carving up a roast: "But Mr. Emerson, if we are to eat meat at all, why should we not eat the best?" I would agree, in that I have often thought a baby's chubby arm looks delicious and (if I ate flesh) good enough to munch on.

Anatomically Unsound: Animals (and man is one of them) are structurally and functionally adapted to a particular mode of nutrition. The rabbit, to which a vegetarian is often disparagingly compared, is of the Rodentia order, feeding entirely on vegetable matter. The pig is Omnivora; its diet is closest to the typical human omnivorous diet of today. The domesticated pig is not particular about what it eats. Like millions of contemporary humans, its diet includes practically anything edible, of both animal and vegetable origin.

Physiologically, a fruit and vegetable diet is more in line with the human anatomy. The teeth, the digestive system, the hands, feet and mammary glands of humans resemble the ape family to a great extent.

Primitive humanity was, no doubt, like the anthropoids, mainly frugiverous.
Robert Briffault, **The Mothers**, 1927

The digestive juices of man are not sufficient to tackle what the carnivores eat. The carnivores secrete hydrochloric acid about ten times as strong as that of humans and have a very short intestinal tract so that meat is quickly digested and expelled. Man's digestive tract is three times as long, holds food for two or three days, forming a putrefying mess if on a meat diet.

The structure of the teeth gives an important clue as to the natural food of a species. Flesh-eating animals have tusks and fangs for tearing and gnawing; herbivores and frugivores have smooth teeth for grinding and chewing. Man and gorilla both belong to the frugivora family. Our front teeth are for biting and our back teeth for crushing and pulping; therefore human diet should be similar to that of the apes: raw fruit, raw vegetables, nuts, shoots and sprouts.

Unhealthy: During World War II, Denmark was put on emergency rations and the king called for a meatless program for a year. Denmark established a world record for lowered death rate that year and a marked decrease in the illness rate. Going back to meat-eating the next year sent the death rate back to the pre-war level.

The strongest of animals, the bull, the elephant, the gorilla, the hippopotamus, are all vegetarian. The camel, also a vegetarian, has long endurance records; the horse and deer have speed records.

A farmer says to me, "You cannot live on vegetable food solely, for it furnishes nothing to make bones with"; and so he religiously devotes a part of his day to supplying his system with the raw materials of bones;; walking all the while he talks behind his oxen, which, with vegetable-made bones, jerks him and his lumbering plough in spite of every obstacle.

Henry David Thoreau, **Walden**, 1854

As to the vaunted necessity for protein and the high protein content in animal flesh and animal products to maintain robust health: protein is certainly required in the body for growth and repair, but is there not a maximum as a well as a minimum beyond which one should not go? Too much protein overtaxes the vital organs. The excess must be eliminated as waste or be stored in the muscles, which become hard and inflexible. One might well ask: How little protein does one require, not how much does one need?

There is protein in nuts, beans, peas, lentils, mushrooms, cheese, milk, eggs, wholemeal cereals, and many green vegetables. Practically no common foodstuff is devoid of some protein. Plants manufacture it from the nitrogen of the air. They make the simpler type of protein, but the same amino acids as in meat.

Vegetable protein is the original source of meat protein. Nuts are not a substitute for meat; meat is a substitute for nuts. All fruits average out with about as much protein as in mother's milk. The banana has more protein than mother's milk. Vegetables average out to about 3 percent protein, nuts to 15 percent and seeds about 20 percent.

If one fed adequately on fresh vegetables, fruits, nuts, seeds and sprouts one could do without animal flesh and dairy products and still be above the minimum necessary intake recommended by orthodox nutritionists.

Unhygienic: It is not only healthier but cleaner to eat fresh vegetables and fruits instead of putrefying meat. Animal carcasses are often full of poisons and sicknesses, and of food additives and chemicals that have been used to fatten or soften or preserve the corruptible flesh. These poisons go into the human bodies that consume the dead meat. With a carnivorous diet the human is a tomb for animal disease. Dead animal bodies contain heavy concentrations of toxic wastes, virulent bacteria and are often diseased with tumors, cancers, tuberculosis, swine fever, and other dangers to health.

Most meats available today are virtually saturated with antibiotics, hormones, tranquilizers, pesticides, dyes, deodorants, and radiation. The majority of processed meats contain preservatives, stabilizers, plastic residue, and other harmful substances.

The Mother Earth News, *No.2, "Meat Is No Treat"*

No one knows better than meat inspectors how much disease there is among animals slaughtered for food. A woman attended a banquet and ordered a vegetable plate. At her side sat a stranger who also chose a vegetable plate. "You too are a vegetarian?" she asked him. "No, madam," he replied, "I am a meat inspector."

Uneconomic: Too many thousands of acres of valuable land are being devoted to pasturage or fodder-feed for animals that are fattened to be eaten by man: over half of all agricultural land in the United States. This land could be planted with crops for direct, first-hand feeding to man, a mush quicker and economical way of obtaining food than at secondhand, through animal's bodies. An estimated 40 percent of the world's livestock production is derived from vegetable sources that could be used for human food.

Vegetarianism could go far toward solving the world food problem by eating lower on the food chain. To feed the world's population more adequately and economically, the enormous quantities of grains, pulses and legumes fed to farm stock animals should be drastically curtailed or eliminated entirely.

Unaesthetic Carcasses that are displayed and hung in butcher shops, or slickly plastic-packaged in supermarkets, would shock any fairly sensitive or artistic person who could bring himself to view the sight objectively. Aesthetically, fruits and vegetables are certainly more attractive than cut-up carcasses and ground-up pieces of flesh, raw and red, or roasted or broiled.

I rarely used animal food, not so much because of any ill effects which I had traced to them, as because they were not agreeable to my imagination. The epugnance to animal food is not the effect of the experience, but is an instinct. I believe that every man who has ever been earnest to preserve his higher or poetic faculties in the best condition has been particularly inclined to abstain from animal food.

Henry David Thoreau, **Walden,** *1854*

Unkind: Let's look at meat-eating from the animal's point of view. They have rights not to be infringed on. They love their lives and their families. Wild creatures are hunted and killed cruelly with no compassion. Domestically-bred animals are wrenched from their families, transported callously and carelessly to abattoirs; there, frenzied with fear at the crowding, the mutual cries and the stench, they are pole-axed, hooked on moving belts for final slaughter, their throats cut, their dangling, twisting, agonized bodies slashed and skinned often before all of life is extinct. I know, because I've seen it on two horrifying visits to slaughterhouses in Chicago twenty-five years ago.

We cannot eat flesh without unkindness and violence and cruelty. Fish are dragged from their natural element with ferociously sharp hooks; whales' gigantic bodies are tracked in the sea and mercilessly stabbed until death; seals are murdered with clubs and stripped half-living of their skins; crabs and lobsters are boiled alive.

What about "humane killing" you may ask. How can one be cruel humanely? Killing is killing. It has been estimated that man kills in one day more cattle than carnivorous animals kill in a hundred years. Let me quote words from lofty philosophers on the cruel and gruesome, and human, custom of slaying and eating our fellow creatures.

Unethical: "How could you select such an occupation?" asked a horrified onlooker to a worker in the stockyards of Chicago. "We're only doing your dirty work, sir," was the scornful and silencing reply. Whoever eats the meat without killing the animal himself is having his dirty work done for him.

We are not only killers; we are slave drivers and exploiters; we are food robbers. We rob the bees for honey; we rob the chickens, for eggs; we rob the cows, for milk. Cattle in the wild suckle their calves for 15 months. Domesticated cows are pushed beyond their normal breeding capacity, separated from their calves often at birth and are fooled into giving us milk instead of to the calves. As to wild poultry, most birds lay four or five eggs a year. Factory farming forces birds to lay hundreds.

Milk is food for the infant of its species. Eggs are food for the embryo bird. Neither should be consumed by human adults.

Slavery of animals to man is one thing. Men also exploit themselves and become slaves to animals. Breeders, milkers, shepherds, graziers, farmers, slaughtermen, all involve labor devoted to being valets and nursemaids to animals. The time and care would be better centered on breeding and caring for better human beings.

We humans are privileged animals. We will not be cooked for a cow's dinner or infected with a disease so that a monkey can find out the cause of its illness; or taught to run round and round in a wheel to make a squirrel laugh; or caged and our throats slit to make us sing sweetly for our supper; or locked behind zoo bars as examples of curious human beings, or our breast-milk stolen to give to calves. Nor will our babies be sent to the slaughterhouse and sliced up for someone's dinner.

All diets are relative to the consciences of the eater. One cannot be perfectly consistent in living, but a more or less harmless way of life is possible, and if not as pure as the purest one can at least try to be as gross as the grossest.

So far, eat we must, in order to survive. Therefore we should look to the less sentient forms of life for sustenance. Life is inherent in every food substance that we imbibe, and one has to kill to eat, whether it be an apple, a tomato, or a blade of grass. By what right do we consume these marvels of nature? Plants have an important place on earth. I salute the trees and apologize if I cut one down. I shrink from picking a daisy or a pansy, or biting into an apple or radish. Who am I to take their lives in their prime?

We should widen the range of human feeling until it encompasses all life on earth, doing the most good to the greatest number and the least harm to the least number. Standards and relative degrees of harm and harmlessness will vary with each one of us. Some will continue to eat fish and fowl while eschewing red meat; some will eat nothing that walks or wiggles–still eating dairy products; some will eat no products at all of the animal kingdom–no eggs, milk, cheese or honey. But we can all be constantly aware of the rights of others, be it baby lamb, bison, fly or cauliflower. We can modify our food habits so that we approach the ideal of living on fruits and nuts and seeds which have finished their life cycle and with which the tree or bush or plant is finished.

The time will come in the world's history, and a movement is setting in that direction even now, when it will be deemed as a strange thing to find a man or a woman who eats flesh as food, as it is now to find a man or a woman who refrains from eating it.

Ralph Waldo Twine, **Every Living Creature**, 1899

The time will come when men will look on the murder of animals a we now look on the murder of men.

Leonardo Da Vinci

Man alone consumes and engulfs more flesh than all other animals put together. He is, then, the greatest destroyer, and he is so more by abuse than by necessity.

George Louis Leclerc De Buffon, **L'Histoire Naturelle**, 1749

Our monstrous habit of bringing millions of animals into existence for the purpose of barbarously slaughtering them, roasting their corpses and eating them.

George Bernard Shaw, **On Going to Church**, 1896

The Animal Rights Position

by Tom Regan

The other animals humans eat, use in science, hunt, trap, and exploit in a variety of ways, have a life of their own that is of importance to them apart from their utility to us. They are not only *in* the world, they are *aware* of it. What happens to them *matters* to them. Each has a life that fares better or worse for the one whose life it is.

That life includes a variety of biological, individual, and social needs. The satisfaction of these needs is a source of pleasure, their frustration or abuse, a source of pain. In these fundamental ways the nonhuman animals in labs and on farms, for example, are the same as human beings. And so it is that the ethics of our dealings with them, and with one another, must acknowledge the same fundamental moral principles.

At its deepest level, human ethics is based on the independent value of the individual: The moral worth of any one human being is not to be measured by how useful that person is in advancing the interests of other human beings. To treat human beings in ways that do not honor their independent value is to violate that most basic of human rights: the right of each person to be treated with respect.

The philosophy of animal rights demands only that logic be respected. For any argument that plausibly explains the independent value of human beings implies that other animals have this same value, and have it equally. And any argument that plausibly explains the right of humans to be treated with respect also implies that these other animals have this same right, and have it equally, too.

It is true, therefore, that women do not exist to serve men, blacks to serve whites, the poor to serve the rich, or the weak to serve the strong. The philosophy of animal rights not only accepts these truths, it insists upon and justifies them. But this philosophy goes further. By insisting upon and justifying the independent value and rights of other animals, it gives scientifically informed and morally impartial reasons for denying that these animals exist to serve us.

Once this truth is acknowledged, it is easy to understand why the philosophy of animal rights is uncompromising in its response to each and every injustice other animals are made to suffer. It is not

larger, cleaner cages that justice demands in the case of animals used in science, for example, but empty cages; not "traditional" animal agriculture, but a complete end to all commerce in the flesh of dead animals; not "more humane" hunting and trapping, but the total eradication of these barbarous practices.

For when an injustice is absolute, one must oppose it absolutely. It was not "reformed" slavery that justice demanded, not "reformed" child labor, not "reformed" subjugation of women. In each of these cases, abolition was the only moral answer. Merely to reform absolute injustice is to prolong injustice.

The philosophy of animal rights demands this same answer–abolition–in response to the unjust exploitation of other animals. It is not just the details of unjust exploitation that must be changed. It is the unjust exploitation itself that must be ended, whether on the farm, in the lab, or among the wild, for example. The philosophy of animal rights asks nothing more, but neither will it be satisfied with anything less.

Ten Reasons For Animal Rights

The philosophy of animal rights is rational.

EXPLANATION : It is not rational to discriminate arbitrarily. And discrimination against nonhuman animals is arbitrary. It is wrong to treat weaker human beings, especially those who are lacking in normal human intelligence, as "tools" or "renewable resources" or "models" or "commodities." It cannot be right, therefore, to treat other animals as if they were "tools," "models" and the like, if their psychology is as rich as (or richer than) these humans. To think otherwise is irrational.

The philosophy of animal rights is scientific.

EXPLANATION : The philosophy of animal rights is respectful of our best science in general and evolutionary biology in particular. The latter teaches that in Darwin's words, humans differ from many other animals "in degree, not in kind." Questions of line drawing to one side, it is obvious that the animals used in laboratories, raised for food, and hunted for pleasure or trapped for profit, for example, are our psychological kin. This is not a fantasy, this is fact, proven by our best science.

The philosophy of animal rights is unprejudiced.

EXPLANATION : Racists are people who think that the members of their race are superior to the members of other races simply because the former belong to the ("superior") race. Sexists believe that the members of their sex are superior to the members of the opposite sex simply because the former belong to the ("superior") sex. Both racism and sexism are paradigms of unsupportable bigotry. There is no "superior" or "inferior" sex or race. Racial and sexual differences are biological, not moral, differences.

The same is true of speciesism–the view that the members of the species *Homo Sapiens* are superior to members of every other species simply because human beings belong to one's own (the "superior") species. For there is no "superior" species. To think otherwise is to be no less prejudiced than racists or sexists.

The philosophy of animal rights is just.

EXPLANATION : Justice is the highest principle of ethics. We are not to commit or permit injustice so that good may come, not to violate the rights of the few so that the many might benefit. Slavery allowed this. Child labor allowed this. Most examples of social injustice allow this. But not the philosophy of animal rights, whose highest principle is that of justice: No one has a right to benefit as a result of violating another's rights, whether that "other" is a human being or some other animal.

The philosophy of animal rights is compassionate.

EXPLANATION : A full human life demands feelings of empathy and sympathy–in a word, compassion–for the victims of injustice, whether the victims are humans or other animals. The philosophy of animal rights calls for, and its acceptance fosters the growth of, the virtue of compassion. This philosophy is, in Lincoln's words, "the way of a whole human being."

The philosophy of animal rights is unselfish.

EXPLANATION : The philosophy of animal rights demands a commitment to serve those who are weak and vulnerable–those who, whether they are humans or other animals, lack the ability to speak for or defend themselves, and who are in need of protection against human greed and callousness. This philosophy requires this commitment, not because it is in our self-interest to give it, but because it is right to do so. This philosophy therefore calls for, and its acceptance fosters the growth of, unselfish service.

The philosophy of animal rights is individually fulfilling.

EXPLANATION : All the great traditions in ethics, both secular and religious, emphasize the importance of four things: knowledge, justice, compassion, and autonomy. The philosophy of animal rights is no exception. This philosophy teaches that our choices should be based on knowledge, should be expressive of compassion and justice, and should be freely made. It is not easy to achieve these virtues, or to control the human inclinations toward greed and indifference. But a whole human life is impossible without them. The philosophy of animal rights both calls for, and its acceptance fosters the growth of, individual self-fulfillment.

The philosophy of animal rights is socially progressive.

EXPLANATION : The greatest impediment to the flourishing of human society is the exploitation of other animals at human hands. This is true in the case of unhealthy diets, of the habitual reliance on the "whole animal model" in science, and of the many other forms animal exploitation takes. And it is no less true of education and advertising, for example, which help deaden the human psyche to the demands of reason, impartiality, compassion, and justice. In all these ways (and more), nations remain profoundly backward because they fail to serve the true interests of their citizens.

The philosophy of animal rights is environmentally wise.

EXPLANATION : The major cause of environmental degradation, including the greenhouse effect, water pollution, and the loss both of arable land and top soil, for example, can be traced to the exploitation of animals. This same pattern exists throughout the broad range of environmental problems, from acid rain and ocean dumping of toxic wastes, to air pollution and the destruction of natural habitat. In all these cases, to act to protect the affected animals (who are, after all, the first to suffer and die from these environmental ills), is to act to protect the earth.

The philosophy of animal rights is peace-loving.

EXPLANATION : The fundamental demand of the philosophy of animal rights is to treat humans and other animals with respect. To do this requires that we not harm anyone just so that we ourselves or others might benefit. This philosophy therefore is totally opposed to military aggression. It is a philosophy of peace. But it is a philosophy that extends the demand for peace beyond the boundaries of our species. For there is a war being waged, every day, against countless millions of nonhuman animals. To stand truly for peace is to stand firmly against speciesism. It is wishful thinking to believe that there can be "peace in the world" if we fail to bring peace to our dealings with other animals.

Ten Reasons Against Animal Rights And Their Replies

You are equating animals and humans, when, in fact, humans and animals differ greatly.

REPLY : We are not saying that humans and other animals are equal in every way. For example, we are not saying that dogs and cats can do calculus, or that pigs and cows enjoy poetry. What we are saying is that, like humans, many other animals are psychological beings, with an experiential welfare of their own. In this sense, we and they are the same. In this sense, therefore, despite our many differences, we and they are equal.

You are saying that every human and every other animal has the same rights, which is absurd. Chickens cannot have the right to vote, nor can pigs have a right to higher education.

REPLY : We are not saying that humans and other animals always have the same rights. Not even all human beings have the same rights. For example, people with serious mental disadvantages do not have a right to higher education. What we are saying is that these and other humans share a basic moral right with other animals–namely, the right to be treated with respect.

If animals have rights, then so do vegetables, which is absurd.

REPLY : Many animals are like us: they have a psychological welfare of their own. Like us, therefore, these animals have a right to be treated with respect. On the other hand, we have no reason, and certainly no scientific one, to believe that carrots and tomatoes, for example, bring a psychological presence to the world. Like all other vegetables, carrots and tomatoes lack anything resembling a brain or central nervous system. Because they are deficient in these respects, there is no reason to think of vegetables as psychological beings, with the capacity to experience pleasure and pain, for example. It is for these reasons that one can rationally affirm rights in the case of animals and deny them in the case of vegetables.

Where do you draw the line? If primates and rodents have rights, then so do slugs and amoebas, which is absurd.

REPLY : It is often not easy to know exactly where to "draw the line." For example, we cannot say exactly how old someone must be to be old, or how tall someone must be to be tall. However, we can say, with certainty, that someone who is eighty-eight is old, and that another person who is 7'1" is tall. Similarly, we cannot say exactly where to draw the line when it comes to those animals who have a psychology. But we can say with absolute certainty that, wherever one draws the line on scientific grounds, primates and rodents are on one side of it (the psychological side), whereas slugs and amoebas are on the other–which does not mean that we may destroy them unthinkingly.

But surely there are some animals who can experience pain but lack a unified psychological identity. Since these animals do not have a right to be treated with respect, the philosophy of animal rights implies that we can treat them in any way we choose.

REPLY : It is true that some animals, like shrimp and clams, may be capable of experiencing pain yet lack most other psychological capacities. If this is true, then they will lack some of the rights that other animals possess. However, there can be no moral justification for causing anyone pain, if it is unnecessary to do so. And since it is not necessary that humans eat shrimp, clams , and similar animals, or utilize them in other ways, there can be no moral justification for causing them the pain that invariably accompanies such use.

Animals don't respect our rights. Therefore, humans have no obligation to respect their rights either.

REPLY : There are many situations in which an individual who has rights is unable to respect the rights of others. This is true of infants, young children, and mentally enfeebled and deranged human beings. In their case we do not say that it is perfectly alright to treat them disrespectfully because they do not honor our rights. On the contrary, we recognize that we have a duty to treat them with respect, even though they have no duty to treat us in the same way.

What is true of cases involving infants, children, and thes other humans mentioned, is no less true of cases involving other animals. Granted, these animals do not have a duty to respect our rights. But this does not erase or diminish our obligation to respect their's.

God gave humans dominion over other animals. This is why we can do anything to them that we wish, including eat them.

REPLY : Not all religions represent humans as having "dominion" over other animals, and even among those that do, the notion of "dominion" should be understood as unselfish guardianship, not selfish power. Humans are to be as loving toward all of creation as God was in creating it. If we loved the animals today in the way humans loved them in the Garden of Eden, we would not eat them.

Only humans have immortal souls. This gives us the right to treat the other animals as we wish.

REPLY : Many religions teach that all animals, not just humans, have immortal souls. However, even if only humans are immortal, this would only prove that we live forever whereas other animals do not. And this fact (if it is a fact) would increase, not decrease, our obligation to insure that this—the only life other animals have—be as long and as good as possible.

If we respect the rights of animals, and do not eat or exploit them in other ways, then what are we supposed to do with all of them? In a very short time they will be running through our streets and homes.

REPLY : Somewhere between 4-5 billion animals are raised and slaughtered for food every year, just in the United States. The reason for this astonishingly high number is simple: there are consumers who eat very large amounts of animal flesh. The supply of animals meets the demand of buyers.

When the philosophy of animal rights triumphs, however, and people become vegetarians, we need not fear that there will be billions of cows and pigs grazing in the middle of our cities or in our living rooms. Once the financial incentive for raising billions of these animals evaporates, there simply will not be billions of these animals. And the same reasoning applies in other cases—in the case of animals bred for research, for example. When the philosophy of animal rights prevails, and this use of these animals cease, then the financial incentive for breeding millions of them will cease, too.

Even if other animals do have moral rights and should be protected, there are more important things that need our attention—world hunger and child abuse, for example, apartheid, drugs, violence to women, and the plight of the homeless. After we take care of these problems, then we can worry about animal rights.

REPLY : The animal rights movement stands as part of, not apart from, the human rights movement. The same philosophy that insists upon and defends the rights of nonhuman animals also insists upon and defends the rights of human beings.

At a practical level, moreover, the choice thoughtful people face is not between helping humans or helping other animals. One can do both. People do not need to eat animals in order to help the homeless, for example, any more than they need to use cosmetics that have been tested on animals in order to help children. In fact, people who do respect the rights of nonhuman animals, by not eating them, will be healthier, in which case they actually will be able to help human beings even more.

from The Animal Rights Position, The Philosophy of Animal Rights *Raleigh, NC: Culture and Animals Foundation. Reprinted by permission of the author and the Culture and Animals Foundation.*

Respect for Animals

interview with Isaac Bashevis Singer

Twice a winner of the National Book Award, Isaac Bashevis Singer was awarded the Nobel Prize for Literature in 1978. Singer's enormous popularity and stature in the United States is the more astonishing since his first language—the language in which he thinks and creates—is Yiddish. He once joked that his writing must be 150 percent better than it appears "because you lose 50 percent in the translation." Even though Singer speaks German and Polish and has a good command of English, he prefers to write in Yiddish because he feels that "it has vitamins that other languages haven't got." Consequently, he is the first writer to have received a Nobel Prize who writes in a language for which there is no country.

Singer was born July 14th, 1904, in Radzymin, Poland. Both of his grandfathers were rabbis as was his father. It is difficult to imagine more unfavorable auspices for a young novelist than to be forced into exile from his native land at the age of 31 with a gift of eloquence in a language that was becoming extinct. Had anyone suggested in 1935 (the year of Singer's emigration to America) that a Polish refugee, writing in a language silenced by the Holocaust, would receive the Nobel Prize for Literature in 1978, Isaac Singer would have been the first to laugh.

How long have you been a vegetarian?
I've been a vegetarian for 14 years.

What do you usually eat in the course of a day?
I eat what I like. In the morning I have some skim milk and hardboiled eggs. For lunch I take a sandwich that consists of toast, sliced tomatoes, and cottage cheese. In the evenings, some vegetables. This is more or less how it goes every day.

Have you felt better since you became a vegetarian?
Since I didn't do it to feel better, I never measure it by that. I feel that I'm right. This is the main thing.

I once read that it was Spinoza's notion that man can do as he likes to animals which repelled you from eating meat.
Yes. I don't say that this passage made me a vegetarian, but I felt, when I read it, a great protest. I thought, if we can do to animals whatever we please, why can't another man come with a theory that we can do to human beings what we please? This did not make

me a vegetarian. I was in my mind a vegetarian before—because when I read this I was revolted. And though I love Spinoza and always admired him (and I still do), I did not like this text.

Many of your own stories treat the subject of vegetarianism. Do you use vegetarian leitmotifs intentionally?
I would say that of course I never sit down to write a story with this intention, with a vegetarian tendency or morality. I wouldn't preach. I don't believe in messages. But sometimes if you believe in something, it will come out. Whenever I mention animals, I feel there is a great, great injustice in the fact they are treated the way they are.

I've noticed that you use butchers and slaughtermen to represent evil.
Well, I'm inclined to do so. If a character's a ruffian, I would make him a butcher—although some of them are very nice people.

In the story Blood, was it your intention to show that people who traffic in animal flesh have something rapacious about them?
What I wanted to show was that the desire for blood has an affinity with lust.

In Blood, the female character, Risha, first seduces the ritual slaughterer Reuben, then insists on killing the animals herself. She sets up as a nonkosher butcher, and, as though following a logical progression, finally becomes a...
She becomes a werewolf.

Do humans who eat meat become predators?
In shedding blood there is always an element of lust.

At the beginning of the story, you mentioned that the Cabalists knew that blood and lust are related, and that's why the commandment "Thou shalt not commit adultery" immediately follows the injunction against killing.
Yes, but I feel so myself. There is always an element of sadism in lust and vice versa.

Do you feel that people who eat meat are just as reprehensible as the slaughterer?
The people who eat meat are not conscious of the actual slaughter. Those who do the hunting, the hunters, are, I would say, in the grip of a sexual passion.

Those who eat meat share in the guilt, but since they're not conscious of the actual slaughter, they believe it is a natural thing. I would not want to accuse them of inadvertent slaughter. But they are not brought up to believe in compassion.

I would say that it would be better for humanity to stop eating meat and stop torturing these animals. I always say that if we don't stop treating these animals the way we do, we will never have any rest.

I think other people are bothered by meat-eating too, but they say to themselves: "What can I do?" They're afraid that if they stop eating meat they will die from hunger. I've been a vegetarian for so many years—thank God I'm still alive!

I've also noticed that in The Slaughterer, *you say that the phylacteries...*

...are made of leather, yes. I'm always conscious of it. Even the Torah is made from hide. And I feel that this somehow is wrong.

Then you say, or have the character in The Slaughter *say, "Father in heaven, Thou art a slaughterer!"*

Didn't we just have an earthquake in Turkey where thousands of innocent people died? We don't know His mysteries and motivations. But I sometimes feel like praying to a vegetarian god.

Do you feel that people who eat meat are evil?

Well, I wouldn't go so far. I don't want to say this about all the people who eat meat. There were many saints who ate meat, very many wonderful people. I don't want to say evil things about people who eat meat. I only like to say that I'm against it. My vegetarianism is in fact a kind of protest against the laws of nature, because actually the animals would suffer whether we ate them or not. Whatever the case, I am for vegetarianism.

In previous interviews you have stated that like the Cabalists you feel that this is a fallen world, the worst of possible worlds.

This is what the Cabalists believe. I don't know all the worlds. All I can see is that this world is a terrible world.

Do you think meat-eating contributes to the triumph of evil throughout the world?

To me, it is an evil thing—slaughter is an evil thing.

Do you think the world might be improved if we stopped the slaughter?

I think so. At least we should try. I think, as a rule, a vegetarian is not a murderer, he is not a criminal. I believe that a man who becomes a vegetarian because he has compassion with animals is not going to kill people or be cruel to people. When one becomes a vegetarian it purifies the soul.

In an interview that you gave to Commentary *in the mid-1960s, you mentioned that you were something of a scholar in spiritual matters.*

Scholar? I wouldn't consider myself a scholar.

Well, do you think that animal souls also participate in the spiritual world?

Well, I have no doubt about it. As a matter of fact, I have a great love for animals that don't eat any meat.

Many of the great poets and philosophers of classical antiquity look back with nostalgia on a golden age in which war, murder, and crime were unknown, food was abundant, and everyone was vegetarian. Do you think that if people became vegetarian again they would become better people?

Yes. According to the Bible, it seems that God did not want people to eat meat. And, in many cases where people became very devout, or very pious, they stopped eating meat and drinking wine. Many vegetarians are anti-alcoholic, although I am not.

I think one loses desire for intoxicants when one becomes a vegetarian; it purifies the body.

I think it purifies the soul.

Do you believe in the transmigration of souls?

There's no scientific evidence of it, but I personally am inclined to believe in it. According to the Cabalists, when people sin, they become animals in the next life, sometimes ferocious animals, like tigers and snakes. I wouldn't be surprised if it were true.

Do you believe in the actual manifestations of demons in the physical world?

I believe it—yes. I mean, I don't know what they are. I'm sure that if they exist, they are part of nature; but I feel that there are beings that we haven't yet discovered. Just as we discovered only about two hundred years ago the existence of microbes and bacteria, there is no reason why we shouldn't one day discover some other beings. We do not know everything that goes on around us.

So you think there are malevolent spirits in the world today?

I think there may be such spirits, or astral bodies—I don't know what to call them. Since I've never seen them or contacted them, everything I say is just guesswork. But I feel there may be entities of which we have no inkling. Just the same, they exist and influence our life just as bacteria and microbes did without our knowing it.

Do you think, on the other hand, that there are benevolent spirits?
Yes, I do. There is a great possibility of it.

Do you wear leather and articles of clothing made from animals?
I try not to, but I can never get the kind of shoes that are not, though I'm going to do something about it. What about you? Do you wear leather shoes?

No, I don't wear anything that could cost an animal his life.
Tell me the name of the place where I can get these shoes that you wear.

I can send you the name of a mail order shoe company where you can get them.
Do me a favor and please do.

I shall. There's a mail-order firm in Patterson, New Jersey—The Haband Co.—which makes shoes of nothing but synthetic leather.
They're not to be gotten in stores?

You can get them, if you're willing to make a canvass of all the stores—which be quite time-consuming—and insist upon buying shoes fashioned entirely from man-made materials.
I never wore furs, and I don't want to wear anything made from animals.

I just think that if one is a vegetarian, one should be consistent.
You are absolutely right, 100 percent.

Animals, My Brethren

by Edgar Kupfer-Koberwitz

The following pages were written in the Concentration Camp Dachau, in the midst of all kinds of cruelties. They were furtively scrawled in a hospital barrack where I stayed during my illness, in a time when Death grasped day by day after us, when we lost twelve thousand within four and a half months.

Dear Friend:

You asked me why I do not eat meat and you are wondering at the reasons of my behavior. Perhaps you think I took a vow—some kind of penitence—denying me all the glorious pleasures of eating meat. You remember juicy steaks, succulent fishes, wonderfully tasted sauces, deliciously smoked ham, and thousand wonders prepared out of meat, charming thousands of human palates, certainly you will remember the delicacy of roasted chicken. Now, you see, I am refusing all these pleasures and you think that only penitence, or a solemn vow, a great sacrifice could deny me that manner of enjoying life, induce me to endure a great resignment.

You look astonished, you ask the question: "But why and what for!" And you are wondering that you nearly guessed the very reason. But if I am, now, trying to explain you the very reason in one concise sentence, you will be astonished once more how far your guessing had been from my real motive. Listen to what I have to tell you:

I refuse to eat animals because I cannot nourish myself by the sufferings and by the death of other creatures. I refuse to do so, because I suffered so painfully myself that I can feel the pains of others by recalling my own sufferings.

I feel happy, nobody persecutes me; why should I persecute other beings or cause them to be persecuted?

I feel happy, I am no prisoner, I am free; why should I cause other creatures to be made prisoners and thrown into jail?

I feel happy, nobody harms me; why should I harm other creatures or have them harmed?

I feel happy, nobody wounds me, nobody kills me; why should I wound or kill other creatures or cause them to be wounded or killed for my pleasure and convenience?

Is it not only too natural that I do not inflict on other creatures the same thing which, I hope and fear, will never be inflicted on me! Would it not be most unfair to do such things for no other purpose than for enjoying a trifling physical pleasure at the expense of others' sufferings, others' deaths?

These creatures are smaller and more helpless than I am, but can you imagine a reasonable man of noble feelings who would like to base on such a difference a claim or right to abuse the weakness and the smallness of others? Don't you think that it is just the bigger, the stronger, the superior's duty to protect the weaker creatures instead of persecuting them, instead of killing them? "Noblesse oblige." I want to act in a noble way.

I recall the horrible epoch of inquisition and I am sorry to state that the time of tribunals for heretics has not yet passed by, that day by day, men use to cook in boiling water other creatures which are helplessly given in the hands of their torturers. I am horrified by the idea that such men are civilized people, no rough barbarians, no natives. But in spite of all, they are only primitively civilized, primitively adapted to their cultural environment. The average European, flowing over with highbrow ideas and beautiful speeches, commits all kinds of cruelties, smilingly not because he is compelled to do so, but because he wants to do so. Not because he lacks the faculty to reflect upon and to realize all the dreadful things he is performing. Oh no! Only because he does not want to see the facts. Otherwise he would be troubled and worried in his pleasures.

It is quite natural what people are telling you. How could they do otherwise? I hear them telling about experiences, about utilities, and I know that they consider certain acts related to slaughtering as unavoidable. Perhaps they succeeded to win you over. I guess that from your letter.

Still, considering the necessities only, one might, perhaps, agree with such people. But is there really such a necessity? The thesis may be contested. Perhaps there exists still some kind of necessity for such persons who have not yet developed into fully conscious personalities.

I am not preaching to them. I am writing this letter to you as an already awakened individual who rationally controls his impulses, who feels responsible—internally and externally—of his acts, who knows that our supreme court is sitting in our conscience. There is no appellate jurisdiction against it.

Is there any necessity by which a fully self-conscious man can be induced to slaughter? In the affirmative, each individual may have the courage to do it by his own hands. It is, evidently, a miserable kind of cowardice to pay other people to perform a blood-stained job, from which the normal man refrains in horror and dismay. Such servants are given some farthings for their bloody work, and one buys from them the desired parts of the killed animal—if possible prepared in such a way that it doesn't any more recall the discomfortable circumstances, nor the animal, nor its being killed, nor the bloodshed.

I think that men will be killed and tortured as long as animals are killed and tortured. There will be wars too. Because killing must be trained and perfected on smaller objects, morally and technically.

I see no reason to feel outraged by what others are doing, neither by the great nor by the smaller acts of violence and cruelty. But, I think, it is high time to feel outraged by all the small and great acts of violence and cruelty which we perform ourselves. And because it is much easier to win the smaller battles than the big ones, I think we should try to get over first our trends toward smaller violence and cruelty, to avoid, or better, to overcome them once and for all. Then the day will come when it will be easy for us to fight and to overcome even the large cruelties. But we are still sleeping, all of us, in habitudes and inherited attitudes. They are like a fat, juicy sauce which helps us to swallow our own cruelties without tasting their bitterness.

I have not the intention to point out with my finger at all that, at definite persons and definite situations. I think it is much more my duty to stir up my own conscience in matters, to try to understand other people better, to get less and less selfish. Why should it be impossible then to act lovingly with regard to more important issues?

That is the point: I want to grow up into a better world where higher law grants more happiness, in a new world where this commandment reigns: You Shall Love Each Other.

from Dachau Diaries, 1956

Posthumous Postscript

Edgar Kupfer, born in 1906 in Koberwitz near Breslau, was a pacifist. Imprisoned in 1940 in Dachau, he was blessed either by the gods or by the guards two years later with a clerical job in the concentration camp storeroom. On stolen scraps of paper and with pieces of pencil, he stealthily scribbled a secret diary. For the next three years he buried his writings, an idea no doubt inspired from burying the dead. On April 29, 1945, Dachau was liberated; Edgar Kupfer was freed.

The *Dachau Diaries* too were freed, and published in 1956. By this time Kupfer-Koberwitz had moved to Chicago, where he lived at St. Stephan's, a stone's throw from the Union Stockyards. From his Dachau notes kept prior to and shortly after the liberation, he wrote an essay on vegetarianism subsequently translated into immigrant English. A carbon copy of the original 38-page typescript from which the following pages are excerpted, along with the four boxes containing the original *Dachau Diaries*, are now preserved in the Special Collection of the Library of the University of Chicago, ironically the same university which formerly housed the Research Laboratories of the American Meat Institute.

As far as can be determined, this marks the first publication in a book of even these few passages selected from the whole diary, either in German or in English. Special thanks is due to the librarians of the Special Collection, without whose help both the manuscript and the shroud surrounding it would never have been known. Permission to publish these segments was sought from all those involved in the donation of "Animals, My Brethren" to the University. But alas, they have died, or have been forgotten by others, or have themselves forgotten.

A Vegetarian Sourcebook

by Keith Akers

Animals do not want to be killed, of course, but in addition to being killed, they suffer a great deal of pain in the process of being turned into food. Of course, their slaughter itself causes a certain amount of pain (more or less, depending on the method of slaughter used). But the process by which the animals are raised in Western societies also causes suffering. Indeed, given the suffering of many animals' day-to-day life, slaughter itself is practically an act of mercy.

In most Western countries, animals are raised on "factory farms." The treatment animals receive in them is solely connected with price. While it is not necessary to be cruel to animals prior to their slaughter, it does save money.

There is no disagreement about the basic facts concerning the ways animals are treated on these factory farms. The nature and types of pain endured by animals in the process of being raised on such farms have been detailed frequently before, most notably in Peter Singer's *Animal Liberation*. I will spare the reader too many of the grisly details, but will indicate the broad outlines of the issue Singer treats so well in his book.

Crowding is the worst problem. Indeed, it is the main cause of the high mortality rate among many factory farm animals. Chickens typically lose 10 percent or 15 percent of their population before they ever get to the slaughterhouse. Veal calves suffer a 10 percent mortality in their brief 15 weeks of confinement. It makes more economic sense to crowd the animals together and increase mortality than to pay the money necessary to maintain all of the animals in more humane conditions.

Chickens are probably the most abused animals. Near the end of its 8- or 9-week life, a chicken may have no more space than a sheet of notebook paper to stand on. Laying hens are crowded into cages so small that none can so much as stretch its wings. This inevitably leads to feather-pecking and cannibalism—the chickens attack and even eat each other. Obviously, such chickens are under a great deal of stress.

The manufacturer's response to this is de-beaking—cutting off most or all of the chicken's beak. Of course, this causes severe pain in the chickens, but prevents the cannibalism.

A similar problem arises when pigs are kept in confinement systems. Pigs, under the stress of the factory farm system, bite each other's tails. The solution, of course, is tail-docking, whereby the tail is largely removed.

About 75 percent of all cattle in the industrialized countries spend the last months of their lives in feed-lots, where they are fattened for slaughter. Cattle usually have at least some degree of freedom for the first months of their lives, veal calves being the exception. Veal calves are kept in very small stalls, prevented even from turning around, and kept deliberately anemic. They are denied any roughage or iron. The purpose of this is solely to keep the flesh pale-looking. It has no effect of the nutritional value of the meat (except perhaps to make it less nutritious); it does not even alter the taste. The only effect this cruel diet has is to produce a pale-colored flesh.

Transportation of animals is frequently another traumatic event in the life of any animal destined for slaughter. Cattle may spend one or two days in a truck without any food, water, or heat—which can be terrifying, and even deadly, in winter time. It is not unusual for cattle to lose 9 percent of their body weight while being transported. About 24 hours or so before slaughter, all the animal's food and water is cut off—there is no point in feeding an animal food which won't be digested before it is killed.

The act of slaughter is not necessarily painful. In many slaughterhouses in the United States, animals must be stunned before having their throats slit. After being rendered unconscious, they are bled to death. The animals must experience awful terror in the minutes or hours before they are killed, smelling the blood of those who have gone before. But the moment of death itself need not be painful at all. Unfortunately, not all slaughterhouses utilize such stunning devices. It is probable, in such cases, that an animal bleeds to death while fully conscious.

The fact of death is almost impossible to minimize in most systems which produce animals for food. In our culture, the use of animals for food in any way usually means putting the animals to death. Even dairy cows and laying hens are likely to wind up in someone's soup once they cease producing. Efficient production of milk, eggs, or meat for humans invariably entails substantial suffering for the animals and—sooner or later—death.

The ugly reality of modern factory farms is an open book, and for this reason I have not gone into detail. Peter Singer's comments are worth quoting at this point:

"Killing an animal is in itself a troubling act. It has been said that if we had to kill our own meat we would all be vegetarians. There may be exceptions to that general rule, but it is true that most people prefer not to inquire into the killing of the animals they eat. Yet those who, by their purchases, require animals to be killed have no right to be shielded from this or any other aspect of the production of the meat they buy. If it is distasteful for humans to think about, what can it be like for the animals to experience it?"

Ethical Significance of these Facts

Among vegetarians there is certainly no consensus on what ethical system, philosophy, or religion one ought to have. Most ethical vegetarians, though, agree on these two points:

• Animals suffer real pain at the hands of meat producers, both from their horrible living conditions and, in some cases, from the way they are slaughtered; and in no case do animals want to die.
• Animals are our fellow creatures and are entitled to at least some of the same considerations that we extend to other (human) fellow creatures; specifically, not to suffer or be killed unnecessarily.

Very few have seriously attacked the first view, that animals suffer real pain or have real feelings. Some have questioned whether animals suffer quite as much pain as humans do, perhaps because animals (allegedly) cannot foresee events in the same way that humans do. Only one major philosopher, Descartes, is said to have held the extreme view that animals have no feelings whatsoever—that they are automatons.

The second issue though, whether animals are our fellow creatures, entitled to the same considerations that we accord other human beings or even pets, is less obvious. This issue requires a more thorough examination.

Are Animals Our Fellow Creatures?

Most people recognize a set of living beings whom they acknowledge to be entitled to a certain amount of consideration of their part. The inhibitions against killing or mistreating one's own family or near relations may very well have a biological basis. Most human beings extend the idea of a "fellow creature" to other humans of their own race or nationality and often to all humans anywhere. The most logical ethical vegetarian position is that this idea should be extended to include animals as well as humans.

Animals are like us in many ways. They have the senses of sight, taste, touch, smell, and hearing. They can communicate, though usually on a more rudimentary level than humans. They experience many of the same emotions that humans do, such as fear or excitement. So why shouldn't animals be considered our fellow creatures?

There are three frequently heard attacks on the idea that animals are our fellow creatures. These kinds of attacks can be summarized as follows:

• Killing for food is natural: "Animals kill other animals. Lions kill zebras, and spiders kill flies. Killing for food is part of nature; it can't be wrong for us to do something which is natural."

• Animals are significantly different from people, so it's all right to kill animals: "We can only have equal considerations for those who are our equals. Animals are not our equals; they are weaker than we are, and they are not rational. Therefore they are not our fellow creatures, and it can't be wrong to eat them."

• To abstain from killing is absurd: "Plants are living creatures too. Perhaps plants have feelings. If one objects to killing, logically one ought to object to eating all living creatures, and thus ought not to eat plants either."

Let us examine these arguments one by one.

Is Killing for Food Natural?

The first argument, perhaps the most sophisticated, concedes that animals may be in some sense our fellow creatures and that animals suffer real pain. But because of the dictates of nature, it is sometimes all right to kill and eat our fellow creatures; or alternatively, it is all right to eat those of our fellow creatures which, as a species, are naturally food for us.

This is quite an admirable argument. It explains practically everything; why we do not eat each other, except under conditions of unusual stress; why we may kill certain other animals (they are in the order of nature, food for us); even why we should be kind to pets and try to help miscellaneous wildlife (they are not naturally our food). There are some problems with the idea that an order of nature determines which species are food for us, but an order against eating certain species may vary from culture to culture.

The main problem with this argument is that it does not justify the practice of meat-eating or animal husbandry as we know it today; it justifies *hunting*. The distinction between hunting and animal husbandry probably seems rather fine to the man in the street, or even to your typical rule-utilitarian moral philosopher. The distinction, however, is obvious to an ecologist. If one defends killing on the grounds that it occurs in nature, then one is defending the practice as it occurs in nature.

When one species of animal preys on another in nature, it only preys on a very small proportion of the total species population. Obviously, the predator species relies on its prey for its continued survival. Therefore, to wipe the prey species out through overhunting would be fatal. In practice, members of such predator species rely on such strategies as territoriality to restrict overhunting, and to insure the continued existence of its food supply.

Moreover, only the weakest members of the prey species are the predator's victims: the feeble, the sick, the lame, or the young accidentally separated from the fold. The life of the typical zebra is usually placid, even in lion country. This kind of violence is the exception in nature, not the rule.

As it exists in the wild, hunting is the preying upon of isolated members of an animal herd. Animal husbandry is the nearly complete annihilation of an animal herd. In nature, this kind of slaughter does not exist. The philosopher is free to argue that there is no moral difference between hunting and the slaughter, but he cannot invoke nature as a defense of this idea.

Why are hunters, not butchers, most frequently taken to task by the larger community for their killing of animals? Hunters usually react to such criticism by replying that if hunting is wrong, then meat-eating must be wrong as well. The hunter is certainly right on one point—the larger community is hypocritical to object to hunting when it consumes the flesh of domesticated animals. If any form of meat-eating is justified, it would be meat from hunted animals.

Is hunting wrong? A vegetarian could reply that killing is always wrong and that animals have a right to live. This would seem to have the odd consequence that it is not only wrong for humans to kill, but that it is wrong for lions to kill zebras, spiders to catch flies, and so on. If animals have a right not to be killed, then they would seem to have a right not to be killed by any species, human or nonhuman.

There are two ways of replying to such an apparent paradox:

—to draw a distinction between necessary and unnecessary killing. Humans have an alternative: they do not have to eat meat. A tiger or a wolf, on the other hand, knows no other way. Killing can be justified only if it necessary, and for humans it is not.

—to accept the challenge, and to agree that the most desirable state of the world is one, in which all killing, even between nonhumans animals, has ceased. Such a world would, perhaps, be like that envisioned by Isaiah in which the wolf would lie down with the lamb....After humans become vegetarians, we can start to work on the wolves.

Are Animals Different from People?

The second argument justifying meat consumption is usually expressed as a sort of reverse social contract theory. Animals are different from people; there is an unbridgeable gulf between humans and animals which relieves us of the responsibility of treating animals in the same way that we would treat humans.

David Hume argues that because of our great superiority to animals, we cannot regard them as deserving of any kind of justice: "Our intercourse with them could be called society, which supposes a degree of equality, but absolute command on the one side, and servile obedience on the other. Whatever we covet, they must instantly resign: Our permission is the only tenure, by which they hold their possessions....This is plainly the situation of men, with regard to animals."

Society and justice, for Hume, presuppose equality. The problem with this theory is that it justifies too much. Hume himself admits in the next paragraph that civilized Europeans have sometimes, due to their "great superiority", thrown off all restraints of justice in dealing with "barbarous Indians" and that men, in some societies, have reduced women to a similar slavery. Thus, Hume's arguments appear to justify not only colonialism and sexual discrimination, but probably also racism, infanticide, and basically anything one can get away with.

Thomas Aquinas provides a different version of the unbridgeable gulf theory. This time it is the human possession of reason, rather than superior force, that makes us so different from animals. Aquinas states that we have no obligations to animals because we can only have obligations to those with whom we can have fellowship. Animals, not being rational, cannot share in our fellowship. Thus, we do not have any duties of charity to animals.

There are two possible responses to this: that the ability to feel, not the ability to reason, is what is ethically relevant; or that animals are not all that different from humans, being more rational than is commonly supposed.

Both of these objections are expressed briefly and succinctly by Jeremy Bentham: "A full-grown horse or dog is beyond comparison a more rational, as well as a more conversable animal, than an infant of a day, or a week, or even a month old. But suppose the case were otherwise, what would it avail? The question is not, 'Can they reason?', nor, 'Can they talk?', but 'Can they suffer?'"

The problem is that none of the differences between humans and animals seem to be ethically significant. Animals are just as intelligent and communicative as small children or even some mentally defective humans. If we do not eat small children and mentally defective humans, then what basis do we have for eating animals? Animals certainly have feelings, and are aware of their environment in many significant ways. So while animals may not have all the same qualities that humans do, there would seem to be no basis for totally excluding them from our consideration.

Equal Rights for Plants?

A third argument seeks to reduce ethical vegetarianism to absurdity. If vegetarians object to killing living creatures (it is argued), then logically they should object to killing plants and insects as well as animals. But this is absurd. Therefore, it can't be wrong to kill animals.

Fruitarians take the argument concerning plants quite seriously: they do not eat any food which causes injury or death to either animals or plants. This means, in their view, a diet of those fruits, nuts, and seeds which can be eaten without the destruction of the plant that bears their food. Finding an ethically significant line between plants and animals, though, is not particularly difficult. Plants have no evolutionary need to feel pain, and completely lack a central nervous system. Nature does not create pain gratuitously but only when it enables the organism to survive. Animals, being mobile, would benefit from having a sense of pain. Plants would not.

Even if one does not want to become a fruitarian and believes that plants have feelings (against all evidence to the contrary), it does not follow that vegetarianism is absurd. We ought to destroy as few plants as possible. And by raising and eating an animal for food, many more plants are destroyed indirectly by the animal we eat than if we merely ate the plants directly.

What about insects? While there may be reason to kill insects, there is no reason to kill them for food. One distinguishes between the way meat animals are killed for food and the way insects are killed. Insects are killed only when they intrude upon human territory, posing a threat to the comfort, health, or well-being of humans. There is a difference between ridding oneself of intruders and going out of one's way to find and kill something which would otherwise be harmless.

These questions may have a certain fascination for philosophers, but most vegetarians are not bothered by them. For any vegetarian who is not a biological pacifist, there would not seem to be any particular difficulty in distinguishing ethically between insects and plants on the one hand, and animals and humans on the other.

from Putnum Books

"Terrorists" For Animal Rights

by Colman McCarthy

Police at the United States Capitol put the nation at risk last Sunday. They allowed an estimated 24,000 terrorists to gather for an afternoon rally on the west lawn of the Capitol. The group was an international assembly of citizens working for animal rights, labeled "terrorists" three days before by Louis Sullivan, secretary of health and human services.

Sullivan, a physician who argues with a broadax more that a scalpel, said the "animal right terrorists" coming to the rally were "on the wrong side of morality." On the right side, Sullivan places—besides himself— medical researchers whose lethal experiments on hundreds of millions of animals have been carried out, until lately, with few constraints beyond amiable peer review, if that.

Sullivan's smear is part of an emerging counteroffensive being waged by those agencies or businesses whose grants and profits are animal-based. The secretary mouthed publicly what many re-searchers in lab coats have been grumbling among themselves for some time: animal right advocates are anti-science fanatics, while we are selfless pursuers of human advancement.

On hand for Sullivan's terrorism speech were several appreciative research organizations as well as some nonmedical slaughterers and tormentors of animals who also see themselves toiling away on behalf of humankind: the American Meat Institute, the National Cattlemen's Association, the National Pork Producers Council, the National Turkey Federation, and the National Broiler Council. A worry arises: If organized protests have lowered fur sales, can meat be next?

In medical research alone, large numbers are involved. The Department of Agriculture reported in 1988 that 140,471 dogs, 42,271 cats, 51,641 primates, 431,457 guinea pigs, 331,945 hamsters, 459,254 rabbits and 178,249 "wild animals" were used experimentally. That figure of 1.6 million animals, which excludes mice and rats, is an annual toll, a small fraction of the estimated 10 million creatures killed daily for food in the United States.

Until the 1970s both commercialists and medical researchers killing animals had little reason to be on the defensive. Meat was not only macho but was promoted as necessary for health, and the only people alarmed at animal experimentation were a few antivivisectionists, usually in England.

The 1970s and '80s saw a flow of books and articles on factory farming, a surge of animal rights and vegetarian magazines, and new animal welfare legislation to protect creatures from carriage horses in Central Park to parrots imported from Central America. In 1980 People for the Ethical Treatment of Animals had a membership of six. Now it's 300,000. In the same decade, the Humane Society of the United States grew from 160,000 to 963,000 members.

Sullivan's labeling these citizens "terrorists" on the "wrong side of morality" is a squeal of panic desperation. If he had more concern for the health of the public than for the health of the medical research and meat industries, he would have skipped the polarizing invective. On animal testing, Sullivan may share the prevailing research opinion that human beings can ethically subject animals to pain that would never be sanctioned for people. But why isn't he raising questions on either the practicality or effectiveness of animal testing? Was it medically necessary for the U.S. Army to pay $2.1 million to Louisiana State University to shoot 700 cats in the head to learn that the animals had post-trauma breathing problems? Was it medically effective to force primates to inhale tobacco smoke to learn that it caused lung cancer?

These are the equivalents of the Pentagon needing $600 toilet seats to defend the free world. University and medical researchers have been as artful as military contractors in enriching themselves with grants to discover the miracle vaccine always just one more animal experiment away. Or two more. Or three more.

The barbarity of using animals in painful tests aside, which is where Sullivan and friends prefer it, the objection of People for the Ethical Treatment of Animals stands: "Despite decades of animal research, no one has been cured of heart disease, multiple sclerosis, spina bifida, muscular dystrophy, diabetes, or cancer of the colon, breast, or uterus." Clean drinking water, food, and already available medicine can prevent nearly all the 60,000 disease-induced deaths that Oxfam reports are occurring daily in the Third World.

Louis Sullivan can keep on with his axings, but too

many citizens are being educated on both the ethics and uselessness of killing animals for human benefit, greed, or pleasure. Changes, brought on by animal rights advocates, have come without commercial devastations. Revlon, Avon, and Mary Kay have recently stopped animal testing. Each had been routinely inflicting their chemicals on animals. Revlon now advertises its products as "cruelty-free."

It was terrorism, all right, behind this conversion-the fearful terror of losing money. Revlon lives. So do some animals.

from Washington Post, *June 16, 1990*

He had grown up in a country run by politicians who sent the pilots to man the bombers to kill the babies to make the world safe for children to grow up in.

Ursula LeGuin

The Art of Loving

by Erich Fromm

Is love an art? Then it requires knowledge and effort. Or is love a pleasant sensation, which to experience is a matter of chance, something one "falls into" if one is lucky? This little book is based on the former premise, while undoubtedly the majority of people today believe in the latter.

Not that people think that love is not important. They are starved for it; they watch endless numbers of films about happy and unhappy love stories, they listen to hundreds of trashy songs about love – yet hardly anyone thinks that there is anything that needs to be learned about love.

This peculiar attitude is based on several premises which either singly or combined tend to uphold it. Most people see the problem of love primarily as that of being loved, rather than that of loving, of one's capacity to love. Hence, the problem to them is how to be loved, how to be lovable. In pursuit of this aim, they follow several paths. One, which is especially used by men, is to be successful, to be as powerful and rich as the social margin of one's position permits. Another, used especially by women, is to make oneself attractive, by cultivating one's body, dress, etc. Other ways of making oneself attractive, used both by men and women, are to develop pleasant manners, interesting conversation, to be helpful, modest, and inoffensive. Many of the ways to make oneself lovable are the same as those used to make oneself successful, "to win friends and influence people." As a matter of fact, what most people in our culture mean by being lovable is essentially a mixture between being popular and having sex appeal.

If two people who have been strangers, as all of us are, suddenly let the wall between them break down and feel close, feel one, this moment of oneness is one of the most exhilarating, most exciting experiences in life. It is all the more wonderful and miraculous for persons who have been shut off, isolated, without love. This miracle of sudden intimacy is often facilitated if it is combined with, or initiated by, sexual attraction and consummation. However, this type of love is, by its very nature, not lasting. The two persons become well-acquainted, their intimacy loses more and more of its miraculous character, until their antagonism, their disappointments, their mutual boredom kill whatever is left of the initial excitement. Yet, in the beginning, they do not know all this: in fact, they take the intensity of the infatuation, this being "crazy" about each other, for proof of the intensity of their love, while it may only prove the degree of their preceding loneliness.

This attitude – that nothing is easier than to love – has continued to be the prevalent idea about love in spite of the overwhelming evidence to the contrary. There is hardly any activity, any enterprise, which is started with such tremendous hopes and expectations and, yet, which fails so regularly, as love. If this were the case with any other activity, people would be eager to know the reasons for the failure and to learn how one could do better – or they would give up the activity. Since the latter is impossible in the case of love, there seems to be only one adequate way to overcome the failure of love – to examine the reasons for this failure and to proceed to study the meaning of love.

The first step to take is to become aware that love is an art, just as living is an art; if we want to learn how to love, we must proceed in the same way we have to proceed if we want to learn any other art, say music, painting, carpentry, or the art of medicine or engineering.

What are the necessary steps in learning any art?

The process of learning an art can be divided conveniently into two parts: one, the mastery of the theory; the other, the mastery of the practice. If I want to learn the art of medicine, I must first know the facts about the human body and about various diseases. When I have all this theoretical knowledge, I am by no means competent in the art of medicine. I shall become a master in this art only after a great deal of practice, until, eventually, the results of my theoretical knowledge and the results of my practice are blended into one – my intuition, the essence of the mastery of any art. But, aside from learning the theory and practice, there is a third factor necessary to becoming a master in any art – the mastery of the art must be a matter of ultimate concern; there must be nothing else in the world more important than the art. This holds true for music, for medicine, for carpentry – and for love. And, maybe, here lies the answer to the question of why people in our culture try so rarely to learn this art, in spite of their obvious failures; in spite of the deep-seated craving for love, almost everything else is considered to be more important than love: success, prestige, money, power – almost all our energy is used for the learning of how to achieve these aims, and almost none to learn the art of loving.

Could it be that only those things are considered worthy of being learned with which one can earn money or prestige, and that love, which "only" profits the soul, but is profitless in the modern sense, is a luxury we have no right to spend much energy on? However true this may be, the following discussion will treat the art of loving in the sense of the foregoing divisions: First, I shall discuss the theory of love – and this will comprise the greater part of the book; and, secondly, I shall discuss the practice of love.

Love is an activity, not a passive affect; it is a "standing in," not a "falling for." In the most general way, the active character of love can be described by stating that love is primarily giving, not receiving.

What is giving? Simple as the answer to this question seems to be, it is actually full of ambiguities and complexities. The most widespread misunderstanding is that which assumes that giving is "giving up" something, being deprived of, sacrificing. The person whose character has not developed beyond the stage of the receptive, exploitative, or hoarding orientation, experiences the act of giving in this way. The marketing character is willing to give, but only in exchange for receiving; giving without receiving for him is being cheated. People whose main orientation is a nonproductive one feel giving as an impoverishment. Most individuals of this type therefore refuse to give. Some make a virtue out of giving in the sense of a sacrifice. They feel that just because it is painful to give, one should give; the virtue of giving to them lies in the very act of acceptance of the sacrifice. For them, the norm that it is better to give than to receive means that it is better to suffer deprivation than to experience joy.

For the productive character, giving has an entirely different meaning. Giving is the mightiest expression of potency. In the very act of giving, I experience my strength, my wealth, my power. This experience of heightened vitality and potency fills me with joy. I experience myself as overflowing, spending, alive, hence as joyous. Giving is more joyous than receiving, not because it is a deprivation, but because in the act of giving lies the expression of my aliveness.

It is not difficult to recognize the validity of this principle by applying it to various specific phenomena. The most elementary example lies in the sphere of sex. The culmination of the male sexual function lies in the act of giving; the man gives himself, his sexual organ, to the woman. At the moment of orgasm, he gives his semen to her. He cannot help giving it if he is potent. If he cannot give, he is impotent. For the woman, the process is not different although somewhat more complex. She gives herself too; she opens the gates to her feminine center; in the act of receiving, she gives. If she is incapable of this act of giving, if she can only receive, she is frigid. With her, the act of giving occurs again, not in her function as a lover, but in that as a mother. She gives of herself to the growing child within her, she gives her milk to the infant, she gives her bodily warmth. Not to give would be painful.

In the sphere of material things, giving means being rich. Not he who has much is rich, but he who gives much. The hoarder who is anxiously worried about losing something is, psychologically speaking, the poor, impoverished man, regardless of how much he has. Whoever is capable of giving of himself is rich. He experiences himself as one who can confer of himself to others. Only one who is deprived of all that goes beyond the barest necessities for subsistence would be incapable of enjoying the act of giving material things. But daily experience shows that what a person considers the minimal necessities depends as much on his character as it depends on his actual possessions. It is well-known that the poor are more willing to give than the rich. Nevertheless, poverty beyond a certain point may make it impossible to give, and is so degrading, not only because of the suffering it causes directly, but because of the fact that it deprives the poor of the joy of giving.

The most important sphere of giving, however, is not that of material things, but lies in the specifically human realm. What does one person give to another? He gives of himself, of the most precious he has, he gives of his life. This does not necessarily mean that he sacrifices his life for the other – but that he gives him of that which is alive in him; he gives him of his joy, of his interest, of his understanding, of his knowledge, of his humor, of his sadness – of all expressions and manifestations of that which is alive in him. In thus giving of his life, he enriches the other person, he enhances the other's sense of aliveness by enhancing his own sense of aliveness. He does not give in order to receive; giving is in itself exquisite joy. But, in giving, he cannot help bringing something to life in the other person, and this which is brought to life reflects back to him; in truly giving, he cannot help receiving that which is given back to him. Giving implies to make the other person a giver also and they both share in the joys of what they have brought to life. In the act of giving, something is born, and both persons involved are grateful for the life that is born for both of them. Specifically with regard to love, this means: love is a power which produces love; impotence is the inability to produce love. This thought has been beautifully expressed by Marx: "Assume," he says, "man as man, and his relation to the world as a human one, and you can exchange love only for love, confidence for confidence, etc. If you wish to enjoy art, you must be an artistically-trained person; if you wish to have influence on other people, you must be a person who has a really stimulating and furthering influence on other people. Every one of your relationships to man and to nature must be a definite expression of your real, individual life corresponding to the object of your will. If you love without calling forth love, that is, if your love as such does not produce love, if by means of an expression of life as a loving person you do not make of yourself a loved person, then your love is impotent, a misfortune." But not only in love does giving mean receiving. The teacher is taught by his students, the actor is stimulated by his audience, the psychoanalyst is cured by his patient – provided they do not treat each other as objects, but are related to each other genuinely and productively.

It is hardly necessary to stress the fact that the ability to love as an act of giving depends on the character development of the person. It presupposes the attainment of a predominantly productive orientation; in this orientation, the person has overcome dependency, narcissistic omnipotence, the wish to exploit others, or to hoard, and has acquired faith in his own human powers, courage to rely on his powers in the attainment of his goals. To the degree that these qualities are lacking, he is afraid of giving himself – hence of loving.

According to what I said about the nature of love, the main conditions for this achievement of love is the overcoming of one's narcissism. The narcissistic orientation is one in which one experiences as real only that which exists within oneself, while the phenomena in the outside world have no reality in themselves, but are experienced only from the viewpoint of their being useful or dangerous to one. The opposite pole to narcissism is objectivity; it is the faculty to see people and things as they are, objectively, and to be able to separate this objective picture from a picture which is formed by one's desires and fears. All forms of psychosis show the inability to be objective, to an extreme degree. For the insane person, the only reality that exists is that within him, that of his fears and desires. He sees the world outside as symbols of his inner world, as his creation. All of us do the same when we dream. In the dream, we produce events, we stage dramas, which are the expression of our wishes and fears (although some-

times also of our insights and judgment) and, while we are asleep, we are convinced that the product of our dreams is as real as the reality which we perceive in our waking state.

Less extreme - or perhaps only less obvious - are the distortions which are commonplace in interpersonal relations. How many parents experience the child's reactions in terms of his being obedient, of giving them pleasure, of being a credit to them and so forth, instead of perceiving or even being interested in what the child feels for and by himself? How many husbands have a picture of their wives as being domineering, because their own attachment to mother makes them interpret any demand as a restriction of their freedom? How many wives think their husbands are ineffective or stupid because they do not live up to a fantasy picture of a shining knight which they might have built up as children?

The lack of objectivity, as far as foreign nations are concerned, is notorious. From one day to another, another nation is made out to be utterly depraved and fiendish, while one's own nation stands for everything that is good and noble. Every action of the enemy is judged by one standard – every action of oneself by another. Even good deeds by the enemy are considered a sign of particular devilishness, meant to deceive us and the world, while our bad deeds are necessary and justified by our noble goals which they serve. Indeed, if one examines the relationship between nations, as well as between individuals, one comes to the conclusion that objectivity is the exception, and a greater or lesser degree of narcissistic distortion is the rule.

To have acquired the capacity for objectivity and reason is half the road to achieving the art of loving, but it must be acquired with regard to everybody with whom one comes in contact. If someone would want to reserve his objectivity for the loved person, and thinks he can dispense with it in his relationship to the rest of the world, he will soon discover that he fails both here and there.

The ability to love depends on one's capacity to emerge from narcissism and from the incestuous fixation to mother and clan; it depends on our capacity to grow, to develop a productive orientation in our relationship toward the world and ourselves. This process of emergence, of birth, of waking up, requires one quality as a necessary condition: faith. The practice of the art of loving requires the practice of faith.

What is faith? Is faith necessarily a matter of belief in God, or in religious doctrines? Is faith by necessity in contrast to, or divorced from, reason and rational thinking? Even to begin to understand the problem of faith one must differentiate between rational and irrational faith. By irrational faith, I understand the belief (in a person or an idea) which is based on one's submission to irrational authority. In contrast, rational faith is a conviction which is rooted in one's own experience of thought or feeling. Rational faith is not primarily belief in something, but the quality of certainty and firmness which our convictions have. Faith is a character trait pervading the whole personality, rather a specific belief.

Some Men Are More Perfect Than Others

by Merle Shain

Our times are obsessed with finding fulfillment, so there are times when some people try too hard, and there are people who want to have the newest feelings just as there are those who want to have the latest model car. You can't play at love any more than you can be proud of your humility, or add water to your perfume and have it smell the same, but men and women both have been known to try.

Love is an infusion of intense feeling, a fine madness that makes you drunk, and when one is in love, life can be a succession of freefalls while working without a net. Love permits the lover to savor rare emotions and dangerous sensations and, because one is never so alive as when one is in love, and never so full of power, there are people hooked on love who wouldn't consider taking drugs.

The energy that runs from lover to lover is an electromagnetic ray that pierces through insensate anesthetized layers, expanding one's perimeters and making one young. Once wounded by love, we are open, so all our defenses escape, making it possible for us to see ourselves. And although that makes us terribly and gloriously vulnerable, it breaks our spirit's fast.

When you fall in love, you feel wiser than others, and larger than life, and the things that happen when you are in love seem too important to be measured by ordinary standards, so lovers often risk everything on an emotional longshot that outsiders are sure can't pay off. The person you can't live without often is one you couldn't live with either, and because it is just as true that reality is what you believe it to be, sometimes a person who wants to believe his beloved beautiful and courageous causes them to be so by believing, making wishes fact.

Love often has more to do with the lover than it has to do with the beloved, and because it does, there are people who prefer to fall in love with someone they hardly know. It can be more exciting to bounce love off an object than to deal with the reality of another whole human being. A fantasy lover has a mystery that can be fleshed out with your own creativity, and you can make it do what you want it to, when you want it to, which isn't true of most real loves, at least not the ones I've known.

There is loving, of course, and being in love, and they are different again which is why one will accept qualities in a lover one wouldn't accept in a spouse. Day-to-day contact has a way of causing the intensity of romantic love to dissipate and sometimes when you get the somebody you have yearned for, most of the magic vanishes with the pain. It's easy to want what you don't have, when you don't have it, and hard not to want something else when you do, so the big love in a lot of lives is the one that got away.

Perhaps the most important thing in any relationship is keeping the lines of communication open. Though this sounds simple, it can be difficult at the pace of life most of us keep, and lots of people who have lived together for years have to make an appointment with each other if they want to talk. There are lots of ways of communicating, of course, and you can sometimes say as much with the laying on of hands as with a three-page letter sent in triplicate and doubled-spaced. But letters are nice, too, and so are fireside chats, and a half hour in bed when the lights are out can make everything right with the world.

Some of us have trouble finding words for what we mean, or we speak in cryptic messages hoping the other person will figure out what we want and rush in to save us from ourselves, and when they miss the message, we feel isolated and alone. It's very important to decode your own messages, like saying "I feel angry" instead of kicking the cat, and people who learn to do this find they are misunderstood less often and, as a fringe benefit, are clawed by fewer cats.

The best men are those who put their cards on the table when something is bothering them, and if possible do it quietly, not blaming anyone, and if they're faced with a hysterical partner, who is not herself, identify with what she feels even when they can't make heads or tails out of what she says.

Women find it very hard to express anger, feeling perhaps that men will lose their love for them the moment they are anything but sweet. But men can usually deal with anger more easily than they can deal with guilt, and women who shout a lot can be shouted back at, which is hard to do with one who weeps.

A man once did something terrible to a girl I know that made her feel awful for a while but, when she pulled herself together, she wrote him a long, very definitely worded letter telling him just what she thought. It was a letter in which she tried to make things clear but at the same time not to whine, and it likely did the trick because he sent her back a note that read, "I thought I'd lost you for all time. Was awfully glad to find you were just pissed off."

If you never get angry, you never know where you stand, and it is also possible that you provoke people into worse and worse behavior just to get your attention or to make sure that you care. People who are loving tell each other what they feel, even when they don't expect the other to share their point of view, and if they don't always get what they want, at least they know what they can expect, and that, while it isn't everything, is at least a start.

One of the problems of the new morality ushered in by "the pill" is that it doesn't have an equivalent for being in the man's tent the next morning chewing on his moccasins – or whatever used to be done – so while, "the pill" has made women freer, it has also freed them to look after their psychosexual needs on their own. And many women who aspired to be "great ladies" found it wasn't so great to be one after all.

Sex deepens love and love deepens sex, so physical intimacy transforms everything and playing with it is playing with fire. Men try to ignore the fact that making love creates bonds, creating dependencies where there were none before, and women who try to ignore it with them deny their basic needs.

I'm not sure there can be loving without commitment, although commitment takes all kinds of forms, and there can be commitment for the moment as well as commitment for all time. The kind that is essential for loving marriages – and love affairs, as well – is a commitment to preserving the essential quality of your partner's soul, adding to them as a person rather than taking away. And if you haven't got that, you haven't got loving, although you might have something else. You could have adventure or a postgraduate course, you might have rehabilitation, or a bit of gossamer to highlight an otherwise somber life, but you don't have loving, and of that you should be sure.

Since the problem is with our expectations rather than with marriage itself, a lot of people are living together today hoping that way they can start fresh. If no one says the word "marriage," it's easier to evolve a plan of your own. There isn't any single formula for

marriage which all couples should find right, and attempting to run your life by your parents' standards or your neighbors' is bound to run aground. Marriages should be as diverse as the people in them are, which means some will be of one kind, and some totally different still. And those who don't want to love, honor and obey, should be able to promise each other anything they choose, without having to ask anyone what they think of that, particularly themselves.

There are many fringe benefits to being alone. You tend to have far more real, intense friendships when you are single, perhaps because you can be more honest when you do not have the marriage or someone else's feelings to protect. That means friends can share a larger part of you, and you of them as well, and friendships can be really intimate rather than activity-oriented associations that only meet to do some special thing.

If one of the problems of marriage is that safety can lead to complacency, then one of the advantages of being single is that one is never safe enough to grow complacent, and constantly having to prove oneself often leads to growth. Being alone means swimming in many waters and that can mean a more interesting life. And, if it is true that a single woman hasn't got one man she can count on, it is also true that, by living on the fringe of many men's lives, she is privy to many ideas and interests denied most married women – and, indeed, most men. Men tell women to whom they are not married truths they cannot tell their wives and fear to tell to men, and what one learns one day from one man makes you more interesting the next day for another – as well as for yourself.

There were women in the golden age of Greece, called hetaerae, who were celebrated by Socrates and philosophers of his time. Although they existed solely for their own pleasure and that of men, they were respected for their independence of mind and spirit and thought of highly by the Greeks. Single women in today's world can function like hetaerae, learning from many and giving back to whom they will, and for the woman who enjoys such a life, it can be a good one, and one both she and society can be the better for.

While married women must adapt to the perimeters of their marriages, single women can expand in all directions, developing as they will. Women who have realized themselves make good companions, and women as well as men find associations with them rewarding and fun - not only because they are more often interesting but because they haven't grown neurotic making a virtue of doing what they most dislike. And time with them is generally given freely, little asked in return.

I remember when I was first married how important it was to me that my husband find me beautiful, talented, womanly and bright. And when he didn't always, I was not these things – as if he'd turned off my light. After we parted and went on to other lives, from time to time a man thought me beautiful and occasionally another found me bright. Until, in time, I was those things even when no one was around and, today, because they are mine, I can give them to whomever I choose. Women who have had a chance to find out who they are don't need as much reassurance from men, having come to terms with themselves, and while it is always nicer to be around people who see you as you want to see yourself, you can't be done in as easily by ones who don't.

There is a lot to be said for being single – and more today than ever before. It is a new world we are living in now and, although there are rules for virginal females under eighteen and for married ones twenty to eighty-five, there are no rules for single women, so we are able to make our own.

Many a superior woman spends her lifetime looking for a man who is more superior instead of for one she likes, not realizing that demanding that a man be superior isn't much different from demanding that he be rich. Men who are required to be superior will always be insecure, and a man who feels his wife should get her identify from his success rather than from her own finds himself having to run all day just to keep up with her demands. Impotence for one is always impotence for both, and men and women who don't recognize this inadvertently become the killers of their own best dreams.

A man who insists that his woman lay her head on his shoulder and lean on him doesn't realize that if she takes her feet off the ground in this position and hangs on, she will be a drag. Psychiatrists are plagued by men who want to know what to do with dependent wives who can't make a move without them, and rising young copywriters are plagued by men who call them after dinner parties to confess that they wish their wives were as interesting and ask if they might have time to meet for a drink. Many marriages between two people become marriages between one and a half very quickly, and people who fear invested the "his and hers" towel culture and are now thrashing around inside.

Women who suffer loud and lengthily and weep copious tears make men feel guilty, beleaguered and anxious to get to the door, and little-girl acts of coyness get them somewhere in the short run but cost them dear in the long. Not only do women despise the men they catch with them and turn them into Jiggs, but men who are manipulated and patronized long enough declare emotional bankruptcy and give up the store.

One of the reasons men fear loving is that they don't want to take responsibility for another total human being. The kind of woman who loves out of need and desperation frightens even the best men off, and women who want someone around they can count on won't feel better until they can count on themselves. The whole superiority-inferiority, passive-submissive business is a bum steer. Women who don't expect the men in their life to give them fulfillment on a silver platter aren't as likely to hold them responsible when it isn't so easy to come by. And men who are not expected to be superior, only human, generally accomplish both more of the time.

Loving someone means helping them to be more themselves, which can be different from being what you'd like them to be, although often they turn out the same. When you ask someone to live through you and for you, they warp like a Japanese tree to suit the relationship which you are, and cease to be what you chose them for, that is, cease to be themselves. So men who are loving like as they love, and somehow they find the courage to let their partners grow in the direction they need to grow, even if that contains the risk that they might grow away.

Good people can't be possessed and those who can, one never wants for long. No one gives you security - you have to do that for yourself. Love can't buy happiness, marriage can't buy happiness, only happiness can buy happiness, so it is also unwise to think of finding happiness in terms of roles.

Being someone's wife or being someone's mother or even being the best plumber or the best brain surgeon may give you some security for a while, even for a long while, but you always have to be ready to find it somewhere else when the time comes, and it tends to come oftener than one would have thought.

Santayana wrote in a essay entitled "Cloud Castles" about the virtue of impermanence, pointing out that clouds are all different and that, as well as there not being two clouds the same, the clouds themselves keep changing and, hence, are never the same for very long. Marriages work best when both the people in them allow each other to be like those clouds, delighting in each other's changes. And those who attempt to find security by eliminating inconsistencies eliminate the miraculous with the same deft hand.

There is no security in a relationship that tries to hold on to what was, nor is there security in the one that dreads what might be. There is only security when we accept what is here now, with its limits and its surprises and, when it goes, in accepting what comes, as we would turn over the pages of a book.

There is a difference between needing and wanting and a difference between wanting and needing and loving, and both partners have a right to what they need, although not always to what they want. Each partner has a right to one life and to that life he has the sole right. He hasn't a right to his spouse's life, and he hasn't a right to his child's, but he has a right to his life, and no one should interfere with that.

It is not possible for one person to meet all of another's needs, and marriage partners who expect this soon find each other wanting. When people don't meet all of our needs, they are not always rejecting us – more often, they are saving themselves – and in a good marriage this is perfectly all right. People who are loving toward each other set up their marriages so that it is possible for both partners to get what they need from life and so that no one is expected to give up his needs to meet those of his spouse. And when their partner meets one of their needs, they accept it as a gift instead of viewing each unmet one as if it were a betrayal.

Our times are obsessed with finding fulfillment, so they are times of more than the usual strain between men and women and a good deal of that strain is blamed on marriage, although it should not be. There was a movie a season or two back called *Lovers and Other Strangers* which had a scene in which a son tries to tell his Italian father that he and his wife of only a few years have decided to get a divorce because, as he puts it, "We feel there must be something more." The father, not understanding what that has to do with anything, answers, his eyebrows raised for an explanation, "We all feel there must be something more," to which his son replies," Then why don't you leave Mom and get out and get it, Dad?" And the old man shoots back, "Because there isn't something more!"

They don't have romantic love with its emphasis on nostalgia, tragedy, and loss in cultures where children are raised by groups of adults instead of parents, so there are those who think romantic love is oedipal love, with the real love object being the image of the parent – ageless, perfect, and unattainable – that the lover hungered for as a child. Falling in love at first sight is transference then, and well it might be, because romantic love – as in knights who served their ladies, as in people who are married but not to each other, as in star-crossed lovers of every kind – tends to be a love that is thwarted, if just slightly, keeping the lovers like those in Keat's Grecian urn, "forever panting, forever young."

There are men who are addicted to the magic of falling in love, and the ego-aggrandizing, intoxicating splendor of it all, and never learn that loving is better still. For them, there is no help for a love that is losing its excitement but to fall in love again, with someone else – and, when that too loses its intensity, with someone else again. You can't maintain a constant state of falling in love, except through artificial means, but loving can go on forever and get better all the time.

How to Love Our Children

by James and Kathleen McGinnis

Children learn and use nonviolent conflict resolution skills only when these skills are taught in an environment encouraging their use. Parents and other caregivers promote peacemaking skills when they make their homes places where affirmation and cooperation—rather than constant criticism and individualism—are the norm. Specific nonviolent conflict resolution or problem-solving skills can be taught from the earliest years, especially if adults allow their children to participate in family decision making.

Peacemaking requires a healthy sense of self-esteem. Self-esteem is essential for developing compassion and caring for others. Peacemaking is sometimes a public and even risky undertaking. No one is capable of going public, taking a stand for their convictions, if they do not feel good about themselves. Without self-esteem, we look for acceptance through conformity; we are afraid to stand out. Nurturing children's sense of self-esteem by affirming their efforts and providing them opportunities to develop their talents is an enormously important part of enabling them to become peacemakers.

Specific possibilities include all the ways we encourage children: posting their artwork in the home, attending school sports or music programs, commenting on their strengths and good efforts more than on their weaknesses, listening carefully to their ideas, asking their advice. Hugs and kisses also help a lot! Birthdays can be a special occasion for affirmation.

The more family members are cooperating, the more peace there will be in the home. Sharing tasks rather than "everyone on their own" helps— whether it is occasional meal preparation, doing dishes, baking holiday goodies, gardening, etc. "Family fix-it nights" when everyone participates in fixing toys, mending clothes, etc., can be occasions for learning new skills and breaking down sex-role stereotypes, as well as teaching cooperation and peace. Encouraging children to share their skills with one another, e.g., helping a younger sibling learn to read, roller-skate, ride a bike, do long division, etc.—is another step. Playing cooperative games as a family and with other families is great fun. Making holiday presents together or writing family letters or making a family greeting card all generate the kind of cooperative spirit essential for being able to resolve family conflicts nonviolently.

Nonviolent conflict resolution skills include listening well, expressing rather than repressing one's feelings and, especially, learning nonhurtful ways to indicate anger, expressing needs and desires in clear terms, weighing a variety of possible solutions to any given conflict, and using negotiating skills. The more that adults can encourage children to use these skills and solve their own problems, rather than always intervene in child/child conflicts with a quick solution, the more opportunities children will have to learn these skills. Thus, the more that parents allow their children to participate in family decision making, the more their children will learn problem-solving skills.

Family meetings are probably the most important single mechanism for promoting peace and cooperation in the home and communicating family values. The more input children have in family decision making, the more likely they are to internalize the values we adults are trying to share and the less resistance we will encounter in trying to live the values of peace, justice and simplicity of lifestyle. These family discussions and decisions force family members to explain their reasons, providing adults especially with a regular opportunity to communicate their values.

Some key guidelines for effective family meetings:

1. Schedule them regularly, so there is some predictability.

2. Schedule them at the most convenient time for all family members.

3. Make the agenda available to everyone. Having a paper posted where everyone can see it helps considerably; otherwise some may forget what they want.

4. Include agenda items that involve family plans, fun events, and family service opportunities. Do not limit the agenda to problems and conflicts, otherwise the experience is always a "heavy" one. No one likes only difficult items, especially at mealtime.

5. Combine family meetings with things that "taste good"—a special dessert, a family game or a fun night, a trip to the ice cream store. The "good" taste addition increases the willingness of children to participate.

6. Rotate leadership, so children get a chance to develop their skills.

7. Be sure that decisions are clear, tasks are assigned, consequences are identified when necessary, and a "check- in" time has been identified, i.e.a time to evaluate how well a particular solution is working.

8. Give everyone a chance to speak; help less verbal members of the family to get their points across.

9. Whenever possible, consider the children's agenda items early in the meeting, so that they experience the process working for them.

10. Do not force the meeting beyond the children's ability or willingness to continue to participate. Carry over the agenda items to the next meeting if necessary. Quality, not quantity of discussion and decision, is the key.

Occasional family reconciliation events can be important sources of peace in the home. Such events reinforce a forgiving, accepting environment in which family members readily apologize and forgive one another. These healing events can be as simple as a five-minute addition to the family meeting at which each member acknowledges and asks forgiveness for one way they have been unhelpful in promoting peace in the home. More elaborate reconciliation events could include spiritual reading, prayer or symbolic actions—such as writing down the negative behaviors on pieces of paper and burning them in the fireplace as a prayer is said for mutual forgiveness and determination to change behaviors.

from "Self-Esteem: Teach Your Children Well," Peacework,
Fort Kamp Publishing Company

Men, Women and the Art of Friendship

by Colman McCarthy

Someday, I'm going to put aside the day's chaos and take time to report the details of a love story between a woman and man who were not lovers but friends. If sexual love is a dosage of intense feelings, a widening of the veins that lets the emotions pass through unclogged from heart to heart, friendship can permit a rarer sensation: raising affections higher than the passings of the emotional.

Lovers have it easy, which is why so many try it: They can mate but not always bond. Friends, in the harder role, bond without mating. Instead of jumping into bed, they jump into life, and find there privacies of the mind and spirit that don't need glands to be aroused. Some wives and husbands marry as best friends and then, blessed, live as better friends.

The woman and man I would write about were friends because their closeness was based on distance. They could stand back. She functioned best as his critic. His main flaw, to her, was that he didn't think he had any flaws. When the air-pumps of public acclaim inflated his ego –because his latest book pleased reviewers or lecture committees invited him to speak on whatever topic he wished–she held up the cue card of friendship: Come off it, pal.

Off he always came–choiceless, really, because, while she looked up to him, she also saw through him. It was her version of a buddy system, the keeping of a rope tied to the hugeness of her friend's male self-importance, so that when he wandered off into believing his notices she could, with gentle protectiveness, pull him back to reality.

That was where he best flourished. He was happily married to a woman much better than he deserved, with part of that betterness being his wife's unjealous expansiveness about his friendship with this woman. Nothing was secretive about the friendship. She wasn't a girlfriend, but a friend who happened to be a woman. Were she a man, the relationship would have been the same. The man's wife–also his best friend–was also close to the woman. After 20 years of marriage, she had learned something about physics as well as love: Her husband's woman friend would never fall for him because her loyalty was in standing up to him.

She was no threat to the couple's marriage. By caring about the husband's professional life, as it filtered through in written and spoken words, she was, perhaps unknowingly, bolstering the marriage. She had been helping the husband to grow up, not grow away.

The matching gift to that generosity was the man's being a support group to the woman. Where she was full-hearted, he was lighthearted. His joking and fooleries were the epidermis that kept life's bogs from getting under her skin. They worked for the same company, but on different floors and separate terrains. All he wanted his coworker to know was that he thought her to be as creative, or more so, than any of his male buddies. She wasn't one of the boys. She was one of the best.

With AIDS and herpes now enforcing the one-person one-bed rule, the art of friendship may be about to enjoy a revival. Are Americans too hurried for the slower pace of working up to be a friend? It appears so. Two people can rush off to Las Vegas or Elkton, Md., to become husband and wife but many can go there 10 times and still be only acquaintances, not friends.

It's impossible to divorce a friend, because friendship means not going away when the other says "go, get lost." It isn't really meant. A friend knows how to decode the message of rejection by going beyond the meaning of words to the words of meaning. Too many of the latter have been said before to be washed away by a moment of anger. Between friends, anger is not harmful because it is a sudden burst of feeling. In marriages, anger can sometimes be the final burst, an eruption of the too-long held back. When friends blow up at each other and retreat for the normal licking of wounds, they can come back scarless: "I'm glad it was nothing serious, that we were only mad at each other."

It was either an Irish mystic or poet, and it's usually one or the other, who said that "a friend is someone who knows the song in your heart and plays back the words when you forget how they go." This weekend, with St. Valentine reminding loved ones to love, some homage is due for friends who befriend. If you have a few someones who can't remember the words of their song, sing them back. It's sweeter than chocolates.

from Washington Post

Preach the Gospel at all times. If necessary, use words.

Francis of Assisi

Letter to Ernesto Cardenal: Guns Don't Work

by Daniel Berrigan

Editor's note:

Ernesto Cardenal had helped establish a Christian community on Solentiname Island in Nicaragua. Some members joined the armed resistance to Samoza, and Cardenal issued a declaration of his support for them and the Sandinista Front.

Dear Brother Ernesto Cardenal,

Your account of events in your community of Solentiname has been widely distributed in the United States, especially by the religious press. One translation appended a word: "It is important for us in this country to be able to listen and not to judge this."

Indeed. But at least we can talk together. Please consider what follows, then, as a continuing reflection on matters you have had the courage to open up, and indeed, to act on.

May I also summon a memory or two, as you do so poignantly in you statement? You visited my brother Philip and myself in jail in February of 1977, when we were locked up after a demonstration at the Pentagon. I hope you could read in our faces all your visit meant; a visit from a fellow priest, a poet, a good communitarian, a struggling friend, whose fame was great but whose human warmth was his best gift. Thank you once more for coming to us.

Then there was our first meeting a few years previous, when you brought the art of Solentiname to New York for an exhibition. I had the joy of greeting you, this poet, the intense quiet Latino, known in the southern countries for his sandals and flowing hair and beard, his kinky myopic eyes; known here for his poetry, his courage.

The shadow of Thomas Merton's death lay heavy on us. I think we were seeking consolation in one another's eyes. And we found it.

I am not going to start with the customary disclaimers about your statement. Such are not only superfluous, they verge on the insulting. What Latino, what Yankee doesn't know by now the deadly mutual interests which in Washington prop up the Nicaraguan military government of the Somozas? And who would regard you—an exile, a priest who must now anoint your forehead with the ashes of your dream—regard your convictions, your choices, with anything but the utmost respect? All this is implicit in friendship itself.

I would like to do you a better courtesy, that of taking you seriously: your words, and the actions which by now, I presume, you have taken.

Let me say too that the questions you raise are among the most crucial that Christians can spell out today. Indeed, in your own country, your life raises them. But you thrust them also at us, and rightly so. They are far more than a matter of domestic importance.

There is, first of all, no parallel in America to the violence you describe—whether of the Somozas or the Sandinistas.

What indeed are a few guns, or even a few hundred guns, in the hands of guerrillas in comparison with the doomsday cache of nuclear horrors lurking in our mountains and bunkers? What reasonable comparison can be made between the sorties of your Frente Sandinista, and the lunar devastation of Vietnam, Laos, Cambodia? On your part, a few deaths, much love, exalted goals. On the part of America—but words fail me.

These things I grant with all my heart. What then nags at me, when I ponder your words? I have some inkling of what you face, what your companions face, the students and workers and peasants of your country. I know that the Somozas, given the leash, could swallow all of you tomorrow. I know that on the same day, the U.S. military could swallow the Somozas who had swallowed you—the mouse within the dog within the python—and hardly feel sated. On the world scale where the stakes are piled high—oil, uranium, laissez-faire larcenies, predatory markets, ripoffs, and standoffs; in a world where the superpowers warily circle one another like urban thugs, nuclear firebombs in hand; in such a world, you or your followers, or even your persecutors, count for very little.

You and the Frente, and the Somozas, could disappear tomorrow. Only a minor breeze would stir the papers on the desk of some sub-secretary of the State Department. A lie or two at a presidential press conference would be your obituary, the Nicaraguan folder transferred to a dead file. The empire, in sum, can take your life, and take your death, and take your theology, and the destruction of your community, and your resistance, all in stride.

I say this in no spirit of cynicism. Merely to suggest that in a way I find both strange and exhilarating, your situation lies quite near the realities of the gospel. It ought not, after all, depress us beyond measure, if the empire finds you and me expendable. That is quite normal and constant in the history of such entities. What is of import finally is whether we are able to salvage something in the open season on humans.

I do not mean salvage our lives; I mean our humanity. Our service to one another, of compassion—our very sanity.

I hope I am inching toward the contents of your letter. You discuss quite freely and approvingly the violence of a violated people, yourselves. You align yourself with that violence, regretfully but firmly, irrevocably.

I am sobered and saddened by this. I think of the consequences of your choice, within Nicaragua and far beyond. I sense how the web of violence spins another thread, draws you in, and so many others for whom your example is primary, who do not think for themselves, judging that a priest and poet will lead them in the true way.

I think how fatally easy it is, in a world demented and enchanted with the myth of shortcuts and definitive solutions, when nonviolence appears increasingly naive, old hat, freakish—how easy it is to cross over, to seize the gun. How easy to conclude: the deck is stacked, first card to last, in favor of the Big Sharks; the outcome of the game, of life itself, is settled before the cards are dealt. Why then isn't taking a few lives (of dubious value at best, torturers, lackeys, police) preferable to the taking of many lives of great value, students, the poor, the victimized and defenseless, the conscientious, those easily identifiable as gospel brothers and sisters? There is, after all, a long tradition of legitimate self-defense.

It may be true, as you say, that "Gandhi would agree with us." Or it may not be true. It may be true, as you imply, that Merton would agree with you. It may be true that Christ would agree with you. I do not believe he would, but I am willing to concede your argument, for the sake of argument.

You may be correct in reporting that "those young Christians fought without hate—and especially without hate for the guards" they shortly killed (though this must be cold comfort to the dead). Your vision may one day be verified of a Nicaragua free of "campesino guards killing other campesinos." The utopia you ache for may one day be realized in Nicaragua: "an abundance of schools, child care centers, hospitals, and clinics for everyone—and most importantly, love between everyone." This may all be true; the guns may bring on the kingdom.

But I do not believe it.

One religious paper here published your words under the following headline: "When they take up arms for love of the kingdom of God." How sublime, I thought, how ironic. We have had "just" wars of the Right, a long history of blood, the blood of colonials and natives and slaves and workers and peasants. But we are through with all that. Now we are enlightened. We are to have "just" wars of the Left!

So the young men of Solentiname resolved to take up arms. They did it for one reason: "on account of their love for the kingdom of God." Now here we certainly speak within a tradition! In every crusade that ever marched across Christendom, murder—the most secular of undertakings, the most worldly, the one that enlists and rewards us along with the other enlistees of Caesar—this undertaking is invariably baptized in religious ideology: the kingdom of God.

The power of such language we know too well. Religious battle cries induct hearts and minds as no secular slogans can. Religious ideology raises its flag in every nation, even as it denies the final authority of every nation. It offers to transcendent longings a task that is simple and forthright: kill. It offers a slogan that is as immediately tactile and hot as a fired gun: kill for the kingdom. And perhaps most important of all, it offers a way out: out of anger, out of frustration, out of poverty, out of political stagnation, out of the harsh and dreadful necessity of love. God wills it! The kingdom requires it!

Blood and iron, nukes and rifles. The leftists kill the rightists, the rightists kill the leftists, both, given time and occasion, kill the children, the aged, the ill, the suspects. Given time and occasion, both torture prisoners. Always, you understand, inadvertently, regretfully. Both sides, moreover, have excellent intentions, and call on God to witness them. And some god or other does witness them, if we can take the word of whatever bewitched church.

And of course nothing changes. Nothing changes in Beirut, in Belfast, or in Galilee, as I have seen. Except that the living die. And that old, revered distinction between combatant and noncombatant, which was supposed to protect the innocent and helpless, goes down the nearest drain, along with the indistinguishable blood of any and all.

Alas, I have never seen anyone morally improved by killing; neither the one who aimed the bullet, nor the one who received it in his or her flesh.

Of course we have choices, of course we must decide. When all is said, we find that the gospel makes sense, that it strikes against our motives and actions or it does not. Can that word make sense at all today, can it be something more than utopian or extravagant? The gospel is after all a document out of a simpler age, a different culture. It may even be our duty to construct for ourselves another ethic, based on our own impasse or insights or ego. And go from there, with whatever assurance we can muster, amid the encircling gloom.

Or on the other hand, we can bow our heads before a few truths, crude, exigent, obscure as they are. The outcome of obedience we cannot know, the outcome of disobedience we can deceive ourselves about, indefinitely and sweetly. Thou shalt not kill. Love one another as I have loved you. If your enemy strikes you on the right cheek, turn to him the other. Practically everyone in the world, citizens and believers alike, consign such words to the images on church walls, or the embroideries in front parlors.

We really are stuck. Christians are stuck with this Christ, the impossible, unteachable, irreformable loser. Revolutionaries must correct him, act him aright. That absurd form, shivering under the crosswinds of power, must be made acceptable, relevant. So a gun is painted into his empty hands. Now he is human! Now he is like us.

Does it all have a familiar ring? In the old empires, the ragged rabbi must be cleaned up, invested in Byzantine robes of state, raised in glittering splendor to the dome of heaven. Correction! correction! we cry to those ignorant gospel scribes, Matthew and the rest. He was not like that, he was not helpless, he was not gentle, he was under no one's heel, no one pushed him around! He would have taken up a gun if one had been at hand, he would have taken up arms, "solely for one reason; on account of his love for the kingdom of God." Did he not have fantasies like ours, in hours out of the public glare, when he too itched for the quick solution, his eyes narrowed like gun sights?

How tricky it all gets! We look around at our culture: an uneasy mix of gunmen, gun makers, gun hucksters, gun researchers, gun runners, guards with guns, property owners with guns. A culture in which the guns put out contracts on the people, the guns own the people, the guns buy and sell the people, the guns practice targets on the people, the guns kill the people. The guns are our second nature, and the first nature is all but obliterated; it is gunned down.

And who will raise it up, that corpse with the neat hole in its temple, ourselves? It is impossible, it is against nature.

Christ asks the literally impossible. And then, our radical helplessness confessed, he confers what was impossible.

Dear brother Ernesto, when I was underground in 1970 with J. Edgar Hoover's hounds on my tail, I had long hours to think of these things. At that time I wrote: "The death of a single human is too heavy a price to pay for the vindication of any principle, however sacred." I should add that at the time, many among the anti-war Left were playing around with bombings, in disarray and despair.

I am grateful that I wrote those words. I find no reason eight years later to amend or deny them. Indeed, in this bloody century, religion has little to offer, little that is not contaminated or broken or in bad faith. But one thing we have: our refusal to take up bombs or guns, aimed at the flesh of brothers and sisters, whom we persist in defining as such, refusing the enmities pushed at us by war-making state or war-blessing church.

This is a long loneliness, and a thankless one. One says "no" when every ache of the heart would say "yes." We, too, long for a community on the land, heartening liturgies, our own turf, the arts, a place where sane ecology can heal us. And the big boot comes down. It destroys everything we have built. And we recoil. Perhaps in shock, perhaps in a change of heart, we begin to savor on our tongues a language that is current all around us: phrases like "legitimate violence," "limited retaliation," "killing for love of the kingdom." And the phrases make sense—we have crossed over. We are now an army, like the pope's army, or Luther's, or the crusaders, or the Muslims. We have disappeared into this world, into bloody, secular history. We cannot adroitly handle both gospel and gun; so we drop the gospel, as impediment in any case.

And our weapons?

They are contaminated in what they do, and condemned in what they cannot do. There is blood on them, as on our hands. And like our hands, they cannot heal injustice or succor the homeless.

How can they signal the advent of the kingdom of God? How can we, who hold them? We announce only another bloody victory for the emperor of necessity, whose name in the Bible is Death.

Shall we have dominion?

Brother, I think of you so often. And pray with you. And hope against hope.

from To Dwell in Peace

Resist Not Evil

by Clarence S. Darrow

The Machinery of Justice

The state furnishes no machinery for arriving at justice. Even if it were possible under any circumstances to judge, and even though men were really criminals, the state has no way of arriving at the facts. If the state pretends to administer justice, this should be its highest concern. It should not be interested in convicting men or punishing crime, but administering justice between men. It is obvious to the most casual observer that the state furnishes no machinery to accomplish this result. The penal law simply takes a man into its hopper and grinds out a criminal at the end. A force of able-bodied, well-fed, well-paid men are kept busy in their search for crime. These men find pecuniary reward in the crime of their fellows. An indictment is easily returned against a friendless man - a suspicion is enough in any case where the victim has no friends. If he is poor, he is at once lodged in jail. Later, he is placed on trial in the courts. When he steps into the dock, both judge and jurors look on him as a guilty man–believe he has committed a crime. He is carefully guarded by officers like a guilty, hunted thing. Arrayed against him is an able prosecutor, well-paid, and having personal and political ambitions dependent on the number of men he grinds into criminals. The prosecutor has ample means for the conduct of the case. The prisoner, helpless enough at best, is rendered absolutely powerless to prepare his case by being lodged in jail. Without money, he has no advocate with either the learning, influence or ability to help his cause. If he is silent, he is convicted. If he speaks, no one believes his words. Innocent or guilty, it is a miracle if he escapes, and in this miracle, the fact of his innocence or guilt plays but the smallest part. Given a few suspicious circumstances, a helpless prisoner, an indictment, and another victim is the sure result. And in the hands of a shrewd lawyer, or under the belief of guilt, any circumstances are suspicious circumstances. Almost all acts are subject to various interpretations, and the guilt or innocence of a circumstance depends not upon the act but upon the mind that passes judgment on the act. We look back with horrors at the criminal courts of England, of Spain, of Italy, even upon our own Puritan judges who sentenced witches to death. These judges were doubtless as intelligent as our own. Their brutal, cruel judgments did not grow from a wicked perverted heart but from the fact that they were passing judgment on their fellow man. These unjust judgments are the fruit of the cruel system of force and barbarism which clothes one man with the authority and power to condemn his fellow man. All prosecutions are malicious, and all judgments are meted out in anger and hatred. Our own judges are constantly showing this. In nearly every instance, they condemn a prisoner to a term of servitude, and when passion has fled and the sane and holy feelings of mercy, of charity, of humanity once more regain their sway, they call on the pardoning power to rescind their cruel acts. In all these cases of pardons, reflection shows the judges that the punishment meted out was at least too severe. The difference is in the frame of mind of the judge when engaged in the business of administering judgment and, when in the mood, for listening to those feelings of human charity which are the diviner part of man.

Punishment, to in any way be justified, should diminish the sum of human misery, the result of the bitterness and hatred of men. But here, as everywhere else, punishment falls short. Wherever the judgment of courts enters, it is to corrupt and to destroy. The misery and suffering entailed on man by scaffolds, racks, blocks, dungeons and jails has never yet begun to be told. Blood and misery and degradation has marked the administration of punishment.

> Since man first penned his fellow men,
> Like brutes, within an iron pen.

Let any reasoning being consider the tens of thousands who have been burned, and hanged, and boiled, and otherwise put to death for witchcraft; the millions for heresy; the thousands of noble victims who have suffered for treason; the victims of fire, of torture, of scaffold, of rack and of dungeon, for all the conceivable crimes since time began. Let him consider the oceans of blood and rivers of tears shed by the force and brutality of the rulers of the world; the cruelty, torture and suffering heaped upon the helpless, the weak, the unfortunate; and then ask himself if he believes that punishment is good. Even could violence ever prevent crime, the brutality, suffering, blood and crime of the rulers has towered mountain high above that of the weak and obscure victims whose wrongs they have pretended to avenge. And this cruelty does not abate. It is simple madness that doubts the justice of past condemnations and believes in the righteous judgments of today. No condemnation is just, and no judgment is righteous. All violence and force are cruel, unjust and barbarous, and cannot be sustained by the judgment of men.

But the evil of judgment and punishment does not end with the unfortunate victim. It brutalizes and makes inhuman all who are touched with its power. Under the influence of punishments, jailers, policemen, sheriffs, detectives and all who deal with prisons are brutalized and hardened. The iniquities produced upon helpless prisoners leave their effects upon the captor as well as the captives. To witness the constant suffering and indignities of prison life is to destroy the finer sensibilities of the soul. Men who are otherwise kind in the various relations of life do not hesitate at cruelty to these despised prisoners whom the law has placed outside its ban. To underfeed and overwork, to insult, degrade and beat are common incidents of prison life, and this, too, not because jailers are naturally cruel and bad, but because prisons are prisons, and convicts are outcasts. Instead of approaching these unfortunates as brothers in fellowship and love, their only concern is to make them feel that the heavy hand of the state has been laid upon them in malice and violence.

However thoroughly the futility, cruelty and injustice of punishment may be shown, men will still persist that it must exist. The thought that society could live without prisons and policemen seems to be beyond the conception of the common man. If punishment has no effect to diminish or prevent crime, then no danger would be incurred to dismiss our jailers and jurors and close our prison doors. The results of this policy can, of course, not be proven absolutely in advance, but so sure as the existence of man is consistent with justice, charity and love, so sure is this policy right and would produce good results. It is not necessary to prove the theory of nonresistance to show that this policy is practical today. Society, as now organized, rests upon violence and wrong. The nonresistant pleads for a better order, one in which the law of love and mercy will be the foundation of every relationship of man with man. The present unjust system is supported by violence and force. The unjust possessions of the rich are kept in their place by soldiers, guns and policemens' clubs. If these were withdrawn, would the weak at once take the earth and all its fullness from those who for ages have ruled the world? No violent and forcible readjustment of this sort could come. Force is wrong both to commit and to redress evil. In the rule of force, the weak must always fall. For the poor and oppressed to advocate the use of force means that they must still be the victims, for the strongest force must win. All that can help the weak is the rule of brotherhood, of love. Unless this can be proved, there is no way to destroy the injustice that is everywhere the rule of life. To make the weak strong, and the strong weak, could neither destroy injustice nor permanently change the wretched order of the world. A bayonet in the hand of one man is no better than in the hand of another. It is the bayonet that is evil and all of its fruits are bad.

The world must learn that violence is wrong. Individuals who understand this truth must take no part in violent acts, whether to enslave or to free. The inherent cohering forces will hold society together and cause man to cooperate for his highest good. A large part of present society is purely voluntary and due to natural law. It is for force and violence and injustice that the aid of the state is called. Society should not punish. The great burden that rests upon production to support armies, courts and prisons with all their endless officers and staggering weight should be taken from the shoulders of the poor. This of itself would so relieve industry and add to the possibilities of life that the very hazardous occupations that we call criminal would almost wholly disappear. The class from which these victims come is known to be the outcast and the poor. A small fraction of the vast sum squandered for violence and force would easily place all these dangerous persons beyond the temptations of criminal activity. Even now, with all the injustice of today, the expenditure of public money to relieve suffering, to furnish remunerative employment, to rationally prevent crime by leaving men with something else to do, would produce better results than all the imagined benefits that follow in the wake of scaffolds and of jails.

The effort of the penal codes has never been to reach any human being before violence is done, except to awe him by the brief transitory show of force; but after the act is done, the state must spend its strength and substance for revenge. Most men are driven to criminal acts from the necessities of life and the hatred bred by the organized force they meet. Remove dire poverty, as could be easily done with a tithe of what is now spent on force; let organized society meet the individual, not with force, but with helpfulness and love, and the inducement to commit crime could not exist. Let society be the friend not the tyrant, the brother not the jailer, and the feeling will be returned a thousandfold. No man or no society ever induced love with clubs and guns. The emblem of the state is the soldier, the policeman, the court, the jail. It is an emblem that does not appeal to the higher sentiments of man - an emblem that so long as it exists will prevent true brotherhood and be a hindrance to the higher sentiments that will one day rule the world.

The concern of society would then be to call back this soul to saner thoughts and a truer, nobler life; not to blacken and destroy, or to plant bitter hatred and despair in the soul of one who might be brought to fine and high realization of human conduct and human life. Under this sort of treatment, a large proportion of those who commit violent deeds would be brought to a full realization of their acts, and they themselves would seek in every way to repair the ill effects of their evil deeds.

The Right Treatment of Violence

Sentimental and humane thoughts and purposes are often, perhaps generally, based on real life, and have a natural reason for their being. To "turn the other cheek" or to "resist not evil" may seem, at first glance, to have no support in the facts of life, but after all that which makes for a higher humanity, a longer life, and a more vigorous community, is the true philosophy. To use violence and force upon the vicious and the weak must produce the evil that it gives. Like produces like. Clubs, jails, harsh language and brutal force inevitably tend to reproduce the same state of mind in the victim of the assault. This is not merely a fact in human nature. It is a fact in all nature, plant, animal and man. So long as the gentle springtime rather than the cruel winter brings vegetable and animal life to an awakening earth, just so long will kindness and love triumph, produce joy and life, where force and violence bring only evil and death. Harsh treatment kills plant life, and kind treatment builds it up. Violence and brutality produce their like in animal life, and kindness tames and subdues. With gentleness and kindness, a swarm of wild bees may be handled and controlled, but approach them with violence and force and each bee is converted into a criminal whose only purpose is to destroy.

With all animal life, the same rule exists; even those beasts whose nature calls for a diet of flesh and blood may be subdued in time by gentleness and love. Man with his higher intellect and better-developed moral being is much more susceptible to kindness and love. Likewise, he more easily learns to fear and hate. Man readily discerns the feelings and judgment of his fellows, and as readily renders judgment in return. The outcast and abandoned form not the slightest exception to the rule - they know and understand the ones who meet them with gentleness and love, for these they make sacrifices, to these they are faithful, to these they exhibit the higher qualities that show the possibilities of the soul. Cases where one convicted of crime comes from a place of safety and risks, his liberty and life to help save his friend are not rare in the least. True comradeship and loyalty is met quite as often here as in the higher walks of life. Nothing is more common in ordinary selfish society than to see one man refuse all aid and help to another in financial need. Many convicts and outcasts could teach a much-needed lesson in loyalty and generosity to the exemplary man.

No amount of treatment can reclaim an evil heart if the treatment is administered without love. As children at school, we knew with our young natural instincts the teacher who loved us and the teacher who despised us - the one who awoke feelings of love and kindness, the other hatred and revenge. No heart is so pure that it may not be defiled and hardened by cruelty, hatred and force, and none so defiled that it may not be touched and changed by gentleness and love. Unless this philosophy of life is true, the whole teaching of the world has been a delusion and a snare. Unless love and kindness tends to love, then hatred and violence and force should be substituted and taught as the cardinal virtues of human life. The mistake and evil of society is in assuming that love is the rule of life and, at the same time, that large classes of people are entirely outside its pale. No parent ever teaches his child any other philosophy than that of love. Even to quarrelsome playmates they are taught not to return blows and harsh language, but to meet force with kindness and with love. The parent who did not depend on love to influence and mold the character of the child rather than force would be regarded not as a real parent but a brute. Force is worse than useless in developing the conduct of the child. It is true that by means of force the little child may be awed by superior brute power, but he gives way only under protest, and the violence that he suppresses in his hand or tongue finds refuge in his heart. Violent acts are not evil - they are a manifestation of evil. Good conduct is not goodness. It is but a manifestation of goodness. Evil and goodness can only be conditions of the inmost life, and human conduct, while it generally reflects this inmost life, may be so controlled as not to manifest the real soul that makes the man.

Every child needs development, needs training to fit him to live in peace and right relations with his fellow man. Every intelligent and right-thinking person knows that this development must be through love, not through violence and force. The parent who would teach his child to be kind to animals, not to ruthlessly kill and maim, would not teach this gentleness with a club. The intelligent parent would not use a whip to teach a child not to beat a dog. The child is not made into the good citizen, the righteous man, by pointing out that certain conduct will lead to punishment, to the jail or the gallows. The beneficence of fear was once considered a prime necessity in the rearing of the child, and this theory peopled the earth with monsters and the air with spooks ready to reach down and take the helpless child when he wandered from the straight and narrow path; but this method of rearing children does not appeal to the judgment and humanity of today. The conduct of children can only be reached for good by pointing to the evil results of hatred, of inharmony, of force, by appealing to the higher and nobler sentiments which, if once reached, are ever present, influencing and controlling life. The code of hatred, of violence and force, too, is a negative code. The child is given a list of the things he must not do, exactly as the man is furnished a list of the acts forbidden by the state. At the best, when the limits of this list are reached and the forbidden things are left undone, nothing more is expected or demanded. But no code is long enough to make up the myriad acts of life. Kindness or unkindness can result in a thousand ways in every human relationship. If the child or the man observes the written code through fear, the unwritten moral code, infinitely longer and more delicate, will be broken in its almost every line. But if the child or the man is taught his right relations to the world and feels the love and sympathy due his fellow man, he has no need of written codes; his acts, so far as those of mortals can be, will be consistent with the life and happiness of his fellow man. And this not through fear, but because he bears the highest attitude toward life.

With our long heredity and our imperfect environment, even if the organized force of the state should disappear, even if the jails and penitentiaries should close their doors, force would only completely die in course of time. Evil environment and heredity may have so marked and scarred some men that kindness and love could never reach their souls. It might take generations to stamp out hatred or destroy the ill effects of life; but order and kindness most surely would result, because nature demands order and tolerance and, without it, man must die. No doubt here and there these so-called evil ones would arouse evil and hatred in return and some sudden act of violence would, for a time, occasionally, be met with violence through mob law in return. But uncertain and reprehensible as mob law has ever been, it is still much more excusable and more certain than the organized force of society operating through the criminal courts. Mob law has the excuse of passion, or provocation, not the criminal nature of deliberation, coldness and settled hate. Mob law, too, generally reaches the object of its wrath, while evidence is fresh and facts are easily understood and unhampered by those rules and technical forms which ensnare the weak and protect the strong. And unjust and unwise as the verdicts of mob law often are, they are still more excusable, quicker, more certain and less erring than the judgments of the criminal courts.

But neither civil law nor mob law is at all necessary for the protection of individuals. Men are not protected because of their strength or their ability to fight. In the present general distribution of weapons, in one sense, every man's life is dependent on each person that he meets. If the instinct was to kill, society as organized presents no obstacle to that instinct. When casual violence results, it is not the weakest or more defenseless who are the victims of the casual violence of individuals. Even the boy at school scorns to war upon a weaker mate. The old, the young, the feeble, children and women, are especially exempt from violent deeds. This is because their condition does not call for feelings of violence, but rather awakens feelings of compassion, and calls for aid and help. The nonresistant ever appears to the courageous and the manly. Without weapons of any kind, with the known determination to give no violence in return, it would be very rare that men would not be safe from disorganized violence. It is only the state that ever lays its hands in anger on the nonresistant.

Neither would nonresistance in the state or individual indicate cowardice or weakness or lack of vital force. The ability and inclination to use physical strength is no indication of bravery or tenacity to life. The greatest cowards are often the greatest bullies. Nothing is cheaper and more common than physical bravery. In the lower animals, it is more pronounced than in man. The bulldog and the fighting cock are quite as conspicuous examples of physical bravery as the prize-fighter or the soldier. The history of all warfare shows either that physical bravery is not an indication of great excellence or that supreme excellence is very common, in fact almost a universal possession. Under the intoxication of patriotism, or the desire for glory, or the fear of contempt, most men will march with apparent willingness into the face of the greatest danger. Often it requires vastly more courage to stay at home than to enlist - more courage to retreat than to fight. Common experience shows how much rarer is moral courage than physical bravery. A thousand men will march to the mouth of the cannon where one man will dare espouse an unpopular cause. An army, well-equipped and ready for action, has less terror for the ordinary man than the unfavorable comment of the daily press. True courage and manhood come from the consciousness of the right attitude toward the world, the faith in one's own purpose, and the sufficiency of one's own approval as a justification for one's own acts. This attitude is not that of the coward, for cowardice is really disapproval of self, a consciousness of one's own littleness and unworthiness in the light of one's own soul, which cannot be deceived.

Intelligent men are willing to accept many truths that they believe are not fitted for the universal acceptance of mankind, and however they may feel that punishment is wrong, they still urge that it will not do to teach this doctrine to the great mass of men and to carry its practice into daily life. But sooner or later, all conduct and all life must rest on truth. It is only fact that can form a basis for permanent theories that tend to the preservation of the race. No one is too poor, or too young, or too vicious to know the truth, for the truth alone is consistent with all facts of life, and this alone can furnish any rule of life. The truth alone can make you free. When society is taught the truth that it is wrong to punish, to use force, to pass judgment on man, it will have no need for jails. The man who really knows and understands this truth can have no malice in his heart, can use no force and violence against his fellow, but will reach him with love and pity. The man or society that understands this truth will know that so-called crime is only so-called crime: that human conduct is what the necessities of life make of the individual soul. Then in reality, as now only partially, men will turn their attention to the causes that make crime. Then will they seek to prevent and cure, not to punish and destroy. Then man will learn to know that the cause of crime is the unjust condition of human life; that penal laws are made to protect earth's possessions in the hands of the vicious and the strong. Man will learn that poverty and want are due to the false conditions, the injustice which looks to human law and violence and force for its safeguard and protection. Men will learn that crime is but the hard profession that is left open to a large class of men by their avaricious fellows. When new opportunities for life are given, a fairer condition of existence will gradually be opened up and the need for violence and the cause of violence will disappear.

Instead of avenging a murder by taking a judge, sheriff, jurors, witnesses, jailer, hangman and the various appendages of the court – by taking these and staining their hands with blood and crime, the world will make the original murder impossible, and thus save the crimes of all. Neither will the vicious control without the aid of law. Society ever has and must ever have a very large majority who naturally fall into order, social adjustment and a rational, permissible means of life. The disorganized vicious would be far less powerful than the organized vicious, and would soon disappear.

Punishment to terrorize men from violating human order is like the threat of hell to terrorize souls into obedience to the law of God. Both mark primitive society, both are degrading and debasing, and can only appeal to the lower instincts of the lower class of men.

Most religious teachers have ceased to win followers by threats of hell. Converts of this sort are not generally desired. The religion that does not approach and appeal to men along their higher conduct is not considered worthy to teach to man. And those souls who cannot be moved through the sentiments of justice and humanity, rather than threats of eternal fire, are very, very rare and even should a soul exist, the fear of hell would cause it still further to shrivel and decay.

Hatred, bitterness, violence and force can bring only bad results – they leave an evil stain on everyone they touch. No human soul can be rightly reached except through charity, humanity and love.

from The Machinery of Justice, *Chapter XV and XVI*
Charles H. Kerr and Co., Chicago, Ill

Dan Berrigan and a Pennsylvania Judge

by Colman McCarthy

A bracing mix of judicial candor and integrity was displayed recently in a Pennsylvania county courtroom. Senior Judge James Buckingham had before the bench eight defendants who were convicted in 1981 of burglary, criminal mischief and criminal conspiracy. A dastardly crew, all. Nine years ago, the sentencing judge threw the book at them, a heavy tome that included three-to-ten-year prison stretches.

On appeal in 1984, the conviction was reversed. Prosecutors then appealed the reversal, with the Pennsylvania Supreme Court ruling favorably for the state. The case was returned to the Superior Court of Pennsylvania, with a resentencing ordered in Montgomery County, Pa. The criminals were the Plowshares Eight, a group of incorrigible peacemakers who, hammers in hands and resistance to war preparation in their hearts, damaged two nuclear missile nose cones, poured blood on documents and prayed for peace. They had slipped into the General Electric plant in King of Prussia, Pa., a bomb-making facility that had helped the nation's sixth largest industrial corporation gross an estimated $11 billion in nuclear warfare systems in 1984-1986. GE has plugged itself into the major instruments of death in the U.S. arsenal: the Trident, MX, Minuteman, Poseidon, Aegis and Tomahawk cruise missiles; the Stealth and B-1 bombers; fighter planes; and Star Wars. In the Washington palm-greasing game, GE is a bright bulb of fluorescent generosity with PAC money and honoraria to its congressional soulmates.

In passing new sentences on the Plowshares Eight, whose members included the Rev. Daniel Berrigan, Philip Berrigan and Sister Anne Montgomery of the Religious of the Sacred Heart, Judge Buckingham declined to throw even a page, much less the previously sanctioned book, at them. They were dismissed on the time they had served awaiting trail in 1980-1981, amounts from 5 days to 17 months.

Buckingham said the crimes were minor and not violent: "The defendants were attempting to make statements. I agree with many of the statements...The nuclear industry is a frightening subject."

The judge has an incorrigibility of his own, an open mind. He broke ranks from most judges in antiwar civil disobedience cases by allowing the eight to speak in court both of their motivations and their vehemence against the American military machine. Not a one of the eight was burdened by reticence, despite the memory of the original sentencing judge in 1981 who treated the defendants as self-anointed, Christ-hounded doomsayers who broke the law and now needed to have the law break them, and without a peep from the docket. That judge was criticized by the Superior Court for his "acrimonious series of confrontations."

Before a calmer judge this time, each of the eight restated what Thoreau, Gandhi, the Rev. Martin Luther King, Jr. and other miscreants had told their courts after guilty verdicts were delivered: Conscience comes before the state, no one is excused from defying unjust laws. The 1980 statement of the group, issued when entering the bomb factory, still held: "In confronting General Electric, we choose to obey God's law of life, rather than a corporate summons to death. Our beating of swords into plowshares is a way to enflesh this biblical call. In our action, we draw on a deep-rooted faith in Christ, who changed the course of history through his willingness to suffer rather than to kill. We are filled with hope for our world and for our children as we join in this act of resistance."

After listening to the Plowshares Eight, Buckingham acknowledged that when he "came down here today my ideas were a little different." The judge praised the defense attorney, Ramsay Clark, a former U.S. attorney general who described the eight as "a gentle, principled, loving and devoted people who have made a stunning difference in the lives of all who know them and, beyond that, in the lives of millions."

Most judges, products first of law schools that require no courses on civil disobedience and then years of not questioning a government that bankrolls the legal slaughter that results from weapons making, disdain such dissidents as the Plowshares Eight. "Who are you to be above the law?" is the rote query. If the question were fairly phrased, it would ask, "Who are you to be above the law that sanctions human annihilation?" Then the answer is rational: "I'm a citizen with a conscience that values life over state-ordered killing."

As surely as the General Electrics keep the assembly lines of death in high gear, protesters keep coming. The Nuclear Resister Newsletter, a Tuscan publication, reports that 37,000 citizens were arrested in the

United States and Canada in the 1980s for antinuclear disobedience.

These citizens are to be honored, their defiance celebrated. They protest legal violence, always the last temple to be stormed because the idolatry of law is America's civil religion. General Electric, godlike, says, "We bring good things to life." Defy the sham of that dictum and some judge may give you life, or three-to-ten years.

Unless we teach our children peace, someone else will teach them violence.

The Town That Defiled the Holocaust

by Grace Scales Yoder

We must set the scene. The year is 1943. Icicles hang like gloom from roofs in the remote French village. In better weather, it is a six-hour drive to Paris. During this dreary winter, however, few persons brave the tortuous roads as far as the next town.

The village is Le Chambon-sur-Lignon, a fleck on the French map with little to distinguish it from similar villages throughout the Cevennes Mountains. Le Chambon is in the free zone; it has escaped German occupation. But not for much longer; the Nazis swarm through central France seeking to eradicate Jews and the underground.

Le Chambon is in Protestant country. In Roman Catholic France, small enclaves of Huguenots still practice the Calvinistic religion of their forebears. These are peasants, but they are performing a heroic task: they are concealing several hundred refugees, most of whom are Jewish.

They do this knowing that anyone caught hiding Jews is subject to arrest, deportation, and even death. The clandestine effort is led by the fiery Huguenot pastor, Andre Trocme and his soft-spoken assistant, Edouard Theis. They collaborate with American Quakers and the Salvation Army.

Vichy officials know that Le Chambon is nicknamed the "Jewish nest in Protestant country," but they have been loathe to prosecute fellow countrymen. So as long as the Chambonese cover their tracks well, Vichy police look the other way.

But not so the Germans. As the Nazi presence grows, the two pastors periodically slip out of town to avoid arrest. But their clandestine network continues. Le Chambon is the main way station in an underground railroad spanning convents and farms from southern France to Geneva.

Some 2,500 Jews will pass through Chambon before the war ends. The 1,000 inhabitants don't expect recognition for their efforts, but in a generation they will nonetheless be immortalized.

Five years ago, Philip Hallie's *Lest Innocent Blood Be Shed* popularized the story of Le Chambon. Hallie, a philosophy professor at Wesleyan University, had become disillusioned – even cynical – as he explored ethical rationalizations for the Holocaust. Le Chambon's weaponless resistance to the Nazis convinced him that humanity is capable of genuine good.

Two years after Hallie's book hits U.S. bookstores, I am in France on a grant to study French Protestantism. Several pastors tell me that Le Chambon is their spiritual capital. I trek to Le Chambon to see whether it is as Hallie portrayed it.

I have written to 82-year-old Edouard Theis, the quieter of the wartime pastor-leaders (Andre Trocme died in the mid-sixties.) Theis has retired to a hamlet 30 minutes from Le Chambon and offers to accompany me on visits to elderly Chambonese who led the refugee effort.

Our first stop is the home of Mme. Barraud, a slender widow no more than four feet eight inches tall. Her story unfolds as it surely must have for Hallie – how she operated a boardinghouse for students who were, in the main, East European refugees; how an anonymous phone call would warn of a raid, and her boarders would flee to the woods as Gestapo trucks pulled in at the presbytery; and finally, how during a raid, her daughter was accidently shot to death.

The conversation veers to Hallie's book. Mme. Barraud says she knows enough English to make out most of it. Her reaction: "What's the big deal? Mr. Hallie acts as if we did something extraordinary. We did the only decent thing."

Everyone I talk with in Le Chambon – including Pastor Theis – shares this business-as-usual attitude about risking one's life for others. Mme. Barraud's modesty aside, Le Chambon's effort truly was exceptional.

But why did it happen? Perhaps the extraordinary effort was rooted in the Reformed faith of the inhabitants. Certainly religious commitment was central to saving the refugees. But there must have been more to the effort. Other towns within a fifty-mile radius – as Protestant as Le Chambon – did little to help refugees. Many Frenchmen willingly hid Jews when they happened by. But Pastors Trocme and Theis did more: they asked the Quakers to send refugees their way.

159

Also, the pastors found money and supplies to make the project feasible, first from Quakers and later from the Cimade, an ecumenical service organization whose sole mission was to help refugees. At the ministers' behest, the Cimade set up a refugee center near Le Chambon. After the Nazis invaded southern France, the Cimade manufactured false identity cards and negotiated with Swiss officials to gain asylum for the refugees, who were led along an underground railroad into Switzerland. Theis worked closely with the group in smuggling refugees. For this, he spent many a night in Swiss jails.

The inhabitants of Le Chambon knew early something of the stake involved in saving Jews. Theis recalls a talk given to regional Reformed Church leaders soon after the 1940 surrender, warning that Germany's anti-Semitic policies could lead to disaster for European Jews. The speaker was Andre Philip, leader in the nascent Resistance movement.

"That meeting convinced Trocme that Le Chambon should become a haven for anyone persecuted during the war," Theis said. Trocme took his idea to the town's officials and the church presbyterial council. Both groups were easily persuaded that Le Chambon should become a refuge.

Miss Lesley Maber, a British teacher who has lived in Le Chambon since the thirties, believes that the Huguenot tradition of clandestine workshop, developed during centuries of persecution, contributed to the Chambonese's sensitivity to persecution of others.

"When I first moved here, I was struck by how the Camisard wars – the oppressions of two hundred years ago – were recounted as if they were yesterday," she says. (The Camisard wars of 1702-1704 pitted make-shift Protestant insurgents against royal French troops, who finally won.)

Andre Chamson, a Cevenole Protestant and member of the elite *Academie Française*, observes that Protestants of southern France are marked by persecution unlike that anywhere else in the world. This theme pervades many of his novels and essays.

Moreover, during the war, the French Reformed Church encouraged its leaders to oppose fascism. The teachings of Swiss theologian, Karl Barth, provided spiritual impetus. His emphasis that one must obey God above all other considerations fitted conveniently with the tales of Camisard insurgence that were still popular in Le Chambon.

Protestants often are regarded as political mavericks in France, fitting in neither Right nor Left. "Here in the south of France," said Jean Valette, a regional director of the Reformed Church, "Protestantism has traditionally been strong. One also finds more local governments opposing the status quo. The two are interrelated."

While Trocme and Theis were hatching a grand scheme for their tiny parish, many French were rationalizing that Germans were fighting the Communists and that it must be a good thing. Vichy was their punishment for the political evils of the thirties - such as paying higher wages to workers and flirting with Communism during the Popular Front years. It was for history to determine which view was right.

Publication of *Lest Innocent Blood Be Shed* has not changed Le Chambon. Though its elderly citizens seek no publicity, they are obviously glad their work is not forgotten. One wonders, though, whether Chambon youth realize what their grandparents did. Le Chambon is still little visited; most strangers are just passing through. Occasional Jews still make a pilgrimage here, if only to read the Hebrew plaque across from the Reformed Church. Perhaps the biggest change since the war is demographic: the population is now about evenly split between Protestants and Catholics.

One leaves believing that the elderly Chambonese—most now in their eighties —would harbor refugees again. But not because an American professor wrote a nice book about them. They would do it because it is the decent thing to do.

As Paster Theis and I finish chatting with Mme. Barraud and gather our things to leave, she invites me to return. "Next time you visit," she says with a heavy Cevenole accent, "Just let me know. I have plenty of room upstairs; I'd love to have you."

She means it.

Lest Innocent Blood Be Shed

by Philip Hallie

Cadaverous as they were – their yellow complexion may have come from the only staple of their diet, rutabagas – the prisoners' camaraderie was magnificent and lifted the three men's hearts.

That first evening in the camp, Trocme, joking with the others, opened up the roll of toilet paper in order to share it with them. On the outer sheets, he found, written in pencil, verses of consolation from the Bible. He stopped laughing, and so did his new friends. Magda believes the Darbystes, who knew the Bible by heart, might have written them; Trocme himself believed it was a member of his parish. But whoever wrote them, those verses reminded Trocme that he was still a part of Le Chambon.

In the course of a few days, the Chambonnais learned much about their fellow inmates. They learned that most of them were the leaders of the most important Communist cells in southwest France; some of these leaders had been interned here since the Hitler-Stalin Pact of 1939. Some of them were Catholics who had opposed Vichy's dictatorial and anti-Semitic policies. And there was one nonbelieving Protestant whose only mark of distinction was that he attached himself to the Chambonnais from the very beginning, only out of greed for the gifts they were getting from the village.

At first, the three nonviolent Protestants were severely criticized by some of these people. Some thought that they were, or at least might well be, moutons (black sheep) who had been placed there to betray the most active resisters by passing information to Vichy about their hopes and hatreds and plans. But these made a small group, or at least a quiet one. The group who openly and regularly attacked the Protestants was the Communists, who were angry and bitter at their nonviolence. "You refuse to kill?" they would say. " Why, in war – and we are in a state of war with Vichy and Germany – that's aiding and abetting the enemy! You're peddling the same old opiate of the people that has kept the masses from moving forward to social justice!"

But it did not take Trocme long to show them that they and their people in Le Chambon were as vigorous and daring in their resistance to Vichy and Germany as the most aggressive inmates in the camp. He had always disliked intensely the connotations of the term "pacifist", with its suggestions of passivity and even retreat, and his few remarks about the activities in the village of Le Chambon swiftly persuaded most of them that, in their own way, by their own principles, the people of the village were doing the best they could against the powers dominating Europe and threatening to dominate the world.

One evening in the course of their first weeks in the camp, Trocme and twenty-nine other prisoners were listening to a BBC broadcast emanating from a radio concealed in a jar. Suddenly, the announcer stopped the quiet flow of information with an announcement: The battle of Stalingrad was over; the Germans had suffered the most terrible defeat in the history of the Third Reich. All of the thirty men in the barracks room burst into cheers.

But the same outward signs concealed basic inward differences among them. Those patriotic followers of de Gaulle, the members of his Secret Army, were full of joy at the prospect of their country's liberation after three years of deprivation, humiliation and death at the hands of the Germans. To them, this was the beginning of France's rebirth. The Communists, most of them Partisan Sharpshooters, cheered for the victory of Russia and of Communism. They saw this not as a national matter, but as one involving all the downtrodden peoples of the world. At last, institutionalized cruelty, capitalistic Fascism, suffered a truly major defeat. For them, this moment was the beginning of a glorious epoch when the weak ones of the earth, the workers of the world, would have their chains smashed by a victorious Communist Russia.

But Trocme, Theis and Darcissac had other thoughts. They too saw Hitler as a monster who had invented and mobilized a great evil; and they too rejoiced at this, his most significant defeat thus far. But, for them, the killing that had created this great victory over murder and humiliation was itself evil. de Gaulle's Secret Army was an army dedicated to military victory by means of killing; the Communists were an international force eager to use any means, including killing and the hatred that motivates killing, to eliminate institutionalized cruelty from the face of the earth; but though the Chambonnais were friends of France and friends of the weak, the poor people of the earth, for them human life was so precious that they found it impossible to justify the killing that had produced this great victory.

Unlike other groups in the camp, political doctrines were not part of their thinking. An intimate, ethical and religious judgment caused their deep ambivalence about the victory at Stalingrad. Trocme had a desire (as he put it in his notebooks) "not to be separated from Jesus." What this meant to him was that God had shown mankind how precious man was to Him by taking the form of a human being and coming down to help human beings find their deepest happiness. Trocme believed also that Jesus had demonstrated that love for mankind by dying for us on the cross. And if these beliefs sounded too mysterious, he knew that Jesus had himself refused to do violence to mankind, refused to harm the enemies of his precious existence as a human being. In short, Jesus was for Trocme the embodied forgiveness of sins, and staying close to Jesus meant always being ready to forgive your enemies instead of torturing and killing them. Trocme could not bear to separate himself from Jesus by ignoring the precious quality of human life that God had demonstrated in the birth, the life and the crucifixion of His son.

When, decades later, I asked Edouard Theis whether he and Trocme believed that the Soviet Union should have used means other than violence to protect herself from the Germans, he answered, "No. They had to use violence then. It was too late for nonviolence. Both the Germans and the Russians were embarques, committed to mass murder – that is, to warfare – and they had to play out their terrible roles upon each other. Besides," he added, "nonviolence involves preparation and organization, methods patiently and unswervingly employed - the Russians knew nothing of all this. Nonviolence must have deep roots and strong branches before it can bear the fruit it bore in Le Chambon. Nonviolence for them would have been suicide; it was too late."

While the cheering was going on, Theis and Trocme could not express these convictions to their newfound friends. But in the course of the weeks that followed that momentous announcement, the old inmates came to understand that the three Huguenots were brave men who had spent the past three years leading a whole village into stubborn, active resistance against the cruel ones of the earth. Bravery, especially humble, efficacious bravery, not simply inner spiritual fortitude, was for most of the inmates an impressive virtue, and so with every passing day, understanding and warmth increased and made the newcomers the spiritual nucleus of the camp.

They envisioned a school that would draw its students and faculty from around the world by virtue of its excellence, by virtue of the fine air of Le Chambon, and by virtue of its freedom from bureaucratic red tape; a school that had a spirit, the spirit of nonviolence, a spirit of internationalism and peace, even though the main function of the curriculum was to be that of preparing teenagers for their baccalaureates.

Such a school would keep the tradesmen and artisans of the village occupied during the winter months if it grew to any appreciable size, since the village was small and isolated, and students, faculty and visitors would have their needs. It would keep the village alive until the tourists came back. But, of equal importance, it would help the world outside Le Chambon by sending into it graduates with a deep understanding of the possibility and meaning of nonviolence in a violent world.

By 1938, Andre Trocme had found the person he needed to help him start the school: his silent, elephantine friend from University of Paris days, Edouard Theis. Theis had experience as a teacher - he had taught in America, Madagascar and the Cameroons. And Theis was a conscientious objector. Part of his livelihood would come from the parish, since he would be half-time pastor at the temple, and another part would come from his activities as first director of the school and teacher of French, Latin and Greek.

In the fall of 1938, the school was tiny, comprising four teachers and eighteen students. There were other teachers, including Mildred Theis and Magda Trocme, but they were not paid. There was patchwork to be done; they had no teacher of the sciences and had to send their students to Roger Darcissac's public Boys' School in order to fill this gap. But this was easy to manage, since Darcissac was secretary of the parish and soon a devoted friend of Trocme. He arranged the whole matter without consulting his superiors in the public school system of France.

Behind the temple there was an annex, divided into sections by very thin walls; here the first language lessons were given, and since one could hear what was happening in the next room about as well as one could hear what was happening in one's own, the place sounded like the Tower of Babel. The temple and its annex were on one side of a busy road, and Darcissac's Boys' School was on the other side of it, facing the temple. The students had to walk around the temple and cross the road in order to study the sciences.

The first few years of the school's history were very

difficult for reasons other than convenience, however. From 1938 to 1940, Hitler's Germany was growing in military power and bellicosity, and fear and hatred of the Germans were rising in France. Conscientious objection to war was being attacked more and more passionately as unpatriotic, dangerous sentimentality. And so when they most needed support, at the founding of the school, Trocme and Theis found themselves deserted by many conscientious objectors, whose patriotism and distrust of Germany were stronger than their love for peace. Many of the pacifists had based their beliefs upon their confidence in the promises of Hitler, but as more and more of those promises were being violated by the Germans, more and more conscientious objectors gave up their nonviolence.

But Trocme's and Theis' nonviolence had a more stable foundation than that of confidence in the Germans. It was based upon the belief that in the Bible, God told us not to kill our fellow man and gave that commandment utter clarity in the life and death of Jesus Christ. And Trocme had a practical belief, a belief that held out for him a promise of success: he believed that love – that feeling, thinking, and acting as if life is precious beyond all price – would manage to find a way to restrain what his notes call "diabolical forces like Nazism."

What saved the school was not only Trocme's clear statement of this position to the parish but also the political structure of the Protestant churches of France. Local independence is crucial in that structure. Parishioners elect a presbyterial council, and this council has very great power. It chooses, oversees and, if need be, dismisses its pastors with no substantial consultation with regional or national synods. The presbyterial council of Le Chambon endorsed Trocme's nonviolence and vowed to support him if war came, and he was legally designated as a conscientious objector. Since such a designation would make him a violator of the law, such a vow on their part expressed great loyalty to their pastor. Just as Trocme would not separate himself from Jesus by hating and killing his fellow man, so the Chambonnais would not separate themselves from their energetic minister.

As Hitler grew in power by actions that dropped nations into his hand like ripe plums, the school grew in size. In a few years, when somebody asked the stationmaster of the tiny railroad station where the Cevenol School was, he would sweep his arms around and say, "The school is everywhere." There were students, faculty and classrooms throughout the village. For their classwork, students usually stayed in a given room, and their teachers came and went, usually

on the run, "like poisoned rats," as the teachers put it.

One of the reasons for the rapid growth of the school was the coming of refugees from Central and Eastern Europe. The love of tyranny and the hatred of the Jew in those places had become clear to them, as clear as the growing military power of Hitler, and so they ran. They ran to many secluded villages in southern France, but in Le Chambon they found not only open doors to homes, but places as teachers and students in the Cevenol School as well. The number of refugees was not great at first (there are no statistics), for the school itself had only forty students, only a few of whom were refugees. The adventure of Le Chambon was barely beginning.

The box-shaped, granite temple of Le Chambon has against its west wall a high wooden pulpit from which the pastor always speaks, after having climbed a staircase to reach it. From that pulpit, Theis and Trocme preached resistance against the hatred, betrayal and naked destruction that Nazi Germany stood for. They insisted, in those times when some nations were trying to appease Hitler, that a nation, like an individual, must do all it can to resist le mal (evil, harmdoing). They attacked the spirit behind the "Keep America out of war" statements that were coming from across the Atlantic; they felt that while evil was being loosed upon the world, neutrality was complicity in that evil.

But their sermons had another aspect: in attacking evil, we must cherish the preciousness of all human life. Our obligation to diminish the evil in the world must begin at home; we must not do evil, must not ourselves do harm. To be against evil is to be against the destruction of human life and against the passions that motivate that destruction.

But the sermons did not propose a neat blueprint for fighting hatred with love. They were not attempts to tell the world or Le Chambon exactly how to overcome Hitler's evil with love. In those last years of the 1930s, the sermons said: Work and look hard for ways, for opportunities to make little moves against destructiveness. The sermons did not tell what those moves should be; they said only that an imitator of Christ must somehow make such moves when the occasion arises. They were preaching an attitude of resistance and of canny, unsentimental watching for opportunities to do something in the spirit of that resistance. Those opportunities soon came.

During the last months of the war, after the Trocmes came back from their exile, Saint-Quentin was like a sprawling hospital. The smells of chemicals and of rotting flesh were everywhere and, at night, trains full of bodies from the front crossed the city to the places where the bodies were to be incinerated. With all this, the hatred of the French toward their German occupiers grew more and more bitter; but, in the midst of all this, Andre Trocme began to have a fundamental, single attitude toward mankind - including the enemies of France, his mother's compatriots, the Germans.

One day, he saw coming toward him a straggling column of wounded German soldiers. The Germans were losing the war and, lacking transportation, the wounded had to drag their broken bodies step-by-step to the hospitals assigned to them. In the first row of the column, the seventeen-year-old boy saw three heavily bandaged men. The man in the middle had, instead of a head, an enormous ball of bandages. He probably could not see, because he stumbled and was being led by his comrades. When he came closer, the boy saw that he had no lower jaw. In its place, there was a ball of linen, and from this ball there hung clots of blood.

Andre Trocme had played at war in the walled garden, and he had heard war being discussed as if it were an heroic duel of honor between good and evil, a duel in which the honor, courage and skill of one adversary sent the other down to deserved defeat. Now that the Germans were losing, this idea of war was a mania in Saint-Quentin; around him there was not only hatred for the crumbling enemy, but triumphant contempt. But he could not hate nor could he despise that man without a jaw. And, for the first time in his life, he found his hatred turning not against the enemy but against the war that had wounded that particular man so terribly. All he could think of as he looked at the blinded, stumbling monster was, "Look there, see what you have done to you brother."

A few days later, he met a German soldier on the staircase of his own house, part of which was being used as military quarters. The German stopped, looked kindly at the lad, and touched his arm. "Are you hungry?" he asked in German, and offered him a bit of Kartoffelbrot, the black potato bread of the German Army.

"No," Andre answered in German, "but even if I were hungry, I would not take bread from you because you are an enemy."

"No! No! I am not your enemy," the soldier said.

"Yes, you are," the young man persisted. "You are my enemy. You wear that uniform and tomorrow you

will perhaps kill my brother, who is a French soldier fighting against you, trying to get you Germans out of our country. Why have you come into our country carrying war and suffering and misery?"

"I am not what you think," he answered. "I am a Christian. Do you believe in God?"

The boy's face brightened slightly - the man was using words he had often heard and uttered throughout his young life.

"At Breslau, we found Christ," the soldier went on, "and we have given Him our life." Then he told Trocme about a certain sect to which he now belonged.

The soldier said, "Men cannot hurt those who have put all their confidence in God. One day a man who hated the work of our sect came into the meeting hall to kill our leader, but his pistol misfired, and we all knew this was a sign from Heaven."

Standing there on the staircase, with his hand on the young man's arm, he went on, "I shall not kill your brother; I shall kill no Frenchman. God has revealed to us that a Christian must not kill, ever. We never carry arms."

"But how can that be?" the boy asked. "After all, you are a soldier."

"Well, I explained all this to my captain, and he has allowed me to go into battle without arms. Usually, telegraphers like me carry a pistol - or a bayonet, at least. I have nothing. I am often in danger when I am in the lines, but then I sing a hymn and I pray to God. If He has decided to keep me alive, He will. If not. . .".

Andre Trocme had met his first conscientious objector. Perhaps if the soldier had been French, the boy would have been indignant at him for refusing to defend his country when Andre's brother was out there fighting for it and for his own life. But here was a German simply refusing to do what he saw as an immoral job. The courage and faith of the man were plain, and the boy invited Kindler (that was his name) to come to the union for the next Sunday service. Kindler accepted the invitation.

Earlier in the war, the boy had walked across Saint-Quentin with some of his German relatives, shame-facedly speaking German with them before his French compatriots. His warmhearted relatives had come to the city toward the beginning of the German occupation of Saint-Quentin to bring the Trocmes much needed food and clothing. These walks had been an agony for the patriotic young Frenchman. Now he was walking across the city at the side of a uniformed German soldier. But something was different - he was beginning to feel that every human being embodied something precious.

When they entered the bare hall of the union, his companions showed their surprise at seeing him bring a German soldier to their services. But when he explained, in the simple language of Kindler himself, that this man was a true Christian, and that he would kill no one because he obeyed Jesus Christ, they immediately adopted Kindler as one of their number, like the believing children they all were.

After the simple Protestant ceremony, Kindler gave him some papers and other private possessions and said that he had to go to the front but he would try to return to pick up his things. "If I am wounded," he said, "or if I am made prisoner, you will hear from me. If I return home, you will hear from me, too. But if you do not hear from me, send these things to my wife at the address I have written on this paper. If you do not hear from me, it is because God has judged it right to take me unto Himself."

No word ever came from Kindler. After a while, the lad sent Kindler's possessions to his family.

The attitude of nonviolence toward all human beings came to Andre Trocme from many sources: his mother's death, which showed him the horrible power of death, his friendships in the union, the sight of that poor monster of a German with a jaw of rags from which hung clots of blood, his own reading of the Sermon on the Mount, and many other experiences. But, in its depths, his nonviolence stayed as simple as Kindler's; it was an attitude toward people, not a carefully-argued theological position. In its depths, it was personal; it had to do with the persons he had known, and these persons were mainly his mother, that stumbling monster and Kindler. Years later, he would study theology in Paris and New York, and he would work to develop persuasive arguments for pacifism. But this work would be primarily for the sake of convincing others. In his own mind, nonviolence was completely expressed in words as simple and direct as Kindler's when he said to the boy, "One must refuse to shoot. Christ taught us to love our enemies. That is His good news, that we should help, not hurt each other."

The German's love and courage had kindled in him a love and a courage that had been waiting for a spark to ignite them.

The story became fuller long after the Liberation in 1944. In the 1960s, Magda and Andre Trocme found themselves in Munich, where Andre was lecturing on nonviolence for the International Fellowship of Reconciliation. Knowing Major Schmehling, who had been a prisoner of war immediately after the Liberation, but who had come back to Le Puy a few years later to receive, in a formal, warmhearted ceremony, the gratitude of the people of the region for all his deeds of kindness, the Trocmes went to visit him one afternoon.

He lived in a house still partially gutted by bombs. They rang his bell and, after a slight hesitation, he recognized them. "Ach! Pastor Trocme!" he said. "Naturally! Come in!"

After a while, Trocme said, "I am here to ask you two questions, Herr Schmehling. The first is: You knew that Le Chambon was a nest of resistance; you knew we had Jews there, and the Maquis nearby. It is true that your German police did us harm, but why did you not send a punitive expedition to destroy the village in those last months? Surely you were doing this elsewhere in France, and in places near Le Chambon. . ."

"Monsieur Trocme," he answered, "it is difficult to answer that question. You know that we had in the department of Haute Loire the Tartar Legion under SS Colonel Metzger." Trocme knew of the man who had been the prosecuting attorney in Le Forestier's trial, and who had been executed for war crimes after the Liberation. "Well," Schmehling went on, "Colonel Metzger was a hard one, and he kept insisting that we move in on Le Chambon. But I kept telling him to wait. At his trial, I had heard the words of Dr. Le Forestier, who was a Christian and who had explained to me very clearly why you were all disobeying our orders in Le Chambon. I believed that your doctor was sincere. I am a good Catholic, you understand, and I can grasp these things."

Schmehling went on, "I told Metzger that this kind of resistance had nothing to do with violence, nothing to do with anything we could destroy with violence. With all my personal and military power, I opposed sending his legion into Le Chambon."

Nonviolent Weapons of the Spirit

by Colman McCarthy

In courses on nonviolence that I've been teaching for the past seven years in high schools and colleges, no question arises more frequently than this: Nonviolence is fine as an abstract intellectual system, but do you seriously believe it would have succeeded in the real world against the Nazis?

The question – usually thrown up as a statement wanting to end the discussion, not broaden it – is currently being answered in a low-budget film, now playing at the Key in Georgetown, that is making its modestly advertised way across the country. *Weapons of the Spirit*, written, directed and produced by Pierre Sauvage, tells the story of Le Chambon, a farming village in central France that nonviolently defied the German Army in the occupation during World War II.

The film–in understated narrative and with simple photography–presents surviving villagers whose fearlessness and quality of love in the early 1940s led them to harbor 5,000 Jewish refugees.

Other villages hid Jews, but they were few and did so only reluctantly. Le Chambon deliberately sought refugees by putting out the word that all were welcome. The Chambonnais were Huguenots–Protestants in a Catholic country who had not forgotten centuries of persecution.

Le Chambon was unique for another reason: It did not adopt pacifism as a strategy the day the Gestapo swept into town. Citizens had embraced it as a way of life years before. Saving Jewish refugees was the external fulfillment of the internal commitment to peace through the strength of nonviolence.

In their defiance of Nazis, the villagers, most of them peasants, were led by their pacifist minister, Andre Trocme. When France surrendered to Germany, he called on his people to resist Nazis with "weapons of the spirit."

Trocme and his family came to Le Chambon in 1934. Part of his ministry was establishing a parish-supported school where the study of nonviolence and pacifism was emphasized. When the Nazis came, the town had a choice for self-defense: violent or nonviolent. It could choose the superior one of nonviolence because it was educated by the pastor in the theories and techniques.

In *Weapons of the Spirit*, villagers, now in their seventies and eighties, recall their nonviolent resistance and harboring of refugees as exercises in common decency, not uncommon valor. What is life for, they had been taught to wonder, if not to risk for others? What is peacemaking for, if not to do it at the moment of crisis. Anyone can be a pacifist between wars.

Two years after Trocme's death in 1971, some of his essays were collected in *Jesus and the Nonviolent Revolution*. The writing is as virile as anything found in Gandhi or Martin Luther King ,Jr. when they wrote of nonviolence. Trocme addressed the question of how to stop the world's Hitlers:

"People say, ' Our nation is about to be exterminated; or the future of our civilization, of our moral values, of true religion, is threatened; or yet, our institutions violate human rights to save human rights, we must temporarily forget our scruples and use violence, sacrificing men to destroy unjust structures, and thus saving the poor from oppression.' For centuries both progressive and reactionary camps have been 'temporarily' choosing violence, 'temporarily' shedding the blood of millions of victims in the name of a better future. Because each side speculates about 'what would happen if we let the enemy win,' they mercilessly sacrifice man, whether friend or enemy...And every generation is faced with new options time after time considered to be so important that it repeatedly believes itself compelled to use violence."

In addition to *Weapons of the Spirit*, the story of Trocme and Le Chambon is told in *Lest Innocent Blood Be Shed* by Philip Hallie. In the 1979 book, Hallie, a professor at Wesleyan University, captures the soul of the pastor much as Pierre Sauvage's film reveals the iron of the villagers: Trocme "believed that decent people who stay inactive out of cowardice or indifference when around them human beings are being humiliated and destroyed are the most dangerous people in the world. His nonviolence was not passive or saccharine, but an almost brutal force for awakening human beings."

After World War II, the historian and military strategist B.H. Liddell Hart interviewed German generals on the different kinds of resistance they met in occupied countries. As practiced in Denmark, Norway, Holland and such places as Le Chambon, nonviolent resistance was effective. The Nazis, Hart writes, had an "inability to cope with it. They were experts in violence, and had been trained to deal with opponents who used that method. But other forms of resistance baffled them...It was a relief to them when resistance became violent."

By defending themselves with love, the strongest weapon of the spirit, the Chambonnais gave the Nazis no relief.

from Washington Post, *February 25, 1990*

But what is war? What is needed for success in warfare? What are the habits of the military? The aim of war is murder, the methods of war are spying, treachery, and their encouragement, the ruin of a country's inhabitants, robbing them to feed the army, and fraud and falsehood termed military craft. The habits of the military class are the absence of freedom, that is, discipline, idleness, ignorance, cruelty, debauchery, and drunkenness. And in spite of all this, it is the highest class, respected by everyone. And he who kills the most people receives the highest awards.

Chapter XXV, War and Peace
Leo Tolstoy

Patriotism or Peace

by Leo Tolstoy

Strange is the egotism of private individuals, but the egotists of private life are not armed, do not consider it right either to prepare or use arms against their adversaries; the egotism of private individuals is under the control of the political power and of public opinion. A private person who with gun in his hand takes away his neighbor's cow, or a desyatina of his crop, will immediately be seized by a policeman and put into prison. Besides, such a man will be condemned by public opinion—he will be called a thief and robber. It is quite different with the states: they are all armed—there is no power over them, except the comical attempts at catching a bird by pouring some salt on its tail—attempts at establishing international congresses, which, apparently, will never be accepted by the powerful states (who are armed for the very purpose that they may not pay any attention to any one), and, above all, public opinion, which rebukes every act of violence in a private individual, extols, raises to the virtue of patriotism every appropriation of what belongs to others, for the increase of the power of the country.

Open the newspapers for any period you may wish, and at any moment you will see the black spot—the cause of every possible war: now it is Korea, now the Pamir, now the lands in Africa, now Abyssinia, now Turkey, now Venezuela, now the Transvaal. The work of the robbers does not stop for a moment, and here and there a small war, like an exchange of shots in the cordon, is going on all the time, and the real war can and will begin at any moment.

If an American wishes the preferential grandeur and well-being of America above all other nations, and the same is desired for his state by an Englishman, and a Russian, and a Turk, and a Dutchman, and an Abyssinian, and a citizen of Venezuela and of the Transvaal, and an Armenian, and a Pole, and a Bohemian, and all of them are convinced that these desires need not only not be concealed or repressed, but should be a matter of pride and be developed in themselves and in others; and if the greatness and well-being of one country or nation cannot be obtained except to the detriment of another nation, frequently of many countries and nations—how can war be avoided?

And so, not to have any war, it is not necessary to preach and pray to God about peace, to persuade the English-speaking nations that they ought to be friendly toward one another, in order to be able to rule over other nations; to form double and triple alliances against one another; to marry princes to princesses of other nations—but to destroy what produces war. But what produces war is the desire for an exclusive good for one's own nation—what is called patriotism. And so to abolish war, it is necessary to abolish patriotism, and to abolish patriotism, it is necessary first to become convinced that it is an evil, and that it is hard to do. Tell people that war is bad, and they will laugh at you: who does not know that? Tell them that patriotism is bad, and the majority of people will agree with you, but with a small proviso. "Yes, bad patriotism is bad, but there is also another patriotism, the one we adhere to." But wherein this good patriotism consists no one can explain. If good patriotism consists in not being acquisitive, as many say, it is nonetheless retentive; that is, men want to retain what was formerly acquired, since there is no country which was not based on conquest, and it is impossible to retain what is conquered by any other means than those by which it was acquired, that is, by violence and murder. But even if patriotism is not retentive, it is restorative—the patriotism of the vanquished and oppressed nations, the Armenians, Poles, Bohemians, Irish, and so forth. This patriotism is almost the very worst, because it is the most enraged and demands the greatest degree of violence.

Patriotism cannot be good. Why do not people say that egotism can be good, though this may be asserted more easily, because egotism is a natural sentiment, with which a man is born, while patriotism is an unnatural sentiment, which is artificially inoculated in him?

It will be said: "Patriotism has united men in states and keeps up the unity of the states." But the men are already united in states—the work is all done: why should men now maintain an exclusive loyalty for their state, when this loyalty produces calamities for all states and nations? The same patriotism which produced the unification of men into states is now destroying those states. If there were but one patriotism—the patriotism of none but the English—it might be regarded as unificatory or beneficent, but when, as now, there are American, English, German, French, Russian patriotisms, all of them opposed to one another, patriotism no longer unites, but disunites. To say that, if patriotism was beneficent, by uniting men into states, as was the case during its highest development in Greece and Rome, patriotism even now, after 1,800 years of Christian life, is just as beneficent, is the same as saying that, since the ploughing was useful and beneficent for the field before the sowing, it will be as useful now, after the crop has grown up.

It would be very well to retain patriotism in memory of the use which it once had, as people preserve and retain the ancient monuments of temples, as mausoleums stand, without causing any harm to men, while patriotism produces without cessation innumerable calamities.

What now causes the Armenians and the Turks to suffer and cut each other's throats and act like wild beasts? Why do England and Russia, each of them concerned about her share of the inheritance from Turkey, lie in wait and do not put a stop to the Armenian atrocities? Why do the Abyssinians and Italians fight one another? Why did a terrible war come very near breaking out on account of Venezuela, and now on account of the Transvaal? And the Chino-Japanese War, and the Turkish, and the German, and the French wars? And the rage of the subdued nations, the Armenians, the Poles, the Irish? And the preparation for war by all the nations? All that is the fruits of patriotism. Seas of blood have been shed for the sake of this sentiment, and more blood will be shed for its sake, if men do not free themselves from this outlived bit of antiquity.

C'est à prendre ou à laisser, as the French say. If patriotism is good, then Christianity, which gives peace, is an idle dream, and the sooner this teaching is eradicated, the better. But if Christianity really gives peace, and we really want peace, patriotism is a survival from barbarous times, which must not only not be evoked and educated, as we now do, but which must be eradicated by all means, by preaching, persuasion, contempt, and ridicule. If Christianity is the truth, and we wish to live in peace, we must but only have no sympathy for the power of our country, but must even rejoice in its weakening, and contribute to it. A Russian must rejoice when Poland, the Baltic provinces, Finland, Armenia, are separated from Russia and made free; and an Englishman must similarly rejoice in relation to Ireland, Australia, India, and the other colonies, and cooperate in it, because the greater the country, the more evil and cruel is its patriotism, and the greater is the amount of the suffering on which its power is based. And so, if we actually want to be what we profess, we must not, as we do now, wish for the increase of our country, but wish for its diminution and weakening, and contribute to it with all our means.

And thus must we educate the younger generations: we must bring up the younger generations in such a way that, as it is now disgraceful for a young man to manifest his coarse egotism, for example, by eating everything up, without leaving anything for others, to push a weaker person down from the road, in order to pass by himself, to take away by force what another needs, it should be just as disgraceful to wish for the increase of his country's power; and, as it now is considered stupid and ridiculous for a person to praise himself, it should be considered stupid to extol one's nations, as is now done in various lying patriotic histories, pictures, monuments, textbooks, articles, sermons, and stupid national hymns. But it must be understood that so long as we are going to extol patriotism and educate the younger generations in it, we shall have armaments, which ruin the physical and spiritual life of the nations, and wars, terrible, horrible wars, like those for which we are preparing ourselves, and into the circle of which we are introducing, corrupting them with our patriotism, the new, terrible fighters of the distant East.

In reply to a prince's question how to increase his army, in order to conquer a southern tribe which did not submit to him, Confucius replied: "Destroy all thy army, and use the money, which thou art wasting now on the army, on the enlightenment of thy people and on the improvement of agriculture, and the southern tribe will drive away its prince and will submit to thy rule without war."

Letter to a Corporal

by Leo Tolstoy

(1899)

You wonder how it is soldiers are taught that it is right to kill men in certain cases and in war, where as in the Scripture, which is acknowledged to be sacred by those who teach this, there is nothing resembling such a permission, but there is the very opposite - a prohibition to commit murder and even any insult against men, a prohibition to do to others what one does not wish to have done to oneself; you ask me whether this is not a deception, and if so, for whose advantage it is practiced.

Yes, it is a deception, which is practiced in favor of those who are accustomed to living by the sweat and blood of other people and who, for this purpose, have been distorting Christ's teaching, which was given men for their good, but which now, in its distorted form, has become the chief source of all the calamities of men.

This happened in the following way:

The government and all those men of the upper classes who adhere to the government and live by the labors of others have to have means for controlling the laboring masses; the army is such a means. The defense against foreign enemies is only an excuse. The German government frightens its nation with the Russians and the French; the French frightens its nation with the Germans; the Russian frightens its nation with the Germans and the French, and so it is with all the nations; but neither the Germans, nor the Russians, nor the French wish to fight with their neighbors and with other nations; they prefer to live in peace with them and are afraid of war more than of anything in the world. But, to have an excuse in their control of the laboring masses, the governments and the upper idle classes act like a gypsy, who whips his horse around the corner and then pretends that he is not able to hold it back. They stir up their people and another government, and then pretend that for the good or for the defense of their nation, they cannot help but declare war, which again is profitable for the generals, officers, officials, merchants and, in general, for the wealthy classes. In reality, war is only an inevitable consequence of the existence of the armies; but the armies are needed by the governments merely for the purpose of controlling their own laboring masses.

It is a criminal business, but the worst thing about it is this, that the governments, to have a rational foundation for their control of the masses, are obliged to pretend that they are professing the highest religious teaching known to men, that is, the Christian, and, in this teaching, educate their subjects. This teaching is, in its essence, opposed, not only to every murder, but even to every violence, and so, to be able to control the masses and be considered Christian, the governments had to distort Christianity and to conceal its true meaning from the masses and thus to deprive men of the good which Christ brought to them.

This distortion of Christianity took place long ago, in the time of the malefactor, Emperor Constantine, who, for this, was canonized a saint. All the subsequent governments, especially our own Russian government, have tried with all their strength to maintain this distortion and not to allow the masses to see the true meaning of Christianity, because, if they saw it, they would come to understand that the governments, with their taxes, soldiers, prisons, gallows and cheating priests, are not only no pillars of Christianity, such as they pretend to be, but its greatest enemies.

In consequence of this distortion, there result those deceptions which startled you so much, and all those terrible calamities from which the masses suffer.

The masses are crushed, robbed, impoverished, ignorant – they are dying out. Why? Because the land is in the hands of the rich; because the masses are enslaved in factories, in plants in their daily occupations; because they are fleeced for the taxes, and the price for their labor is lowered, and the price for what they need is raised. How can they be freed? Shall the land again be taken away from the rich? But if that is done, the soldiers will come, will kill off the rioters and will lock them up in prisons. Shall the factories, the plants, be taken away? The same will happen. Stick out in a strike? But that will never happen – the rich can stick out longer than the laborers, and the armies will always be on the the side of the capitalists. The masses will never get away from that want in which they are held, so long as the armies shall be in the power of the ruling classes.

But who are the armies which hold the masses in this slavery? Who are those soldiers who will shoot at the peasants who have taken possession of the land, and at the strikers, if they do not disperse, and at the smugglers, who import wares without paying the revenue - who will put into prisons and keep there those who refuse to pay the taxes? These soldiers are the same peasants whose land has been taken away, the same strikers who want to raise their wages, the same payers of the taxes who want to be freed from these payments.

Why do these men shoot at their brothers? Because it has been impressed upon them that the oath which they are compelled to take upon entering military service is obligatory for them, and that they may not kill men in general, but may kill them by command of the authorities, that is, the same deception which startled so much is practiced upon them. But here arises the question – how can people of sound mind, who frequently know the rudiments and are even educated, believe in such a palpable lie? No matter how little educated a man may be, he nonetheless cannot help knowing that Christ did not permit any murder, but taught meekness, humility, forgiveness of offenses, love of enemies; he cannot help but see that, on the basis of the Christian teaching, he cannot make a promise in advance that he will kill all those whom he is commanded to kill.

Thus, the deception of the soldiers, which consists in this, that they are impressed with the idea that it is possible without sinning to kill men by command of the authorities, does not stand alone, but is connected with a whole system of deceptions, without which this particular deception would be ineffective.

Advice to a Draftee

by Leo Tolstoy

This letter by Leo Tolstoy dramatizes the frequent fact that what is past is prologue. Written in 1899 to a desperate young candidate for conscription, Tolstoy's words will seem to some to bear a relevance to America.

Count Tolstoy's letter was addressed to a young Hessian ,named Ernst Schramm, whose earlier correspondence with the great writer has been lost; Schramm evidently wrote a second time in an effort to evade Tolstoy's argument that he refuse conscription. The letter printed here is Tolstoy's response to Shramm's second letter, and it seems to have terminated the exchange. In reading Tolstoy's words against killing, one should bear in mind that both parties understood that the Hessian army in 1899 was a peacetime army, but that the penalty for evading conscription was death. Tolstoy addressed the letter to Schramm in Darmstadt, and the Hessian post office forwarded it to Aschaffenburg in Bavaria, leaving us to infer that Schramm decided not to join up but to change countries instead.

In my last letter, I answered your question as well as I could. It is not only Christians but all just people who must refuse to become soldiers – that is, to be ready on another's command (for this is what a soldier's duty actually consists of) to kill all those one is ordered to kill. The question as you state it – which is more useful, to become a good teacher or to suffer for rejecting conscription? – is falsely stated. The question is falsely stated because it is wrong for us to determine our actions according to their results, to view actions merely as useful or destructive. In the choice of our actions, we can be led by their advantages or disadvantages only when the actions themselves are not opposed to the demands of morality.

We can stay home, go abroad or concern ourselves with farming or science according to what we find useful for ourselves or others; for neither in domestic life, foreign travel, farming nor science is there anything immoral. But under no circumstance can we inflict violence on people, torture, or kill them because we think such acts could be of use to us or to others. We cannot and may not do such things, especially because we can never be sure of the results of our actions. Often, actions which seem the most advantageous of all, turn out in fact to be destructive; and the reverse is also true.

The question should not be stated: Which is more useful, to be a good teacher or to go to jail for refusing conscription? But rather: What should a man do who has been called upon for military service – that is, called upon to kill or to prepare himself to kill?

And to this question, for a person who understands the true meaning of military service and who wants to be moral, there is only one clear and incontrovertible answer: such a person must refuse to take part in military service no matter what consequences this refusal may have. It may seem to us that this refusal could be futile or even harmful, and that it would be a far more useful thing, after serving one's time, to become a good village teacher. But, in the same way, Christ could have judged it more useful for himself to be a good carpenter and submit to all the principles of the Pharisees than to die in obscurity as he did, repudiated and forgotten by everyone.

Moral acts are distinguished from all other acts by the fact that they operate independently of any predictable advantage to ourselves or to others. No matter how dangerous the situation may be of a man who finds himself in the power of robbers who demand that he take part in plundering, murder, and rape, a moral person cannot take part. Is not military service the same thing? Is one not required to agree to the deaths of all those one is commanded to kill?

But how can one refuse to do what everyone does, what everyone finds unavoidable and necessary? Or must one do what no one does and what everyone considers unnecessary or even stupid and bad? No matter how strange it sounds, this strange argument is the main one offered against those moral acts which in our times face you and every other person called up for military service. But this argument is even more incorrect than the one which would make a moral action dependent upon considerations of advantage.

If I, finding myself in a crowd of running people, run with the crowd without knowing where, it is obvious that I have given myself up to mass hysteria; but if by chance I should push my way to the front, or be gifted with sharper sight than the others or receive information that this crowd was racing to attack human beings and toward its own corruption, would I really not stop and tell the people what might rescue them? Would I go on running and do these things which I knew to be bad and

173

corrupt? This is the situation of every individual called up for military service, if he knows what military service means.

I can well understand that you, a young man full of life, loving and loved by your mother, friends, perhaps a young woman, think with a natural terror about what awaits you if you refuse conscription; and perhaps you will not feel strong enough to bear the consequences of refusal, and knowing your weakness, will submit and become a soldier. I understand completely, and I do not for a moment allow myself to blame you, knowing very well that in your place I might perhaps do the same thing. Only do not say that you did it because it was useful or because everyone does it. If you did it, know that you did wrong.

In every person's life there are moments in which he can know himself, tell himself who he is, whether he is a man who values his human dignity above his life, or a weak creature who does not know his dignity and is concerned merely with being useful (chiefly to himself). This is the situation of a man who goes out to defend his honor in a duel or a soldier who goes into battle (although here the concepts of life are wrong). It is the situation of a doctor or a priest called to someone sick with plague, of a man in a burning house or a sinking ship who must decide whether to let the weaker go first or shove them aside and save himself. It is the situation of a man in poverty who accepts or rejects a bribe. And in our times, it is the situation of a man called to military service. For a man who knows its significance, the call to the army is perhaps the only opportunity for him to behave as a morally free creature and fulfill the highest requirement of his life – or else merely to keep his advantage in sigh, like an animal and thus remain slavishly submissive and servile until humanity becomes degraded and stupid.

For these reasons, I answered your question whether one has to refuse to do military service with a categorical "yes" – if you understand the meaning of military service (and if you did not understand it then, you do now) and if you want to behave as a moral person living in our times must.

Please excuse me if these words are harsh. The subject is so important that one cannot be careful enough in expressing oneself so as to avoid false interpretation.

War and Peace

Leo Tolstoy

After passing a chasseur regiment and in the lines of the Kiev grenadiers—fine fellows busy with similar peaceful affairs—near the shelter of the regimental commander, higher than and different from the others, Prince Andrew came out in front of a platoon of grenadiers before whom lay a naked man. Two soldiers held him while two others were flourishing their switches and striking him regularly on his bare back. The man shrieked unnaturally. A stout major was pacing up and down the line, and regardless of the screams, kept repeating:

"It's a shame for a soldier to steal; a soldier must be honest, honorable, and brave, but if he robs his fellows, there is no honor in him, he's a scoundrel. Go on! Go on!"

So the swishing sound of the strokes, and the desperate but unnatural screams, continued.

"Go on, go on!" said the major.

A young officer with a bewildered and pained expression on his face stepped away from the man and looked round inquiringly at the adjutant as he rode by.

Prince Andrew, having reached the front line, rode along it. Our front line and that of the enemy were far apart on the right and left flanks, but in the center where the men with a flag of truce had passed that morning, the lines were so near together that the men could see one another's faces and speak to one another. Besides the soldiers who formed the picket line on either side, there were many curious onlookers who, jesting and laughing, stared at their strange foreign enemies.

Since early morning – despite an injunction not to approach the picket line – the officers had been unable to keep sightseers away. The soldiers forming the picket line, like showmen exhibiting a curiosity, no longer looked at the French but paid attention to the sightseers and grew weary waiting to be relieved. Prince Andrew halted to have a look at the French.

"Look! Look there!" one soldier was saying to another, pointing to a Russian musketeer who had gone up to the picket line with an officer and was rapidly and excitedly talking to a French grenadier.

"Hark to him jabbering! Fine, isn't it? It's all the Frenchy can do to keep up with him. There now, Sidorov!"

"Wait a bit and listen. It's fine!" answered Sidorov, who was considered adept at French.

The soldier to whom the laughers referred was Dolokhov. Prince Andrew recognized him and stopped to listen to what he was saying. Dolokhov had come from the left flank where their regiment was stationed, with his captain.

"Now then, go on, go on!" incited the officer, bending forward and trying not to lose a word of the speech which was incomprehensible to him. "More, please: More! What's he saying?"

Dolokhov did not answer the captain; he had been drawn into a hot dispute with the French grenadier. They were naturally talking about the campaign. The Frenchman, confusing the Austrians with the Russians, was trying to prove that the Russians had surrendered and had fled all the way from Ulm, while Dolokhov maintained that the Russians had not surrendered but had beaten the French.

"We have orders to drive you off here, and we shall drive you off," said Dolokhov.

"Only take care you and your Cossacks are not all captured!" said the French grenadier.

The French onlookers and listeners laughed.

"We'll make you dance as we did under Suvorov. . . [*on vous fera danser*]," said Dolokhov.

"*Qu'est-ce qu'il chante?* [What's he singing about?]" asked a Frenchman.

"It's ancient history," said another, guessing that it referred to a former war. "The Emperor will teach your Suvara as he has taught the others. . ."

"Bonaparte. . ." began Dolokhov, but the Frenchman interrupted him.

"Not Bonaparte. He is the Emperor! *Sacre nom..!*"

cried he angrily.

"The devil skin your Emperor."

And Dolokhov swore at him in coarse soldier's Russian and shouldering his musket walked away.

"Let us go, Ivan Lukich," he said to the captain.

"Ah, that's the way to talk French," said the picket soldiers. "Now, Sidorov, you have a try!"

Sidorov, turning to the French, winked, and began to jabber meaningless sounds very fast: "Kari, mala, tafa, safi, muter, Kaska," he said, trying to give an expressive intonation to his voice.

"Ho! ho! ho! Ha! ha! ha! Ouh! ouh!" came peals of such healthy and good-humored laughter from the soldiers that it infected the French involuntarily, so much so that the only thing left to do seemed to be to unload the muskets, explode the ammunition, and all return home as quickly as possible.

But the guns remained loaded, the loopholes in blockhouses and entrenchments looked out just as menacingly, and the unlimbered cannon confronted one another as before.

from War and Peace, *excerpts from Book Two*

Napoleon

by Leo Tolstoy

On the 29th of May, Napoleon left Dresden, where he had been spending three weeks surrounded by a court that included princes, dukes, kings, and even one emperor. Before his departure, Napoleon took a gracious leave of the princes, kings and emperor deserving of his favor, and sternly upbraided the kings and princes with whom he was displeased. He made a present of his own diamonds and pearls – those, that is, that he had taken from other kings – to the Empress of Austria. He tenderly embraced the Empress Marie Louise – who considered herself his wife, though he had another wife still living in Paris – and left her, so his historian relates, deeply distressed and hardly able to support the separation. Although diplomats still firmly believed in the possibility of peace, and were zealously working with that object, although the Emperor Napoleon, with his own hand, wrote a letter to the Emperor Alexander calling him "Monsieur mon frere," and assuring him with sincerity that he had no desire of war, and would always love and honor him, he set off to join the army, and at every station gave such commands, hastening the progress of his army from west to east. He drove in a traveling carriage, drawn by six horses and surrounded by pages, adjutants and an armed escort, along the route by Posen, Thorn, Danzig and Konigsberg. In each of these towns, he was welcomed with enthusiasm and trepidation by thousands of people.

The army was moving from west to east, and he was driven after by continual relays of six horses. On the 10th of June, he overtook the army and spent the night in the Vilkovik forest, in quarters prepared for him on the property of a Polish count.

The following day, Napoleon drove on ahead of the army, reached the Niemen, put on a Polish uniform in order to inspect the crossing of the river, and rode out on the river bank.

When he saw the Cossacks posted on the further bank and the expanse of the steppes – in the midst of which, far away, was the holy city, Moscow, capital of an empire, like the Scythian empire invaded by Alexander of Macedon – Napoleon surprised the diplomatists and contravened all rules of strategy by ordering an immediate advance, and his troops began crossing the Niemen the next day.

Early on the morning of the 12th of June he came out of his tent, which had been pitched that day on the steep left bank of the Niemen, and looked through a field glass at his troops pouring out of the Vilkovik forest, and dividing into three streams at the three bridges across the river. The troops knew of the Emperor's presence, and were on the lookout for him. When they caught sight of his figure in the greatcoat and hat standing apart from his suite in front of his tent on the hill opposite, they threw up their caps and shouted, "Vive l'Empereur!" And one regiment after another, in a continuous stream, flowed out of the immense forest that had concealed them, and split up to cross the river by the three bridges. "We shall make some way this time. Oh, when he takes a hand himself, things begin to get warm! Name of God! . . . There he is! . . . Hurrah for the Emperor! So those are the Steppes of Asia! A nasty country it is, though. Good-bye, Beauche; I'll keep the finest palace in Moscow for you. Good-bye! Good luck! . . . Have you seen the Emperor? Hurrah for the Emperor! If they make me governor of the Indies, Gerard, I'll make you minister of Cashmere, that's settled. Hurrah for the Emperor! Hurrah! Hurrah! Hurrah! The rascally Cossacks, how they are running. Hurrah for the Emperor! There he is! Do you see him? I have seen him twice as I am seeing you. The little corporal. . . I saw him give the cross to one of the veterans . . . Hurrah for the Emperor!" Such was the talk of old men and young, of the most diverse characters and positions in society. All the faces of those men wore one common expression of joy at the commencement of a long-expected campaign, and enthusiasm and devotion to the man in the gray coat standing on the hill opposite.

On the 13th of June, Napoleon mounted a small thoroughbred Arab horse and galloped towards one of the bridges of the Niemen, defended all the while by shouts of enthusiasm, which he obviously endured simply because they could not be prevented from expressing in such shouts their love for him. But those shouts, invariably accompanying him everywhere, wearied him and hindered his attending to the military problems which beset him from the time he joined the army. He rode over a swaying bridge of boats to the other side of the river, turned sharply to the left, and galloped in the direction of Kovno, preceded by horse guards, who were breathless with delight and enthusiasm, as they cleared the way before him. On reaching the broad river Niemen, he pulled up beside a regiment of Polish Uhlans on the bank.

"Vive l'Empereur!" the Poles shouted with the same enthusiasm, breaking their line and squeezing against each other to get a view of him. Napoleon looked up and down the river, got off his horse, and sat down on a log that lay on the bank. At a mute sign from him, they handed him the fieldglass. He propped it on the back of a page who had run up delighted. He began looking at the other side, then, with absorbed attention, scrutinized the map that was unfolded on the logs. Without raising his head, he said something, and two of his adjutants galloped off to the Polish Uhlans.

"What? What did he say?" was heard in the ranks of the Polish Uhlans as an adjutant galloped up to them. They were commanded to look for a fording-place and to cross to the other side. The colonel of the Polish Uhlans, a handsome old man, flushing red and stammering from excitement, asked the adjutant whether he would be permitted to swim across the river with his men instead of seeking for a ford. In obvious dread of a refusal, like a boy asking permission to get on a horse, he asked to be allowed to swim across the river before the Emperor's eyes. The adjutant replied that probably the Emperor would not be displeased at this excess of zeal.

No sooner had the adjutant said this than the old whiskered officer, with happy face and sparkling eyes, brandished his sabre in the air shouting "Vive l'Empereur!" and commanding his men to follow him, he set spurs to his horse and galloped down to the river. He gave a vicious thrust to his horse, that foundered under him, and plunged into the water, making for the most rapid part of the current. Hundreds of Uhlans galloped in after him. It was cold and dangerous in the middle of the rapid current. The Uhlans clung to one another, falling off their horses. Some of the horses were drowned, some, too, of the men; the others struggled to swim across, some in the saddle, others clinging to their horses' manes. They tried to swim straight across, and although there was a ford half a verst away, they were proud to be swimming, and drowning in the river before the eyes of that man sitting on the log and not even looking at what they were doing. When the adjutant, on going back, chose a favorable moment and ventured to call the Emperor's attention to the devotion of the Poles to his person, the little man in the gray overcoat got up, and summoning Berthier, he began walking up and down the bank with him, giving him instructions, and casting now and then a glance of displeasure at the drowning Uhlans who had interrupted his thoughts.

It was no new conviction for him that his presence in any quarter of the earth, from Africa to the Steppes of Moscow, was enough to impress men and impel them to senseless acts of self-sacrifice. He sent for his horse and rode back to his bivouac.

Forty Uhlans were drowned in the river in spite of the boats sent to their assistance. The majority struggled back to the bank from which they had started. The colonel, with several of his men, swam across the river and with difficulty clambered up the other bank. But as soon as they climbed out in drenched and steaming clothes, they shouted, "Vive l'Empereur!" looking ecstatically at the place where Napoleon had stood, though he was no longer there, and at that moment thought themselves happy.

In the evening, between giving two orders - one for hastening the arrival of the counterfeit rouble notes that had been prepared for circulation in Russia, and the other for shooting a Saxon who had been caught with a letter containing a report on the disposition of the French army - Napoleon gave a third order for presenting the colonel, who had quite unnecessarily flung himself into the river, the order of the Legion d'Honneur, of which he was himself the head. *Quos vult perdere, dementat.*

Tolstoy and the Larger Vision

by Colman McCarthy

One night in early 1851, in a Russian military camp on the outer rim of organized life and circled by gore-minded Moslem soldiers, a young man despaired of his future. A chronic card-player, drinker and womanizer, he put in his diary a thought shared by countless other militarized young men before and since: "How on earth have I ended up here? I don't know. Why? I even know less." To ease his despair and keep busy his spitfire mind, 23-year-old Leo Tolstoy kept detailed, intricate notes on what he saw, heard and felt among the people of the Caucasus. It was therapy-by-writing, the first words from a pen that was to produce some of the world's most sweeping and most read novels.

In a few weeks, the centenary of Tolstoy's "War and Peace" will be celebrated; many of those for whom Tolstoy is important will re-read this book and take up again with the others. A New York radio station, the lively WBAI-FM, plans to read over the air the entire "War and Peace" non-stop, a pleasure expected to last four or five around-the-clock days. Even more topical, perhaps, is the influence of Tolstoy on those caught up in real war and peace; many conscientious objectors are telling draft boards that their moral refusal to kill other human beings in war is based on the writings of Tolstoy.

The most common pictures show a thin rock-faced old man, hair shooting from his head like a fire hazard, but with searing, deep set eyes that look out from a never-resting soul. That may have been Tolstoy the writer of genius, but the non-writer, the man of guilts and sins, was far different. The contradictions run through his life like crossties on a railroad of wildness. He fought for freedom of the oppressed outside the home, but inside he often ran his family like a gone-mad czar. He warned others that "to marry a woman of society is to swallow the whole poison of civilization" but chose for his own wife an upper-class girl. For much of his life, Tolstoy pined after a socialism that would give ownership of the meadows and forests to everyone, while regularly making land deals that added to his already large holdings. He saw himself as sensitive and intelligent but he called Shakespeare's plays "a boundless tedium." Yet, as if fully aware of his own hypocrisy – thus taking the treachery out of it – Tolstoy could write: "Every man lies twenty times daily."

The great and heavy labor of "War and Peace" took nearly seven years of writing. The bone structure of the story was Russia's war with Napoleon in 1812, but the muscles and sinews of character portrayal are the story's movement. "Napoleon, Alexander, Kutuzov and Talleyrand are not the heroes of my book," said Tolstoy. "I shall write the story of people living in the most privileged circumstances, with no fear of poverty or constraint, free people, people who have none of the flaws that are necessary to make a mark on history."

In the most recent and perhaps most exhaustive biography of Tolstoy, Henri Troyat wrote that the novelist "was deeply attached to to ideas in 'War and Peace.' But it is not his ideas that have guaranteed the posterity of the book; it is the fact that, in spite of the historical, military and philosophical considerations that encumber it, the book is a hymn to man and nature whose like has not been seen in the literature of the world."

As with many fiction writers, Tolstoy's imaginative world was created from the real world. Heroine Natasha was partly a copy of sister-in-law Tanya, whom the novelist adored. Friends, aunts, uncles, cousins-all were illuminated in print by the sun of Tolstoy's pen. For his two heroes, Andrey Bolkonsky and Pierre Bezukhov, the writer drew on himself, as if proclaiming-with accuracy-that he had double the personality of most men. Andrey, a taut pragmatist conditioned to the world's cruelty, went into the army, as did Tolstoy, to prove his courage. Pierre, a tender, affectionate man, soft-hearted and softer headed, believed, as did Tolstoy, "we must love, we must have faith . . ." Of the two, only Pierre found peace.

Many issues of mid-19th century Russia are surprisingly similar to those in America today: freedom of the press, government reform, women's rights, reclaiming the poor, court reorganization. Russian critics of "War and Peace" hooted Tolstoy for being too remote from real problems like these. This was a standard charge, both about Tolstoy then and about many thinkers now-the get-with-it argument so cherished by liberals and sophomores foamed up about "relevance." In reality, no one feels the times more acutely than he who seeks to get beneath the acts and habits of men and understand the eternal laws that motivate them: fear, love, pride, hope, greed, ingnorance.

Enriched rather than drained by life as it passed by, Tolstoy was soon able to write a second epic novel, *Anna Karenina*. With little competition from American novelists today, with their zoom-lens delight in bedrooms, Tolstoy's study of three couples is still perhaps the world's greatest love story. Three kinds of marriages-perhaps the only three kinds-are detailed: the broken one between Anna and the clammy bureaucrat Karenin, the dried-up but surviving marriage of the Oblonskys and the innocent, happy marriage of Kitty and Levin. As in the earlier novel, the characters who best survive are not the proud and glittering, like Anna, but Kitty and Levin, the naive, shuffling-along pair whose simplicity of heart is stronger than all the world's busy sorrow combined.

A brooding, seeking man with no rest from the world or himself, Tolstoy thrived in later life on manual labor-mowing hay fields, wood chopping, caring for cattle. The muzhiks, or peasants, with whom Tolstoy worked and constantly idealized seemed not only to have the answers to life-they didn't really-but their company was naturally better for a writer. "Continual association with professors," he wrote, "leads to prolixity, love of long words and confusion, but with muzhiks, to conciseness, beauty of language and clarity."

After a brief conversion to organized religion, Tolstoy came to loathe both the doctrines of faith and the priests who preached them. His complaints against the church were correct and are not at all dated today-a rich, aloof institution, preaching peity but all the while blessing the state and its mischeif.

The value of Tolstoy's non-fiction is its message of nonviolence. He spoke out against British and American use of force in the Transvaal and the Philippines: "They are horrible, these wars that the English and Americans are waging in a world in which even school-children condemn war." Typically, he had no master plan to end war, only a simple personalistic formula-"The freeing of men from servitude, from ignorance, can not be obtained by revolution, syndicates, peace congresses, but simply by the conscience of each one of us forbidding to participate in violence and asking in amazement, why are you doing that?"

Tolstoy died in 1910, revered, famous and worn out, the storehouse of his mind long filled with the best thoughts and hopes. Few of the latter have come true-war still smothers peace and everything else. Yet those who unashamedly think that love is more essential for social change than politics and programs cling to Tolstoy as never before. A firm grip is best; as a major theme of Tolstoy's said, being ahead of the times often means being against the times.

Until now, study and research on nonviolence have enjoyed little institutional support from government, the university, or the church in the United States. Teaching nonviolence has been left to a handful of groups with limited personnel and financial support, such as the American Friends Service Committee, the Fellowship of Reconciliation, the War Resisters League, and the Catholic Worker Movement. As of 1995, only one U.S. college--Colorado College--offers even a minor in nonviolence.

Michael True

Nonviolence as Strategy and Commitment
by Robert A. Seeley

The difficulty with considering nonviolence as one strategy among others, as "pragmatic" nonviolent strategists are prone to do, is twofold. On the one hand, widespread use of nonviolence would transform the system and human relations in ways which, though not totally foreseeable, would differ sharply from the effects of any chosen military strategy. On the other hand, effective nonviolent action is difficult or impossible without a firm commitment to nonviolent discipline – a commitment generally going beyond that required to choose one strategy as against another. Thus, Gandhi says that nonviolence begins in the mind, and, if it does not, it is likely to fail.

From the pragmatic point of view, however, maintenance of nonviolent discipline is also essential. A break in the discipline would allow an occupying army an opportunity for violent repression. As Liddell Hart says:

[The German generals] were experts in violence, and had been trained to deal with opponents who used that method. But other forms of resistance baffled them - and all the more in proportion as the methods were subtle and concealed. It was a relief to them when resistance became violent, and when nonviolent forms were mixed with guerrilla action, thus making it easier to combine drastic suppressive action against both at the same time.

Thus, for nonviolent resistance to be most effective, deep commitment to nonviolent discipline is needed and, preferably, training in maintaining it.

The Dynamics of Nonviolence

Gene Sharp, one of the major theorists of nonviolence, has said that nonviolence involves a kind of "moral jiu-jitsu." This characterization, though terse, encapsulates the particular nature of nonviolent action. Nonviolence is not passive. Though it can involve persuasion, it is not merely this. Nor is it a form of coercion like that used by the military. Nonviolence seeks to establish a human bond between the resister and those being resisted. In the long run, this changes the oppressor and can transform the system which has created the oppression in the first place.

The most basic assumption of nonviolent theory, and especially of nonviolent civilian defense, is that government – and, by extension, occupation – functions only with the consent of the governed. This means literal physical cooperation. If such cooperation is withdrawn in a nonviolent way, the government faces two choices. It can modify its policies or it can repress the resistance. The latter choice is not, in general, attractive because the resisters have provided no excuse for violence. To enforce repression against unarmed people who resist without fighting back, risks undermining the morale of the occupying army. This is too real a risk for many regimes to take. Nonviolence, which uses "go-slow" tactics and other more subtle forms of resistance, can baffle an occupying force, since it can make ordinary administration difficult or impossible while providing no focus for repression.

This does not suggest that nonviolent resisters will not suffer terribly. Gandhi's movement and King's movement accepted great suffering as the price of their freedom. But in the end, both prevailed because it became impossible to enforce repression against people who would not respond to it with violence.

Techniques of Nonviolence

Gene Sharp lists 198 distinct nonviolent techniques which have been used in history. Sharp summarizes these techniques as follows:

• Protest and persuasion: Including leafletting, picketing, marches and teach-in.
• Social noncooperation: Including student strikes and social boycotts.
• Economic noncooperation: Including war tax resistance, consumer boycotts, and labor strikes.
• Political noncooperation: Including draft resistance and refusal to obey unjust laws.
• Nonviolent intervention: Civil disobedience generally, nonviolent blockages, sit-ins and nonviolent obstructions.

Some pragmatic strategists include sabotage of property as a nonviolent technique. While arguable, this position poses serious difficulties. In a property-conscious society, sabotage of property is often considered a form of violence which justifies violent repression. Thus, the use of property sabotage carries risks which outweigh its potential benefits.

Far less dangerous and more clearly acceptable is sabotage of bureaucratic systems. This technique is frequently not only low in risk but completely legal. An example is the breakdown of the Selective Service System in the early 1970s, which was brought on by a combination of civil disobedience and mass use of rights which were provided by law. In this event, the hundreds of thousands of legal appeals filed by men subject to the draft were probably the determining factor in making the draft unworkable.

In the occupation or totalitarian situation, sabotage of bureaucratic systems may take the form of a perfectly legal slowdown undertaken in a cordial and smiling way. It may include losing papers, "accidentally" erasing computer tapes and so on. The possibilities are limited primarily by the imagination of the nonviolent resister. Such actions would be difficult to repress, and they would make administration of the government a matter of extreme difficulty. In order to be most effective, however, they should be part of a coordinated campaign so that if one resister is fired from a bureaucratic job, the next person in the post will continue the resistance, perhaps in different ways.

Obstacles to Nonviolent Defense

The obstacles to the use of nonviolence as defense are not those usually cited by militarists. They relate instead to the more general problems of defense in modern warfare and to acceptability of nonviolence to governments as they are now constituted.

Military defense is extremely costly in material and human terms. More than that, however, it is impossible in the case of missile attack, and to a lesser extent, in aerial bombardment generally. This is also true of nonviolent defense for there is no complete effective defense against such attack.

None of this invalidates nonviolence. It suggests, however, that nonviolent defense of one's country is not sufficient to end war or increase national security. What is required is a strategy which will prevent missiles from being deployed and launched in the first place. Military defense and preparations for it cannot provide such a strategy. They are built around deployment of missiles and the threat to use them. Thus, while it provides no defense against aerial attack, in the long run, nonviolence offers the real hope of stopping such attacks before they begin – which is the only way they will be stopped.

A far more serious obstacle to widespread use of nonviolent resistance is the fact that it is a technique based not in an elite or a government but in the population at large. It cannot work without popular participation. Thus, it is the only inherently democratic form of national defense. Moreover, because it seeks to change those who enforce the system being resisted, to break through to them as human beings, nonviolence, in principle, undercuts all oppressive systems.

This is an obvious threat to governments, which even among the democracies engage in some degree of repression. Although a democratic government operates to a greater or lesser extent by popular consent, it does not empower the public in the way that nonviolent training would. Thus, it is an open question whether any current government would accept nonviolent defense as national policy – not because such defense would fail, but because a people trained in nonviolent resistance would be a constant check on government abuses. From the government's point of view, an obedient and disciplined army which follows its leader without question would be far more desirable than a nonviolently-trained citizenry which can, if it chooses, block government actions it finds unacceptable.

This suggests strongly that nonviolent strategists must look beyond the question of national defense to the larger question of transformation of the war system itself. If governments will not adopt nonviolent defense then the public must learn to defend itself against the government's military follies.

This is in fact being done. In Europe, the nonviolent peace movement seeks to interpose itself as a neutral force between the Eastern and Western alliances. It does this in the name of Europe, but even more so in the interest of humanity. Based on this model, nonviolence would be not simply a "better" form of national defense, but a defense for humanity against the destructive forces the nations are now empowered to unleash.

Transformation of the system thus becomes the overriding goal of nonviolent action. National defense is of far less importance for if the war system does not change, there will sooner or later be no nations to defend.

Nonviolence and the United States

Despite the difficulties of considering nonviolence solely as a form of national defense, it is worthwhile to imagine how civilian resistance could be used in one country. This can show the feasibility of nonviolent defense, and it can also show how one country's adoption of nonviolent defense could begin to transform the war system.

Paradoxically, one obvious candidate for successful nonviolent defense is also the greatest military power: the United States. Strategically, the United States is well-situated for any form of defense. It is bordered on the north and south by friendly neighbors and on the east and west by oceans thousands of miles wide. The nearest hostile bases are in Cuba, ninety miles from American shores. The United States is geographically large, politically complex and administered by bureaucracies which an invader could not replace without extreme difficulty.

All this means that the defense of the United States could be accomplished with far smaller military forces than are currently at the president's disposal. It also means that the country is ideally situated for nonviolent defense.

There is, as noted earlier, no adequate defense against aerial attack, particularly missile attack. An invader would, however, gain little by such an attack. If the bombardment were conventional, the attacker could not expect to annihilate all defenders; the history of aerial bombardment shows that this has never occurred. An occupational army following after the bombardment would find defenders (either nonviolent or military) still alive, while means of transportation, roads and so on, would be severely damaged. This would make occupation against any form of resistance difficult. If the bombardment were a large-scale nuclear attack, it would render most of the United States uninhabitable and, as shown in the article "Nuclear Weapons and War", might precipitate a "nuclear winter" and amount to suicide for the attacker.

Despite the objections to a preliminary bombardment, such tactics are common military practice and would be likely in any conventional attack on the United States. The logistics of the occupation that followed, however, would frighten any sane general. An army is only as good as its line of supply and cannot easily cross three thousand miles of ocean, let alone sustain itself, once at its destination. Its troops would be far from home and thus liable to drastic declines in morale. Confronted with a nonviolently trained citizenry, they would face the choice of regularly using violence against unarmed people or seeing the occupation's administration break down. Their own bombardment would have made getting around and obtaining local supplies far more difficult. The occupying army would be dependent on a three-thousand-mile line of supply. They would be forced to unload their own ships, arrange their own transportation, and perhaps set up their own administration. This would lead to the phenomenon that Liddell Hart called "over-stretch." For a military force, overstretch leads to collapse.

It is impossible to predict whether any of this would in fact occur should the United States adopt nonviolent defense. The difficulties of an invasion and the possibility of widespread citizen resistance would, in all likelihood, be strong deterrents in themselves.

The positive effects of a nonviolent policy would, however, be incalculable. U.S. military forces would no longer be available to intervene in civil wars. The United States would no longer threaten the world with mass destruction. And abandonment of violence would lead to an immediate decrease in the general level of violence in the world – by, for example, stopping U.S. arms sales. America's role as world policeman, with all its terrible results, would end.

Whether the change in U.S. policy would lead to a larger transformation in the world system is unknowable. One can only speculate. However, the United States is not about to adopt a nonviolent policy. Quite the contrary. Thus, like the peace movement elsewhere, the American peace movement cannot look to its government to change the system. It must instead seek, as it has done, to change the system directly.

Two Spurious Objections

It is commonly suggested that Gandhi and, to a lesser extent, Martin Luther King, Jr., succeeded with their nonviolent campaigns only because they were dealing with civilized oppressors or, in the case of King, a country in which the basic law and social consensus favored them. Critics of nonviolence also suggest that because nonviolent strategies often depend on influencing public opinion, nonviolence is somehow a failure. Nothing could be further from the truth.

Gandhi's nonviolent campaign succeeded despite British civilization. The British record, particularly in the nineteenth century, had been as bloody and racist as that of most other nations, save Hitler's Germany and Stalin's Russia. In repressing a Moslem revolt, British troops slaughtered ten thousand Dervishes at Omdurman (1896): the architect of the slaughter, Lord Kitchener, earned a peerage for his troubles. British troops had repressed violent rebellions in India with heavy casualties for the rebels. They showed little compunction about firing into crowds of unarmed Indian civilians during Gandhi's campaign. Thus, the suggestion that the British were especially civilized, while flattering to the British, is unsupported by the facts.

So, too, with King's campaign, which while its aims were far more limited, encountered entrenched and violent opposition that led to beatings, jailings and even death for nonviolent resisters. Nor did the social consensus favor King's campaign. Though his name is remembered now with a holiday, Martin Luther King, Jr. was considered by many to be a dangerous radical while he was alive and was harassed by the FBI. His support among the general population was by no means widespread, and racism, in various forms, persists in the United States today. King's campaign succeeded because of the power of nonviolence and the steadfastness of its resistance, not because he reflected an existing consensus.

The argument that nonviolence somehow does not work if it seeks to change public opinion is unworthy of extensive comment. It is perfectly true that Gandhi tried to influence British public opinion and that King sought to change American public opinion. This was an effective and nonviolent way of achieving their goals. When a military force uses similar tactics, it is called "psychological warfare" and is considered a respectable tactic even though it seldom works.

The ability of nonviolent movements to change public hearts and minds is, in fact, one of their strengths. Violence, whether in India or in the southern United States, would have failed utterly in this regard and led to bloody repression of the two movements. It is hardly surprising that a military force generally fails to influence enemy public opinion, while a nonviolent movement succeeds more frequently than not.

By changing the hearts and minds of people in Britain, Gandhi gained independence. King made major gains for civil rights in the same way. These results hardly show that nonviolence fails; they are instead one of the enduring strengths of nonviolent action.

Nonviolence and Revolution

Critics of nonviolence argue that it cannot overthrow an entrenched, ruthless and unjust power structure. According to this argument, nonviolence, though in principle revolutionary, cannot reasonably promise success if those in power have no scruples.

Questions about the best methods for achieving social change are difficult and painful not only for pacifists but for all who seek justice and peace. They are also, however, impossible to answer with certainty. No route to social change can guarantee success. On the contrary: Movements, whether violent or nonviolent, frequently fail or lose their initial impetus. Ideals are betrayed; liberation becomes oppression. History provides ample evidence that justice is never easily or perfectly achieved.

The difficulty of social change, however, is not a defect of nonviolence. It is part of the human condition. We cannot predict all of the consequences of our acts. When a movement seeks major social change, it cannot determine the outcome; it can control only the means used to seek that outcome. If those means are violent, the movemen–whether it succeeds or fails–will do extensive damage to people or property or both. Violence, far from building a movement for social change, frequently increases factionalism and destroys the movement from within. The aftermath of violence is bitterness and division. The aftermath of failed violence is almost always increased government repression. This destruction is not an accidental by-product. It is a consequence of the means chosen.

A simple example will illustrate. A nonviolent sit-in may not achieve its objectives, but it will not destroy the building where it takes place. Nor, unless it is met with police violence, will it result in death or injury. But a time bomb placed in the same building will inevitably do damage to the building and to anyone who happens to be within range of the explosion. Government repression, decrease in popular support for social change, media fascination with the violent and spectacular all make peace and justice more difficult to achieve. The consequences of violence are all too evident from history.

It is clear that violence is, at best, an untrustworthy and risky means of achieving social change. More significantly, the use of violence does nothing to change the balance of power between the established order and those who seek change. The established order is based on violence. It is far better armed than those who would overthrow it.

from The Handbook of Nonviolence

The Technique of Nonviolent Action
by Gene Sharp

A ruler's power is ultimately dependent on support from the people he would rule. His moral authority, economic resources, transport system, government bureaucracy, army, and police—to name but a few immediate sources of his power—rest finally upon the cooperation and assistance of other people. If there is general conformity, the ruler is powerful.

But people do not always do what their rulers would like them to do. The factory manager recognizes this when he finds his workers leaving their jobs and machines, so that the production line ceases operation; or when he finds the workers persisting in doing something on the job which he has forbidden them to do. In many areas of social and political life comparable situations are commonplace. A man who has been a ruler and thought his power sure may discover that his subjects no longer believe he has any moral right to give them orders, that his laws are disobeyed, that the country's economy is paralyzed, that his soldiers and police are lax in carrying out repression or openly mutiny, and even that his bureaucracy no longer takes orders. When this happens, the man who has been ruler becomes simply another man, and his political power dissolves, just as the factory manager's power does when the workers no longer cooperate and obey. The equipment of his army may remain intact, his soldiers uninjured and very much alive, his cities unscathed, the factories and transport systems in full operational capacity, and the government buildings and offices unchanged. Yet because the human assistance which had created and supported his political power has been withdrawn, the former ruler finds that his political power has disintegrated.

Nonviolent Action

The technique of nonviolent action, which is based on this approach to the control of political power and the waging of political struggles, has been the subject of many misconceptions: for the sake of clarity the two terms are defined in this section.

The term technique is used here to describe the overall means of conducting an action or struggle. One can therefore speak of the technique of guerrilla warfare, of conventional warfare, and of parliamentary democracy.

The term nonviolent action refers to those methods of protest, noncooperation, and intervention in which the actionists, without employing physical violence, refuse to do certain things which they are expected, or required, to do; or do certain things which they are not expected, or are forbidden, to do. In a particular case there can of course be a combination of acts of omission and acts of commission.

Nonviolent action is a generic term: it includes the large class of phenomena variously called nonviolent resistance, satyagraha, passive resistance, positive action, and nonviolent direct action. While it is not violent, it is action, and not inaction; passivity, submission, and cowardice must be surmounted if it is to be used. It is a means of conducting conflicts and waging struggles, and is not to be equated with (though it may be accompanied by) purely verbal dissent or solely psychological influence. It is not pacifism, and in fact has in the vast majority of cases been applied by nonpacifists. The motives for the adoption of nonviolent action may be religious or ethical or they may be based on considerations of expediency. Nonviolent action is not an escapist approach to the problem of violence, for it can be applied in struggles against opponents relying on violent sanctions. The fact that in a conflict one side is nonviolent does not imply that the other side will also refrain from violence. Certain forms of nonviolent action may be regarded as efforts to persuade by action, while others are more coercive.

Methods of Nonviolent Action

There is a very wide range of methods, or forms, of nonviolent action, and at least 197 have been identified. They fall into three classes – nonviolent protest and persuasion, noncooperation, and nonviolent intervention.

Generally speaking, the methods of nonviolent protest are symbolic in their effect and produce an awareness of the existence of dissent. Under tyrannical regimes, however, where opposition is stifled, their impact can in some circumstances be very great. Methods of nonviolent protest include marches, pilgrimages, picketing, vigils, "haunting" officials, public meetings, issuing and distributing protest literature, renouncing honors, protest emigration, and humorous pranks.

The methods of nonviolent noncooperation, if sufficient numbers take part, are likely to present the opponent with difficulties in maintaining the normal efficiency and operation of the system; and in extreme cases the system itself may be threatened. Methods of nonviolent noncooperation include various types of social noncooperation (such as social boycotts); economic boycotts (such as consumers' boycott, traders' boycott, rent refusal, and international trade embargo); strikes (such as the general strike, strike by resignation, industry strike, go-slow, and economic shutdown); and political noncooperation (such as boycott of government employment, boycott of elections, administrative noncooperation, civil disobedience, and mutiny).

The methods of nonviolent intervention have some features in common with the first two classes, but also challenge the opponent more directly; and, assuming that fearlessness and discipline are maintained, relatively small numbers may have a disproportionately large impact. Methods of nonviolent intervention include sit-ins, fasts, reverse strikes, nonviolent obstructions, nonviolent invasion, and parallel government.

The exact way in which methods from each of the three classes are combined varies considerably from one situation to another. Generally speaking, the risks to the actionists on the one hand, and to the system against which they take action on the other, are least in the case of nonviolent protest, and greatest in the case of nonviolent intervention. The methods of noncooperation tend to require the largest numbers, but not to demand a large degree of special training from all participants. The methods of nonviolent intervention are generally effective if the participants possess a high degree of internal discipline and are willing to accept severe repression; the tactics must also be selected and carried out with particular care and intelligence.

Several important factors need to be considered in the selection of the methods to be used in a given situation. These factors include the type of issue involved, the nature of the opponent, his aims and strength, the type of counteraction he is likely to use, the depth of feeling both among the general population and among the likely actionists, the degree of repression the actionists are likely to be able to take, the general strategy of the overall campaign, and the amount of past experience and specific training the population and the actionists have had. Just as in military battle weapons are carefully selected, taking into account such factors as their range and effect, so also in nonviolent struggle the choice of specific methods is very important.

Mechanisms of Change

In nonviolent struggles there are, broadly speaking, three mechanisms by which change is brought about. Usually there is a combination of the three. They are conversion, accommodation, and nonviolent coercion.

George Lakey has described the conversion mechanism thus: "By conversion we mean that the opponent, as the result of the actions of the nonviolent person or group, comes around to a new point of view which embraces the ends of the nonviolent actor." This conversion can be influenced by reason or argument, but in nonviolent action it is also likely to be influenced by emotional and moral factors, which can in turn be stimulated by the suffering of the nonviolent actionists, who seek to achieve their goals without inflicting injury on other people.

Attempts at conversion, however, are not always successful, and may not even be made. Accommodation as a mechanism of nonviolent action falls in an intermediary position between conversion and nonviolent coercion, and elements of both of the other mechanisms are generally involved. In accommodation, the opponent, although not converted, decides to grant the demands of the nonviolent actionists in a situation where he still has a choice of action. The social situation within which he must operate has been altered enough be nonviolent action to compel a change in his own response to the conflict; perhaps because he has begun to doubt the rightness of his position, perhaps because he does not think the matter worth the trouble caused by the struggle, and perhaps because he anticipates coerced defeat and wishes to accede gracefully or with minimum of losses.

Nonviolent coercion may take place in any of three circumstances. Defiance may become too widespread and massive for the ruler to be able to control it by repression; the social and political system may become paralyzed; or the extent of defiance or disobedience among the ruler's own soldiers and other agents may undermine his capacity to apply repression. Nonviolent coercion becomes possible when those applying nonviolent action succeed in withholding, directly or indirectly, the necessary sources of the ruler's political power. His power then disintegrates, and he is no longer able to control the situation, even though he still wishes to do so.

Just as in war danger from enemy fire does not always force front line soldiers to panic and flee, so in nonviolent action repression does not necessarily produce submission. True, repression may be effective, but it may fail to halt defiance, and in this case the opponent will be in difficulties. Repression against a nonviolent group which persists in face of it and maintains nonviolent discipline may have the following effects: it may alienate the general population from the opponent's regime, making them more likely to join the resistance; it may alienate the opponent's usual supporters and agents, and their initial uneasiness may grow into internal opposition and at times into noncooperation and disobedience; and it may rally general public opinion (domestic or international) to the support of the nonviolent actionists; though the effectiveness of this last factor varies greatly from one situation to another, it may produce various types of supporting actions. If repression thus produces larger numbers of nonviolent actionists, thereby increasing the defiance, and if it leads to internal dissent among the opponent's supporters, thereby reducing his capacity to deal with the defiance, it will clearly have rebounded against the opponent.

Naturally, with so many variables (including the nature of the contending groups, the issues involved, the context of the struggle, the means of repression, and the methods of nonviolent action used), in no two instances will nonviolent action "work" in exactly the same way. However, it is possible to indicate in very general terms the ways in which it does achieve results. It is, of course, sometimes defeated: no technique of action can guarantee its user short-term victory in every instance of its use. It is important to recognize, however, that failure in nonviolent action may be caused, not by an inherent weakness of the technique, but by weakness in the movement employing it, or in the strategy and tactics used.

Strategy is just as important in nonviolent action as it is in military action. While military strategic concepts and principles cannot be automatically carried over into the field of nonviolent struggle, since the dynamics and mechanisms of military and nonviolent action differ greatly, the basic importance of strategy and tactics is in no way diminished. The attempt to cope with strategic and tactical problems associated with civilian defense (national defense by prepared nonviolent resistance) therefore needs to be based on thorough consideration of the dynamics and mechanisms of nonviolent struggle; and on consideration of the general principles of strategy and tactics appropriate to the technique—both those peculiar to it and those which mat be carried over from the strategy of military and other types of conflict.

Development of the Technique

Nonviolent action has a long history but because historians have often been more concerned with other matters, much information has undoubtedly been lost.

Even today, this field is largely ignored, and there is no good history of the practice and development of the technique. But it clearly began early. For example, in 494 B.C. the plebeians of Rome, rather than murder the Consuls, withdrew from the city to the Sacred Mount where they remained for some days, thereby refusing to make their usual contribution to the life of the city, until an agreement was reached pledging significant improvements in their life and status.

A very significant pre-Gandhian expansion of the technique took place in the 19th and early 20th centuries. The technique received impetus from three groups during this period: first from trade unionists and other social radicals who sought a means of struggle—largely strikes, general strikes, and boycotts—against what they regarded as an unjust social system, and for an improvement in the condition of working men; second, from nationalists who found the technique useful in resisting a foreign enemy—such as the Hungarian resistance against Austria between 1850 and 1867, and the Chinese boycotts of Japanese goods in the early 20th century; and third, on the level of ideas and personal example, from individuals, such as Leo Tolstoy in Russia and Henry David Thoreau in the U.S.A., who wanted to show how a better society might be created.

With Gandhi's experiments in the use of nonviolent action to control rulers, alter policies, and undermine political systems, the character of the technique was broadened and refinements were made in its practice. Many modifications were introduced: greater attention was given to strategy and tactics; the armory of methods was expanded; and a link was consciously forged between mass political action and the ethical principle of nonviolence. Gandhi, with his political colleagues and fellow Indians, demonstrated in a variety of conflicts in South Africa and India that nonviolent struggle could be politically effective on a large scale. He termed his refinement of the technique "satyagraha," meaning roughly insistence and reliance upon the force of truth. "In politics, its use is based upon the immutable maxim, that government of the people is possible only so long as they consent either consciously or unconsciously to be governed."

from The Politics of Nonviolent Action

Nonviolent Civilian Defense

by Liane Ellison Norman

You want us to lie down and let the Russians trample over us, critics say of peace workers. There's some justice in this view: we've opposed particular wars or preparations for wars. But we've not sufficiently explored ways to *replace* warfare, which has historically been the principal *recorded* means whereby nations, states, princes or parties within states have contended for both noble and ignoble ends–defense as well as conquest, liberty and justice as well as hegemony and despotism. In our hatred of war, we've ignored the needs it has satisfied.

War at its Old Germanic linguistic roots means confusion, discord and strife. But war is also associated with splendid panoply and poetry. "Once more into the breach, dear friends," urges the warrior King Henry V, appealing to the tradition that burnishes the reputation of battle. Our culture tells us that though war is hell, it is honorable. It occasions solidarity, heroism, spectacle, comradeship, self-sacrifice and vitality.

War is thought to work, despite evidence that there's always at least one losing side, that each war concludes by making the next more likely. And when, for participants, experience tarnishes war, culture tells us that there's no other way to pursue certain objectives.

Long-standing ambivalence about war has tightened like thumbscrews since 1945, when it became evident that nuclear weapons could do in seconds the damage it had taken decades–even centuries–to do in earlier times; could destroy not only populations and their works, but the very environment on which life depends. We who deplore violence have seized on each new piece of evidence that war is insupportable to make our point. But, say the dubious, so long as the world is not made up of saints, you cannot dismantle arms nor do away with war.

It's worth listening to our critics. History suggests it's realistic to be concerned about both conquest and tyranny. If we had neither weapons nor soldiers, what would we do if an enemy tried to conquer us? What would we do if our government suspended civil liberties, imprisoned, tortured and executed people like us? Women know that to accommodate bullying makes them silent partners in violence. Peace, given such realities, smacks of weakness, cowardice, appeasement and submission.

Our language both reflects and shapes the problem. Peace means the absence or cessation of war, a negative definition. How can we have both peace *and* the power to stand up to conquerors and tyrants?

I ask my students to draw a picture of peace, not an easy task, for while we use the term "power" with confidence, it's an elusive idea. One student draws God threatening a father who has his arm raised with a club to beat his son–my student. This picture crudely expresses a common notion about power: that in the nature of things, power resides at the top of some kind of hierarchy and that it involves the ability to hurt and/or humiliate. Those with high position have power *because* they can do violence. Parents, teachers, religious leaders and employers can make us do their bidding because they can punish us if we don't. This view of power is a widespread article of faith.

Looked at more closely, however, the power exercised by those *in* power is both *dependent* and *fragile*. No head of state governs singlehandedly. She has aides and advisors to help formulate and transmit policy to bureaucracies; secretaries to answer the telephone, write letters and file records; tax collectors to provide revenues; experts of all varieties (planners, economists, engineers, construction crews, garbage collectors, mail deliverers, cooks, cleaners); police to enforce and courts to interpret the laws; and citizens, who by and large obey the laws, cooperate, submit to the general order.

The power to govern depends on the willingness of people to be governed. If they withdraw their consent, even in significant part, no head of state can govern. In other words, citizens provide their leaders with power and can regulate its use. Those *in* power can use sanctions against the dissident and disobedient–or at least a representative sample–but even sanctions require obedience to carry out.

For example, the federal government says Central American refugees are illegal aliens and requires that law-enforcement officials help catch and punish them. But a large number of cities have declared themselves sanctuaries, which means that city employees will not assist the government in carrying out its policy. The

New York Times (December 27, 1985) proclaims editorially that "Cities Can't Make Immigration Law." But cities, along with individual citizens *make* law all the time when they *comply* with it. "If the law displeases them, let them petition Washington, " scolds the *Times*, which nearly always reinforces the view that power rests only at the top. The cities, like the churches which have offered sanctuary, like those who once harbored runaway slaves en route to freedom or those who made white lightning during prohibition, refuse obedience to the federal government and laws they judge to be oppressive. Government is limited by the power of the people.

What really frightens power-at-the-top people is that citizens and localities may discover how powerful they are. However, with the discovery that they can resist the policies of their own government comes the insight that the same citizens and localities can formulate a defense that does not depend upon the kind of organized, legalized violence we call war.

To design a nonviolent defense requires thinking about conquest, victory and defeat. Though it seems to be about battlefields, war is really about *who* is to govern *what* and *how*. Conquest is meaningless unless the conqueror is able to govern: victory means that one or more of the contending parties acknowledges defeat, concedes the right of the victor to govern. One army may rout another, but unless the population represented by the defeated army permits itself to be governed by the conquerors, there is no conquest.

A conqueror can punish or kill those–or some of those–who resist, just as he does in battle. But conquerors do not bring with them whole regimes to govern, enforce and implement: even if they had the requisite human power, newcomers would not know *how* to make a conquered system operate. The conquerors, instead, have to persuade local people to run things for them by intimidation or reward. If the "conquered" refuse, braving threat or punishment, the "conquerors" are stymied. Increased oppression meant to persuade the population to obey may backfire: any regime that has to rely on excessive punishment to govern loses legitimacy and increases resistance. Precisely the same general principles apply to domestic tyranny as to foreign imposition: dictators, wherever they originate, rely on cooperation and consent, whether given with enthusiasm or fear.

Nonviolent defense strategy is to deny enemy objectives, to make the task of controlling a population and its institutions impossible. Historic instances–of the Danes and Norwegians in World War II, of the Czechs in 1968, of the Indians under Gandhi, of many others as documented by Gene Sharp–are more suggestive than conclusive: they represent spontaneous rather than well developed strategies, relying more on ingenuity and courage than preparation and discipline. But that very spontaneity, ingenuity and courage suggest that *with* preparation and discipline, with advance planning, with reinforcement by education and popular culture, nonviolent strategies can provide defense against both foreign conquest and domestic tyranny.

Nonviolent defense strategies cannot be used against nuclear weapons: but then, neither can violent defense strategies. But a country that ceases to menace others while maintaining its capacity to defend itself can afford to give up its nuclear weapons, which though expensive, undermine rather than provide security. While nuclear weapons provide a fundamentally incredible deterrent, nonviolent strategies *can* be used to deter an enemy by making clear in advance that the nonviolently-prepared country will make the task of conquest and governance costly, impossible and unpopular. But nonviolent defense *cannot be perverted to offense*. While a country, region or people can protect themselves using nonviolent means, they *cannot* invade and intimidate using the same means.

A nonviolent defense strategy does not require that other nations relinquish violence: it can be used against violent, brutal and ruthless enemies. Nonviolent combatants need not be nice, cussedness being more to the point than saintliness. The effectiveness of their strategy does not require the moral conversion of the enemy. However, by depriving enemies of the arguments they rely on to justify otherwise outlawed acts of brutality, nonviolence undermines their conditioning. Recognizing that adversaries also have the power to withdraw their consent humanizes them, offering them options they may, as individuals, not have considered. This is what the advice to love one's enemies means in tactical terms.

Young men have to be *broken* of their humanity to be made soldiers. Nonviolent defense requires no such rupture of human inclinations, but rather a strengthening thereof. Nonviolent civilian, or popular, defense does not delegate society's dirty and dangerous work to adolescent boys, but relies on people to defend themselves–taking their share of casualties. Such strategies do not require temporarily setting aside civilian values, but fortify them. Violent revolutions habitually fail because the arts of war are ill-suited to post-revolutionary order: violent revolution spawns counterrevolutionaries eager to avenge their losses, and those who win by violence can rarely be kind. Nonviolent defensive and revolutionary strategies are inherently democratic, for those doing the defending learn the skills, develop the stamina and support systems necessary to the withdrawal of consent not only from foreign tyrants and their agents but from tyrants closer to home as well. Thus nonviolent policies demand legitimacy now rather than eventually. Further, nonviolent strategies promote the continuous renewal of democratic principles, relying on the genius and know-how of ordinary people and providing them with the means to rectify wrongs long before desperation makes them reckless.

Most societies teach people to be powerless. This is convenient for those who want to wield power *over* others, but is in the long run self-defeating because it prepares them to submit. The more powerless people think they are, the more easily they can be conquered. The *New York Times* sees no recourse but courteous petitions to those *in* power: the same habit of mind might well lead the *Times* to defer to a conqueror. The cities which defy the federal government in the matter of sanctuary are better prepared to resist foreign or domestic tyranny. Few parents, frustrated by a two-year-old resisting a snowsuit, teach the child to note and learn from that exercise of power. Few teachers, faced with students coughing in unison, use the occasion to teach the lesson of resistance and solidarity. It takes confident, secure adults and leaders to teach power and the discernment to use it well. However, violence springs from insecurity and the sense of weakness rather than security and strength: Rambo is a fantasy of power, not the real thing.

Some say that there's no evidence that nonviolent strategies for defense would work. It's true that we haven't tested such strategies consciously enough to know for sure whether they would always do the trick: nor does warfare. It's also true, however, that we *have* tested organized violence, and while wars have won some gains, the price has been terrific. Part of that price has been the failure to develop other means of serious struggle.

And so we find ourselves in a corner: war has become too dangerous to use and we haven't as a civilization developed an alternative. But we have the opportunity, even this late in the day, to work together, hawks and doves, each with our partial understanding of the truth, to develop the means to make peace strong and strength peaceful.

from "Peace Through Strength," Civilian Based Defense, *Vol.3, No.2, March 1986. Reprinted as "Nonviolent Civil Defense" by permission of the author and the Civilian-Based Defense Association.*

Look to the Future, Then Learn from the Past

by Dudley Weeks

Every relationship and every conflict has a past, present, and future, and resolving conflicts effectively requires that we deal with all three. The conflict partnership process encourages us to use positive power to focus on what I call the present-future, and to learn from the past.

The past provides an experiential landscape for the present and the future, but the past is *not* the soil in which the present and future are irrevocably rooted. The present brings past memories onto new ground and tills that fresh soil with improved tools, always mindful that the future will reap what the present has sown. The present and the future are inseparable, and the future develops in the womb of the present. They are all linked: past, present, and future. Blending the three into a dynamic reach for improvement is the essence of being.

We will begin by dealing with how the past can impede conflict resolution. Then we will explore how we can learn from the past. Finally, we will look at the present-future and explore how focusing on this time frame helps us to deal with present conflicts and improve the future relationship.

Here are a few of the more prevalent ways we allow the past to impede effective conflict resolution.

People sometimes allow the past to hold present and future possibilities prisoner by thinking that because they did not deal well with a conflict in the past, they cannot deal effectively with a current conflict. In this pattern, people think that because they were unable to deal with problems in the past, or because they have in the past defined their relationship as a struggle for dominance and advantage over the other party, it is futile to believe that they can ever act differently or even try to apply improved relationship and conflict resolution skills.

This negative use of the past is, in effect, a self-deprecating and self-*dis*empowering pattern. It implies that people are incapable of growing and improving. Of course, those who use this pattern usually say it is the other party who is incapable of improving, but such a stance hinders the development of positive power and positive influence in both parties. However, when one party moves beyond this negative use of the past and takes the lead in demonstrating improved relationship

and conflict resolution behavior, the other party usually begins to feel more hopeful that improved behavior *can* be implemented.

People sometimes see only the past negative behavior of their conflict partner, refusing to see the positive potential, even if their partner's present behavior is encouraging. This particular pattern seems to be one of our favorite ways of using the past to obstruct both the improvement of relationships and the actualization of the positive potential of conflict resolution. Examples abound. Perpetually harping on one or two incidents of a conflict partner's especially negative behavior in the past when dealing with a current conflict, regardless of her or his stated willingness to avoid repeating that behavior, is one example. Another is evident when people and groups are perpetually held accountable for past mistakes or inadequacies, even though they have tried to make amends and have not repeated those mistakes.

Another example involves perceiving people as they were at a past age and never allowing them the possibility and right to grow up, to change and improve. Sons and daughters who have reached maturity but are still seen by a parent as "my little boy or girl" in need of protection are being perceived as the role they once were, not as the human beings they now are and can be.

People sometimes blame themselves for what they were or did at some time in the past and continue to punish their own lives and their relationships in a subconscious attempt at penance. Perhaps no misuse of the past is more agonizing and complex than allowing a past mistake to cover with guilt and shame one's own self-image in the present and future. People involved in such a pattern often become obsessed with a past mistake and ignore how they can improve in the present. They may even strike out at any person or event that reminds them of that past mistake.

People sometimes are unwilling to let go of a particular demand or behavior they expressed in the past, even though that demand or behavior is no longer relevant or helpful in the present. I'm sure we've all heard people say, "I've done things that way all my life and I'm not going to change now!", or, "If I go back on that demand now, it will make me look weak." There are usually several hidden reasons underlying this use of the past to justify a continuation of damaging or ineffective behavior in the present.

One of these reasons is that people do not want to admit that a past behavior pattern or demand was damaging or ineffective. They see that as an admission of failure. Another is that some people feel they have little insight or confidence in designing alternatives to ineffective or harmful patterns. Still another is that certain narrow, vested self-interests are *perceived* as being served by a continuation of the past behavior or demands. Finally, people sometimes hold onto old behavior patterns or demands because they fear the unknown of trying new patterns or making effective, shared-need, positive-power proposals rather than demands.

Impeding conflict resolution by holding onto past patterns is evident, for example, when a parent invests a great deal of energy and money in a daughter's education toward becoming a doctor or teacher and then cannot accept the daughter's decision that teaching or medicine is not the most fulfilling profession for her. The parent stubbornly tries to force her not to change directions, or charges the daughter with being a failure.

Another example is a business that, for twenty years, has kept a particular organizational pattern, and now, when that policy is proving unpopular and counterproductive among the work force, refuses to change because that is the way they have always done things or because it would take too much time and expense to change.

People assume that because something has always been done a certain way, it somehow means it's the best way This obstructing use of the past might be called the wisdom-of-the-ages syndrome. Just because a particular behavior pattern, or business policy, or family habit has been around for some time does not automatically mean it is best. It may have been appropriate for the past, but is it appropriate for today and tomorrow?

Involved in this pattern is that complex and resilient phenomenon we call tradition. Tradition certainly has its place, but in conflict resolution we need to rely on effective *skills* not just tradition. Sometimes traditional ways of conducting a relationship or dealing with conflict have, in part, *contributed* both to the conflict and to an inability to resolve it.

People sometimes romanticize or glorify the past to such a degree that present behavior or relationships can never compare favorably with that past behavior or that past relationship. Pleasant memories do not make demands or require attention to needs. They do not prove bothersome, stubborn, or intransigent. They do not have budget deficits, confused policies, or unfavorable public opinion. They don't even call us in the middle of the night seeking help on a matter we feel totally incompetent to address. Pleasant memories just float in a lovely morning sky, reminding us of better times as we struggle through the storms and stresses of our present lives.

In other words, we not only use the past unwisely by carrying its *negative* behavior into the present and future, we sometimes use the past unwisely by creating glorified interpretations of the past that cause us to see the present and future as undervalued comparisons to the good old days. Pleasant memories of a past time, event, behavior, or relationship are wonderful and cherished gifts, *but we must beware of using them as nostalgic hindrances to resolving conflicts effectively and making the present and future the best we possibly can.*

from "Look to the Future, Then Learn from the Past"
The Eight Essential Steps To Conflict Resolution

Charles Grassley and the Pentagon Hogs

by Colman McCarthy

Hoisting his corn-fed hulk over the fence and into the sty, the farmer walks among his rooting hogs. The black and white-belted Yorkshires, fat and getting fatter, eat in gluttonous zeal the best grist growable on this 240-acre farm in the rural outback of northeast Iowa.

The farmer–51, black-haired, and wearing a mud-splattered shirt–stands next to a trough and pats his hogs. They snort, squeal and scurry in the muck. But he has them under control. This is a man who understands hog psychology.

He ought to. The farmer is Charles Grassley, Iowa's senior senator and conservative Republican who in the past two years has been going into the sty of military excess where the fattest breed on earth–the money hog–feeds at the Pentagon trough, the world's deepest. Grassley, a member of the Senate Budget Committee, has been the most vocal Republican in Washington to call for a freeze on military spending.

Last month, he wrote in the *Des Moines Register* and the *Wall Street Journal* that the Pentagon's budget has "become the nation's largest entitlement program, and has nursed a new generation of welfare queens: the defense industry."

Such language–which is as close to a barnyard epithet as the evangelical Baptist will get–is not a sudden outburst. Grassley has been developing in a gradual germination. He voted 15 times in favor of the MX missile, standing as tall as an Iowa cornstalk when it came to loyalty to Ronald Reagan. Then, in June of 1984, he changed his mind and began voting against the MX.

What happened? He began studying the Pentagon's procurement policies and learned that military contractors were routinely putting a move on the public. Last month, he explained his anti-MX votes: "I discovered from Air Force documents that work-to-date by the 14 associate contractors for the MX was taking up to 17 times as many direct labor hours as the contractors' own standards determined it should have taken. The average factory efficiency rate of those 14 contractors...was 48 percent. In other words, 48 percent of the taxpayers' dollars were funding efficiency, and 52 percent were funding inefficiency. We paid for in-house work for 2.1 equivalent units, on average, and got only one."

In New Hartford, the grass-roots Grassley jokes easily about how his militancy is being perceived as a drift to the left. He tells of his conservative right-of-right brother on a farm down the road who thinks the senator is something of a pinko. In fact, Grassley voted 78 percent of the time with Reagan in the past two years. That is down from about 85 percent from a previous period, a drop which signifies apostasy only to the fanatical wing of the New Right.

The Old Right is alarmed for other reasons. Sen. Barry Goldwater wrote a 2,000 word reply to Grassley's pro-freeze articles. What Washington sophisticates of the left were snickering when Grassley came to the Senate in 1980 – the guy's a yokel, an airhead – Goldwater was suggesting now. The Arizonan lectured Iowans that their senator "does his state and our nation a disservice when he passes off his simplistic, self-serving advocacy as reasoned analysis."

Goldwater sought to bomb Grassley's thinking back to the stone age with a further assault: "Superficial impulsive schemes like Sen. Grassley's defense freeze are better suited to bumper stickers than the realities of the dangerous world in which we live."

Goldwater had a final put-down: Grassley isn't a member of the Armed Services Committee–Goldwater is the chairman–so what can he know?

"He doesn't have access to all the information required to discuss the defense budget," said the chairman who gives access to any general, admiral or military supplier who screams communists are coming.

Among his New Hartford hogs and while showing a visitor to a barn where the shoats are sleeping and to a pen where a boar is grunting, Grassley prefers to talk about the farm and the beauty of Iowa's springtime than the snipes from Goldwater. This is home on the weekend, a moment for renewal of the spirit through contact with the earth.

Iowans, heartened that their farmboy is becoming a national figure, are rallying to Grassley's defense. A letter to the *Register* last week said that "Goldwater brings out that old argument that Grassley is not a member of the committee so he 'does not have access to all the information.' This 'big-daddy-knows-best' and, you'd agree-with-him-if-you-had-the-secret-information-he-has' argument simply does not wash with those of us who were adults during the Vietnam War. Besides, this is a cheap shot which attempts to put Grassley down."

The senator is up right now: in popularity and influence. He is currently the liberals' favorite conservative, a fate he can live with. Goldwater and the Pentagon are dismissing him as a rube, but Grassley's attacks on waste, fraud and excess are seeds sure to grow. He is betting the farm.

Nonviolence offers no guarantees. But the curious thing is that people who do violence don't receive guarantees either. Statistics show that you have a better chance of coming out alive in a nonviolent battle.

Joan Baez

What Would You Do If?

by Joan Baez

"OK, You're a pacifist. What would you do if someone were say, attacking your grandmother?"

"Attacking my poor old grandmother?"

"Yeah, You're in a room with your grandmother and there's this guy about to attack her and you're standing there. What would you do?"

"I'd yell, 'Three cheers for Grandma!' and leave the room."

"No, seriously. Say he had a gun and he was about to shoot her. Would you shoot him first?"

"Do I have a gun?"

"Yes."

"No. I'm a pacifist, I don't have a gun."

"Well, say you do."

"All right. Am I a good shot?"

"Yes."

"I'd shoot the gun out of his hand."

"No, then you're not a good shot."

"I'd be afraid to shoot. Might kill Grandma."

"Come on. OK, look. We'll take another example. Say you're driving a truck. You're on a narrow road with a sheer cliff on your side. There's a little girl standing in the middle of the road. You're going too fast to stop. What would you do?"

"I don't know. What would you do?"

"I'm asking you. You're the pacifist."

"Yes, I know. All right, am I in control of the truck?"

"Yes."

"How about if I honk my horn so she can get out of the way?"

"She's too young to walk. And the horn doesn't work."

"I'll swerve around to the left of her, since she's not going anywhere."

"No, there's been a landslide."

"Oh. Well, then I would try to drive the truck over the cliff and save the little girl."

Silence.

"Well, say there's someone else in the truck with you. Then what?"

"What's my decision have to do with my being a pacifist?"

"There's two of you in the truck and only one little girl."

"Someone once said, 'If you have a choice between a real evil and a hypothetical evil, always take the real one.'"

"Huh?"

"I said why are you so anxious to kill off all the pacifists?"

"I'm not. I just want to know what you'd do if—"

"If I was with a friend in a truck driving very fast on a one-lane road approaching a dangerous impasse where a 10-month-old girl is sitting in the middle of the road with a landslide one side of her and a sheer drop-off on the other."

"That's right."

"I would probably slam on the brakes, thus sending my friend through the front windshield, skid into the landslide, run over the little girl, sail off the cliff, and plunge to my own death. No doubt Grandma's house would be at the bottom of the ravine and the truck would crash through her roof and blow up in her living room where she was finally being attacked for the first, and last, time."

"You haven't answered my question. You're just trying to get out of it. ..."

"I'm really trying to say a couple of things. One is that no one knows what he'll do in a moment of crisis. And that hypothetical questions get hypothetical answers. I'm also hinting that you have made it impossible for me to come out of the situation without having killed one or more people. Then you can say 'Pacifism is a nice idea, but it won't work.' But that's not what bothers me."

"What bothers you?"

"Well, you may not like it because it's not hypothetical. It's real. And it makes the assault on Grandma look like a garden party."

"What's that?"

"I'm thinking about how we put people through a training process so they'll find out the really good, efficient ways of killing. Nothing incidental like trucks and landslides. Just the opposite, really. You know, how to growl and yell, kill and crawl and jump out of airplanes. Real organized stuff. Hell, you have to be able to run a bayonet through Grandma's middle."

"That's something entirely different."

"Sure. And don't you see that it's so much harder to look at, because it's real, and it's going on right now? Look. A general sticks a pin into a map. A week later a bunch of young boys are sweating it out in a jungle somewhere, shooting each other's arms and legs off, crying and praying and losing control of their bowels. Doesn't it seem stupid to you?"

"Well, you're talking about war."

"Yes, I know. Doesn't it seem stupid?"

"What do you do instead, then? Turn the other

cheek, I suppose."

"No. Love thine enemy but confront his evil. Love thine enemy. Thou shalt not kill."

"Yeah, and look what happened to him."

"He grew up."

"They hung him on a damn cross is what happened to him. I don't want to get hung on a damn cross."

"You won't."

"Huh?"

"I said you don't get to choose how you're going to die. Or when. You can only decide how you're going to live. Now."

"Well, I'm not going to go letting everybody step all over me, that's for sure."

"Jesus said, 'Resist not evil.' The pacifist says just the opposite. He says to resist evil with all your heart and with all your mind and body until it has been overcome."

"I don't get it."

"Organized nonviolent resistance. Gandhi. He organized the Indians for nonviolent resistance and waged nonviolent war against the British until he'd freed India from the British Empire. Not bad for a first try, don't you think?"

"Yeah, fine, but he was dealing with the British, a civilized people. We're not."

"Not a civilized people?"

"Not dealing with a civilized people. You just try some of that stuff on the Russians."

"You mean the Chinese, don't you?"

"Yeah, the Chinese. Try it on the Chinese."

"Oh dear. War was going on long before anybody dreamed up communism. It's just the latest justification for self-righteousness. The problem isn't communism. The problem is consensus. There's a consensus out that it's OK to kill when your government decides who to kill. If you kill inside the country you get in trouble. If you kill outside the country, right time, right season, latest enemy, you get a medal. There are about 130 nation-states, and each of them thinks it's a swell idea to bump off all the rest because he is more important. The pacifist thinks there is only one tribe. Three billion members. They come first. We think killing any member of the family is a dumb idea. We think there are more decent and intelligent ways of settling differences. And man had better start investigating these other possibilities because if he doesn't, then by mistake or by design, he will probably kill off the whole damn race."

"It's human nature to kill."

"Is it?"

"It's natural. Something you can't change."

"If it's natural to kill why do men have to go into training to learn how? There's violence in human nature, but there's also decency, love, kindness. Man

organizes, buys, sells, pushes violence. The nonviolent wants to organize the opposite side. That's all nonviolence is—organized love."

"You're crazy."

"No doubt. Would you care to tell me the rest of the world is sane? Tell me that violence has been a great success for the past 5,000 years, that the world is in fine shape, that wars have brought peace, understanding, brotherhood, democracy, and freedom to mankind, and that killing each other has created an atmosphere of trust and hope. That it's grand for one billion people to live off of the other two billion, or that even if it hasn't been smooth going all along, we are now at last beginning to see our way through to a better world for all, as soon as we get a few minor wars out of the way."

"I'm doing OK."

"Consider it a lucky accident."

"I believe I should defend America and all that she stands for. Don't you believe in self-defense?"

"No, that's how the Mafia got started. A little band of people who got together to protect peasants. I'll take Gandhi's nonviolent resistance."

"I still don't get the point of nonviolence."

"The point of nonviolence is to build a floor, a strong new floor, beneath which we can no longer sink. A platform which stands a few feet above napalm, torture, exploitation, poison gas, A- and H-bombs, the works. Give man a decent place to stand. He's been wallowing around in human blood and vomit and burnt flesh screaming how it's going to bring peace to the world. He sticks his head out of the hole for a minute and sees an odd bunch of people gathering material and attempting to build a structure above ground in the fresh air. 'Nice idea but not very practical,' he shouts and slides back into the hole. It was the same kind of thing when man found out the world was round. He fought for years to have it remain flat, with every proof on hand that it was not flat at all. It had no edge to drop off or sea monsters to swallow up his little ship in their gaping jaws."

"How are you going to build this practical structure?"

"From the ground up. By studying, learning about, experimenting with every possible alternative to violence on every level. By learning how to say no to the nation-state, no to war taxes, 'NO' to the draft, 'NO' to killing in general, 'YES' to the brotherhood of man; by starting new institutions which are based on the assumption that murder in any form is ruled out; by making and keeping in touch with nonviolent contacts all over the world; by engaging ourselves at every possible chance in dialogue with people, groups, to try to begin to change the consensus that it's OK to kill."

"It sounds real nice, but I just don't think it can work."

"You are probably right. We probably don't have enough time. So far we've been a glorious flop. The only thing that's been a worse flop than the organization of nonviolence has been the organization of violence."

from The Kingdom of God Is Within You

A Question of Adhesion
(Finding The Right Glue)
By Joan Baez

Last fall, during a two-month tour of the U.S., I called my good friend, Washington columnist, Colman McCarthy. Colman teaches a high school class on nonviolence, so we arranged an hour-long seminar with his students after my Washington concert. Looking back on it, I think that I got more out of that one-hour meeting than I did out of anything else I did during the tour.

The students in the group were racially, economically, and politically mixed, fairly knowledgeable, and very bright. Their discussion of social issues, viewed in the context of nonviolence (or otherwise), was honest, astute, intelligent, but most striking of all, characterized by a sort of dignified cynicism and resignation.

They were also refreshingly inquisitive. Some of the questions (theirs and mine) which arose:

What did I think were the real reasons that the administration sent troops to Lebanon, invaded Grenada, and meddles and manipulates events and affairs in Central and Latin America? Is it a real fear of communism? Or is President Reagan just looking for the best way to get votes? Does any member of the administration, State Department, or CIA really believe we are acting for the good of humankind?

Why is the perception of suffering, repression and torture so dramatically influenced by unrelated perceptions of geography and ideology? Why are the practices of some abusers tolerated while others are vehemently denounced.

Why is the Freeze, the only viable "movement" in the United States today, almost exclusively an adult movement? Why won't kids leave their classes, their computers and their video games and get involved? Is this apathy of Americans—kids and grown-ups—a result of a genuine fear that any political involvement comes at the risk of economic security, or are they simply too self-centered to care?

To most of these questions, there were no specific answers—just general (and inadequate) responses.

As we discussed the subject of the general lethargy within the United States, someone suggested that the overwhelming reaction of the European public against missiles in their "own backyard" was, in part, because the missiles belonged to somebody else and that one reason Americans weren't outraged and terrified by our own missile-dotted terrain was that ours are "nice American missiles."

It seemed that these kids were all coping, each in his or her own private way, with the fear of nuclear holocaust, which has to affect everyone's behavior, whether they accept or deny the reality of the situation—and that the job of coping is taking up a lot of energy. One girl talked about her inability to read a newspaper or watch the news on television because it was too emotionally demanding. If she exhausted her feelings on the morning news, she feared she wouldn't have enough left to react to those things that ought to matter to her. Even the death of a relative, she confided, might not stir her from the indifference that seemed to consume her after watching the news.

But of all that we talked about that evening, the one thought that struck me most, and which moved me to realize that it was time to reorganize my life once again, was a very simple one. It came from a sixteen-year-old boy whose "punk" styles included blonde spikes in his hair, black jeans and a leather jacket; he sat casually near me on a couch, his motorcycle helmet in his lap. He called himself Dante, and he was clearly well-liked by the rest of the class. He had mused, participated, joked, and now seemed to sum things up. "You see," he said, "you guys in the sixties had everything. You had the music, the issues, the symbols, the momentum. You had each other; you had glue. We are missing that. We don't have any glue."

There was unanimous agreement in the room and I saw instantly that this statement rang true not only for young people, but certainly for me, and, as I have found since that evening, for practically everyone I meet. We are all so caught up in our individual problems and struggles that we have no attachment to others whose problems and struggles are so very much like our own. We need some common bonding ingredient—some social and political "glue."

When I asked Dante if he'd be interested in taking risks if he felt that he were not alone, he said "sure."

Following that conversation, at the remaining concerts on the tour, I began testing this notion. "I know that there are intelligent people all over the world," I would say. "It's just that we have to discover each other." Audiences seemed to respond with enthusiasm, anticipation and relief.

This response brought to mind the ideas expressed by British historian, E.P. Thompson, whose "Letter to America" appeared in our last newsletter. Thompson wrote of the need for an international peace movement. Perhaps there is a way to develop real solidarity against violence, terror and oppression, which could cut across international borders. If the call and ensuing actions were strong enough, they would appeal to all ages.

Of course, there are many different kinds of glue. Perhaps the current wave of nationalistic frenzy in the United States can be interpreted in terms of instant glue–a sort of national Elmer's glue-all. But building a humane, nonviolent, life-supporting movement will take a much more permanent, stronger-bonding, more substantial kind of glue.

My head is spinning with ideas of how to approach this overwhelming task. As I write this, I am on my way to Germany, France, England, New York, Washington and elsewhere to speak with some of the people whose experience in and understanding of the process of nonviolent change I most respect. Hopefully, by the next newsletter, we – with any suggestions that you can offer to us – will have begun to formulate a plan to determine how I, with the help of Humanitas, can best play a part in the effort to find a moral equivalent, in the year 1984, to Gandhi's spinning wheel.

Humanitas International, *1984*

The Courage of Conviction

Joan Baez

It is not only the purity of her voice and the power of her songs, but her commitment to human rights, that have won Joan Baez an international following since she first burst upon the scene at the 1959 Newport (Rhode Island) Folk Festival. At the zenith of her popularity in the 1960s, she served as a role model for a generation of students who appreciated her idealism, sincerity and compassion. The Baez trademarks – long hair, informal dress, and guitar – became a uniform of the young rebel. For the student activists of the period who relied on violence, however, she had no sympathy. Her radicalism was firmly grounded in nonviolence, stemming from her traditional pacifistic beliefs. Over the years, she has experimented with every possible alternative to violence (including serving time in prison for civil disobedience) while lending her voice to the civil rights and the anti-war movements and the causes of American farm workers and prisoners, Cambodian refugees, Latin American desaparecidos, and disarmament. In 1979, she founded Humanitas International to address human-rights violations. Under its aegis, she continues to travel throughout the world, singing and advocating nonviolence like one of the warriors of the sun, "fighting postwar battles that somehow never got won."

When my son, Gabriel, was about nine, and we were sitting on the back porch watching the sunset, he asked me if I believed in God. I went on a long spiel about how Quakers say that there is that of God in every man and maybe the best way to translate that is that of "good" – I said it sounds like God – and he said, "But do you believe in God?" So I asked him, "Do you mean the man in the long robe and the white beard?" and he said, "Yeah." That's what he understood to be God, and he wanted to know if that is what I understood as well. "No," I told him, "I don't believe in that." And I tried to explain to him that what I do believe in is a force, a spiritual force, something that guides me.

Now this force does permit me to make choices. I can choose whether I'm going to do a wise thing or something really stupid. But at some point, it doesn't give me a choice. And, occasionally, I reach that point. I don't think that the events of my life are preordained, but they're definitely guided. Anyway, I hope they're guided because I'd have a hell of a time trying to figure it out all by myself.

For me, there is no separation between my spiritual and metaphysical beliefs and my ideological and political beliefs. When I'm trying to decide what direction to take in my life, for example, I go to a Quaker meeting and wait for direction – or perhaps it would be better to say "search for direction." And I do the same thing at home. I've taught myself to slow down enough in the mind, because the methodical process of thinking doesn't get me there. Plotting and planning and thinking have never gotten me anywhere. If I've had a good idea, it's been an inspiration that has come at the end of a great deal of plotting and planning and thinking, but usually the inspiration has had absolutely nothing to do with all the thoughts that I had. Whether it is political action or artistic creation, it must be the same process. It seems to me that of those songs that have been any good, I have not had much to do with the writing of them. The words have just crawled down my sleeve and come out on the page.

I really do think that if we can use the word "God" to describe this source of inspiration, and I'd be happy to, it must be the power of love, it must have something to do with love and caring that wins out over all of our craziness and jumbled thoughts and ill intentions and neurosis and all the rest. If you can care on top of all that stuff or through that stuff, then that is what keeps you engaged in the outside world and not just turned in on yourself and unaware of other people. It has to do with passion for love and life.

What's more important to me is maintaining a connection between myself and the things that I do to bring about a better world. That seems to be what I was put here for. For instance, at those times that I've tried doing music without politics – politics meaning my involvement with people and social change – the music has lost its glow. I've done lots of things in my lifetime, and I know that I am least happy when I am least involved in social action. But when I seem to be on the track that's really mine, it has been because my activities were closest to pure Gandhian nonviolent action. I have rarely felt as content, as energized, as satisfied, or as fulfilled personally as when I marched with Dr. Martin Luther King, Jr. in Grenada, Mississippi, took the hands of little black kids and walked with them to their school, and confronted the white cops who viewed us hatefully as we tried to make contact with them as feeling, individual human beings.

The attachment to nonviolent action is spiritual –

coming out of an old-fashioned Quaker heritage. What people do in a Quaker meeting is sit around as a group listening for the word of God to guide them. Alone, I am nothing. That's why I can speak immodestly, but with total humility, about my voice, and about some of the things that I've done because I consider that when I achieved anything, it was the result of something speaking through me. You could say that I've been a conduit, and that, most of the time, whatever I have done, it was not my idea at all; it was something that happened and it has to do with being inspired. That something could be called "God."

Somebody recently asked me if I had ever had any doubts about how I had lived my life, if I had ever thought to myself, "I'm uncertain about everything that I've done before in my life; I don't know about everything that I've believed before in my life." I had never thought about that before, but when I reflected on it, I realized that I had never had any doubts because I don't think I ever believed anything. I've just done it. I mean I haven't had a belief system except for a faith in nonviolence. I've had faith in it, I've done it, and what I have done, I have seen work.

Of course, I have seen places where it was impossible for nonviolent action to "work" because the situation had gone beyond the point where it could work. It hasn't made me turn against it, because I'm not about to take up armed struggle. It's just been kind of disheartening, knowing that what we've created in this world is a situation in which nonviolence as a social and political tool barely has a chance even to be planted, let alone flower. But if, looking back over the years, I ask myself if I think that I should have done it another way, or if I did the wrong thing, or if maybe I've got it all wrong and that human life is not important after all and killing each other is all in the natural order of things, the answer is "no." I've never had that sort of cataclysmic disillusionment. Sometimes I think whales are nicer and kinder and more tolerant and brighter than people, and I might wonder why I didn't spend any time for the last twenty years trying to save the whales. But I have priorities. Anyway, whales sing better than I do, so I'd probably be jealous.

I wish I belonged to a church. My life would be a whole lot easier if I had the pattern of an organized religion, which I could go through and have faith in and be sure of and something I could pray to with more certainty than I do now. I don't have enough faith. I wish that, somehow or other, it had been arranged that I had more of a structure to lean on. I mean, even symbols would be nice. It would be easier for me to ground myself. Of all the structures I've tried, the Quaker meeting makes the most sense to me. It's something resembling a structure. And I like what happens there. At a Quaker meeting, you can be and feel whatever you want. But I have had to discipline myself in whatever I've done all my life because I have not taken to other people's disciplines. I guess what I'm saying is that if something could force a discipline on me and I liked it, it would just make life easier – that's all.

As it is, I have to find the answers on my own. But as long as one keeps searching, the answers come. And to me that search has a great deal to do with nonviolence – with the things that are worth caring for: human life and respect for human life. This leads me automatically to the basic and most important rule: Thou shalt not kill. And so you spend your life looking for ways to work out conflict and to put that commandment into practice on a wide and practical scale.

Backstage with Joan Baez

by Colman McCarthy

I can't tell you how boring it would be for me," said Joan Baez, "to give a concert and not have it be connected with people's lives and people's suffering and real issues. There's no music for me outside of that."

For two hours, Joan had performed for 3,000 people at Constitution Hall, one of 27 singing dates in her seven-week tour just completed. Her soprano voice remains unaffectedly pure. Now, though, the concert was over, and Joan was in a backstage reception room with 25 high-school students. Last spring, they were in my pacifism class at School Without Walls. We had studied an essay on peace that Joan wrote in 1966, when, as today, she was in a fierce hurry to get on with it.

A few weeks before she came to Washington, Joan, a woman of generosity, gave an emphatic "yes" when I asked if she would meet with my students. I had come to know her years before when she would pass on information about political prisoners. She had a moral firmness that I have known in few others.

Bring your kids to the concert, she said, and we can talk and relax after. That was a large gift in itself, but Joan then gave them $240 worth of front-row tickets.

The students loved her singing, and backstage they connected quickly with her mind. She was not a star now. She was a constellation of ideas, questions, opinions, and reconsiderations. During the concert, Joan surprised many in the audience by dedicating a song, "Goodnight Saigon," to the Marines in Lebanon and their families: "That may sound strange coming from me, but I really am a person who is committed to the sanctity of all human life, especially young men who need not have died in their prime."

In spirals of anecdotes and theories, she built a case that gradually peaked into the high ideal that radical nonviolence is the best and only answer worth offering to children. "I understand any kid who looks at the news in the morning and says, 'I wanna smoke dope for the rest of my life.' It's so huge what we're facing, so scary." Joan said it was her commitment to offer to young people alternatives to despair.

Briefly into her talk, Joan, who sat atop a dressing table, asked for questions. Draft registration was first. "The draft has no right to exist," she answered. "Nobody has the right to tell you how you are going to live your life. What they'll tell you is, you have to preserve democracy around the world. But you can't bring democracy into an undemocratic set-up. And the least democratic set-up I can think of, offhand, besides possibly the U.S.S.R., is an army." She advised the students to study the alternative options to the draft, including jail if that's what it comes to.

As a pacifist, was she ever afraid of violence? "The fear is always there," she said. She told stories of being in Hanoi during the Vietnam War and taking to the shelters to avoid being killed by American pilots dropping bombs on the city. She had had bomb threats in Belfast, police-state threats in Argentina and Chile, billy-club threats in Mississippi. "You learn to pray," she said.

One student wondered what Joan believed "U.S. interests" means, considering that the phrase is used repeatedly in foreign policy discussion. "What do you think they are?" she asked the student. He said they were so "ambiguous and vague" that "I have no idea." Joan replied, "I agree with you. I don't know what they mean."

On tax resistance as a way of protesting the government's military policies, Joan said that she refused to cooperate with the IRS in the 1960s and that it may be time to say "no" again. "It may be much more of a risk this time. I also have to decide that if I end up in jail, is that worth it? Probably yes. It's probably the best thing I can do."

None of this was too heavy for the students. Joan's radical nonviolence was not irrelevant to their lives. Some let her know that in their gut they felt the same revulsion to the world's violence that Joan felt when she was a teenager going to Quaker meeting houses. She sensed then that only pacifism and organized resistance to violence was the answer. She has given her life, and her talent, to it.

When she was last in Washington, Joan had called. We met and spent time talking about her just completed trips to Latin America. There, she had been seeking to renew the energy of her folksinging with its only strength, the folk. In Argentina, she sang at a Mass for the mothers of citizens who had disappeared. In Brazil, she met with labor leaders who had been punished for striking. In Chile, she sang in a free concert for a Santiago human rights group.

The primitivist governments in each of these countries found Baez and her music too threatening. She was denied permission to give commercial concerts. Banned in public, she sang in private - in churches, homes, and anyplace else where people gathered to ease their anguish about the systematic violence that is crushing them daily. Joan sang their own songs of hope to them, as well as those that have risen up from the repressed in other countries.

Amid the torturing and silencing that is standard equipment in these countries, Joan, even if she weren't a glowing artist of independent mind, would have still been a worrisome figure for the governments. She is the president of Humanitas International, a human rights organization. Based in Menlo Park, California, it already has 5,000 paying members. It is different from similar groups because Joan is an activist, not a theoretician. She will turn up in a Chile or a Northern Ireland, just as she went in 1979 to the refugee camps in southeast Asia. She has denounced the "Stalinist leadership" in Vietnam as vehemently as the oligarchy in El Salvador.

Humanitas International, she says, is "quite simply, for the right to life. We recognize that Somalian refugees, Salvadoran peasants, and Cambodian children are not concerned with the fine points of Marxism or capitalism - they are struggling for their survival. And if what we can do in our small way aids in that struggle, then all our efforts are worthwhile."

Those words have meaning. Aside from her persistent idealism and her commitment to nonviolence, Joan is matched by few performing artists for using talent on behalf of the world's poor.

Backstage at Constitution Hall, Joan spoke to the students not as children but as adults with crucial choices to make. They were grateful. They didn't want prolix philosophizing or another there-are-no-easy-answers lecture. Joan gave them what they wanted: a call to action, a call to conscience.

from Washington Post

Love without courage and wisdom is sentimentality, as with the ordinary church member. Courage without love and wisdom is foolhardiness, as with the ordinary soldier. Wisdom without love and courage is cowardice, as with the ordinary soldier. Therefore one who has love, courage and wisdom is one in a million who moves the world, as with Jesus, Buddha and Gandhi.

Ammon Hennacy

The Nonviolent Alternative

by Thomas Merton

Nonviolence is not simply a way of proving one's point and getting what one wants without being involved in behavior that one considers ugly and evil. Nor is it, for that matter, a means which anyone can legitimately make use of according to his fancy for any purpose whatever. To practice nonviolence for a purely selfish or arbitrary end would, in fact, discredit and distort the truth of nonviolent resistance.

Nonviolence is perhaps the most exacting of all forms of struggle, not only because it demands first of all that one be ready to suffer evil and even face the threat of death without violent retaliation, but because it excludes mere transient self-interest from its considerations. In a very real sense, he who practices nonviolent resistance must commit himself not to the defense of his own interests or even those of a particular group: he must commit himself to the defense of objective truth and right and, above all, of *man*. His aim is then not simply to "prevail" or to prove that he is right and the adversary wrong, or to make the adversary give in and yield what is demanded of him.

Nor should the nonviolent resister be content to prove *to himself* that *he* is virtuous and right, and that *his* hands and heart are pure even though the adversary's may be evil and defiled. Still less should he seek for himself the psychological gratification of upsetting the adversary's conscience and perhaps driving him to an act of bad faith and refusal of the truth. We know that our unconscious motives may, at times, make our nonviolence a form of moral aggression and even a subtle provocation designed (without our awareness) to bring out the evil we hope to find in the adversary, and thus to justify ourselves in our own eyes and in the eyes of "decent people." Wherever there is a high moral ideal, there is an attendant risk of pharisaism, and nonviolence is no exception. The basis of pharisaism is division: on one hand this morally or socially privileged self and the elite to which it belongs. On the other hand, the "others," the wicked, the unenlightened, whoever they may be, Communists, capitalists, colonialists, traitors, international Jewry, racists, etc.

A test of our sincerity in the practice of nonviolence is this: are we willing to *learn something from the adversary?* If a *new truth* is made known to us by him or through him, will we accept it? Are we willing to admit that he is not totally inhumane, wrong, unreasonable, cruel, etc.? This is important. If he sees that we are completely incapable of listening to him with an open mind, our nonviolence will have nothing to say to him except that we distrust him and seek to outwit him. Our readiness to see some good in him and to agree with some of his ideas (though tactically this might look like a weakness on our part) actually gives us power: the power of sincerity and of truth. On the other hand, if we are obviously unwilling to accept any truth that we have not first discovered and declared ourselves, we show by that very fact that we are interested not in the truth so much as in "being right." Since the adversary is presumably interested in being right also, and in proving himself right by what he considers the superior argument of force, we end up where we started. Nonviolence has great power, provided that it really witnesses to truth and not just to self-righteousness.

The dread of being open to the ideas of others generally comes from our hidden insecurity about our own convictions. We fear that we may be "converted"– or perverted–by a pernicious doctrine. On the other hand, if we are mature and objective in our open-mindedness, we may find that viewing things from a basically different perspective–that of our adversary– we discover our own truth in a new light and are able to understand our own ideal more realistically.

Our willingness to take *an alternative approach* to a problem will perhaps relax the obsessive fixation of the adversary on his view, which he believes is the only reasonable possibility and which he is determined to impose on everyone else by coercion.

The key to nonviolence is the willingness of the nonviolent resister to suffer a certain amount of accidental evil in order to bring about a change of mind in the oppressor and awaken him to personal openness and to dialogue. A nonviolent protest that merely seeks to gain publicity and to show up the oppressor for what he is, without opening his eyes to new values, can be said to be in large part a failure. At the same time, a nonviolence which does not rise to the level of the personal, and remains confined to the consideration of nature and natural necessity, may perhaps make a deal but it cannot really make sense.

Conflict will never be abolished but a new way of

solving it can become habitual. Man can then act according to the dignity of that adulthood which he is now said to have reached–and which yet remains, perhaps, to be conclusively proved. One of the ways in which it can, without doubt, be proved is precisely this: man's ability to settle conflicts by reason and arbitration instead of by slaughter and destruction.

The distinction suggested here, between two types of thought–one oriented to nature and necessity, the other to person and freedom–calls for further study at another time. It seems to be helpful. The "nature-oriented" mind treats other human beings as objects to be manipulated in order to control the course of events and make the future for the whole human species conform to certain rather rigidly determined expectations. "Person-oriented" thinking does not lay down these draconian demands, does not seek so much to *control* as to *respond*, and to *awaken response*. It is not set on determining anyone or anything, and does not insistently demand that persons and events correspond to our own abstract ideal. All it seeks is the openness of free exchange in which reason and love have freedom of action. In such a situation the future will take care of itself.

Nonviolence must be aimed, above all, at the transformation of the present state of the world, and it must, therefore, be free from all occult, unconscious connivance with an unjust use of power. This poses enormous problems–for if nonviolence is too political, it becomes drawn into the power struggle and identified with one side or another in that struggle, while, if it is totally apolitical, it runs the risk of being ineffective or, at best, merely symbolic.

Here the human dignity of nonviolence must manifest itself clearly in terms of a freedom and a nobility which are able to resist political manipulation and brute force and show them up as arbitrary, barbarous and irrational. This will not be easy. The temptation to get publicity and quick results by spectacular tricks, or by forms of protest that are merely odd and provocative but whose human meaning is not clear, may defeat this purpose.

The realism of nonviolence must be made evident by humility and self-restraint which clearly show frankness and open-mindedness and invite the adversary to serious and reasonable discussion.

Instead of trying to use the adversary as leverage for one's own effort to realize an ideal, nonviolence seeks only to enter into a dialogue with him in order to attain, together with him, the common good of *man*. Nonvio-

lence must be realistic and concrete. Like ordinary political action, it is no more than the "art of the possible." But precisely the advantage of nonviolence is that it has a *more humane notion of what is possible*. Where the powerful believe that only power is efficacious, the nonviolent resister is persuaded of the superior efficacy of love, openness, peaceful negotiation and, above all, of truth. For power can guarantee the interests of *some men* but it can never foster the good of *man*. Power always protects the good of some at the expense of all the others. Only love can attain and preserve the good of all. Any claim to build the security of *all* on force is a manifest imposture.

It is here that genuine humility is of the greatest importance.

Message to Poets

by Thomas Merton

We who are poets know that the reason for a poem is not discovered until the poem itself exists. The reason for a living act is realized only in the act itself. This meeting is a spontaneous explosion of hopes. That is why it is a venture in prophetic poverty, supported and financed by no foundation, organized and publicized by no official group, but a living expression of the belief that there are now in our world new people, new poets who are not in tutelage to established political systems or cultural structures– whether communist or capitalist–but who dare to hope in their own vision of reality and of the future. This meeting is united in a flame of hope whose temperature has not yet been taken and whose effects have not yet been estimated, because it is a new fire. The reason for the fire cannot be apparent to one who is not warmed by it. The reason for being here will not be found until all have walked together, without afterthought, into contradictions and possibilities.

We believe that our future will be made by love and hope, not by violence or calculation. The Spirit of Life that has brought us together, whether in space or only in agreement, will make our encounter an epiphany of certainties we could not know in isolation.

The solidarity of poets is not planned and welded together with tactical convictions or matters of policy, since these are affairs of prejudice, cunning and design. Whatever his failures, the poet is not a cunning man. His art depends on an ingrained innocence which he would lose in business, in politics or in too organized a form of academic life. The hope that rests on calculation has lost its innocence. We are banding together to defend our innocence.

All innocence is a matter of belief. I do not speak now of organized agreement, but of interior personal convictions "in the spirit." These convictions are as strong and undeniable as life itself. They are rooted in fidelity to *life* rather than to artificial systems. The solidarity of poets is an elemental fact like sunlight, like the seasons, like the rain. It is something that cannot be organized, it can only happen. It can only be "received." It is a gift to which we must remain open. No man can plan to make the sun rise or the rain fall. The sea is still wet in spite of all formal and abstract programs. Solidarity is not collectivity. The organizers of collective life will deride the seriousness or the reality of our hope. If they infect us with their doubt we shall lose our innocence and our solidarity along with it.

Collective life is often organized on the basis of cunning, doubt and guilt. True solidarity is destroyed by the political art of pitting one man against another and the commercial art of estimating all men at a price. On these illusory measurements, men build a world of arbitrary values without life and meaning, full of sterile agitation. To set one man against another, one life against another, one work against another, and to express the measurement in terms of cost or of economic privilege and moral honor is to infect everybody with the deepest metaphysical doubt. Divided and set up against one another for the purpose of evaluation, men immediately acquire the mentality of objects for sale in a slave market. They despair of themselves because they know they have been unfaithful to life and to being, and they no longer find anyone to forgive the infidelity.

Yet their despair condemns them to further infidelity: alienated from their own spiritual roots, they contrive to break, to humiliate and to destroy the spirit of others. In such a situation there is no joy, only rage. Each man feels the deepest root of his being poisoned by suspicion, unbelief and hate. Each man experiences his very existence as guilt and betrayal, and as a possibility of death: nothing more.

We stand together to denounce the shame and the imposture of all such calculations.

If we are to remain united against these falsehoods, against all power that poisons man and subjects him to the mystifications of bureaucracy, commerce and the police state, we must refuse the price tag. We must refuse academic classification. We must reject the seductions of publicity. We must not allow ourselves to be pitted one against another in mystical comparisons–political, literary or cultural orthodoxies. We must not be made to devour and dismember one another for the amusement of their press. We must not let ourselves be eaten by them to assuage their own insatiable doubt. We must not merely be for something and *against* something else, even if we are for "ourselves" and against "them." Who are "they"? Let us not give them support by becoming an "opposition," which assumes they are definitively real.

Let us remain outside "their" categories. It is in this sense that we are all monks: for we remain innocent and invisible to publicists and bureaucrats. They cannot imagine what we are doing unless we betray ourselves to them, and even then they will never be able.

They understand nothing except what they themselves have decreed. They are crafty ones who weave words about life and then make life conform to what they themselves have declared. How can they trust anyone when they make life itself tell lies? It is the businessman, the propagandist, the politician, not the poet, who devoutly believes in "the magic of words."

For the poet, there is precisely no magic. There is only life in all its unpredictability and all its freedom. All magic is a ruthless venture in manipulation, a vicious circle, a self-fulfilling prophecy.

Word-magic is an impurity of language and of spirit in which words, deliberately reduced to unintelligibility, appeal mindlessly to the vulnerable will. Let us deride and parody this magic with other variants of the unintelligible, if we want to. But it is better to prophesy than to deride. To prophesy is not to predict, but to seize upon reality in its moment of highest expectation and tension toward the new.

This tension is discovered not in hypnotic elation but in the light of everyday existence. Poetry is innocent of prediction because it is itself the fulfillment of all the momentous predictions hidden in everyday life.

Poetry is the flowering of ordinary possibilities. It is the fruit of ordinary and natural choice. This is its innocence and dignity.

Let us not be like those who wish to make the tree bear its fruit first and the flower afterward–a conjuring trick and an advertisement. We are content if the flower comes first and the fruit afterward, in due time. Such is the poetic spirit.

Let us obey life, and the Spirit of Life that calls us to be poets, and we shall harvest many new fruits for which the world hungers–fruits of hope that have never been seen before. With these fruits, we shall calm the resentments and the rage of man.

Let us be proud that we are not witch doctors, only ordinary men.

Let us be proud that we are not experts in anything.

Let us be proud of the words that are given to us for nothing, not to teach anyone, not to confute anyone, not to prove anyone absurd, but to point beyond all objects into the silence where nothing can be said.

We are not persuaders. We are the children of the Unknown. We are the ministers of silence that is needed to cure all victims of absurdity who lie dying in a contrived joy. Let us then recognize ourselves for who we are: dervishes mad with secret therapeutic love which cannot be bought or sold, and which the politician fears more than violent revolution, for violence changes nothing. But love changes everything.

We are stronger than the bomb.

Let us then say "yes" to our own nobility by embracing the insecurity and abjection that a dervish existence entails.

In the Republic of Plato there was already no place for poets and musicians, still less for dervishes and monks. As for the technological Platos, who think they now run the world we live in, they imagine they can tempt us with banalities and abstractions. But we can elude them merely by stepping into the Heraklitean river which is never crossed twice.

When the poet puts his foot in that ever-moving river, poetry itself is born out of the flashing water. In that unique instant, the truth is manifest to all who are able to receive it.

No one can come near the river unless he walks on his own feet. He cannot come there carried in a vehicle.

No one can enter the river wearing the garments of public and collective ideas. He must feel the water on his skin. He must know that immediacy is for naked minds only, and for the innocent.

Come, dervishes: Here is the water of life. Dance in it.

Excerpts of this essay first appeared in Americas, *April 16, 1964. The essay was subsequently published* in toto *in* Raids on the Unspeakable *(New York: New Directions, 1966)*

Education and Success

by Thomas Merton

The danger of education, I have found, is that it so easily confuses means with ends. Worse than that, it quite easily forgets both and devotes itself merely to the mass production of uneducated graduates– people literally unfit for anything except to take part in an elaborate and completely artificial charade which they and their contemporaries have conspired to call "life."

A few years ago, a man who was compiling a book entitled *Success* wrote and asked me to contribute a statement on how I got to be a success. I replied indignantly that I was not able to consider myself a success in any terms that had a meaning to me. I swore I had spent my life strenuously avoiding success. If it so happened that I had once written a best seller, this was a pure accident, due to inattention and naivete, and I would take very good care never to do the same again. If I had a message to my contemporaries, I said, it was surely this: Be anything you like, be madmen, drunks and bastards of every shape and form, but at all costs avoid one thing: success. I heard no more from him and I am not aware that my reply was published with the other testimonials.

Thus, I have undercut all hope of claiming that Columbia made me a success. On the contrary, I believe I can thank Columbia, among so many other things, for having helped me learn the value of unsuccess. Columbia was for me a microcosm, a little world, where I exhausted myself in time. Had I waited until after graduation, it would have been too late. During the few years in which I was there, I managed to do so many wrong things that I was ready to blow my mind. But fortunately I learned, in so doing, that this was good. I might have ended up on Madison Avenue if I hadn't. Instead of preparing me for one of those splendid jobs, Columbia cured me forever of wanting one. Instead of adapting me to the world downtown, Columbia did me the favor of lobbing me half–conscious into the Village, where I occasionally came to my senses and where I continued to learn. I think I have sufficiently explained, elsewhere, how much I owed, in this regard, to people like Mark Van Doren (who lived around the corner from me in the Village) and Joseph Wood Krutch (who became, as I have become, a hermit). Such people taught me to imitate not Rockefeller but Thoreau. Of course, I am not trying to say that one has to be Thoreau rather than Rockefeller, nor am I slyly intimating that I have discovered a superior form of resentment, an off-beat way of scoring on everybody by refusing to keep score.

What I am saying is this: The score is not what matters. Life does not have to be regarded as a game in which scores are kept and somebody wins. If you are too intent on winning, you will never enjoy playing. If you are too obsessed with success, you will forget to live. If you have learned only how to be a success, your life has probably been wasted. If a university concentrates on producing successful people, it is lamentably failing in its obligation to society and to the students themselves.

Now I know that even in the thirties, at Columbia, the business of wanting to be a success was very much in the air. There was, in fact, a scandal about the yearbook senior poll. The man who was voted "most likely to succeed" was accused of having doctored the results in his own favor after a surreptitious deal with the yearbook staff member who was voted "best dressed." Incidentally, I was voted best writer. I was not accused of trickery, but everyone understood that the vote, which had been between me and Hank Liebermann, had been decided by my fraternity brothers. (Incidentally, whatever became of the man "most likely to succeed"?)

In any case, no one really cared. Since that time many of my classmates have attained to eminence with all its joys and all its sorrows, and the ones I have seen since then are marked by the signature of anguish. So am I. I do not claim exemption. Yet I never had the feeling that our alma mater just wanted us to become well-paid operators, or to break our necks to keep on the front pages of the *Times*. On the contrary–maybe this is a delusion, but if it is a delusion it is a salutary one–I always felt at Columbia that people around me, half amused and perhaps at times half incredulous, were happy to let me be myself.

from Collected Essays

Rediscovering Thomas Merton

by Colman McCarthy

Who was Thomas Merton?

The commonplace answer, the one most of us would give, is that he was a man who renounced his worldly ways in the early 1940s and entered a Trappist monastery, there to serve God until he died in 1968.

How handily a life can be summed up! In Merton's instance, it is even easier because, we assume, once a person commits himself to the intense spiritual life of Trappist monasteries, that's it. What more can be said?

In 1941, when Merton entered Our Lady of Gethsemani in Kentucky, the Order of Cistercians of the Strict Observance had been changeless for centuries. To take on its rigors was to become changeless yourself, the only growth being spiritual growth. Everything else went. To become a Trappist was to put a final paragraph on your life story.

None of that holds for Thomas Merton, and that is surely an understatement. The 54 years of his life – 27 out of the monastery and 27 in – were an astonishing flurry of activity that produced an amazing outflow of changes and contradictions. In his later years, it was as though Merton sensed that he had become a symbol of stability to the millions of his readers. But he wanted no part of the symbolism because it meant he would have to become lifeless.

If people wanted to romanticize Father Louis (his Trappist name) as a holy monk on a mountaintop or as a professional prayer man who was undistracted by worldly pursuits, well, that was their choice. But for Merton, the image was phony. As he wrote in his journal, *The Sign of Jonas*: "People are starving to death and freezing and here I sit with a silver spoon in my mouth and write books and everybody sends me fan mail telling me how wonderful I am for giving up so much."

The monk's appreciation for the irony of things was a quality bound to be dominant in a person whose mind and heart were constantly bouncing off walls of contradiction.

A few of the obvious ones:

To many of the readers of his 50 books and 250 articles, Merton was the last word on authentic spirituality. Yet he wrote to ask for guidance from Rosemary Radford Ruether, the American theologian who currently teaches in Chicago: "Do you think you could help me once in a while? I do not intend to be very demanding on your time, but I would like to feel that I can resort to you for suggestions and advice. Not so much for my work, as just to help me think."

Merton celebrated his turning from secular pleasures in his best-selling autobiography, *The Seven Storey Mountain*, but in a well-hushed trip to New York City in 1964, he was not only overjoyed to be sprung from the monastery for a few days, but he discovered that the world wasn't so wicked after all. "The people walking on Fifth Avenue were beautiful," he wrote. New York "is a stately and grown up city, a true city, life-size, anything but soulless. New York is feminine. It is she, the city. I am faithful to her. I have not ceased to love her to the last gasp of this ball-point pen."

Merton relished his solitude; he finally moved out of the community to live alone in a hermitage on a lonely part of the monastery property. But he was often as busy as a trainmaster routing visitors in and out of his life. Along with friends from the publishing world and Columbia University, where he had studied, he welcomed people as diverse as Jacques Maritain and Joan Baez, Daniel Berrigan, and John Howard Griffin. His correspondents were all over the globe: oriental mystics, South American poets, Henry Miller, Cardinal Montini, poets, pacifists, and strangers who wrote to him because he seemed to be a person who would understand their troubles.

Sometimes the strain of correspondence became too much, as he confessed in a letter to Henry Miller: "People going down for the third time think a letter will keep them afloat. But often what they are going in is itself an illusion. Sometimes I answer, sometimes I can't, and I mean not to worry about it. There is a destiny involved there too. But there is no question that we spend our lives battling mountains of crap, and this is no mean exercise."

If those quotes and correspondence suggest a "different" Merton, it is because some serious biographers lately have been digging out new material. The latest is Monica Furlong, a British writer who had access to

Merton's papers at Bellarmine College in Louisville and St. Bonaventure University in New York.

In *Merton: A Biography*, Furlong writes that much of Merton's "struggle on the long road to becoming a contemplative had to do with the problem of identity. The hermit, or just the man who tries to explore solitude, finds himself no longer reassured by the affirmation of others, and may suffer deeply from the emptiness caused by loneliness, feeling that he has ceased to exist. On the far side of this emptiness, Merton believed, there is an identity scarcely dreamed, an identity to be found only in the religious search, and one that sets the contemplative free to love his or her fellow human beings."

Other biographers have said the same. In *Man Before God*, Frederic Kelly said that "no social commentator in modern times has combined such a deeply contemplative view of reality on such a broad range of topics over such a long period as has Thomas Merton."

What the biographers are telling us is something that readers of Merton will understand for themselves soon after they get into his work: however creative and compassionate he was, he was still struggling to make sense out of the same problems that hound the rest of us.

For someone who had radically changed the ways of his own life—from an oat-sowing student who fathered a child (later killed, with his mother, in a London air raid in World War II) to a recognized spiritual master—Merton overflowed with soft empathy for others who found the going rough.

In 1966, in a Christmas letter to friends, Merton counseled that the "heart can be filled with much pain even when things are exteriorly 'all right.' It becomes all the more difficult because today we are used to thinking that there are explanations for everything. But there is no explanation of most of what goes on in our own hearts, and we cannot account for it all. No use resorting to the kind of mental tranquilizers that even religious explanations sometimes offer. Faith must be deeper than that, rooted in the unknown and in the abyss of darkness that is the ground of our being. No use teasing the darkness to try to make answers grow out of it. But if we learn to have a deep inner patience, things solve themselves, or God solves them, if you prefer. But do not expect to see how. Just learn to wait, and do what you can to help other people. Often in helping someone else we find the best way to bear with our own trouble."

This wasn't a Holy Joe sermon. Merton himself had waited through years of hard pain, much of it coming from the superiors of his own order. His abbot, a wily and conservative character who guarded Merton's image as shrewdly as he marketed the monastery's cheese and fruitcake, kept him under special wraps. Dom James Fox took it as all but a holy cause to restrain Merton when in the mid-1950s he began seriously considering changing to another, more reclusive, order. He put out the word: good Father Louis is a bit neurotic and is having emotional problems.

A few years later, when Merton sought permission to attend outside conferences or to visit other monasteries (routine activities for others in the order), Dom James said no. It was already questionable enough that Merton was writing about civil rights, war and social justice, all of it prompting the *National Catholic Reporter* to call Merton "the public monk." But how would it look if Merton were turned loose? Wouldn't the public delight in following the city capers of the monk whose image was largely built on solitude and silence? And what, the abbot wondered, would become of holy Gethsemani and its reputation for piety? The prospects were frightening. It would take Merton about a week to write his first life-in-the-city book, *The Seven Storey Tenement*, and another week for every Trappist to read it. The same crowd who piled in to Gethsemani on a Merton book would now be flocking out on a Merton book. And who would be left to bake the fruitcakes?

The subterfuge and snideness by which his abbot controlled Merton became unofficial penances. But however much he grumbled about the shabby treatment he received, he did not let the unfairness embitter him.

Rather than withdraw, Merton followed his own advice. He expanded and became concerned with the suffering of others.

Part of that meant being available to the members of his own community. Among the fathers and brothers of Gethsemani, Merton was revered for the sharing of his gifts. A priest and psychiatrist at Gethsemani wrote that Merton "was a true brother. In our community, he was surely one of the best loved of people. His whole manner was pen and outgoing and so constantly enthusiastic that he quickly formed community."

Perhaps Merton formed community in another way, by writing *Seven Storey Mountain* and seeing the book become, for many people, a recruiting pamphlet for the Trappist life. Twenty years after it came out, when Merton was seasoned and well beyond the first fervor in which he wrote of his conversion, he told an interviewer: I left the book behind many years ago…It is a youthful book, too simple, in many ways, too crude. Everything is laid out in black and white . . . [it deals in] a clean-cut division between the natural and the supernatural, God and the world, sacred and secular, with boundary lines that were supposed to be quite evident. Since those days, I have acquired a little experience, I think, and have read a few things and tried to help other people with their problems. Life is not as simple as it once looked in *Seven Storey Mountain*. Unfortunately, the book was a best seller, and has become a kind of edifying legend or something. This is a dreadful fate. I am doing my best to live it down."

Part of that living down drew Merton into social issues, helping him to fulfill "my intention to make my entire life a rejection of, a protest against, the crimes and injustices of war and political tyranny." In a searing essay, which took as a departure the fact that a psychiatrist had examined Adolf Eichmann, the Nazi mass killer, and pronounced him sane, Merton wrote that "the sanity of Eichmann is disturbing. We equate sanity with a sense of justice, with humaneness, with prudence, with the capacity to love and understand other people. We rely on the sane people of the world to preserve it from barbarism, madness, destruction. And now it begins to dawn on us that it is precisely the sane ones who are the most dangerous… Those who have invented and developed atomic bombs, thermonuclear bombs, missiles; who have planned the strategy for the next war, who have evaluated the various possibilities of using bacterial and chemical agents; these are not the crazy people, they are the sane people. The ones who cooly estimate how many millions of victims can be considered expendable in a nuclear way, I presume they do all right with the Rorschach ink blots too. On the other hand, you will probably find that the pacifists and the ban-the-bomb people are, quite seriously, just as we read in *Time* magazine, a little crazy."

During the 1950s and 1960s, when the power of Merton's writing was a trusted force, one of the intellectual comforts was in believing that not only was this gentle and knowledgeable man on the scene but that he would probably be with us for a long time. Living in a rural monastery, where he sometimes chopped wood and spread manure over the fields for physical exercise, Merton was one person in whom the blows and crashes of modern life would bring on no mid-life coronary. He seemed as safe for old age as the prophets. For decades to come, he would be talking to us – exhorting, stirring and blessing – like a patriarch seeking a covenant.

If we knew better the way things go in this world,

Merton's death at 53 would have been less a disquieting event. The manner of his dying was beyond imagining: by electrocution in a Bangkok hotel room after touching the faulty wiring of a fan.

He had gone to Asia to visit some authorities on Oriental mysticism with whom he had been corresponding for years. The trip was no lark; Merton had spent several years, for example, meditating on the sayings and parables of Chuang Tzu, the Taoist sage who lived in Plato's time. Merton's interest in Zen was not the coffeehouse mysticism fashionable in America in the late 1960s (and lingering well into the 1970s). For a start, he understood that the spiritual discipline of Zen is impossible without a matching of moral discipline.

It may well have been that Merton's trip to the East was a moment of rejuvenation, after a stroke of good luck that saw his old abbot resign and be replaced by a man more sympathetic to Merton's travel requests. But it is impossible to read the *Asian Journal* without sensing that his understanding of the East was that of someone looking for what Merton called "a new language of prayer." He wrote as a visitor who was intent on taking something home with him that would be lasting: "I think we have now reached a state of long overdue religious maturity at which it may be possible to remain perfectly faithful to a Christian and Western monastic commitment, and yet learn in depth from, say, a Buddhist or Hindu discipline and experience. I believe that some of us need to do this to improve the quality of our own monastic life and even to help in the task of monastic renewal which has been undertaken within the Western church."

As with many persons who did most things well, time is still needed on judgments on what Merton did best. He was a spiritual seeker who, in the tradition of St. John of the Cross and Ruysbroek, elevated religion well beyond the merely pious. He could write strong poetry, as Mark Van Doren said, in which "all the senses work together to one end, the letting of things declare themselves." His social criticism was grounded in pacifism. He suspected the idea that a return to paradise is imminent if only the world would get out of America's way.

However the judgments turn out, evidence exists that Merton saw himself as fragmented by having several vocations within a vocation. A self existed and a God existed, and the point of living is to increase the closeness of the two.

In an essay, "Is the Contemplative Life Finished?"

Merton wrote that what must happen in the monastaries is much the same that must happen everywhere else, in our homes, schools and worksites: "What each of us has to do and what I have to do is to buckle down and really start investigating new possibilities in our own life; and if new possibilities mean radical changes, all right. Maybe we need radical changes for which we have to struggle and sweat some blood. . . But on the other hand, let these be real changes and not just neurotic upheaval."

Thomas Merton currently has two of kinds of readers. One group has been with him all along, friends and followers who put up with the mediocrity of many of his books – the little ground-out devotionals – but who cherish such fecund works as *Conjectures of a Guilty Bystander* and *The Behavior of Titans*. The other group includes those for whom Merton is a new voice recently discovered, perhaps having heard him for the first time in school or in early adulthood when the need for authenticity and guidance runs deep.

Merton, whatever his role in an individual's life, was not a man apart. He saw himself simply, as a "self-questioning human person who, like all his brothers, struggles to cope with a turbulent, mysterious, demanding, frustrating, confused existence."

That is the starting point for everyone – and the ending point, too. The quality of the movement in between measures the worthiness of the struggle.

from Washington Post

Few of us will ever do great
things, but all of us can do small things in a great way.

Volunteers for Peace

by Gerard T. Rice

Shortly after the Peace Corps had been launched, Vice-President Lyndon Johnson took Sargent Shriver aside and gave him some advice on the selection of Volunteers. "Do it like I did the Texas Youth Conservation Corps," said Johnson. "Keep out the three Cs." "The three Cs?" asked a puzzled Shriver. "The three Cs," Johnson repeated: "The communists, the consumptives and the cocksuckers."* In his own inimitable fashion, the Vice-President was telling Shriver that if the wrong type of person were selected to go overseas, the Peace Corps would face embarrassment at home and abroad. Yet Shriver had to recruit, train, and select thousands of young people to go to exotic Third World countries and perform tasks which few Americans had attempted before. The only way of learning was by trial and error.

Shriver's "Report to the President" of February 1961 had left the opportunity for service open to any American over the age of eighteen. Within early Peace Corps councils it had been argued that service should be restricted to skilled technicians and to those with specific academic qualifications. Shriver disagreed; he felt that many useful jobs in the developing countries could be done by the average, well-motivated American. In the area of people-to-people contact, he believed that an unskilled but enthusiastic generalist could do at least as well as a skilled but diffident technocrat. "There was no point in having Ph.D.'s in the boondocks," he said.

Shriver's sentiment reinforced Kennedy's original aim of giving as many young Americans as possible the chance to serve at a grassroots level in Third World countries. As a traveler himself, Kennedy realized the potential benefit of crossing cultural frontiers. His Cow Palace proposal had been aimed primarily at the college senior completing a liberal arts degree–bright, healthy, interested in world affairs, and well-educated in a general sense. B.A. generalists would also be more likely to sacrifice two or three years of their lives to service in a developing country than technicians already embarked upon a career. Nevertheless, critics were skeptical of the abilities of the inexperienced generalists and of the wisdom of Shriver's decision to build the Peace Corps around them. Shriver told Kennedy he was certain that the Peace Corps could attract "cream-of-the-crop, talented, fit, well-adjusted and devoted American men and women."

The truth is that the Peace Corps owes much of its success to its birth in a political campaign...Because of the response of the American people President Kennedy decided to establish the Peace Corps as one of his first major acts. This is an example of what Martin Buber calls "the meeting of idea and fate in a creative hour." It is the way ideas are born in American politics.

Sargent Shriver—First Director of the Peace Corps

Despite Shriver's confidence, the Peace Corps experienced some initial difficulty in finding sufficient numbers of suitable applicants. In those early, frenetic days when an organization had to be built, programs developed, and Congress faced, recruitment had been left to take care of itself. The popular interest in Kennedy's new idea had been such that Shriver and his colleagues had assumed that Volunteers would appear in droves without an intensive recruitment campaign. Indeed, the Peace Corps' policy position was that it did not "recruit" but merely supplied information to prospective applicants. Shriver did not want the Peace Corps to become engaged in a "we need recruits" campaign; accordingly, he issued a stern warning that the Peace Corps should never attempt to enlist people in the manner of the U.S. Marine Corps. The agency waited and hoped that enough people would answer Kennedy's call.

I'd never done anything political, patriotic, or unselfish because nobody ever asked me to. Kennedy asked.

A Peace Corps Volunteer

John F. Kennedy liked to remind young Americans that they lived " at a very special moment in history— Latin America, Africa, the Middle East and Asia are caught up in the adventures of asserting their independence and modernizing their old way of life." He saw the United States, with its anti-colonial heritage and tremendous economic power, as the natural sponsor of the emerging nations. Through the Peace Corps, he sought to identify America with the revolution of rising expectations taking place in the world.

Many of the new Third World leaders believed that Kennedy was indeed on their side. They accepted the Peace Corps as a manifestation of his empathy with them. "For the first time we found in the United States a man who felt as we did, who suffered with us," explained Juan Bosch, president of the Dominican Republic. "And the Peace Corps, what is it? Kennedy in action."

Because of the Third World's admiration and affection for Kennedy, his sudden death in November 1963 dealt the Peace Corps a particularly cruel blow. The seven thousand Volunteers then in service witnessed at first hand the unprecedented phenomenon of Kennedy's popularity as a figure of hope among the world's forgotten and destitute. In a letter to Peace Corps headquarters, a Volunteer described the reaction to Kennedy's assassination in a small, isolated village of Borneo:

Living in a community where the native people live in relative seclusion, and know only smatter- ings of worlds affairs, I was surprised to look up and find several local boys standing at my door saying that they had heard on a radio that "my President and dear friend had been shot and they were sorry for me because they knew I would be sad." A mourning party was arranged...and the natives living in the Borneo interior were reminded that John F. Kennedy was more than an important President and world leader in some faraway capital; he will be remembered as the man who sent his personal representative to live and teach in their village and who showed them some concrete evidence of the American willingness to improve the universal dignity of man.

Volunteers from all over the globe wrote to Washington expressing their sense of personal loss." In the recent days of sadness I have been trying to sort out some of the significant things about Mr. Kennedy's presidency," wrote Volunteer Michael Woldenberg. "It was not until Kennedy's administration," he concluded, "that the people of America could feel that, through a government program, they had definite ties with other peoples of the world." To volunteer Maureen Carroll, the one source of consolation at Kennedy's death was that she had been "in the chorus that answered him...I am proud to have been a part of an already-established living memorial to Kennedy: the Peace Corps.

The Peace Corps was never to recapture the vigor and enthusiasm that characterized it in the Kennedy years. It carried on; moreover, by 1966 it had doubled in size and Lyndon Johnson called for twenty thousand Volunteers by 1970. As the 1960s progressed however, Johnson and all Americans, especially young Americans, were torn apart by the war in Vietnam. When the first conference of returned volunteers was held in

1965, many returnees were outspoken in their criticism of the war; some new Volunteers began to carry their protest overseas with them. On the domestic side, the Peace Corps recruiters were challenged to justify how one could help a government work for peace in the Third World while that same government was engaged in a bloody war in the Third World. As cynicism took hold, many young Americans applied for the Peace Corps only because they hoped it would save them from the draft.

Although the Peace Corps became ensnared by the problems which afflicted America in the later 1960s, there was no doubt that Kennedy had sparked the imagination of a generation and made many of them aware of the potential of personal action. "My three years in the Peace Corps taught me that you can never know when your individual effort will make a difference," said Senator Paul Tsongas in later years. I have relearned the lesson many times since then."

Throughout the 1960s there was strong evidence of a desire by the generation of Americans in their 20s and 30s to participate in the great issues of their time—through the war on poverty, the civil rights crusade, the anti-war protest. Collectively, they added up to a movement among America's young people. While Kennedy personally provided much of the inspiration behind the movement, the Peace Corps was in its vanguard. As journalist Jack Newfield put it: "Kennedy liberated energies bottled up for a decade...he held up a vision of social idealism, represented by the Peace Corps."

Who Volunteered and Why

By 1963, seven thousand Americans were sharing the Peace Corps experience; but there was no such thing as a "typical" Volunteer. Shriver believed that anyone who decided to give up two years of his or her life to service in a developing country was extraordinary. There were, however, several characteristics which many Volunteers had in common. He or she (the male to female ratio was 3:2) was usually a recent graduate in the liberal arts, unmarried, and aged between twenty-two and twenty-eight. Volunteers were sometimes referred to as the "in-betweeners." Most had just finished college but were as yet undecided whether to pursue a career or continue on to graduate school. Some were already involved in further education. For others, immediate job prospects were uncertain and the Peace Corps provided a useful breathing space at a critical juncture in their lives.

Two thirds of all Volunteers were Democrats rather than Republicans, reflecting the Peace Corps' liberal ethos. The large number of Republicans, however, was indicative of the agency's bipartisan political appeal. In terms of regional appeal, the West Coast always led in the number of Volunteers (evidence of Kennedy's sound political intuition in choosing San Francisco for his first public espousal of the Peace Corps). Next to California came the big industrial states of the East and Midwest–New York, Illinois, Pennsylvania, Ohio, Massachusetts, and Michigan. The Southern states lagged far behind. The segregationist policies of many of their colleges prevented the Peace Corps from using them as recruiting or training grounds. By the end of 1962, not a single college or university in the South had a Peace Corps training contract. The Peace Corps did contract with black universities in the North.

The reasons why Volunteers chose to join the Peace Corps was one of the questions most commonly asked of them. Since their motivations were usually complex, the question was not easily answered. A 1962 study analyzed applicants' responses to a question in the Volunteer Questionnaire: "What do you hope to accomplish by joining the Peace Corps?" Answers were widespread ranging from: to help the poorer countries; to develop or improve as an individual; to get to know and understand other countries; and to further my career. Few applicants gave just one reason and most claimed their motives were mixed. The most recurrent answer was "to help people and humanity in general"; next was "to improve international relations and promote international understanding." At the bottom of the list were "to travel and have an adventure" and "to fight communism."

Although these sets of reasons were sometimes at opposite ends of the spectrum, applicants often combined both types in their answers. Moreover, after some experience in the field, Peace Corps officials preferred to see a mixture, believing that Volunteers who were too single-minded in their motivation had to be looked at carefully. As Burdick and Lederer explained:

Better a Peace Corps Volunteer with a capacity to admit his mixed motivations. Such Peace Corps Volunteers may be better able to adjust to the realities of life in the Peace Corps than those who say the come primarily to the Peace Corps for purely altruistic motives. In addition, too strong protests of commitment may be covering up less desirable characteristics.

One sixty-year-old Volunteer got tired of being constantly asked why she had joined the Peace Corps. Finally, when a reporter again wondered why she would want to travel to Africa after teaching school for thirty years in Kansas, she responded: "Young man, have you ever taught school for 30 years in Kansas?"

A major factor in persuading young Americans to join the Peace Corps was the special affinity which many of them felt with John F. Kennedy. "Here was a man with whom I, and all young people, could identify," wrote Duncan Yaggy, who volunteered in the summer of 1961, " a man who suddenly made being an American an exciting idea." Paul Tsongas, who volunteered in 1962 (and went on to become a Democratic senator for Massachusetts), recalled that Kennedy's influence was the "major factor" motivating him to overcome all obstacles in his path–including the grave doubts of his Republican father. In the early 1960s, the President inspired many others to join the agency which he had created. On the day after Kennedy's assassination, the Peace Corps was flooded with requests from young people on college campuses all over America. In the week after Dallas, the all-time record number of applications was received: 2,550. This response led one young Peace Corps official to conclude that Volunteers were really "the last of the old-fashioned patriots," answering Kennedy's call to do something for their country.

Aside from these broad generalizations about motives, few Volunteers cared to pinpoint any single reason for their decision to join the Peace Corps. Volunteer David Schickele said that a "favorite parlor sport" among trainees was to dream up "cocky answers to a question that was put to us 17 times a day by the professional and idly curious alike: why did you join the Peace Corps?" Most Volunteers considered it a simplistic and infuriating question. Lyndon Johnson deliberately avoided asking it when he met a group of trainees at the Peace Corps' Puerto Rico camp in July 1962. Instead, he suggested that the next time someone asked them the question, they should turn it around, "like Thoreau turned Emerson's question around. Emerson had paid a visit to his friend in the Concord jail. 'My dear Thoreau,' Emerson said, 'Why are you here?' To which Thoreau replied, 'My dear Emerson, why are you not here?'"

Should it come to it, I had rather give my life trying to help someone than to give my life looking down a gun barrel at them.

David Crozier—the first Volunteer to die in service

While the Peace Corps had a number of other significant effects on the United States–as the country's most innovative language-learning institution, for example–the greatest impact was on the Volunteers themselves. They usually felt they had undergone a dramatic change overseas. As one returnee put it: "Whatever we were before, and none of us can quite remember, that's all gone." This personal transition was impossible to quantify. "Until one has had the experience," wrote Neil Boyer, a Volunteer who later joined the State Department, "one cannot realize how important two years can be in a lifetime."

Coming home, Volunteers had to face the painful process of readjusting to aspects of their society that they had previously accepted as "American." Many found the old ways exceedingly difficult to accept. The founders of the Peace Corps had expected that Volunteers would gain a useful familiarity with the Third World; they had not anticipated that many would undergo an intense personal experience that would profoundly alter their view of their own society. For many it was a cathartic experience. "The thing about the Peace Corps," said one returnee, "is that it doesn't end after two years; it lasts a lifetime." Newell Flather, a Volunteer in the first teaching program in Ghana, claimed that the Peace Corps opened his and many Americans' minds to the possibility of personal growth and change. "The Peace Corps gets people at a very formative age and gives them new ideas," he said. "For many it is the opening of a new frontier of the psyche." Flather, who admitted going to Ghana as a rather quiet and reserved graduate student, returned to help form the radical Committee of Returned Volunteers and, later, play a leading role in Oxfam America.

The story of Paul Tsongas of Massachusetts was another dramatic example of how volunteers underwent personal change overseas. Tsongas had never been outside the eastern seaboard when he applied to the Peace Corps in 1961. "I had a very insulated existence," he said later. "I was in the first group that went overseas, and I didn't know what the hell I was getting myself in for." Tsongas spent three years teaching math and science in Ghion, Ethiopia. As he recalled it:

I ended up in a village in Ethiopia with five other Peace Corps Volunteers, and I didn't go anywhere on vacations, just stayed in the village. I broke away from the others and set up house by myself, with my students. I took the ten best kids in the school and I lived with them, just a total immersion in their culture. And, you know, nothing I've ever done before or since has given me the same feeling.

When he came home from Ethiopia, Tsongas felt completely out of place. Studying at Yale Law School, he described his first year home as "catastrophic." Such was the force of his " reverse culture shock" that he developed a slight speech impediment. Although it took him some time to readjust to the "American way," the Peace Corps had sparked his political and intellectual interests. He quickly moved up the ladder from

Lowell city councilor to Middlesex county commissioner to U.S. Representative. Finally, he won a seat in the Senate in 1978. Tsongas cited the Peace Corps as "the formative experience of my life. And if I have a meeting with someone and find out he's a former Peace Corps Volunteer, there's an instant sort of attachment." One such attachment was Christopher Dodd of Connecticut, a former Volunteer in the Dominican Republic; he too was elected to the U.S. Senate in 1978.

Many former Volunteers also maintained ties to their Peace Corps host communities. A 1979 survey found that some two-thirds of all returned Volunteers kept up their overseas contacts. On occasion, returnees joined together in the United States to give emergency assistance to countries where they had once lived and worked. In 1968, Volunteers went back to Nigeria as workers with an ad hoc committee for Nigeria/Biafra Relief (jointly established by a group of former Peace Corps Volunteers and American Friends Service Committee volunteers). Several former Volunteer groups also organized refugee committees, raising money and resources for medical and health programs administered by missions and relief agencies in Ethiopia, Somalia, and Afghanistan.

When Joe Walsh returned to Guatemala in 1978, where he had been a Volunteer in the early 1960s, he found that a native couple he had known had died, leaving a young son to fend for himself. Walsh adopted the boy and took him back with him to Massachusetts. Many other Volunteers kept up correspondence or visited their former counterparts. In this respect, the Peace Corps had a continuing impact down the years — for Volunteers and their hosts. "Volunteers are personally concerned with the vital interests of the people of 46 nations with which our country has had little contact–except for a few economic interests or where Communism scared us in," observed returnee Roger Landrum in 1965. "We are sons and daughters of America but we are in a sense also sons and daughters of a thousand towns and villages scattered around the world."

"Volunteers joined the Peace Corps to shape, teach, influence and help other people," wrote Bill Moyers in 1963. "They joined to leave something behind...It is in the nature of a man to want to leave some monument, however small, however insignificant, however intangible." Moyers and his colleagues had no illusions about what the Peace Corps might accomplish. Along with Kennedy, they hoped only that "In some small village, Volunteers will lay a seed which will bring a rich harvest for us all in later days."

In terms of national economic development, the Peace Corps' effects were not great. However, by concentrating on human resource development in small communities, its impact belied its size. In the 1980s, the World Bank conceded that "Nothing can make widespread absolute poverty melt away overnight...but the most valuable resource any country has is its people, the means and the end of economic advance." The Peace Corps had recognized this point since its inception. Bringing only themselves as resources, Volunteers had an impact on the people they worked with.

Host nationals readily acknowledged that the Peace Corps' strength was the individual working at the personal level with materials that were locally available on projects that would continue after they left. "We have a saying in Tagalog," said Emanuel Pelaez, vice-president of the Philippines, *"Ang bato na matigas ay maaagnas din so kapapatak ng ulam"* (Even the hardest stone will wear away under constant drops of rain). "Your labors in our fields and barrios," he told a group of Volunteers, "will be like those constant drops of rain slowly but surely eroding the boulders of poverty, ignorance and disease which block the road to greatness and prosperity in this country."

From the very start the question of motives was raised i.e., "Why did you join the Peace Corps?" Everyone seemed to want to know...Invariably we gave these queries an unfriendly response —partly because they soon acquired the hollow ring of cliche, partly because the reasons were complex, profound and personal and partly, perhaps because we weren't quite sure of the answer ourselves.

John Demos–Volunteer in Ghana

Official: "How will you describe your Peace Corps experience?"

Volunteer: "Well, I won't sell it." (Pause)

Official: "What will you say?"

Volunteer: "I'll tell them what it was like." (Pause)

Official: "Such as?"

Volunteer: "The best goddam experience a young man can have. Worth four years of college."

For what should a volunteer be prepared? He should be prepared for a delightful, warm, friendly, appreciative and fun-loving people, and for the nerve-racking frustration that arises out of incomprehension and consistent failure. He should be prepared for a rewarding experience which will live with him as long as he is on this earth.

A Peace Corps Volunteer in Sierra Leone

Volunteers Forever

by Sargent Shriver

Today I recommend that we remember our beginning. We are dedicated to the pursuit of peace—which means we oppose the idea that war is inevitable. We believe that with God's help we can get rid of war. We are a corps, a band of brothers and sisters, united in the conviction that, if we work hard enough, we truly can avoid war–and achieve peace. And we all think that everyone in the Peace Corps, and everyone who has ever worked in the Peace Corps, is a special person, who, given a chance, will overcome any problem! In believing this about each other, in believing this about all Peace Corps people, we are giving reality to the words of Martin Luther King, Jr. He said:

"Everybody can be great because everybody can serve. You don't have to have a college degree to serve. You don't have to make your subject and your verb agree to serve. You don't have to know about Plato or Aristotle to serve. You don't have to know Einstein's theory of relativity to serve. You don't have to know the second theory of thermodynamics and physics to serve. You only need a heart full of grace and a soul regenerated by love."

So, in 1985, we look back across a quarter of a century of grace and soul—and we know how fortunate we are. In the Peace Corps, we have known the summer heat of the Sahara, the biting cold of the Alte Plano, the endless rain of the monsoons in Asia, and the even greater obstacles caused by bureaucratic inertia.

And what a precious gift it has all been! For we have also seen the smile on the face of a child who has just learned to read; the energy of people in a dusty village who have just learned that they can lift the dead hand of hopelessness; the wondrous sense of powerless people taking destiny into their own hands for the first time. We have been pioneers of the Peace Corps world–and, in that new world, we have seen the worst that happens to fellow human beings in daily acts of indifference and even evil; but we have also seen what is, what can be, the best in ourselves and others. We have seen into our own souls, even as we have felt our eyes misting and our hearts touched when it was time to say goodbye. But, for Veterans of the Peace Corps enlisted in the cause of peace, whatever we do when the first tour is over, there is never a final "goodbye." We are Peace Corps volunteers forever, and we will never be the same again.

In that spirit, let us resolve to continue and complete our real tours of duty—which are not for two years—but for all the years of our lives—until the peace we dreamed of when we signed up for the Corps, is finally won.

from an address entitled "Volunteers Forever",
25th Anniversary of the Peace Corps
University of Michigan, October 7, 1985

Sargent Shriver, Enduring Peacemaker

by Colman McCarthy

When the Peace Corps turned 25 the other day, the calendar had another date worth celebrating: the 70th birthday of Sargent Shriver, the program's director for its first six years and its most fired-up defender and promoter for the next 19. The Peace Corps and Shriver, certified imperishables, remain unslowed by the passage of time. Each still stirs with the idealism that marked their peak in the 1960s. Each has yet to be tempered by the what's-in-it-for-me spirit of the '80s.

Last week,, the Peace Corps was preparing for its next 25 years by working toward the congressionally sanctioned goal of having 10,000 volunteers in the field. Shriver, who was the federal government's original Department of Energy, had hiked off to China across South Korea to organize some Special Olympics events. Without doubt, he was selling the East on high hurdles, his own specialty the first days of the Peace Corps.

Fate delivered back then the kind of opponents who guaranteed success. Richard Nixon, speaking in the 1960 campaign, said that John Kennedy's idea of the Peace Corps was no more than a "fast and flashy technique of proposing a program that looks good on the surface, but which is inherently dangerous." The *Wall Street Journal*, dealing in the same sarcasm that is its editorial-page tone today, asked: "What person can really believe that Africa aflame with violence will have its fires quenched because some Harvard boy or Vassar girl lives in a mud hut and speaks Swahili?" The Daughters of the American Revolution asked Congress to kill the pending Peace Corps legislation. Rep. Otto Passman, who in 1961 worked to cut funds for the program, was saying in 1972: "If I had to meet my Maker in three minutes, and the last decision the Good Lord would let me make...it would be to abolish the Peace Corps. Then I could die in peace."

In early 1961, with legs the equal of his lungs, Shriver visited each congressional office to win support for the Peace Corps. Even the agency's name prompted arguments. Shriver recalls: "'Peace Corps' was not the most popular title. Among the most experienced advisers, that title was scoffed at. They wanted a solid bureaucratic title–like the Agency for Overseas Voluntary Service. Conservatives opposed the word 'peace.' They maintained it sounded soft, wishy-washy, vague and weak. The communists, they said, had corrupted the word peace by applying it to every political initiative and even to every war they got involved in. The left wing disliked the word 'corps.' It sounded too militaristic. The famous German Africa Corps, victorious almost everywhere under General Rommel, was fresh in their mind. 'Corps' sounded like a scourge. Finally, I decided we'd use both words, put them together and get the best out of both of them: Peace because that truly was our business, and Corps because it showed that we were not individualists but a group."

Today the group numbers 5,500 active volunteers serving in 62 countries and 120,000 former volunteers who went to 88 countries. In Washington, nine directors were to follow Shriver. In the quarter-century that saw at least two dozen members of Congress sent to prison or shamed by scandal into retirement, and the jailing of the Nixon gang, the Peace Corps leadership has not suffered one resignation due to corruption or deceit.

The tension on the program has been its proximity to an American foreign policy that is based on the force of weapons and domination rather than the Peace Corps' force of altruism and cooperation. Thousands of volunteers have been troubled by the obvious inconsistency of going abroad to create the conditions of peace but realizing that the big money from America to the Third World goes for military aid.

The imbalance is also at home. The current Peace Corps budget is still less than what the Pentagon spends on its soldier boy recruitment ads. The volunteers who came home 20 years ago as opponents of the Johnson war in Southeast Asia are echoed by volunteers returning today who oppose the Reagan war in Central America. Twenty-five years ago, Shriver wrote to John Kennedy: "What the world most needs from this country is better understanding of the world."

That sounds naive in these times when American foreign policy is guided by pushers of U.S. superiority who see no need to answer to anyone, much less to listen to the world's poor for guidance. This mentality was also present in the Kennedy White House. It created the Green Berets, saw the New Frontier as extending to Vietnam and called Shriver and Peace Corps "boy scouts." Some justice exists. The best and the brightest are now seen, in history's surer light, as the worst and the dullest.

The Peace Corps and Shriver, and their band of 125,500 idealists, have earned kinder treatment. They are in the history books as true peacemakers. They provide one of the better reasons that make the reading of American history bearable.

from "America's True Peacemakers", The Washington Post
22 November 1985

SUGGESTED TOPICS FOR RESEARCH PAPERS

Small is Beautiful and *A Guide for the Perplexed* are classic texts on economic nonviolence. The author, E.F. Schumacher, was philosophically aligned with Gandhi. Apply Schumacher's thoughts to today's world of economic injustice where 40,000 people die every day from hunger and malnutrition while governments spend $2 billion a day ($800 million a day in the United States alone) on military programs.

We have some idea of the problems and frictions faced by Desmond Tutu with the whites of South Africa. But what of his difficulties with blacks? Explore Tutu's relations with other anti-apartheid leaders. Refer to news stories, as well as his two books, *Hope and Suffering* and *Crying in the Wilderness*.

Examine the politics of Jeannette Rankin, the Montanan who was the first woman elected to Congress–in 1917. She was a pacifist and a feminist. What was the effect of her twice voting against American involvement in World War I and II? How did her dissent affect Congress, herself and the peace movement?

Has the Peace Corps been a success? It celebrates its 30th anniversary in 1991. Write a brief history of the program, including a tale or two about its first director, Sargent Shriver, and Loret Ruppe, the tireless director from 1981-1988. Explore how the Peace Corps experience affected the host countries and the American volunteers who went abroad and came back.

Scott Nearing was perhaps the purest practitioner of nonviolence America has ever had. At age 45, after being fired from a professorship in Pennsylvania, he left rat-race academia and settled in Vermont, then Maine, and lived off the land for the next 55 years. His books range from *Living the Good Life*, which he wrote with his sparkling wife, Helen, to *The Making of a Radical*, a classic text. Write a profile of the Nearings and their thinking.

Research the nonviolent civil disobedience of the Ploughshares activists, who keep trying to be modern Isaiahs by converting nuclear weapons into plowshares. Refer to the writings of Daniel and Philip Berrigan, as well as Judge Miles Lord of Minneapolis.

Must being born be violent and traumatic? In the 1970s, Frederick Leboyer answered no. He is an obstetrician who assisted more than 10,000 deliveries. His book, *Birth Without Violence*, argues the case that the first breaths of a human being can, and should, occur in an atmosphere of peace and gentleness, not pain, noise, bright lights, confusion, slaps to the behind and delivery-room fear. Analyze Leboyer's thinking, and relate it to the current home-birth and midwife movement.

Erasmus was a contemporary of Luther, Thomas More, Machiavelli, Calvin and Henry VIII. Some crew! Erasmus, in the minds of many, endures as the greatest of these because of his writings on peace. Analyze one or two of his peace essays. What was his relationship with Luther? And Thomas More?

Trace the American Friends Service Committee (Nobel Peace Prize winners in 1947) back through the Quakers to William Penn among the Delawares in colonial Pennsylvania when, for a brief moment, the continent had a "peaceable kingdom."

Few in this country are more fervent in seeking peace through nonviolence and world government than Garry Davis. Review his books, *My Country is the World* and *World Government: Ready or Not*. Davis is either one of the earth's certified loonies or he is profoundly sane. Which, in your view, is he?

Only a few years ago, the animal rights movement was the preserve of alleged flakes and flukes. Now it is mainstream folk who refuse to eat, wear, ride, dissect, experiment on, imprison, hunt, trap, sell, own or breed animals. What's going on? Refer to Tom Regan's *The Case for Animal Rights*, one of the best books available on nonviolence and animals.

The peace movement is also the economic conversion movement–shifting the United States from a war preparation and war-making economy to one of economic strength through jobs that feed, clothe and house people, not bomb or destroy them. Develop this theme.

Take a look at the peace writings of Clarence Darrow, one of the world's most influential lawyers. Examine his famous work, "Resist Not Evil," and apply it to today's violent world.